Introduction to European Tax Law: Direct Taxation

Third edition

Edited by

Michael Lang
Pasquale Pistone
Josef Schuch
Claus Staringer

The College of Law
of England and Wales
2 BUNHILL ROW
LONDON
EC1Y 8HQ

Introduction to European Tax Law: Direct Taxation

Third edition

Edited by

**Michael Lang
Pasquale Pistone
Josef Schuch
Claus Staringer**

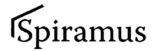

First published by Spiramus Press, 2008

This third edition published January 2013

© LINDE VERLAG Ges.m.b.H., Wien 2013
1210 Wien, Scheydgasse 24, Tel.: 0043/1/24 630
www.lindeverlag.at
ISBN Linde Verlag: 978-3- 7073-2211-8
ISBN Spiramus: 978-1-907444- 68-5

British Library Cataloguing-in-Publication Data.

A catalogue record for this book is available from the British Library.
The right of Michael Lang, Pasquale Pistone, Josef Schuch and Claus
Staringer to be identified as the authors of this work has been asserted by
them in accordance with the Copyright, Designs and Patents Act, 1988.

Typeset by:
EXAKTA GmbH, 1180 Wien, Hasenauerstraße 67
Druck: Hans Jentzsch & Co. GmbH.
1210 Wien, Scheydgasse 31

Printed in Great Britain by: Berforts Information Press, UK

Preface
3rd edition

The development of European Union tax law has picked considerable speed over the past two years. A constant and periodical update is therefore essential for all those who want to keep a focused view of the actual limits set to the exercise of national taxing powers and the correct interpretation and application of primary and secondary Union law in tax matters. For the same reason an update was necessary also for this textbook. This edition records a still growing trend for negative integration of direct taxes, which broadens the spectrum of areas within which settled case law on fundamental freedoms exists, features a higher number of infringement procedures and a sharp increase in the relevance and application of the prohibition of State aids, which suggested a structural change to Chapter three of the book. Over the same period, tax directives have been upgraded in order to bring mutual assistance back in line with the most advanced international standards. A further growth of positive integration of direct taxes is expected in the near future to take place through enhanced cooperation, perhaps supplemented by soft some coordination contour measures.

This third edition provides a concise analysis of such developments to the extent that they reached a reasonable level of stability by 1 October 2012. All efforts were made in order to avoid that the growth of European tax integration would result in a corresponding increase in the dimensions of this textbook. The reader-friendly approach was improved by supplementing the table of cases (listed in alphabetical order and including reference to the marginal numbers of the textbook in which each case is addressed) with an analytical index. The editors and authors are confident that also this edition of the book will give its readers a useful tool to navigate through the mazes of European tax law. As for the previous editions, all suggestions on further improvement to the book are warmly welcome.

The editors and authors would like to take this opportunity to thank Margaret Nettinga for linguistic editing and Eline Huisman for her active coordination of the book.

Vienna, 6 November 2012

Michael Lang
Pasquale Pistone
Josef Schuch
Claus Staringer

Preface
2nd edition

The number of judgments of the European Court of Justice in the field of direct taxation continues to grow at a stable pace, bringing technical legal complexity to a system which is reaching maturity on several issues, as proven by the significantly increased number of infringement procedures over the past two years. Global tax transparency is catalyzing the political consensus required for upgrading tax directives that enhance cooperation among Member States. By contrast, the other areas of direct taxation remain largely tied to the schemes of the early days in the history of European tax law, although progress in positive integration in such areas is equally important. The increased complexity of European tax law represents a major barrier to access by all those who are experts in either taxation or European law, but are still not familiar with the legal issues arising from their combination. Similar problems also arise for scholars and practitioners around the world who have realized that European tax law is no longer relevant only for a small academic European tax circle, but has turned into a strategic element for international tax planning in relations with the European Union countries. This textbook has been designed to address such persons and needs, no matter whether students or experienced professionals in Europe or third countries. This second edition updates and upgrades the first one, trying to enhance its use by adding flow charts and a table of cases, while keeping its original structure based on marginal numbers and bold typing, as well as its concise drafting.

We are confident that it will meet the needs of its readers and are grateful for suggestions on how to further improve it.

This book would not have been possible without the active involvement of Karoline Spies and the careful linguistic editing of Margaret Nettinga. We also wish to thank Rita Szudoczky for kindly being available to give us her views on the textbook during her research period at the WU as well as those who have contributed to it.

Vienna, April 2010

Michael Lang
Pasquale Pistone
Josef Schuch
Claus Staringer

Preface
1st edition

Direct taxation is still within the competence of the Member States. However, European law has become increasingly influential in this area as well. Most provisions of European law are directly applicable. They thus have an immediate impact on taxpayers and tax authorities when applying domestic tax law.

This book will serve as an introduction to European direct taxation for both students and practitioners. However, we hope that this book will also be of assistance to experts in European law who have so far considered tax law (and in particular direct taxation) as too technical a domain, as well as to tax law experts who have so far been not familiar with the problems of compatibility with European law. Our intention was not to focus on a specific national tax system. Therefore, we hope that students and practitioners throughout Europe (and outside Europe as well) will find this book helpful.

This book is the result of a joint project that has been conducted at the Institute for Austrian and International Tax Law (WU) in Vienna. All authors are part of the research team of the Institute. We would like to thank Kasper Dziurdź, who did essential work in the preparation and publication of this book, and Margaret Nettinga, who contributed greatly by editing and polishing the texts of the authors. Above all, sincere thanks to the publishers Linde and Spiramus, who generously agreed to include the publication in their catalogue.

Vienna, June 2008

Michael Lang
Pasquale Pistone
Josef Schuch
Claus Staringer

Contents

List of Abbreviations

Art. or Arts.	Article or Articles
BB	Betriebsberater
Bulletin	Bulletin for International Taxation, Bulletin for International Fiscal Documentation
CCCTB	Common Consolidated Corporate Tax Base
CFC	Controlled Foreign Corporation
CMLR	Common Market Law Review
Commission	European Commission (formerly Commission of the European Communities)
Council	Council of the European Union
DB	Der Betrieb
DStR	Deutsches Steuerrecht
DTC	Double Taxation Convention
EGC	European General Court (formerly Court of First Instance)
EC	European Community, EC Treaty
ECJ	European Court of Justice
ECOFIN	Economic and Financial Affairs Council
ed.	edition
ed. or eds..	editor or editors
EEA	European Economic Area
EEC	European Economic Community
EFTA	European Free Trade Area
e.g.	for example
EPA	European Partnership Agreement
EStAL	European State Aid Law Quarterly
ET	European Taxation
etc.	et cetera
EU	European Union
EuZW	Europäische Zeitschrift für Wirtschaftsrecht
FJ	Finanz Journal
FR	Finanz-Rundschau
GeS	GeS aktuell (Zeitschrift für Gesellschafts- und Steuerrecht)
i.e.	that is
IStR	Internationales Steuerrecht
IWB	Internationale Wirtschaftsbriefe
ITPJ	International Transfer Pricing Journal
JFC	Journal of Financial Crime
JIBL	Journal of International Banking Law
JIBLR	Journal of International Banking Law and Regulation
JIFM	Journal of International Financial Markets

JTPF	Joint Transfer Pricing Forum
m.no. or m.nos.	marginal number or marginal numbers
MS	Member State of the European Union
OECD	Organisation for Economic Co-operation and Development
OECD Model or OECD MC	OECD Model Tax Convention on Income and on Capital
OJ	Official Journal
ÖStZ	Österreichische Steuerzeitung
p. or pp.	page or pages
para. or paras.	paragraph or paragraphs
PE	permanent establishment
RdW	Recht der Wirtschaft
SCE	Societas Cooperativa Europaea
SE	Societas Europaea
et seq.	and the following
StuW	Steuer und Wirtschaft
suppl.	supplement
SWI	Steuer und Wirtschaft International
TIEA	Tax Information Exchange Agreement
TEU	Treaty on European Union
TFEU	Treaty on the Functioning of the European Union
TNI	Tax Notes International
UCITS	undertaking for collective investment in transferable securities
VAT	Value Added Tax
v	versus
WHT	withholding tax

I. The Sources of EU Law Relevant for Direct Taxation

Łukasz Adamczyk

Literature: Mulders, Compensation of losses within the EC, *EC Tax Review* 1996, p. 123; Dougan, Cutting your losses in the enforcement deficit: a community right to the recovery of unlawfully levied charges, *Cambridge Yearbook of European Legal Studies* (1998) p. 233; Gammie/Lodin, *Home State Taxation* (2001); Leegaard, Impact of the European Economic Area Agreement on Direct Taxation: A Norwegian Perspective, *ET,* 2002, p. 111; de Goede, European Integration and Tax Law, *ET* 2003, p. 204; Dassesse, Taxes paid in violation of EU law: How far back can a taxpayer claim reimbursement?, *Bulletin* 2004, p. 512; Gudmundsson, European Tax Law in the relations with the EFTA Countries, *Intertax* 2006, pp. 58–85; Niżnik, EU Corporate tax harmonization: Road to nowhere?, *Tax Notes International* 2006, p. 975; Jans, State Liability: In search of dividing line between national and European law, in Obradovic/Lavranos (eds.) *Interface between EU law and national law* (2007) p. 285; O'Shea, Tax Harmonization vs. Tax Coordination in Europe: Different Views, *Tax Notes International* 2007, p. 811; Weatherill, *Cases and Materials on EU Law* (2007); Bezborodov, Freedom of Establishment in the EC Economic Partnership Agreements: in Search of its Direct Effect on Direct Taxation, *Intertax* 2007, pp. 658–712; Terra/Wattel, *European Tax Law* (2005) and (2008); Lang/Pistone/Schuch/Staringer (eds.) *Common Consolidated Corporate Tax Base (CCCTB)* (2008); Dourado/da Palma Borges (eds.) *The Acte Clair in EC Direct Tax Law* (2008); Pistone (ed.) *Legal Remedies in European Tax Law* (2009).

Case Law: ECJ 5 February 1963, 26/62, *Van Gend en Loos* [1963] ECR 1; ECJ 15 July 1964, 6/64, *Costa v E.N.E.L.* [1964] ECR 585; ECJ 11 July 1968, 4/68, *Internationales Handelsgesellschaft* [1968] ECR 563; ECJ 12 November 1969, 29/69, *Stauder v Ulm* [1969] ECR 419; ECJ, 5 May 1970, 77/69, *Commission v Belgium* [1970] ECR 237; ECJ 4 December 1974, 41/74, *Van Duyn v Home Office* [1974] ECR 1337; ECJ 16 December 1976, 33/76, *Rewe* [1976] ECR 1989; ECJ 9 March 1978, 106/77, *Simmenthal* [1978] ECR 629; ECJ 5 April 1979, 148/78, *Publico Ministero v Ratti* [1979] ECR 1629; ECJ 9 February 1982, 270/80, *Polydor Limited and RSO Records v Harlequin Records Shops and Simons Records* [1982] ECR 329; ECJ 6 October 1982, 283/81, *CILFIT* [1982] ECR 3415; ECJ 9 November 1983, 199/82, *San Giorgio* [1983] ECR 3595; ECJ 25 July 1991, C-208/90, *Emmott* [1991] ECR I-4269; ECJ 19 November 1991, joined cases C-6/90 and C-9/90, *Francovich* [1991] ECR I-5357; ECJ 17 October 1996, joined cases C-283/94, C-291/94 and C-292/94, *Denkavit International, VITIC Amsterdam and Voormeer* [1996] ECR I-5063; ECJ 12 May 1998, C-336/96, *Gilly* [1998] ECR I-2823; ECJ 15 September 1998, C-231/96, *Edis* [1998] ECR I-4951; ECJ 29 April 1999, C-224/97, *Erich Ciola and Land Vorarlberg* [1999] ECR I-2517; ECJ 11 May 2000, C-37/98, *R v SSHD ex parte Abdulnasır Savaş* [2000] ECR I-2927; ECJ 24 September 2002, C-255/00, *Grundig Italiana* [2002] ECR I-8003; ECJ 23 September 2003, C-452/01, *Ospelt* [2003], ECR I-9743; ECJ 30 September 2003, C-224/01, *Köbler* [2003] ECR I-10239; ECJ 2 October 2003, C-147/01, *Weber's Wine Word* [2003] ECR I-11365; ECJ 9 December 2003, C-129/00, *Commission v Italy* [2003] ECR I-14637; ECJ 13 January 2004, C-453/00, *Kühne & Heitz* [2004] ECR I-837; ECJ 7 September 2004, C-319/02, *Manninen* [2004] ECR 7477; ECJ 23 February 2006, C-471/04, *Keller* [2006] ECR I-2107; ECJ 13 June 2006, C-173/03, *Traghetti del Mediterraneo* [2006] ECR I-5177; ECJ 13 March 2007, C-524/04, *Test Claimants in the Thin Cap Group Litigation* [2007] ECR I-2107; ECJ 13 April 2007, C-470/03, *A.G.M. – COS. MET Srl* [2007] ECR I-2749.

1. The Nature of the EU Law System

a) Supremacy

1 As the EC Treaty (the predecessor of the Treaty on the functioning of the European Union (hereinafter TFEU)) was silent on the issue of relation between the

EU law and national legal orders, the ECJ has had to clarify it. In the *Costa v Enel* case the Court made clear that "... **the law stemming from the Treaty ... could not ... be overridden by domestic legal provisions ...**" and in the case of a conflict between a EU law provision and a national provision the former takes precedence over the latter.[1] Later, the Court further clarified that every national court is obliged to apply EU law "in its entirety and protect rights which the latter confers on individuals and must accordingly set aside any provision of national law which may conflict with it, whether prior or subsequent to" the EU law provision.[2] In addition, the Court held that an EU law provision even takes precedence over a national constitutional provision.[3] According to the subsequent jurisprudence of the ECJ, the national administration is also required to ensure the supremacy of EU law over national law.[4]

b) Direct Effect

A **directly effective provision** of EU law confers **legally enforceable rights** on an individual so that he may rely on these before a national court or a national administrative authority. As a result of the supremacy theory, a national provision that is in conflict with a directly effective EU law provision has to be set aside. **2**

A **directly applicable provision** of EU law constitutes a **part of national law**.[5] This means that they are **automatically effective** in the national legal orders without a need to enact implementation measures. The TFEU expressly recognizes the direct applicability of provisions of EU Regulations. However, the TFEU remains silent on the direct effect of treaty provisions, directives and the international agreements concluded by the EU. For this reason, the Court has had to elaborate on these issues. **3**

i. Direct Effect of the TFEU Treaty Provisions

As for the direct effect of an EC Treaty (now the TFEU) provision, it was the renowned *Van Gend & Loos* decision that has proved to be crucial.[6] In this judgment the Court held that the **EC Treaty (now the TFEU) constitutes more than an international agreement** since the Member States have limited their sovereign rights in certain fields by transferring powers to the EU institutions, creating thereby a new, *sui generis*, system of law. The Court recognized that the provisions of the Treaty are directly effective and that there is no need to implement them into domestic law. **4**

---

[1] ECJ 15 July 1964, 6/64, *Costa v E.N.E.L.* [1964] ECR 585.
[2] ECJ 9 March 1978, 106/77, *Simmenthal* [1978] ECR 629, para. 21.
[3] ECJ 11 July 1968, 4/68, *Internationale Handelsgesellschaft* [1968] ECR 563.
[4] ECJ 29 April 1999, C-224/97, *Erich Ciola and Land Vorarlberg* [1999] ECR I-2517.
[5] Weatherill, *Cases and Materials on EU Law* (2007) p.129.
[6] ECJ 5 February 1963, 26/62, *Van Gend en Loos* [1963] ECR 1.

5   In order to be directly effective, a TFEU provision has to fulfil the following conditions:

- it must be **clearly** and **precisely** worded,
- it must be **unconditional** and **independent** from any national implementation measure.

ii. Direct Effect of the EU Directives' Provisions

6   Since Member States are responsible for implementing the directives into domestic law, there is an inherent risk of possible incorrect implementation or non-implementation, which might undermine the uniformity of EU law application. Therefore, it is extremely important for individuals to be entitled in any case to rely on the "true meaning" of a directive provision. In the *Van Duyn* case the Court ruled there that "it would be incompatible with the binding effect attributed to a directive [...] to exclude in principle, the possibility that the obligation which it imposes may be invoked by those concerned. [...] It is necessary to examine in every case, whether the nature, general scheme and wording of the provision in question are capable of having direct effects on relations between Member States and individuals".[7] In the *Ratti* case the ECJ established that Member States may not rely on a non-implemented directive against its own citizens (the *estoppel* principle).[8] In addition, the Court clarified that an individual may rely on a an unconditional and sufficiently precise provision of the directive if the time limit for implementation has elapsed and the Member State has not implemented the directive[9] or has failed to do so correctly.[10]

7   In principle, an individual may not rely on a non-implemented or incorrectly implemented directive against another individual ("**horizontal direct effect**"). The Court holds that legal certainty prevents the directives from creating obligations for individuals without being implemented into EU law. However, under certain circumstances, the Court is prepared to recognize some effects of a non-implemented or incorrectly implemented directive for an individual. Consequently, *Wattel* argues that, for instance, it would be possible for a parent company to sue a subsidiary regarding the application of a withholding tax on dividends provided under national law that is not in line with the Parent-Subsidiary Directive.[11]

iii. Direct Effect of the EU International Agreements' Provisions

8   As regards international agreements, the Court has been willing to accept that their specific provisions are capable of having direct effect, as long as the following three conditions are met:

---

[7] ECJ 4 December 1974, 41/74, *Van Duyn v Home Office* [1974] ECR 1337.

[8] ECJ 5 April 1979, 148/78, *Publico Ministero v Ratti* [1979] ECR 1629.

[9] ECJ 19 January 1982, 8/81, *Becker* [1982] ECR 53.

[10] ECJ 17 October 1996, joined cases C-283/94, C-291/94 and C-292/94, *Denkavit International, VITIC Amsterdam and Voormeer* [1996] ECR I-5063.

[11] Terra/Wattel, *European Tax Law* (2008) p. 88.

- **clear and precise wording of a given provision,**
- **lack of conditionality and independence** of any national implementation measure
- **the object and purposes** do not preclude their direct effect.[12]

c) Legal Remedies

The following remarks explain how rights **arising from EU law can be en-** **9** **forced** (see m.nos. 14 et seq.) and how breaches of EU law are redressed (see m nos. 22). **For a further understanding** the relevant EU institutions for direct taxation and their competences are listed below (see m.nos 10 et seq.).

i. EU Institutions

Art. 13 of the Treaty on European Union (TEU) provides for institutions of the **10** European Union. Three of them, namely the European Parliament, the Council and the European Commission, may have an impact on the shape of EU direct taxation, even if powers in the field of direct taxation remain mostly in the hands of the Member States.

The **European Parliament** and the **Council** can be seen as two chambers of **11** the legislative branch of the EU with its competences being officially distributed between both institutions. The Treaty of Lisbon has somehow also strengthened the powers of the European Parliament in fields that may be relevant for direct taxation, as the amendment on Arts. 64 and 65 TFEU (ex Arts. 57 and 58 EC) may prove. However, some relevant differences can still be noted in comparison to national in comparison to those given to national legislatures, such as for instance the fact that in principle the power of legislative initiative is neither for the Parliament, nor for the Council, but is instead exclusively reserved to the European Commission. Therefore, while Parliament can amend and reject legislation, the Commission is needed to start off the legislative procedure.

Besides its competences in legislative process, the **European Commission** **12** monitors the Member States' compliance with EU law and, whenever it finds that a Member States does not comply with it, may initiate an infringement procedure. Moreover, the Commission often issues non-binding soft law measures directed to Member States.

In its quality of single judicial body competent to interpret EU law the role of **13** the **Court of Justice of the European Union** is to ensure that EU law is observed. In doing so, the Court reviews the legality of the acts of the institutions of the European Union (including when it acts as appellate body for the decisions of the European General Court in domains such as, for instance, State aids), controls the Member States' compliance with obligations under the Treaties and in-

---

[12] ECJ 9 February 1982, 270/80, *Polydor Limited and RSO Records v Harlequin Records Shops and Simons Records* [1982] ECR 329, para. 12; ECJ 11 May 2000, C-37/98, Savaş [2000] ECR I-2927, para. 39.

terprets EU law at the request of the national courts and tribunals with the aim of ensuring the uniform application and interpretation of EU law.

ii. The Enforcement of EU Law

14 Like every legal system, EU law possesses mechanisms to ensure its proper enforcement. Accordingly, there are **two ways of protecting rights arising from EU law**. The measures incompatible with EU law may be challenged either at the EU level under an infringement procedure or at the national level by nationals invoking directly effective EU law provisions before a national court.[13]

a. European Union Level

15 The Commission serves as the guardian of the Treaties and the watchdog of Member States' compliance with European Union law. Usually, **an infringement procedure** comes into play when a Member State has enacted or kept in force domestic provisions incompatible with EU law or if a Member State has failed to implement a directive in a timely or accurately fashion. If an individual whose rights are infringed by a given national provision or by the lack of action by a Member State (non-implementation of a directive) makes a complaint to the Commission, it is under no obligation to commence an action, but this complaint may serve as an "inspiration" to start an infringement procedure. The Commission has recently more often employed this procedure in order to tackle potential infringements of the fundamental freedoms by the national direct tax provisions. This increasing activity has resulted so far in several cases decided by the ECJ and in even more still pending before the Court.[14]

16 Once the Commission considers that a Member State has breached the EU law it is obliged, in accordance with **Art. 258 TFEU** (ex Art. 226 EC), to launch an **infringement procedure**. As a first step the Commission should notify the Member State involved of its reservations. Having received observations from a Member State, it should deliver a reasoned opinion. Unless the Member State complies with the position presented in the reasoned opinion within the period laid down therein, the case may be brought before the ECJ.

17 Under **Art. 260(1) TFEU** (ex Art. 228(1) EC), once the Court finds the Commission action well grounded, the Member State involved is under an obligation to amend its domestic legislation so as to make it EU-compatible. Failure to do so within a reasonable time triggers another action of the Commission, on the basis of **Art. 260(2) TFEU** (ex Art. 228(2) EC). If the Commission considers

---

[13] It should be noted that, in principle, a Member State national enjoys a right to rely on EU law before a national administrative body, which is, on the other hand, obliged to comply with EU law. However, the administrative body is not entitled to refer a preliminary question to the ECJ.

[14] See the list of cases relevant for direct taxation available at http://ec.europa.eu/taxation_customs/resources/documents/taxation/gen_info/tax_law/legal_proceedings/court_cases_direct_taxation_en.pdf.

that the Member State concerned has not taken the necessary measures to comply with the judgment of the Court, it may bring the case before the Court after giving that State the opportunity to submit its observations. The Commission must specify the amount of the "lump-sum payment or penalty payment" to be paid by the Member State concerned which it considers appropriate in the circumstances. If the Court finds that the Member State concerned has not complied with its judgment, it may impose a "lump-sum or penalty payment" on it.

In accordance with **Art. 259 TFEU** (ex Art. 227 EC), it is possible for a **18** Member State to bring **a case before the ECJ against another Member State** for its breach of EU law. This procedure has not been frequently put into use and has never so far been used in direct tax cases. However, it seems that this provision may unexpectedly prove helpful for a Member State in a case involving a direct tax issue. Imagine a situation where Member State A has to credit Member State B taxes imposed on dividends received by its resident.[15] Member State A feels that its residents are discriminated against by Member State B, which imposes higher taxation on dividends received by non-residents than on dividends obtained by its residents. From Member State A's point of view elimination of discrimination of its residents and lowering the tax burden borne by them in Member State B means less tax credit to be given. Therefore, Member State A may have good reasons to bring a case against Member State B before the ECJ.

b. National Level (Preliminary Reference Procedure)

The enforcement of EU law on the national level consists in the combined result **19** of the principles of direct effect and of supremacy as well as a preliminary reference procedure. Under **Art. 267 TFEU** (ex Art. 234 EC), the ECJ has jurisdiction to give **preliminary rulings** concerning the interpretation of the TFEU. The aim of this provision is to ensure the uniform application of EU law throughout all Member States. When a question concerning the application or interpretation of EU law is raised before a court or a tribunal, it *may* request the ECJ to give preliminary ruling thereon if it believes that such a ruling is necessary for delivering a decision. However, when such a situation occurs before a court or a tribunal against whose decisions no legal remedies are available in national law (for example, a Supreme Court or a Constitutional Court), it is obliged to pose questions to the ECJ.

A national court does not have to make reference to the ECJ in a case which **20** requires EU law interpretation when the *acte clair* and *acte éclairé* **doctrine** applies. This doctrine was forged in the *CILFIT* case where the Court recognized the national court's discretion to ascertain whether a decision on questions of EU law is necessary to enable it to give a judgment.[16] Therefore, once a national

---

[15] ECJ 7 September 2004, C-319/02, *Manninen* [2004] ECR 7477.
[16] ECJ 6 October 1982, 283/81, *CILFIT* [1982] ECR 3415.

court has established that an EU law issue is irrelevant for the outcome of the case, it does not have to refer the case to the ECJ.[17] Moreover, the national court is under no obligation to do so also when "the EC provision in question has already been interpreted by the Court" (*acte éclairé*) or "the correct application of EC law is so obvious as to leave no scope for reasonable doubts" (*acte clair*).[18]

21   The *acte clair* and *acte éclairé* **doctrine** allows a national court a large area of discretion regarding the necessity of referring the preliminary ruling. On the one hand, it speeds up the enforcement of EU law by allowing national courts to decide cases with EU law aspects without time-consuming preliminary references to the ECJ. On the other hand, the national courts in several Member States have reportedly been misusing this doctrine with the result of leaving the ECJ outside the litigation process even with respect to cases involving unclear EU law issues.[19]

iii. Effectiveness of EU law

a. Procedural Aspects of Redressing Breaches of EU Law

22   It is settled ECJ case law that, in the absence of EU measures, a Member State should remedy a breach of EU law on the basis of national provisions and designate the competent courts as well as set out the detailed procedural rules for restitution proceedings (**principle of national procedural autonomy**).[20] This principle is, however, subject to two important limitations. Firstly, "the substantive and procedural conditions for reparation of loss and damage laid down by the national law of the Member States must not be less favourable than those relating to similar domestic claims"[21] (**principle of equivalence**). Secondly, those conditions "must not be so framed as to make it virtually impossible or excessively difficult to obtain reparation"[22] (**principle of effectiveness**).

23   The Court applied the **principle of equivalence** in the *Edis* case where it held that if a tax has been imposed in violation of EU law a taxpayer will be able to successfully bring an action for recovery of the tax only in accordance with the national procedural rules that govern the recovery of taxes unduly paid, including time limits applicable to such actions.[23] The exception to this principle was established in the *Emmot* case where the ECJ ruled that the fact that the

---

[17] ECJ 6 October 1982, 283/81, *CILFIT* [1982] ECR 3415, para. 21.
[18] ECJ 6 October 1982, 283/81, *CILFIT* [1982] ECR 3415, para. 21.
[19] For more on this issue, see Dourado/da Palma Borges (eds.) *The Acte Clair in EC Direct Tax Law* (2008).
[20] ECJ 16 December 1976, 33/76, *Rewe* [1976] ECR 1989, para. 5; ECJ 24 September 2002, C-255/00, *Grundig Italiana* [2002] ECR I-8003, paras. 33 and 42.
[21] ECJ 19 November 1991, joined cases C-6/90 and C-9/90, *Francovich* [1991] ECR I-5357, para. 43.
[22] Ibidem.
[23] ECJ 15 September 1998, C-231/96, *Edis* [1998] ECR I-4951, paras. 17–19. See also Dassesse, *Bulletin* 2004, p. 511.

provisions of a directive were not duly (or timely) transposed into national law prevents a Member State from invoking a time limit provided by its domestic law as long as the Member State has not properly implemented the provisions of the directive into its domestic law.[24]

At the core of the dispute in *Weber's Wine World* was the Austrian provision **24** shortening the **time limit for claiming unduly paid taxes** with the exception of taxes paid in violation of the Constitution. The Court held that the principles set by the national law regarding time limits applicable to refunds of taxes paid unconstitutionally have to apply also with respect to taxes imposed in violation of EU law.[25]

On the other hand, in certain circumstances the **principle of effectiveness** **25** requires that a final administrative decision issued by a national administration authority has to be reversed. In the *Kühne & Heitz* case a Dutch company had to pay back export subsidies already received due to the erroneous interpretation of EU law adopted by the Netherlands authorities and the Netherlands courts. The ECJ ruled in favour of the claimant by holding that EU law obliges national authorities to **"review a final administrative decision** where an application for such review is made to it, in order to take account of the interpretation of the relevant provision given in the meantime by the Court where

- under national law, it has the power to reopen that decision;
- the administrative decision in question has become final as a result of a judgment of a national court ruling at final instance based on a misinterpretation of Community law without asking the Court for a preliminary ruling;
- the person concerned complained to the administrative body immediately after becoming aware of that decision of the Court."[26]

It is believed that the decision in the *Kühne & Heitz* case may prove helpful for a **26** taxpayer in forcing the tax authorities to rescind a ruling denying a taxpayer's earlier claim for a tax paid in violation of EU law when it subsequently turns out that the taxpayer's position was well grounded.[27]

The judgment in the *Kühne & Heitz* case stirred up a lot of discussion about **27** the relationship between the finality of administrative decisions and the principles of effectiveness and supremacy of EU law. It also has pushed the national courts to ask the ECJ to clarify whether the *res iudicata* principle may fend off the EU law.

As a rule, res iudicata holds firmly. It was confirmed in the *Kapferer* case **28** where the Court made clear that a national court is not under obligation to ignore its procedural provisions in order to void a final court judgment, even though

---

[24] ECJ 25 July 1991, C-208/90, *Emmott* [1991] ECR. See also Dassesse, *Bulletin* 2004, p. 512.
[25] ECJ 2 October 2003, C-147/01, *Weber's Wine Word* [2003] ECR I-11365, para. 117.
[26] ECJ 13 January 2004, C-453/00, *Kühne & Heitz* [2004] ECR I-837, para. 28.
[27] Dassesse, *Bulletin* 2004, p. 513.

this judgment is contrary to the EU law.[28] However, this principle is subject to exceptions that are permanently extended by the ECJ.

29   In the *Lucchini* case the ECJ decided that the EU law precludes the application of a provision of national law which seeks to lay down the principle of *res judicata* in so far as the application of that provision prevents the recovery of State aid granted in breach of EU law which has been found to be incompatible with the common market in a decision of the Commission which has become final.[29]

30   In the *Fallimento Olimpiclub* case the ECJ ruled that the interpretation of the *res judicata* principle following which final judgments on tax obligations in period X are also binding in period Y infringes the principle of effectiveness and, therefore, should be ignored.[30]

b. Remedies against Breaches of EU Law

31   In principle, a taxpayer who has paid taxes in violation of EU law has two kinds of claims at his disposal. Firstly, entitlement to **claim a refund** of charges levied by a Member State in breach of EU law stems from rights conferred on nationals by directly effective EU law provisions prohibiting such charges.[31] Secondly, an individual is also entitled to obtain compensation for losses resulting indirectly from payment of unduly charges, for example **interest on reimbursed charges** resulting from the unavailability of sums of money as a result of tax being levied prematurely.[32] This second claim comes into play only as a corollary of a Member State's liability for a breach of EU law.

32   One should not overlook the Court's decision in *Littlewoods Retail and Others* where it was held that a taxable person who overpaid tax under national law provisions that are contrary to the EU law should be reimbursed together with interest on the amount of the overpayment. The interest should be calculated as simple interest unless in the case of similar claims based on domestic law a taxpayer is entitled to receive a more generous remedy (for instance, compound interest), in which case this more favorable treatment should be extended to reimbursement of taxes paid in violation of EU law.[33]

33   Member States tend to preclude the individuals' right to a refund of unduly levied charges that have been subsequently passed down the economic chain so that their economic burden is borne by third parties and a refund would prompt **unjust enrichment** of the claimant. This unjust enrichment argument was initially

---

[28]   ECJ 16 March 2006, C-234/04, *Kapferer* [2006] ECR I-2585.

[29]   ECJ 18 July 2007, C 119/05, *Lucchini* [2007] ECR I 6199.

[30]   ECJ 3 September 2009, C-2/08, *Fallimento Olimpiclub* [2009] ECR I-7501.

[31]   ECJ 9 November 1983, 199/82, *San Giorgio* [1983] ECR 3595; see also Dougan, *Cambridge Yearbook of European Legal Studies* (1998) p. 233 et seq.

[32]   ECJ 13 March 2007, C-524/04, *Test Claimants in the Thin Cap Group Litigation* [2007] ECR I-2107, para. 112.

[33]   ECJ 19 July 2012, C-591/10, *Littlewoods Retail and Others* (not yet published).

accepted by the Court, but later has been subjected to several conditions and effectively watered down.

In order to successfully claim remedies for sustained losses the Member **34** State's liability must first be established in the case at hand. The Court developed the principle of the **Member State's liability for breach of EU law** in *Francovich* by holding that "it is a principle of Community law that the Member States are obliged to make good loss and damage caused to individuals by breaches of Community law for which they can be held responsible".[34] It is settled case law that the following **conditions** have to be met **in order for a Member State to be held liable**:

- the rule of law infringed must be intended to confer rights on individuals,
- the breach of EU law has to be "sufficiently serious",
- a causal link must exist between the breach of the State's obligation and the loss and damage suffered by the injured parties.

National rules establishing **stringent conditions of liability of a Member State** **35** are unacceptable under EU law as they could jeopardize the right to compensation for breach.[35] On the other hand, more lenient state liability conditions are accepted if they ensure a more effective application of EU law.[36]

In addition, one may not overlook that **state liability for breach of EU law** **36** can arise **not only out of activities of legislative organs** of a Member State. In this respect, it should be noted that "a Member State's failure to fulfil obligations may, in principle, be established under Article 226 EC whatever the agency of that State whose action or inaction is the cause of the failure to fulfil its obligations, even in the case of a constitutionally independent institution".[37] Accordingly, the Court has recently extended the principle of state liability to include the judiciaries of Member States. In the *Koebler* case the Court ruled that Member States are liable for damages of individuals caused by "manifest infringements" of EU law by their highest courts.[38] In the *Commission v Italy* case the ECJ held Italy liable for infringement of EU law by its national courts.[39] From the *Commission v Spain* case one may deduce that a single judgment of the supreme court of a Member State which is not in line with EU law suffices to claim Member State liability.[40] Very recently, a state official's statement that was

---

[34] ECJ 19 November 1991, joined cases C-6/90 and C-9/90, *Francovich* [1991] ECR I-5357, para. 37.
[35] See Jans, in Obradovic/Lavranos (eds.) *Interface between EU law and national law* (2007) p. 285; see also ECJ 13 June 2006, C-173/03, *Traghetti del Mediterraneo* [2006] ECR I-5177.
[36] Jans, in Obradovic/Lavranos (eds.) *Interface between EU law and national law* (2007) p. 286.
[37] ECJ, 5 May 1970, 77/69, *Commission v Belgium* [1970] ECR 237, para. 15.
[38] ECJ 30 September 2003, C-224/01, *Köbler* [2003] ECR I-10239.
[39] ECJ 9 December 2003, C-129/00, *Commission v Italy* [2003] ECR I-14637.
[40] ECJ 12 November 2009, C-154/08, *Commission v Spain* [2009] (not yet published).

contrary to EU law was found a sufficient base for establishing liability of a Member State.[41]

2. The Sources of EU Direct Tax Law

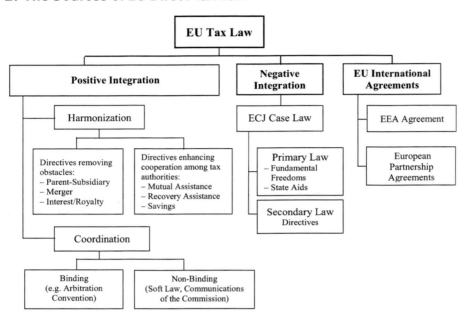

a) Primary Law

37 In contrast to indirect taxes, **direct taxes** are not expressly dealt with by the TFEU. This fact is usually explained in two ways. Firstly, at the time the Treaty of Rome was signed (1957) direct taxes apparently were not seen as necessarily important for the establishing of the internal market and, consequently, were left outside the scope of the EC Treaty (the predecessor of the TFEU).[42] Secondly, having in mind that direct taxes may serve as useful tools of pursuing various economic or social aims, Member States' reluctance to give up their competence seems quite understandable. Consequently, direct taxation remains within the competence of Member States.

38 In the absence of specific provisions, **Art. 115 TFEU** (ex Art. 94 EC) seems to be an appropriate **legal basis** for possible harmonization in the field of direct taxes. It authorizes the Council to issue directives to approximate laws, regu-

---

[41] ECJ 13 April 2007, C-470/03, *A.G.M. – COS. MET Srl* [2007] ECR I-2749, para. 96.

[42] It should be noted that the 1953 Tinbergen report, laying conceptual grounds for creation of the EC, did not acknowledge harmonization of direct taxes as necessary in developing the single market.

lations and provisions directly affecting the establishment and functioning of the internal market. Such directives may be only adopted on the basis of **unanimity** in the Council. Therefore, it is rather difficult to push forward European tax harmonization as every measure has to satisfy all Member States, which, in the light of serious differences between national tax policies (for instance, low tax countries vs. high tax countries), appears more than difficult. A legal basis for harmonization of direct taxes unfortunately cannot be seen in **Art. 114 TFEU** (ex Art. 95 EC). This provision may come into play where a difference between the legal orders of Member States is distorting the conditions of competition in the common market and this distortion needs to be eliminated. Accordingly, the Council, acting together with the European Parliament, by a qualified majority on a proposal from the Commission is entitled to issue the necessary directives. However, the procedure envisaged in this article does not apply to tax provisions.[43]

It should be noted that the EC Treaty contained **Art. 293** providing that the **39** Member States must as far as necessary enter into negotiations to secure the **abolition of double taxation**. Such a provision does not exist in the TFEU. However, as this provision was devoid of direct effect and merely constituted a political declaration,[44] the effect of its deletion should not be overestimated or perceived as a sign of removing the abolition of double taxation from the political agenda of the EU.[45]

Quite unexpectedly the most relevant primary law provisions for direct taxes **40** have turned out to be the **fundamental freedoms** as interpreted by the ECJ (see Chapter II, m.nos 96 et seq.), which set limits as to the boundaries for exercising national tax jurisdictions (known as **negative integration**).

Furthermore, State aid rules (Art. 107 and 108 TFEU, ex Art. 87 and 88 EC) **41** have played an increasingly important role in the field of direct taxes, whereas recent judgments from EU courts have determined the boundaries of the direct effect of such rules on direct taxes and secured an effective review of the EU Commission activity's in this domain (see Chapter III, m.nos 299 et seq.).

b) Secondary Law

i. Level of Harmonization

As stated above, when the EC was created, **harmonization** of direct taxes as **42** such was not considered to be an aim of the EC. Nevertheless, at a certain level of development of the Single Market, it turned out that, at least to some extent, harmonization is also required in this field, namely insofar as common rules

---

[43] Art. 114(2) TFEU (ex Art. 95(2) EC).
[44] ECJ 12 May 1998, C-336/96, *Gilly* [1998] ECR I-2823, para. 17.
[45] See in this respect Tax Policy Work Programme by Commissioner Algirdas Šemeta available at http://ec.europa.eu/commission_2010-2014/semeta/headlines/speeches/2010/02/speech_1602b.pdf.

are indispensable for securing the elimination of obstacles within the internal market. Naturally, there have been different views in the Commission and Member States regarding how much harmonization is needed. As a result, the introduction of common rules for all EU Member States (known as **positive integration**) in the field of direct taxes was mainly realized by means of tax coordination, i.e. without the creation of secondary EU law (known as **tax harmonization**).

ii. Directives

43 Directives can be grouped according to their actual function into two main categories, namely whether they remove a tax obstacle within the internal market, or whether they have been designed mainly for the purpose of enhancing cooperation among the tax authorities and they secure a more proportionate impact on the exercise of rights granted by primary law.

a. Directives Removing Obstacles

44 The **Parent-Subsidiary Directive**[46] was adopted by the Council on 23 July 1990 based on a proposal presented by the Commission in 1969. It allows for, under certain conditions, elimination of withholding taxes on outbound dividends distributed by a subsidiary to its parent within the EU. Moreover, it prescribes measures so as to avoid economic double taxation of dividends in the hands of a parent company. On 22 December 2003 the Council adopted a new directive amending the Parent-Subsidiary Directive[47] (see Chapter IV, m.nos. 429 et seq.).

45 The **Merger Directive**[48] was also accepted by the Council on 23 July 2003 based on a proposal presented by the Commission in 1969. It provides for deferral (by rollover relief) of tax claims that become due at the level of a company or a shareholder in the case of the cross-border mergers, (partial) divisions, transfers of assets and exchanges of shares taking place within the EU. Taxation of the capital gains is deferred until a later disposal of the asset (actual realization of profits). On 17 October 2003 the Commission adopted a proposal amending the Merger Directive.[49] A modified version of this proposal was subsequently adopted by the Council[50] (see Chapter V, m.nos 450 et seq.).

---

[46] Council Directive 90/435/EEC of 23 July 1990 on the common system of taxation applicable in the case of parent companies and subsidiaries of different Member States, OJ L 225 of 20 August 1990, pp. 6–9.

[47] Council Directive 2003/123/EC of 22 December 2003 amending Directive 90/435/EEC on the common system of taxation applicable in the case of parent companies and subsidiaries of different Member States, OJ L 7 of 13 January 2004, pp. 41–44.

[48] Council Directive 90/434/EEC of 23 July 1990 on the common system of taxation applicable to mergers, divisions, transfers of assets, and exchanges of shares concerning companies of different Member States, OJ L 225 of 20 August 1990, pp. 1–5.

[49] See COM(2003) 613 final.

[50] Council Directive 2005/19/EC of 17 February 2005 amending Directive 90/434/EEC 1990 on the common system of taxation applicable to mergers, divisions, transfers of assets and

The aim of the **Interest and Royalty Directive**[51] is to eliminate certain ob- **46**
stacles to the cross-border activity of multinationals. It provides, under certain
conditions, for no withholding tax on interest and royalty payments between associated companies (see Chapter VI, m.nos. 574 et seq.).

b. Directives Enhancing Cooperation among Tax Authorities

The **Mutual Assistance Directive**[52] was issued on 9 December 1977 as the first **47**
directive in the field of direct taxes. It deals with mutual administrative assistance between the competent tax authorities and authorizes them to exchange
information (upon request, spontaneously or even automatically) relevant for determining a taxpayer's assessment. In 2009 the European Commission presented
a proposal for a completely new Directive on administrative cooperation in the
field of taxation,[53] which was subsequently adopted (see Chapter VIII, m.nos 647
et seq.).

The **Recovery Assistance Directive**,[54] setting up a legal framework for mutual **48**
assistance between Member States in recovering claims, initially covered agricultural levies and customs duties as sources of EU revenue (traditional own
resources)[55] and later extended to indirect taxation. As of 1 July 2002 the directive was extended to include the possibilities to also recover taxes on income and
capital as well as taxes on insurance premiums. In 2009 the European Commission put forward a proposal for a completely new directive concerning mutual
assistance for the recovery of tax claims,[56] that was subsequently enacted (see
Chapter VIII, m.nos. 693 et seq.).

---

exchanges of shares concerning companies of different Member States, OJ L 58 of 4 March
2005, pp. 19–27.

[51] Council Directive 2003/49/EC of June 2003 on a common system of taxation applicable to
interest and royalty payments, OJ L 157 of 26 June 2003, pp. 49–54.

[52] Council Directive 77/799/EEC of 19 December 1977 concerning mutual assistance by the
competent authorities of the Member States in the field of direct taxation, OJ L 336 of
27 December 1977, pp. 15–20.

[53] Proposal of 2 February 2009 for a Council Directive on administrative cooperation in the
field of taxation, COM(2009) 29 final.

[54] Council Directive 2001/44/EC of 15 June 2001 amending Directive 76/308/EEC on mutual
assistance for the recovery of claims resulting from operations forming part of the system
of financing the European Agricultural Guidance and Guarantee Fund, and of agricultural
levies and customs duties and in respect of value added tax and certain excise duties, OJ
L 175 of 28 June 2001, pp. 17–20.

[55] Council Directive 76/308/EEC of 15 March 1976 on mutual assistance for the recovery of
claims resulting from operations forming part of the system of financing the European
Agricultural Guidance and Guarantee Fund, and of the agricultural levies and customs duties OJ L 73 of 19 March 1976, pp. 18–23.

[56] Proposal of 2 February 2009 for a Council Directive concerning mutual assistance for the
recovery of claims relating to taxes, duties and other measures, COM(2009) 28 final. See
for a detailed analysis on the proposed Directive Caram, *Intertax* 2009, p. 639 et seq.

49   The **Savings Directive**[57] seeks to ensure a minimum level of taxation of interest received by individual taxpayers. For this reason, each Member State is responsible for collecting the relevant information from the paying agents in its territory about interest payments made to beneficial owners residing in other Member States. A special regime excluding the obligation to carry out an automatic exchange of information was included in the original version of the Directive for Austria, Belgium and Luxembourg. The same regime was also the object of the Savings Agreements concluded by the EU and its Member States with Switzerland on 26 October 2004 as a part of a package of measures containing third states' measures equivalent to those adopted under the Savings Directive. Such agreements have been also concluded with Andorra, Lichtenstein, Monaco and San Marino (see Chapter VII, m.no 610 et seq.).

iii. Regulations

50   There is no single EU Regulation entirely devoted to direct taxes. However, Art. 7(2) of **Regulation 492/2011** on freedom of movement for workers within the EU requires that all workers who are nationals of a Member State enjoy in the territory of other Member States the same tax benefits as host state nationals working there.[58] One should not also overlook in this respect regulations on *Societas Europaea*[59] and *Societas Cooperativa Europaea*.[60]

c) Tax Coordination

51   Tax coordination as such does not give rise to the production of EU law, but rather hard rules (known as **binding coordination**) and soft rules (known as **non-binding coordination**), which EU Member States have in common and are therefore obliged to comply with. Nevertheless, the fact that it does not represent EU law in strict terms is important for the perspective of excluding the ECJ jurisdiction on it.

i. Soft Law

52   The European Commission has issued several **non-binding recommendations and communications** with the aim of promoting Member States' voluntary com-

---

[57] Council Directive 2003/48/EC of June 2003 on taxation of savings income in the form of interest payments, OJ L 157 of 26 June 2003, pp. 38–48.

[58] Council Regulation (EC) No. 1612/68 of 15 October 1968 on freedom of movement for workers within the Community, OJ, English Special Edition 1968 (II), p. 475.

[59] Council Regulation (EC) No 2157/2001 of 8 October 2001 on the Statute for a European company (SE) accompanying by Council Directive 2001/86/EC of 8 October 2001 supplementing the Statute for a European company with regard to the involvement of employees.

[60] Council Regulation (EC) No 1435/2003 of 22 July 2003 on the Statute for a European Co-operative Society (SCE) accompanying by Council Directive 2003/72/EC of 22 July 2003 supplementing the Statute for a European Cooperative Society with regard to the involvement of employees.

pliance with EU law. Even though such documents may serve well as guidance for Member States when applying EU law, sadly their relevance has been so far ignored by them. Perhaps it will be different with the Commission initiatives within the framework of the coordination action (see m.nos. 90 et seq.).

ii. The Arbitration Convention

The Member States concluded the **Arbitration Convention** on 23 July 1990 to **53** provide for binding arbitration when the tax authorities fail to find a solution within two years to the double taxation arising within a multinational group due to different views of the tax authorities of the Member States concerned about the prices charged for transactions within this group. It should be noted that, even though the Commission preferred the form of a directive, the Member States selected a form of agreement which does not fall within the jurisdiction of the European Court of Justice. This convention is possibly the only example of binding coordination in the field of direct taxes (see Chapter IX, m.nos. 727 et seq.).

d) The EU International Agreements

Art. 217 TFEU (ex Art. 310 EC) clearly entitles the EU to conclude **agreements** **54** **with third states or international bodies** (hereinafter: "international agreements"). So far, the EU itself has concluded very few international agreements concerning tax law issues. However, certain provisions of the EU international agreements may have important consequences for the direct tax systems of Member States.[61]

i. European Economic Area Agreement

The **European Free Trade Area (EFTA)** was created in 1960 as a free trade **55** zone offering an alternative means of economic integration than that of the European Economic Community. **The European Economic Area (EEA)** Agreement was invented as a mechanism allowing Members States of the EFTA to actively participate in the process of the European economic integration without losing any political competences. The EEA Agreement entered into force on 1 January 1994. One year later, three Member States of the EFTA (Austria, Finland and Sweden) joined the European Union. Currently, the EFTA consists only of Norway, Lichtenstein, Iceland and Switzerland (the last state is not a member of the EEA since it rejected the EEA Agreement in a referendum in 1992). The EFTA Court is entitled to give opinions upon questions referred by the EFTA countries' courts.[62] The **EFTA Court opinions**, unlike the ECJ judgments under Art. 267

---

[61] For more on this issue, see Bezborodov, Freedom of Establishment in the EC Economic Partnership Agreements: in Search of its Direct Effect on Direct Taxation, *Intertax* 2007, pp. 658–712.

[62] Art. 34 of the ESA/Court Agreement.

TFEU (ex Art. 234 EC), do not bind the national courts. It should be noted that the EFTA countries' courts are not obliged in any case to ask the EFTA Court for an opinion and they may freely interpret the EEA Agreement. Nevertheless, generally the EFTA states' national courts follow the decisions of the EFTA Court.

56   The **structure of the EEA Agreement** resembles that of the TFEU. First of all, the prohibition of discrimination on grounds of nationality is envisaged.[63] There are also provisions concerning the fundamental freedoms as well as on competition and State aid law.[64] In the *Ospelt* case the ECJ held that "one of the principal aims of the EEA Agreement is to provide for the fullest possible realisation of the free movement of goods, persons, services and capital within the whole European Economic Area, so that the **internal market** established within the European Union is **extended to the EFTA States**" and, consequently, decided that the provisions of the EEA should be interpreted is a similar fashion as the corresponding provisions of the TFEU.[65] In the *Keller Holding* case[66] the ECJ for the first time applied the EEA to a direct tax case.

ii. European Partnership Agreements (EPA)

57   Furthermore, the EU and its Member States have concluded several international agreements with third countries for the purpose of making them share to a greater or lesser extent the goals of the internal market. In several (but not all) cases such agreements contain directly applicable provisions. Examples of this kind are the **EPA with Russia** (perhaps the most advanced one so far), EPAs with other economies in transition, the **Euromediterranean Agreement** and the agreements with several developing countries.

58   Although such agreements have not been designed to deal specifically with tax issues, their general wording may be in principle reconciled with their application to direct taxes unless they contain a specific carve-out clause.

3. The European Commission's Positive Integration Efforts

a) Historical Overview

i. Early Harmonization Proposals (up to the 1990s)

59   In early 1960s it became obvious that the lack of direct tax harmonization constitutes an obstacle to the creation of a true single market. For this reason, in 1962 **the Neumark Report** came up with a single corporate tax rate based on a

---

[63] Art. 4 EEA.

[64] Art. 8 EEA provides for the free movement of goods, Art. 28 provides for the free movement of workers, Art. 32 provides for the freedom of establishment, Art. 36 provides for the freedom to provide services and Art. 40 provides for the free movement of capital.

[65] ECJ 23 September 2003, C-452/01, *Ospelt* [2003] ECR I-9743, paras. 29 and 32.

[66] ECJ 23 February 2006, C-472/04, *Keller Holding* [2006] ECR I-2107.

split-rate system (0% on retained earnings, 15%–25% on distributed profits) without giving credits to shareholders against their personal income tax liability.

In 1975 the Commission made a proposal for a **directive on harmonization** 60 **of corporate and capital income taxes**. It was based on a uniform credit system with a corporate income tax rate between 45 % and 55 % on retained earnings and distributed profits, a fully deductible withholding tax of 25 % on dividends as well as credits available to shareholders from 45 % to 55 % of the distributed profits. This proposal was rejected by the European Parliament.

In 1969 the proposals for the **Parent-Subsidiary Directive** and the **Merger** 61 **Directive** were made public. Modified versions of these proposals were adopted in 1990. In 1990 the Commission put forward a proposal for a **directive on cross-border loss relief** which, due to lack political support, was eventually abandoned.[67]

In March 1992 a committee chaired by Onno Ruding presented a report com- 62 missioned by the Commission on company taxation in Europe (also known as the **Ruding Report**).[68] The report identified several differences between the na- tional tax systems regarding models of taxation of distributed company profits, the way of providing double taxation relief, the level of statutory tax rates, the definition of the tax assessment base, the level of the rates of withholding taxes. In addition, several differences in the tax treatment of cross-border investments in comparison to the tax treatment of domestic investments were mentioned as well as the impossibility of cross-border compensation of losses incurred by a foreign subsidiary with profits of a domestic parent, the discriminatory effects of imputation systems (granting the imputation credit only to resident share- holders), non-elimination of international double taxation, and lack of credit for foreign withholding taxes.

The **recommendations** made by the Ruding Report are based on three 63 principles: a source state entitlement, non-discrimination and reciprocity. The Report strongly recommended elimination of the double economic taxation of cross-border income flows and approximation of corporation taxes. As regards the two general recommendations, several more specific proposals were put forward. Consequently, with respect to the elimination of the double taxation, the following suggestions were made (none of them were immediately put into motion):

- abolition of withholding taxes on dividends paid by subsidiaries to parent companies but maintaining source taxation on dividends paid to other reci-

---

[67] Proposal of 28 November 1990 for a Council Directive concerning arrangements for the taking into account by enterprises of the losses of their permanent establishments and sub- sidiaries situated in other Member States, COM(1990) 595 final, OJ C 53 of 28 February 1991, p. 30.

[68] Commission of the European Communities, *Report of the Committee of Independent Experts on Company Taxation* (1992).

pients unless they prove their identity and their residence in an EU Member State,

- elimination of double economic taxation of dividends in the parent company state, although the choice of method (the exemption method or the credit method) was left for Member States,
- the speedy introduction of the Interest and Royalty Directive (then a proposal) and extension of its subjective scope as well as the lowering of thresholds,
- extension of the Arbitration Convention to all Member States (the Commission was asked, among other things, to set up a procedure in order to avoid transfer pricing disputes).

ii. The Action against Harmful Tax Competition

64 The background of the EU's **action against harmful tax competition** dates back to the 1980s when several Member States, in order to attract foreign capital, introduced favourable tax regimes. Such regimes include "coordination centres", holding companies, finance companies, exempt companies.

65 In October 1997 the Commission issued a paper entitled "**Towards tax co-ordination in the European Union**".[69] It proposes a four-track approach to tackle harmful tax competition. Three of the proposed measured deal with direct tax matters:

- the Code of Conduct for Business Taxation, together with the Notice of the Commission on how the EC State aid rules, must be understood and applied in the field of company taxation,
- measures ensuring the effective taxation of capital income, especially in the form of interest on savings (a proposal for the Savings Directive),
- measures eliminating withholding taxes on cross-border payments of interest and royalties between companies (a proposal for the Interest and Royalty Directive).

66 **An amended version of the Code of Conduct** was adopted by the Council in the form of a resolution on 1 December 1997.[70] It constitutes a non-binding political declaration. Harmful tax measures are "measures (including administrative practices) which affect or may affect in a significant way the location of business activity in the Community" and which provide for a significantly lower effective level of taxation than the general level of taxation in the Member State concerned.

67 The Code of Conduct lists the following characteristics as crucial for **establishing the harmfulness of a tax measure**:

---

[69] COM(1997) 495.
[70] OJ C 2 of 6 January 1998, p. 1.

- a measure is only available for non-residents for transactions with non-residents (**off-shore feature**)
- the measure does not affect the domestic tax base (**ring-fencing**)
- the tax advantage is granted regardless of any actual economic activity in a state (**lack of substance**)
- rules for the determination and allocation of profits are applied that **do not follow** internationally accepted standards like the OECD Transfer Pricing Guidelines
- **lack of transparency** caused, for example, by negotiability of the tax burden.

Under the Code of Conduct, Member States undertook **a political commitment** to wipe out any harmful tax measures from their tax systems and not to introduce such new measures. In addition, each Member State may demand that any measure of another Member State be discussed and it may make comments on it. *Wattel* points out that the Code of Conduct does not challenge competitive tax systems with low tax rates but its sword is rather directed to "tax measures departing from the normal tax system, favouring certain mobile investments".[71]   **68**

In order to examine any national measures that might possibly be regarded as harmful a group of high-level representatives of Member States chaired by Mrs. Dawn Primarolo was set up (the **Primarolo group**). This group issued its final report on 23 November 1999. It discussed and applied criteria set in the Code of Conduct to potential harmful tax measures of Member States. In addition, it also presented a black list of certain national measures together with reservations of the respective Member States in the form of footnotes.   **69**

The group scrutinized **over 200 national measures** and identified **66 of them as harmful** (40 in EU Member States, 3 in Gibraltar and 23 in dependent or associated territories). Among them, one can find holding company regimes (for example, in Austria, Denmark, Luxembourg), coordination centre regimes (Belgium, Germany, Luxembourg), headquarters and logistics centre regimes (France), the international finance service centre (Ireland).   **70**

Despite reluctance or even hostility on the side of some Member States, the ECOFIN Council achieved an **interim agreement** and decided on phasing-out certain measures. Until 31 December 2010 extensions were granted in respect of the following regimes: **71**

- Belgian coordination centres,
- Irish foreign income rules,
- Luxembourg 1929 holding companies,
- Netherlands group financing regimes,
- Portuguese Madeira free zone regime (in this case until the end of 2011).[72]

---

[71] Terra/Wattel, *European Tax Law* (2008) p. 199.
[72] In June 2007 the European Commission approved under EC State aid rules a scheme providing tax reductions worth EUR 300 million until 2020 to companies setting up in the free

72 It goes without saying that in the post-crisis era EU Member States desperately searching for new revenue sources take tougher position on tax havens and uncooperative jurisdictions. In the future this may crystallize into legislative initiative on the EU level. For the time being, one should not overlook that the new EU Commissioner for Taxation has put tackling tax evasion, avoidance and harmful tax competition at the EU and at international level by promoting the **principles of good governance** (transparency, exchange of information and fair tax competition) in the tax area on the top of his agenda.[73]

iii. Towards an Internal Market without Tax Obstacles

73 On 23 June 2001 the Commission released a communication entitled **"Towards an Internal Market without Tax Obstacles"** setting its tax priorities for the next years.[74] With respect to income tax it makes clear that this sphere should remain an exclusive competence of Member States and only specific actions are required in order to eliminate obstacles concerning the fundamental freedoms and to ensure an effective taxation. As regards corporate taxation, the Commission announced that instead of drafting ambitious direct-tax harmonization plans it would focus on solutions more likely to gain political acceptance. First of all, the Commission declared its intention to combat breaches of the fundamental freedoms and the State aid rules more frequently by means of infringement proceedings before the ECJ. Secondly, more soft law (recommendations, interpretations and guidance on the application of ECJ case law) was promised. Last but not least, the Commission made public its wish to make use of enhanced cooperation whereby at least eight Member States may cooperate more closely in certain areas after approval by a qualified majority in the Council.

74 More detailed plans regarding corporate taxation contained in a policy document on corporate tax policy and a study on company taxation were issued on **23 October 2001**. Taking account of the Lisbon strategy to make the EU "the most competitive and dynamic knowledge-based economy in the world" the Commission proposed a two-route approach, built on: targeted, short-term measures and consolidation/common tax base. The targeted measures included proposed improvements of the Parent-Subsidiary Directive and the Merger Directive (including introducing specific provisions dealing with the tax treatment of *Societas Europae*), establishment of the EU Joint Transfer Pricing Forum, a greater coordination of tax treaties within the EU and with third states.

---

zone of Madeira (ZFM) between 2007 and 2013. The granting of the aid is subject to requirements to create jobs and strict safeguards as to the implementation of the aid. See the official press release IP/07/891.

[73] See in this respect the Commission Communication on Promoting Good Governance in Tax Matters, Brussels, 28.4.2009 COM(2009) 201 final and Tax Policy Work Programme by Commissioner Algirdas Šemeta available at http://ec.europa.eu/commission_2010-2014/semeta/headlines/speeches/2010/02/speech_1602b.pdf.

[74] COM(2001) 582 final.

b) Current Proposals for Harmonization

The greatest problem of **multinationals** operating in more than one Member **75** State is the fact that their activities **fall within several tax jurisdictions**. This results in a number of negative consequences ranging from **severe compliance costs** (the need to comply with several different legal regimes) to **a lack of cross-border relief**. This last phenomenon can be especially painful as one could imagine a situation where in a given tax year a multinational would have to pay taxes on profits earned in some jurisdictions even though its overall pan-European result is negative. This situation can also dissuade investors from investing in Europe as they do not experience similar problems in other big world economies like Japan or the US.

In order to tackle this problem the Commission has come up with the idea **76** of providing companies with **a consolidated corporate tax base for their EU-wide activities**. In 2001 the Commission started studying various concepts allowing for introducing a common tax base for European companies. The following ideas were presented as potentially feasible solutions:

- **Compulsory Harmonized Tax Base**
- **European Union Company Tax**
- **Home State Taxation**
- **Common Consolidated Corporate Tax Base**

The **Compulsory Harmonized Tax Base** entails a single corporate tax base for **77** all EU companies and abolition of national rules defining the corporate tax base. If introduced, this system would be mandatory for all EU-based companies. Initially, the Commission considered it to be a first step towards a Common Consolidated Tax Base, but later decided that there was no need for intermediate measures.

The **European Union Company Tax** constituted the most ambitious project **78** of harmonization of corporate taxation leading in fact to its integration within the EU. Under the European Union Company Tax system, both tax bases and tax rates would be the same in all Member States. In addition, assessment as well as collection would be done at the EU level. EU taxpayers would pay a European Union Company Tax on their consolidated EU profits directly to an EU body. This body would be responsible for apportioning the tax revenue among the Member States where taxpayer's activities are carried out on the basis of a formula. In the literature this concept is seen as the most unrealistic among those considered by the Commission since it would lead to a complete elimination of national sovereignty in direct tax matters, something Member States would not appreciate.[75] Therefore, it is unsurprising that the Commission failed to develop this concept any further.

---

[75] Terra/Wattel, *European Tax Law* (2005) p. 297.

79   The underlying idea of **Home State Taxation** is based on the principle of mutual recognition, which has been accepted within the EU framework by the ECJ.[76] Accordingly, the tax system of the Member State of the parent company would govern the determination and allocation of profits to subsidiaries and permanent establishments located in other Member States. The group would be treated as a unity and taxed on consolidated profits irrespective of the number or legal form of secondary establishments (a subsidiary or a branch). Profits would be calculated in accordance with the parent company's home state tax law provisions and, subsequently, divided among the Member States involved on the basis of a specific formula. The portion of the profit of a group of companies allocated to a Member State is to be taxed at its own tax rate. At present, despite earlier announcements, it seems that work on this project has ceased.

i. Common Consolidated Corporate Tax Base

80 Under the Common Consolidated Corporate Tax Base (hereinafter: CCCTB), firstly, **a consolidated tax base of a group of companies** would be established and, secondly, it would be divided among jurisdictions on the basis of a **formula apportionment**. Finally, the part of a tax base allocated to a Member State would be taxed at its own tax rate.[77] In 2004 the Commission set up the Common Consolidated Corporate Tax Base Working Group composed of Member States' experts, occasionally joined by business and academic representatives and chaired by an official from the Commission. The Working Group had been meeting to discuss the future shape of the project. In 2007 the European Commission disclosed several details concerning a proposal for the CCCTB. Finally, in 2011 the EU Commission presented a proposal of Directive on a Common Consolidated Corporate Tax Base (CCCTB) [hereinafter **the CCCTB Proposal**].[78]

81   The creation of an optional **common corporate tax base for EU-based business operators** is envisaged.[79] CCCTB will apply on the basis of worldwide taxation; however, much of this income will be exempt. A group would cover an EU-resident parent and its EU-resident subsidiaries[80] (including permanent establishments) regardless of whether the EU-resident parent is controlled by a non-EU-resident company. It would also include a group of EU-resident sub-

---

[76] The development of the Home State Taxation concept is credited to Malcolm Gammie and Sven Olof Lodin. See Gammie/Lodin, *Home State Taxation* (2001).

[77] For more information, see Lang/Pistone/Schuch/Staringer (eds.) *Common Consolidated Corporate Tax Base (CCCTB)* (2008).

[78] http://ec.europa.eu/taxation_customs/resources/documents/taxation/company_tax/common_tax_base/com_2011_121_en.pdf. For a broader overview see: J. Lamotte, New EU Tax Challenges and Opportunities in a (C)CCTB World, *European Taxation*, 6/2012, p. 271 et seq.

[79] Arts. 6 and 104 of the CCCTB Proposal.

[80] As defined in art. 2 of the CCCTB Proposal, having one of the legal forms listed in Appendix I and being liable to one of the corporate taxes listed in Appendix II of the CCCTB Proposal.

sidiaries (or permanent establishments) remaining under the common control of a non-EU-resident parent. The consolidation is to be mandatory for all companies having opted for CCCTB who have a qualifying subsidiary or a permanent establishment in another state in the EU (the "all-in" or "all-out" principle). For a subsidiary to qualify for consolidation over 50% of its voting rights have to be directly or indirectly controlled by a parent company or it must have an ownership right amounting to more than 75% of the company's capital or more than 75% of the rights giving entitlement to profits, provided that the thresholds have been met for the entire tax period and for a minimum uninterrupted period of nine months.[81]

The CCCTB Proposal provides for detailed rules on the computation of income, thereby not adhering to many Member States' practice of taking accounting principles as the starting point for computation taxable income.[82] The tax base is to be calculated as revenues less exempt revenues, deductible expenses (incurred by the taxpayer with a view "to obtaining or securing income, including costs of research and development and costs incurred in raising equity or debt for the purposes of the business") and other deductible items.[83] Exempt revenues consist of capital gains earned upon the disposal of shares, dividends (no specific holding threshold or holding period required), income attributed to a third-country PE.[84] However, a switch-over applies if a PE or a company distributing dividends or in which shares are disposed of is located in low-tax jurisdiction. In addition, loss carry forward relief, naturally including cross-border loss relief, without time limits is allowed.[85] Last but not least, in calculating the consolidated tax base, profits and losses arising from transactions directly carried out between members of a group are to be left out.[86] **82**

The CCCTB involves a revolutionary change: this is the switch of the method used for allocation of income from arm's length method to a **formula apportionment method**. This method envisages apportionment based on a formula including company factors involved in the conduct of business by companies. On the basis of a formula apportionment the consolidated tax base of the group is to be shared by using weighted factors. The most crucial issue is the selection of these factors and determination of relevance attributed to each of them. An ideal formula would ensure a fair division of the tax base and afford protection from income shifting. The CCCTB Proposal envisages using a **multiple-formula** based on the following factors: **labour, capital and sales**. Each of these factors is deemed to have the same weight. **83**

---

[81] Art. 59 of the CCCTB Proposal.
[82] Art. 9 of the CCCTB Proposal.
[83] Art. 10 of the CCCTB Proposal.
[84] Art. 11 of the CCCTB Proposal.
[85] Art. 43 of the CCCTB Proposal.
[86] Art. 59 of the CCCTB Proposal.

84   As for the **labour factor,** composed of one half of the total amount of the payroll of a group member as its numerator and the total amount of the payroll of the group as its denominator, and as to the other half, made up of the number of employees of a group member as its numerator and the number of employees of the group as its denominator it is suggested to measure it by means of two equally weighted elements: payroll of the workforce and number of employees. In order to appropriately determine this factor, three elements have to be precisely defined: the workforce, the cost of workforce, and the location of the work force. The workforce should cover all persons employed by a given entity. The cost of the workforce is the remuneration that is tax deductible. As for the location of the workforce the actual place of providing services by employees would be decisive.

85   The **assets factor** is to be calculated as the average value of all fixed tangible assets owned, rented or leased by a group member as its numerator and the average value of all fixed tangible assets owned, rented or leased by the group as its denominator".[87] For reasons of practicality and simplicity only fixed tangible assets (i.e. land, buildings, plant, machinery, equipment) are proposed to be included whereas intangible assets as well as financial and current assets (including inventory) would be left out. The only exception to this rule is the inclusion in assets of the factor of research, advertising, marketing and development costs incurred by an entity over the six years preceding its entry into a new or existing CCCTB group.

86   The **sales factor** is defined as "the total sales of a group member (...) as its numerator and the total sales of the group as its denominator".[88] Sales would be measured at destination (taking into account the place in which the goods are ultimately delivered).

ii. The EU Joint Transfer Pricing Forum (JTPF)

87   In the wake of the Communication "Towards an Internal Market without tax obstacles" in June 2002 the Commission formally established **the EU Joint Transfer Pricing Forum.** It consists of one expert from the tax administrations of each Member State and ten experts from business. They are joined by representatives from applicant countries and the OECD Secretariat acting as observers. The Joint Transfer Pricing Forum is expected to work on the basis of consensus and produce pragmatic, non-legislative solutions within the framework of the OECD Transfer Pricing Guidelines for the practical problems posed by transfer pricing practices in the EU.

88   Until now the Forum's work resulted in the preparation of two codes of conduct. In 2004 the Joint Transfer Pricing Forum issued the recommendation for the **Code of Conduct for the effective implementation of the Arbitration**

---

[87] Art. 92 of the CCCTB Proposal.
[88] Art. 95 of the CCCTB Proposal.

Convention and certain related issues of the mutual agreement procedure under double tax treaties between Member States.[89] This proposal was accepted by the Council on 7 December 2004. Another document developed by the Joint Transfer Pricing Forum – the **Code of Conduct on transfer pricing documentation for associated enterprises in the European Union** was adopted by the Council on 27 June 2006.[90] This document sets standards for the documentation that multinationals must provide to tax authorities on their pricing of cross-border intra-group transactions ('transfer pricing' documentation). It is well known that companies carrying out cross-border activities within the EU face onerous and divergent documentation obligations in the different Member States involved. The latter code is expected to reduce significantly tax compliance costs resulting from trading with associated enterprises in other Member States. It goes without saying that each code is merely a political commitment and is not legally binding on Member States.

On 26 February 2007 the Commission adopted a Communication on the work of the JTPF in the field of dispute avoidance and resolution procedures including guidelines for **Advance Pricing Agreements** (APAs) within the EU.[91] The Guidelines seek to avoid transfer pricing disputes and associated double taxation by providing detailed rules on how an efficient APA process should work. Moreover, they set out the framework for the over-all procedure and also provide details of how some specific problems could be resolved.

c) Current Proposals for Tax Coordination

The first Commission efforts to encourage Member States to **coordinate direct tax issues** date back to early 1990s when some non-binding recommendations were released. The first one concerns the tax treatment of non-resident individuals.[92] The second deals with the taxation of small and medium-sized enterprises.[93] Member States have remained rather unimpressed by all these documents. Later, the Commission re-branded a recommendation into a communication and issued "The Communication on Dividend Taxation of Individuals in the Internal

---

[89] Code of conduct for the effective implementation of the Convention on the elimination of double taxation in connection with the adjustment of profits of associated enterprises (2006/C 176/02), OJ C 176 of 28 July 2008, p. 8.

[90] Resolution of the Council and of the representatives of the governments of the Member States, meeting within the Council, of 27 June 2006 on a code of conduct on transfer pricing documentation for associated enterprises in the European Union (EU TPD) OJ C 176 of 28 July 2008, p. 1.

[91] Commission Communication COM(2007) 71 of 26 February 2007 on the work of the Joint Transfer Pricing Forum in the field of dispute avoidance and resolution procedures including guidelines for Advance Pricing Agreements within the EU.

[92] Commission Recommendation 94/79/EC of 21 December 1993 on the taxation of certain items of income received by non-residents in a Member State other than that in which they are resident, OJ L 39 of 10 February 1994, pp. 22–28.

[93] Recommendation 94/390/EC, OJ L 177 of July 1994, p. 1.

Market".[94] This paper was not much appreciated by the Member States either until the ECJ reinforced it with its judgments. However, these experiences have not gone in vain as recently the Commission gave up the idea of promoting its own ideas through soft law in favour of showing Member States how to comply with ECJ case law.

91   Recently, the Commission released a communication on **"Coordinating Member States' Direct Tax Systems in the Internal Market"**.[95] The communication begins by noting that at present Member States do not take cross-border situations into consideration when designing their direct tax systems. This approach results, therefore, in a different treatment of cross-border situations which often is incompatible with EU law. For this reason, the Commission believes that there is a need for more tax coordination among Member States' tax systems. Its new attitude is based on basic principles: removing discrimination and double taxation, preventing abuse and double non-taxation as well as reducing compliance costs for taxpayers who are subject to more than one tax system. It is recognized that in some instances tax coordination can be brought about by unilateral, bilateral or multilateral measures (for example, by concluding DTCs). However, in some cases measures adopted at the EU level (for instance, directives) are necessary. In the Commission's opinion, the biggest problem Member States face is the correct understanding of the implication of the ECJ case law, especially with respect to the very recent judgments. The Commission strongly believes that "appropriate co-ordination and co-operation between Member States can enable them to attain their tax policy goals and protect their tax bases, while ensuring elimination of discrimination and double taxation and reducing compliance costs".[96]

92   The new strategy presented by the Commission is extremely interesting as it is built on accepting Member States' competence in the field of direct taxation. In the absence of harmonized measures, the Commission wishes to introduce more coordination between Member States' tax systems. So far within the framework of the coordination process three communications on specific issues have been issued: the tax treatment of losses in cross-border situations[97] and exit taxation and the need for co-ordination of Member States' tax policies,[98] the application of anti-abuse measures in the area of direct taxation – within the EU and in relation to third countries.[99] These communications illustrate the Commission's willingness to help Member States to understand the ECJ jurisprudence and show them how they can bring national law in line with the fundamental

---

[94] COM(2003) 810 final.
[95] COM(2006) 823 final, section 2.1.
[96] COM(2006) 823 final, section 2.1.
[97] COM(2006) 824 final.
[98] COM(2006) 825 final.
[99] COM(2007) 785 final.

freedoms. Sadly, since 2007 the Commission has not issued any new coordination communications and it seems that its activity in this area has been stopped for unknown reasons.

The renewal of interest in tax coordination has arisen as a way to tackle the **93** financial crisis of the Eurozone. The Euro Summit, held on 26 October 2011, called for "pragmatic coordination of tax policies in the euro area" as an element of stronger economic policy coordination to support fiscal consolidation and economic growth by noting, among other things, legislative work on the Commission proposals for a CCCTB.[100]

Against this backdrop, the French-German attempt at coordination of their **94** direct tax systems should be pointed out.[101] The Green Paper published by the German Ministry of Finance provides for measures that need to be taken in order to align the tax bases of corporate income taxpayers in Germany and France. These measures include proposed changes in German tax law concerning the rules on group taxation, the treatment of portfolio dividends and loss deduction and in French tax law relevant for the corporate tax rate, the treatment of interest expenses, the rules on depreciation and amortization and partnerships. It appears that Mr Francois Hollande's election as the French president in May 2012 terminated or at least suspended this ambitious project.

d) The Financial Transaction Tax (FTT)

The Commission Proposal for a Council Directive on a common system of **95** financial transaction tax[102] is the latest development in the area of tax coordination. Since the financial sector played a major role in the crisis and has received substantial government support, there is a strong consensus that the financial sector should now make a fair contribution to public finances.[103] For this reason, the European Commission put forward a proposal for a financial transaction tax (FTT) on 28 September 2011. The proposed tax[104] would generate significant revenues for the EU budget and help to ensure greater stability of financial markets, without posing undue risk to EU competitiveness.

While it has been difficult to convince all 27 Member States of the need for a FTT, on 9 October 2012 it was declared that at least 11 Member States support the introduction of a common financial transaction tax via enhanced cooperation.[105]

---

[100] Euro Summit Statement http://www.consilium.europa.eu/uedocs/cms_data/docs/pressdata/en/ec/125644.pdf, p. 29.

[101] For a broader overview see N. Gaoua, A. Perdelwitz, Green Paper on Convergence in the Field of Corporate Taxation, *European Taxation*, 8/2012, p. 428 et seq.

[102] COM(2011) 594 final.

[103] COM(2011) 594 final, section 1.1.

[104] For more details on the proposed scope of this tax, see the Commission Proposal COM(2011) 594 final.

[105] Seven EU Member States have already submitted requests to the European Commission for a proposal to introduce a FTT via enhanced cooperation (Austria, Belgium, France,

Since then, the European Commission has concluded, through a Council Decision, that all legal conditions for an enhanced cooperation are met. Those Member States willing to move ahead with an EU FTT are thus allowed to do so.

Germany, Greece, Portugal and Slovenia). Estonia, Italy, Slovakia and Spain have pledged to follow soon.

II. The Relevance of the Fundamental Freedoms for Direct Taxation

Vanessa E. Englmair

Literature: Hinnekens, Compatibility of Bilateral Tax Treaties with European Rules, *EC Tax Review* 1995, p. 202; Vogel, Problems of a Most-Favoured-Nation Clause in Intra-EU Treaty Law, *EC Tax Review* 1995, p. 264; Essers/De Bont/Kemmeren (eds.) *The Compatibility of Anti-Abuse Provisions in Tax Treaties with EC Law* (1998); Mohamed, *European Community Law on the Free Movement of Capital and the EMU* (1998); Helminen, *The Dividend Concept in International Tax Law* (1999); Avery Jones, A Comment on "Progressive Taxation of Non-Residents and Intra-EC Allocation of Personal Tax Allowances, *ET* 2000, p. 375; van Thiel, *Free Movement of Persons and Income Tax Law: The European Court in Search of Principles* (2001); Pistone, *The Impact of Community Law on Tax Treaties* (2002); Hinnekens, The search for the framework conditions of the fundamental EC Treaty principles as applied by the European Court to Member States' direct taxation, *EC Tax Review* 2002, p. 112; Dourado, From the Saint-Gobain to the Metallgesellschaft case: scope of non-discrimination of permanent establishments in the EC Treaty and the most-favoured-nation-clause in EC Member States tax treaties, *EC Tax Review* 2002, p. 147; Gammie, The Role of the European Court of Justice in the Development of Direct Taxation in the European Union, *Bulletin* 2003, p. 86; Lyal, Non-discrimination and direct tax in community law, *EC Tax Review* 2003, p. 68; Gutmann/Hinnekens, The Lankhorst-Hohorst case; The ECJ finds German thin capitalization rules incompatible with freedom of establishment, *EC Tax Review* 2003, p. 90; Wattel, Corporate tax jurisdiction in the EU with respect to branches and subsidiaries; dislocation distinguished from discrimination and disparity; a plea for territoriality, *EC Tax Review* 2003, p. 194; Ståhl, Free movement of capital between Member States and third countries, *EC Tax Review* 2004, p. 47; Englisch, Fiscal Cohesion in the Taxation of Cross-Border Dividends (Part I and II), *ET* 2004, pp. 323 and 355; Schnitger, The CLT-UFA Case and the "Principle of Neutrality of Legal Form", *ET* 2004, p. 522; Mason, *Primer on Direct Taxation in the European Union* (2005); Vanistendael, Cohesion: the phoenix rises from his ashes, *EC Tax Review* 2005, p. 208; De Graaf/Janssen, The implications of the judgement in the *D* case: the perspective of two non-believers, *EC Tax Review* 2005, p. 173; O'Shea, The ECJ, the 'D' case, double tax conventions and most-favoured nations: comparability and reciprocity, *EC Tax Review* 2005, p. 190; Peters/Gooijer, The Free Movement of Capital and Third Countries: Some Observations, *ET* 2005, p. 475; Kofler/Schindler, "Dancing with Mr D": The ECJ's Denial of Most-Favoured-Nation Treatment in the "D" case, *ET* 2005, p. 530; Weber, *In Search of a (New) Equilibrium between Tax Sovereignty and the Freedom of Movement in the EC* (2006); Aarnio, Treatment of permanent establishments and subsidiaries under EC law: towards a uniform concept of secondary establishment in European tax law?, *EC Tax Review* 2006, p. 18; Cordewener, The Future of Most-Favoured-Nation Treatment in EC Tax Law – Did the ECJ Pull the Emergency Brake without Real Need? – Part 1, *ET* 2006, p. 239; Brokelind, The ECJ Bouanich Case: The Capital Gains and Dividend Classification of Share Buy-Backs in Swedish Tax Law, *ET* 2006, p. 268; Lang, Direct Taxation: Is the ECJ Heading in a New Direction, *ET* 2006, p. 421; Lang, Limitation of the Temporal Effects of Judgments of the ECJ, *Intertax* 2007, p. 230; Lang/Schuch/Staringer (eds.) *Tax Treaty Law and EC Law* (2007); Lang/Schuch/Staringer (eds.) *ECJ – Recent Developments in Direct Taxation 2007* (2007), *2008* (2008), *2009* (2009) and (2010); Weber, *The Influence of European Law on Direct Taxation – Recent and Future Developments* (2007); Terra/Wattel, *European Tax Law* (2008); Hinnekens/Hinnekens (eds.) *A vision of taxes within and outside the European borders* (2008); Dourado (ed.) *The Interpretation of Direct Taxation Issues by the ECJ – The Meaning and Scope of the Acte Clair Doctrine* (2008); Lang, ECJ case law on cross-border dividends – recent developments, *EC Tax Review* 2008, p. 67; Wimpissinger, Cross-border transfer of losses, the ECJ does not agree with Advocate General Sharpston, *EC Tax Review 2008, p. 173;* Meussen, European Union: Columbus Container Services: a victory for the Member States' fiscal autonomy, *ET* 2008, *p. 169;* Smit/Kiekebeld, *EC free movement of capital, corporate income taxation and third countries: four selected issues* (2008); O'Shea, Freedom of establishment tax jurisprudence: Avoir fiscal re-visted, *EC Tax Review* 2009, p. 259; Verdoner, The Coherence Principle under EC Tax Law, *ET* 2009, p. 274; Lang, Recent Case Law of the ECJ in Direct Taxation: Trends, Tensions, and Contradictions, *EC Tax Review* 2009, p. 98; Dourado/Pistone, Looking Beyond Cartesio: Reconciliatory Interpretation as a Tool to Remove Tax Obstacles on the Exercise of the Primary Right of Establishment by Companies and Other Legal Entities, *Intertax* 2009, p. 342; Bammens/De Broe, Truck Center Belgian Withholding Tax on Interest Payments to Non-resident Companies Does Not violate EC Law: A Critical Look at the ECJ's Judgement in Truck Center, *EC Tax Review* 2009, p. 131; Cordewener, Free Movement of Capital between EU Member States and Third Countries: How far has the Door Been Closed?, *EC Tax Review* 2009, p. 260; CFE – Comment by the CFE Task Force on ECJ Cases on the Judgment in Belgium SPF Finance vs. Truck Center SA, Case C-282/07, Judgment of 22 December 2008, *ET* 2009, p. 491; Lang, Recent Case Law of the ECJ in direct Taxation: Trends, Tensions, and Contradictions, *International Taxation* 2010, p. 439; Meussen, The SGI Case: ECJ Approves Belgian System of Selective Profit Corrections in Relation to Foreign Group Companies, *ET* 2010 (Volume 50), No. 6; CFE – Opinion Statement of the CFE on *X Holding* (C-337/08), *ET* 2011, p. 150; Smit, The Haribo and Österreichische Salinen Cases: To What Extent Is the ECJ Willing To Remove International Double Taxation Caused by Member States?, *ET* 2011, p. 275; Gabert, Council Directive 2011/16/EU on Administrative Cooperation in the Field of Taxation, *ET* 2011, p. 342; CFE – Opinion Statement of the CFE on the Decision of the European Court of Justice of 10 February 2011 in Joint Cases C-436/08 and C-437/08, *Haribo* and Österreichische Salinen, and the Tax Treatment of Inbound Dividends in the European Union and in Relations with EEA and Third Countries, *ET* 2011, p. 472; Kofler, Tax Treaty "Neutralization" of Source State Discrimination under the EU Fundamental Freedoms?, *Bulletin* 2011, p. 684.

1. The Fundamental Freedoms

a) General

Direct taxation falls within the **competence** of the Member States. Because of **96** their sovereignty they are free to determine the taxable base as well as the tax rate in the area of direct taxes. Only a few areas of direct taxation are harmonized by EU directives; these are dealt with in Chapters IV et seq. (m.nos. 429 et seq.).

97   Even though Member States are exclusively competent for direct taxation, the ECJ has held in its settled case law that the Member States must nonetheless exercise that competence **consistently with EU law** and avoid any discrimination on grounds of nationality.[106]

98   EU law comprises a general non-discrimination provision, Art. 18 TFEU (ex Art. 12 EC), the free movement and residence of EU citizens under Art. 21 TFEU (ex Art. 18 EC) and the **five fundamental freedoms**, the free movement of goods, the free movement of workers, the freedom of establishment, the freedom to provide services and the free movement of capital. It is the last four fundamental freedoms in particular that have an impact on direct taxation. The articles of the Treaty on the Functioning of the European Union (TFEU) were renumbered by the Treaty of Amsterdam and the Treaty of Lisbon. The articles for the fundamental freedoms are currently Arts. 28 et seq. TFEU (ex Arts. 23 et seq. EC) for the free movement of goods, Arts. 45 et seq. TFEU (ex Arts. 39 et seq. EC) for the free movement of workers, Arts. 49 et seq. TFEU (ex Arts. 43 et seq. EC) for the freedom of establishment, Arts. 56 et seq. TFEU (ex Arts. 49 et seq. EC) for the freedom to provide services and Arts. 63 et seq. TFEU (ex Arts. 56 et seq. EC) for the free movement of capital and payments.

99   All freedoms are **directly applicable within the internal market.** If national legislation of a Member State infringes the fundamental freedoms, the Member State is prohibited to apply the discriminatory legislation.

100   To find out whether a national provision is an impediment to EU law, national courts may ask the ECJ for a **preliminary ruling**. Thereby, the national court presents the national legislation to the ECJ and asks whether the legislation is in line with the fundamental freedoms. It should be noted that lower national courts may ask the ECJ for a preliminary ruling in the case of doubts on the compatibility of the national legislation with EU law, whereas national supreme courts are obliged to do so. Supreme courts may only abstain from starting a preliminary ruling procedure if they have no doubt as to the compatibility of the national legislation with EU law. This is known as the *acte clair* doctrine.[107]

101   In addition to preliminary references of national courts, the Commission has the option of starting an **infringement procedure** against a Member State if it is of the opinion that national legislation of that Member State infringes EU law. Member States have the right during this procedure to respond to the arguments of the Commission. If a Member State is not able to convince the Commission of the compatibility of its national legislation with EU law, the Commission has to refer the case again to the Member State before it may present it to the ECJ, which will then have the competence to decide the case (see m.nos. 14 et seq.).[108]

---

[106] See ECJ 28 January 1986, 270/83, *Commission v France ("Avoir Fiscal")* [1986] ECR 273, para. 13.

[107] *Dourado, The Interpretation of Direct Taxation Issues by the ECJ – The Meaning and Scope of the Acte Clair Doctrine* (2008).

[108] In the last years the number of infringement procedures against Member States increased

Decisions of the ECJ do not just have effect on the current and future application of domestic legislation but also have **retroactive effect**. ECJ case law may therefore have an influence on assessments of previous years. The reason for the retroactive effect is that the ECJ interprets EU law as being effective since its coming into force.[109] Nevertheless, restrictions concerning time constraints may exist under national procedural law.

102

In order to find out whether a provision of national law is in line with the fundamental freedoms, the ECJ applies the following scheme:

103

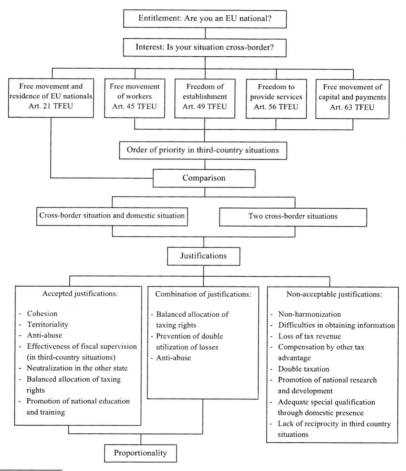

Entitlement: Are you an EU national?

Interest: Is your situation cross-border?

| Free movement and residence of EU nationals Art. 21 TFEU | Free movement of workers Art. 45 TFEU | Freedom of establishment Art. 49 TFEU | Freedom to provide services Art. 56 TFEU | Free movement of capital and payments Art. 63 TFEU |

Order of priority in third-country situations

Comparison

| Cross-border situation and domestic situation | Two cross-border situations |

Justifications

Accepted justifications:	Combination of justifications:	Non-acceptable justifications:
- Cohesion - Territoriality - Anti-abuse - Effectiveness of fiscal supervision (in third-country situations) - Neutralization in the other state - Balanced allocation of taxing rights - Promotion of national education and training	- Balanced allocation of taxing rights - Prevention of double utilization of losses - Anti-abuse	- Non-harmonization - Difficulties in obtaining information - Loss of tax revenue - Compensation by other tax advantage - Double taxation - Promotion of national research and development - Adequate special qualification through domestic presence - Lack of reciprocity in third country situations

Proportionality

---

significantly; for the pending procedures see: http://ec.europa.eu/taxation_customs/common/infringements/infringement_cases/bycountry/index_en.htm.

[109] Only in very exceptional cases does the ECJ admit limits to the retrospective application of the fundamental freedoms: see ECJ 6 March 2007, C-292/04, *Meilicke* [2007] ECR I-1835, paras. 35 et seq.

b) Free Movement and Residence of EU Nationals

104 Art. 21 TFEU (ex Art. 18 EC) sets out the right of every national of the EU to **move and reside freely** within the territory of the Member States. This general rule may be applied by any EU national and prohibits any restrictions and discrimination which may hinder nationals to move and reside freely within the EU. This general rule has to be read in conjunction with Art. 18 TFEU (ex Art. 12 EC) which in general prohibits any discrimination on grounds of nationality but may only be applied if no other more specific provision of the TFEU may be applied.

105 Whereas Art. 18 TFEU (ex Art. 12 EC) does not require the national himself to move cross-border, Art. 21 TFEU (ex Art. 18 EC) does. Therefore, Art. 21 TFEU (ex Art. 18 EC) may only be applied if the national himself moves across the border.[110]

106 Furthermore, Art. 21 TFEU (ex Art. 18 EC) finds specific expression in Art. 45 TFEU (ex Art. 39 EC) in relation to the free movement of workers. The free movement of workers may only be applied if an occupational activity is carried out. Consequently, if a national has no intention to work in another Member State, he may not rely on the free movement of workers but on the general provision under Art. 21 TFEU (ex Art. 18 EC).

107 According to the ECJ case law, Art. 21 TFEU (ex Art. 18 EC) is applicable if the worker exercised the right to reside in another Member State only after retirement without intention to work in that other Member State and is discriminated by the Member States in which he has worked.[111] In this case, the cross-border element is fulfilled and the national no longer pursued an occupational activity.

c) Free Movement of Workers

108 Arts. 45 et seq. TFEU (ex Arts. 39 et seq. EC) provide for the free movement of workers within the EU. Any **discrimination based on nationality** of workers of the Member States must be abolished. This comprises employment, remuneration and other conditions of work and employment.

109 According to the case law, the essential characteristic of the **employment relationship** is that for a certain period of time a person performs services for and under the direction of another person in return for which he receives remuneration.[112]

110 National provisions on income tax are covered by the principle of non-discrimination. The ECJ has held that the principle of equal treatment with regard to remuneration would be rendered ineffective if it could be undermined by discriminatory national provisions on income tax. In Regulation 1612/68 of

---

[110] ECJ 12 July 2005, C-403/03, *Schempp* [2005] ECR I-06421.

[111] ECJ 9 November 2006, C-520/04, *Turpeinen* [2006] ECR I-10685.

[112] See ECJ 3 July 1986, 66/85, *Lawrie-Blum* [1986] ECR 2121, para. 17.

15 October 1968 on the free movement of workers within the EU repealed by Regulation 492/2011 of 5 April 2011 on freedom of movement for workers within the Union Text with EEA relevance,[113] it is laid down that workers who are nationals of a Member State are to enjoy, in the territory of another Member State, the **same tax benefits** as nationals working there.

d) Freedom of Establishment

Arts. 49 et seq. TFEU (ex Arts. 43 et seq. EC) provide for the freedom of establish- **111** ment within the EU. This fundamental freedom comprises the **right of individuals** to take up and pursue activities as a self-employed person in another Member State as well as the right to set up and manage undertakings in another Member State. Furthermore, this fundamental freedom **applies to companies** and grants them the right to set up agencies, branches or subsidiaries in another Member State.[114]

Whether a person or company that acquires a participation in a company **112** established in another Member State exercises the freedom of establishment depends on the extent to which it may **influence and control** the foreign company.

In the *Baars* case[115] the ECJ decided that a holding in the capital of a com- **113** pany established in another Member State which gives the shareholder a definite influence over the company's decisions and allows him to determine its activities exercises his right of establishment. For the application of the freedom of establishment this **control test** has to be fulfilled. In subsequent case law the Court confirmed this principle and filled it in concrete terms. Examples are the *Cadbury Schweppes* case[116] and the *Thin Cap Group Litigation* case[117] where the Court decided that the British controlled foreign corporation (CFC) rules, as well as the British thin capitalization rules, fall within the freedom of establishment as the rules are only applicable if a qualified participation is held in a foreign company that provides a definite influence. In recent decisions the ECJ has applied the control test in third-country cases to apply an order of priority between the freedom of establishment and the free movement of capital (see m.nos. 122 et seq.).

e) Freedom to Provide Services

The freedom to provide services is dealt with in Arts. 56 et seq. TFEU **114** (ex Arts. 49 et seq. EC). It prohibits any discrimination of nationals of a Member

---

[113] Council Regulation (EEC) No. 1612/68 of 15 October 1968 on freedom of movement for workers within the Community, OJ English Special Edition 1968 (II), p. 475; Regulation (EU) No 492/2011 of 5 April 2011 on freedom of movement for workers within the Union. Text with EEA relevance. OJ L 141, 27 May 2011, p. 1.

[114] ECJ 23 February 2006, C-471/04, *Keller Holding* [2006] ECR I-2107.

[115] ECJ 13 April 2000, C-251/98, *Baars* [2000] ECR I-2787, para. 22.

[116] ECJ 12 September 2006, C-196/04, *Cadbury Schweppes* [2006] ECR I-7995.

[117] ECJ 13 March 2007, C-524/04, *Test Claimants in the Thin Cap Group Litigation* [2007] ECR I-02107.

State in providing services in another Member State. The TFEU provides that **'services'** in particular include: Activities of an industrial character; Activities of a commercial character; Activities of craftsmen; Activities of the professions. The ECJ decided in its case law that e.g. **public education services** financed, entirely or mainly, by public funds are **excluded** from the definition of services. In this case the State is fulfilling its duties towards its own population and is not seeking to engage in gainful activities.[118]

115 The freedom to provide services includes the **active provision of services**, where the provider moves to the beneficiary of the services and the **freedom of persons to go to another Member** State, where the provider of the services is established, in order to enjoy the services there. The freedom to provide services confers rights not only on the provider of services but also on the recipient.

f) Free Movement of Capital

116 Arts. 63 et seq. TFEU (ex Arts. 56 et seq. EC) deal with the free movement of capital. Art. 63 TFEU (ex Art. 56 EC) provides that all restrictions on the movement of capital and payments **between Member States and between Member States and third countries** are prohibited. This fundamental freedom is the only one that applies not only within the European Union but also vis-à-vis third states.

117 The ECJ clarified the status of **overseas countries or territories (OCTs)** that are territories which have a special relation with Denmark, France, the Netherlands and the United Kingdom and which are listed in Annex II to the TFEU. The Court decided that OCTs are not considered to be Member States but third countries, with the result that the general provisions of the Treaty do not apply to them. OCTs may only benefit from the provisions of the TFEU if Union Law expressly provides for this.[119]

118 There is no definition of the term **'movement of capital'** in the Treaty but the ECJ has confirmed that the nomenclature of the capital movements set out in Annex I to Directive 88/361/EEC of 24 June 1988[120] is relevant for the interpretation of Arts. 63 et seq. TFEU (ex Arts. 56 et seq. EC), although the Directive was adopted under the former Art. 67 EC. The nomenclature lists examples of capital movements but is non-exhaustive.[121]

119 Art. 64 TFEU (ex Art. 57 EC) narrows the scope of the free movement of capital between Member States and third countries. It is referred to as a **standstill clause** and allows the application of discriminatory provisions vis-à-vis third states which existed on 31 December 1993 involving direct investment –

---

[118] ECJ 20 May 2010, C-56/09, *Zanotti* [2010] ECR I-4517, para. 31.

[119] See ECJ 5 May 2011, C-384/09, *Prunus* (not yet published) para. 29.

[120] Council Directive 88/361/EEC of 24 June 1988 for the implementation of Article 67 of the Treaty, OJ L 178 of 8 July 1988, pp. 5-18.

[121] See ECJ 18 December 2007, C-101/05, *A* [2007] ECR I-11531.

including in real estate – establishment, the provision of financial services or the admission of securities to capital markets (see m.nos. 214 et seq.).

2. The Fundamental Freedoms Under Union Law Compared to EEA Law

The rules under the EEA Agreement and the EC Treaty that are **identical in** **120** **substance** have to be **interpreted uniformly**.[122] Nevertheless, differences between the internal market and the EEA may lead to different interpretative results.[123] In recent case law, the EFTA Court and the ECJ held that a uniform interpretation of rules identical in substance is needed. The EFTA Court held in its opinion in the *Fokus Bank ASA*[124] case that "the EEA Agreement provides for the fullest possible realization of the free movement of goods, persons, services and capital within the whole European Economic Area, so that the internal market established within the European Union is extended to the EFTA States". In a recent decision the ECJ confirmed these findings.[125] The ECJ confirmed that Art. 40 EEA Agreement has the same legal scope as the substantially identical provision of Art. 63 TFEU (ex Art. 56 EC).[126] The Court also confirmed its findings concerning Arts. 28 and 31 EEA Agreement, which correspond to Arts. 45 and 49 TFEU (ex Arts. 39 and 43 EC).[127]

Nevertheless, in **third-country situations, the legal context may be different** **121** than in intra-EU situations.[128] As regards the argument on the difficulties in obtaining information, the ECJ already decided that this ground might serve as justification in third-country situations whereas it is not accepted in EU situations.[129]

3. Order of Priority of the Fundamental Freedoms

a) General

Within the internal market there is a **convergence of the fundamental freedoms**. **122** The ECJ in general applies the same pattern for all the freedoms to examine whether or not a national provision constitutes an infringement. That the Court

---

[122] For the ECJ case law see e.g.: ECJ 23 February 2006, C-471/04, *Keller Holding GmbH* [2006] ECR I-2107, para. 48; for the EFTA Court case law see e.g.: EFTA Court 23 November 2004, E-1/04, *Fokus Bank ASA*, para. 23; EFTA Court 12 December 2003, E-1/03, *EFTA Surveillance Authority*, para. 27.

[123] EFTA Court 14 June 2001, E-6/00, *Tschannett*, para. 7; EFTA Court 14 June 2001, E-5/00, *Josef Mangold*, para. 7; EFTA Court 14 June 2001, E-4/00, *Johann Brändle*, para. 7.

[124] EFTA Court 23 November 2004, E-1/04, *Fokus Bank ASA,* paras. 22 et seq.

[125] ECJ 11 June 2009, C-521/07, *Commission vs. Netherlands* [2009] ECR I-04873, paras. 32 et seq.

[126] ECJ 5 May 2011, C-267/09, *Commission vs. Portugal* (not yet published) para. 50.

[127] ECJ 20 January 2011, C-155/09, *Commission vs. Greece* (not yet published) para. 62.

[128] See ECJ 5 May 2011, C-267/09, *Commission vs. Portugal* (not yet published) para. 54.

[129] For further details see chapter II.7.c)ii and chapter II.7.e).

examines the case in the light of one or the other fundamental freedoms therefore has no consequences on the result within the internal market. Consequently, in situations in which the Court comes to the conclusion that a national law may simultaneously hinder the exercise of two or more freedoms, it refers to one fundamental freedom and concludes that there is no need to examine an infringement under another fundamental freedom if such an infringement is already determined under the prior one.[130]

123   Within the internal market there is no need for an order of priority of the fundamental freedoms. The only **priority rule** is provided for in Art. 18 TFEU (ex Art. 12 EC), which in general prohibits any discrimination on grounds of nationality. The fundamental freedoms as *leges speciales* derogate to Art. 18 TFEU (ex Art. 12 EC) as *lex generalis* (*lex specialis derogat legi generali*).

124   Art. 57 TFEU (ex Art. 50 EC) provides that services are 'services' "in so far as they are not governed by the provisions relating to freedom of movement of goods, capital and persons." At first glance, this provision seems to provide that the freedom to provide services applies only as alternative to the other freedoms. In the *Fidium Finanz* case[131] the Court decided that this provision relates to the **definition of the term 'services' but does not establish any order of priority** between the freedom to provide services and the other fundamental freedoms. Furthermore, Art. 58(2) TFEU (ex Art. 51(2) EC) does not provide for an order of priority. It primarily is addressed to the EU legislature and can be explained by the fact that the freedom to provide services and the free movement of capital may be developed differently.[132]

125   Furthermore, Arts. 49 (2) and 65 (2) TFEU (ex Arts. 43(2) and 58(2) EC), which are cross-references between the freedom of establishment and the free movement of capital, **do not establish any rules of priority**.

126   In a **third-country situation** it becomes crucial whether or not there is an order of priority. The only freedom that applies vis-à-vis third states is the free movement of capital. The other freedoms apply only to intra-Union situations.

127   In general, the fundamental freedoms are designed to regulate different situations and they each have their own field of application. But it is possible that a case may involve **more than one fundamental freedom.** Consequently, in a third-country situation it is of great relevance whether the free movement of capital has priority over the freedom to provide services or the freedom of establishment. A national provision concerning both the free movement of capital and the free movement of workers probably will not exist as these two freedoms have completely different fields of application.

---

[130] See e.g. ECJ 18 November 1999, C-200/98, *X AB and Y AB* [1999] ECR I-8261, para. 30; ECJ 6 June 2000, C-35/98, *Verkooijen* [2000] ECR I-4071, para. 63; ECJ 7 September 2006, C-470/04, *N.* [2006] ECR I-7409, para. 29.

[131] ECJ 3 October 2006, C-452/04, *Fidium Finanz* [2006] ECR I-9521, para. 32.

[132] ECJ 3 October 2006, C-452/04, *Fidium Finanz* [2006] ECR I-9521, para. 33.

b) Freedom to Provide Services over Free Movement of Capital

In the *Fidium Finanz* case[133] the Court had to decide on the **priority of the free-** **128** **dom to provide services or the free movement of capital**. Fidium Finanz was a Swiss company that granted credits mainly to German residents. Under German national law, Fidium Finanz was required to obtain authorization in order to grant credits whereas such an authorization is not required for German companies or other EU companies granting the same credits.

The Court decided that in the case of **simultaneous application** of the free- **129** dom to provide services and the free movement of capital, it may examine the national measure in relation to only one of those two freedoms if it appears that "one of them is **entirely secondary** in relation to the other and may be considered together with it".[134]

The ECJ referred to the **purpose of the provision** and held that it intended to **130** supervise the provision of such services and to authorize them only for undertakings that guarantee conducting such transactions properly. Consequently, the freedom to provide services prevails over the free movement of capital as the restriction of the cross-border financial traffic, falling within the scope of Art. 63 TFEU (ex Art. 56 EC), is **"merely an unavoidable consequence"** of the restriction on the freedom to provide services. It follows that it is not necessary to consider whether the rule infringes Art. 63 TFEU (ex Art. 56 EC). As a result, none of the freedoms were applicable to the third-country situation at issue.

It has to be emphasized that the Court referred to the **object and purpose** of **131** the respective national provision for answering the question of the order of priority.[135]

c) Freedom of Establishment over Free Movement of Capital

In the order in *Lasertec*[136] the Court provided a clear decision on the **order of** **132** **priority** between the freedom of establishment and the free movement of capital.

First, it has to be said that it is remarkable that the ECJ gave an **order** and not **133** a decision in this case, which is done if a question referred to the Court for a preliminary ruling is identical to a question on which the Court has already ruled or where the answer to such a question may be clearly deduced from existing case law. The Court had never before provided a decision on the order of priority of Art. 49 and Art. 63 TFEU (ex Art. 43 and Art. 56 EC) in a third-country situation. The cases to which the Court referred to justify the order were exclusively intra-Union cases.

---

[133] ECJ 3 October 2006, C-452/04, *Fidium Finanz* [2006] ECR I-9521.
[134] ECJ 3 October 2006, C-452/04, *Fidium Finanz* [2006] ECR I-9521, para. 34.
[135] ECJ 1 July 2010, C-233/09, *Dijkman* [2010] ECR I-6649, para. 26.
[136] ECJ 10 May 2007, C-492/04, *Lasertec* [2007] ECR I-3775.

134   Lasertec Germany held two thirds of the nominal capital in Lasertec Switzerland. The Swiss company granted a credit to the German company for which interest was paid. As the debt/equity ratio of 3:1 of the German company was exceeded, the interest paid by the German company was partly re-characterized as dividends. Consequently, only part of the interest was deductible as expenses at the level of the German company. The German thin capitalization rules were only applicable to circumstances in which the non-resident lending company had a **substantial holding** in the nominal capital of the resident borrowing company, namely a holding of over 25 %. Even though the holding was below this threshold, the rules were applicable if it nevertheless conferred a '**dominant influence over the company**'.

135   The Court decided in the *Lasertec* case that according to the **purpose of the legislation** – only participations which involve a dominant influence are involved – and the fact that two thirds of the nominal capital was held by the non-resident company in the German company the issue falls within the scope of Art. 49 TFEU (ex Art. 43 EC). The national provision may also have discriminatory effects under Art. 63 TFEU (ex Art. 56 EC) but these effects must be seen as an '**unavoidable consequence**' of the discrimination of Art. 49 TFEU (ex Art. 43 EC) and, consequently, there is no need to apply the free movement of capital. As the freedom of establishment applies solely to intra-Union issues, there was no fundamental freedom applicable to this case. The same result was achieved by the Court in the Swedish *A and B* case[137] in which the Swedish national rule discriminated against the Swedish company that planed to set up a permanent establishment in Russia and in the *Stahlwerk Ergste Westig* case,[138] which also concerned the setting-up of a permanent establishment, but in the United States.

136   The main question in the *Glaxo Wellcome* case[139] was the issue whether or not the old German depreciation provisions were in line with the fundamental freedoms of the TFEU. According to the German provisions, depreciations of shares in the subsidiary upon distribution of dividends were allowed. However, if shares of foreign companies were acquired, such depreciations on the value of the shares were not allowed. The ECJ explicitly mentioned that the **purpose of the national legislation** has to be taken into consideration in order to decide which fundamental freedom of the EC Treaty applies. Thereby the ECJ decided that since the purpose of the legislation at issue in the main proceedings is to prevent non-resident shareholders from obtaining an undue tax advantage directly through the sale of shares with the sole objective of obtaining that advantage, and not with the objective of exercising the freedom of establishment or as a result of exercising that freedom, it must be held that the free-movement-of-capital aspect of that legislation prevails over that of the freedom of establishment. The

---

[137] ECJ 10 May 2007, C-102/05, *A and B* [2007] ECR I-3871.

[138] ECJ 6 November 2007, C-415/06, *Stahlwerk Ergste Westig* [2007] ECR I-151.

[139] ECJ 17 September 2009, C-182/08, *Glaxo Wellcome* [2009] ECR I-8591.

national provision may also have a discriminatory effect under Art. 49 TFEU (ex Art. 43 EC) but these effects must be seen as the '**unavoidable consequence**' of the discrimination under Art. 63 TFEU (ex Art. 56 EC). Consequently, the freedom of establishment did not apply in this case.

To summarize, it can be said that the Court has developed a **new rule of** 137
priority. Whenever the discriminatory effects of a national provision are within the scope of two fundamental freedoms and one of them is **predominantly affected**, the other one is only affected as an 'unavoidable consequence' and consequently does not apply. In recent case law, the Court confirmed this new concept and emphasized that the **purpose** of the respective legislation is decisive.[140]

4. Addressees of the Non-Discrimination Rules

Even though, according to their wording, the fundamental freedoms are directed 138
to prohibiting discrimination only in the **host state**, the ECJ has decided that they also prohibit the **home state** from hindering nationals or companies in exercising their fundamental freedoms.[141] Therefore, nationals and companies have to be treated in the host Member State in the same way as nationals of that state and the home state is prohibited from hindering the establishment in another Member State of one of its nationals or of a company incorporated under its legislation.

Typical examples of national provisions of the **host state** hindering the person 139
to exercise his fundamental freedoms are source taxation provisions on a gross basis that apply only to non-resident taxpayers whereas resident taxpayers are assessed on a net basis.[142]

Typical examples of national provisions of the **home state** hindering the 140
establishment in another Member State are **exit tax provisions,** on which the ECJ gave decisions in the *Lasteyrie du Saillant* case,[143] the *N.* case[144] and the *National Grid Indus* case.[145] In these cases the Court came to the conclusion that the taxation of hidden reserves of certain assets at the moment a person crosses the border is a hindrance to the exercise of the fundamental freedoms.

---

[140] ECJ 21 January 2010, C-311/08, *Société de Gestion Industrielle* [2010] ECR I-487, para. 25; ECJ 10 February 2011, C-436/08 and 437/08, *Haribo Lakritzen and Österreichische Salinen* [2011] ECR I-305, para. 35; 15 September 2011, C-132/10, *Halley* (not yet published) para. 17; ECJ 15 September 2011, C-310/09, *Accor* (not yet published) para. 31.

[141] The non-discrimination article under Art. 24 of the OECD Model has a similar scope but is restricted to the host state. Under Art. 24 of the OECD Model, the home state is not prohibited from discriminating.

[142] ECJ 12 June 2003, C-234/01, *Gerritse* [2003] ECR I-5933, para. 28; ECJ 3 October 2006, C-290/04, *Scorpio* [2006] ECR I-9461, para. 46; ECJ 15 February 2007, C-345/04, *Centro Equestre* [2007] ECR I-1425, paras. 23 et seq.

[143] ECJ 11 March 2004, C-9/02, *Lasteyrie du Saillant* [2004] ECR I-2409.

[144] ECJ 7 September 2006, C-470/04, *N.* [2006] ECR I-7409.

[145] ECJ 29 November 2011, C-371/10, *National Grid Indus* (not yet published).

5. The Non-Discrimination Principle

141 In applying the concept of non-discrimination, the ECJ takes the following steps. It first determines whether or not **two situations are comparable**. It may compare the factual cross-border situation with a hypothetical national situation or a factual cross-border situation with another hypothetical cross-border situation.

142 Subsequently, on the question whether or not the domestic provision constitutes an infringement of the fundamental freedoms, it determines whether different rules apply to comparable situations or the same rules apply to different situations. Both **discrimination of the first and the second order** lead to discrimination of the fundamental freedoms.[146]

143 An infringement of the fundamental freedoms may be **justified**. In addition to grounds explicitly foreseen in the TFEU, the Court has accepted other grounds in the area of public interest put forward by the Member States in the proceedings.[147]

144 The last step of the Court's examination is to determine whether discrimination complies with the **principle of proportionality**.[148]

6. The Search for the Correct Comparison

a) Direct and Indirect Discrimination

145 According to the case law of the Court from the 1980s, the non-discrimination provisions of the fundamental freedoms not only prohibit direct discrimination by reason of nationality but also **indirect discrimination**, which by the application of other criteria of differentiation leads to the same result.

146 More precisely, the Court has held that national rules of a kind whereby a distinction is drawn on the **basis of residence** in that non-residents are denied certain benefits that are, conversely, granted to persons residing within the national territory, are liable to operate mainly to the detriment of nationals of other Member States. Non-residents are in the majority of cases foreigners. In those circumstances, tax benefits granted only to residents of a Member State may constitute indirect discrimination by reason of nationality.

147 In some cases the ECJ did not refer to discrimination but rather to **restrictions**. Restrictions make cross-border situations 'less attractive'. In the legal literature it is debated whether the restriction concept is a different concept from the **non-discrimination** concept. It is argued that under the restriction concept no pair of comparison is required for the determination of an infringement of the fundamental freedoms, whereas such a pair of comparison is inherent to the

---

[146] See e.g. ECJ 14 November 2006, C-513/04, *Kerckhaert-Morres* [2006] ECR I-10967, para. 19.

[147] See m.nos. 223 et seq.

[148] See m.nos. 286 et seq.

non-discrimination concept. The counter-argument is that even in a restriction scenario the situation in which the fundamental freedoms are carried out may be compared with the situation in which the taxpayer remains in his home country and, consequently, restrictions would form part of the broader term 'discrimination'.[149] For tax law purposes, the differentiation between restriction and discrimination may hardly be of any relevance.

Many countries do not **tax on the basis of nationality but rather on the basis of residence**. Direct discrimination therefore occurs less often than indirect discrimination.   **148**

In the case of companies, the **registered office** of the company serves in the same way as nationality in the case of individuals as the connecting factor with the legal system of a Member State.[150]   **149**

b) Cross-Border Situation and Domestic Situation

i. General

The classic pair of comparison is that of a person who exercises its freedoms compared to a person who remains in the home state. The **factual cross-border situation** is therefore compared with the **hypothetical situation** of a taxpayer who remains in the home state.   **150**

In this regard, it should be noted that in tax law the residence of a taxpayer may constitute a factor that may justify national rules involving different treatment for resident and non-resident taxpayers. This means that the **situation of residents and non-residents is not, as a rule, comparable**. The ECJ often refers to this general statement in its case law. Nevertheless, in many cases, by referring to the **aim and purpose of the domestic tax provision**, the ECJ concluded that residents and non-residents are in comparable situations.[151]   **151**

From the perspective of the **home state** the Court e.g. held in the *Marks & Spencer* case[152] that "... **residence is not always a proper factor for distinction**. In effect, acceptance of the proposition that the Member State in which a company seeks to establish itself may freely apply to it a different treatment solely by reason of the fact that its registered office is situated in another Member State would deprive Article 43 EC of all meaning." This principle was repeated by the ECJ in other cases.[153]   **152**

---

[149] See Hohenwarter, in Lang/Schuch/Staringer (eds.) *Tax Treaty Law and EC Law* (2007) p. 99, with further references.

[150] See e.g. ECJ 22 December 2008, C-282/07, *Truck Center SA* [2008] ECR I-10767, para. 32.

[151] ECJ 14 February 1995, C-279/93, *Schumacker* [1995] ECR I-225, para. 32.

[152] ECJ 13 December 2005, C-446/03, *Marks & Spencer* [2005] ECR I-10837, para. 37.

[153] ECJ 12 December 2006, C-374/04, *Test Claimants in Class IV of the ACT Group Litigation* [2006] ECR I-11673, para. 43; ECJ 22 December 2008, C-282/07, *Truck Center SA* [2008] ECR I-10767, para. 32; ECJ 18 June 2009, C-303/07, *Aberdeen Property* [2009] ECR I-5145, para. 38.

153   The *Marks & Spencer* case concerned the British group relief system and applied only to domestic subsidiaries with the consequence that losses of these subsidiaries could be transferred to other British group subsidiaries or to the British group parent company and set off against their profits. Losses of foreign subsidiaries were not able to be set off against profits of another British group subsidiary or the group parent. Even though British subsidiaries are taxed on the profits and losses, whereas profits of foreign subsidiaries are not taxable in the United Kingdom, the Court nevertheless decided that a **domestic group parent with a domestic group subsidiary** is in a situation comparable to a **domestic group parent with an EU group subsidiary**. As the two comparable situations were treated differently, the Court decided that the British group relief system constitutes discrimination. The same principle was applied by the Court in the *X Holding* case in which the Netherlands group taxation system was at stake.[154]

154   In the *Persche* case[155] the ECJ again decided from the perspective of the **home state.** Under German national law, deductions of gifts to bodies recognized as charitable were only allowed if the gifts were made to such resident bodies but were permitted if they were made to such non-resident bodies. The ECJ decided that these rules lead to a different treatment of two comparable situations and consequently were discriminatory.

155   The ECJ has also held from the perspective of the **host state,** e.g. in the *Biehl* case.[156] Mr Biehl was a resident of Luxembourg where he pursued an activity as an employed person. His Luxembourg employer deducted sums by way of income tax from his salary. From the final tax assessment it emerged that the amount deducted exceeded the total amount of his liability to tax. Before Mr Biehl could ask for **repayment of the excessive tax**, he moved to Germany. In Luxembourg repayments of taxes were only granted to residents. As Mr Biehl had become a non-resident in Luxembourg, the repayment was denied by the Luxembourg authorities. The Court decided that in this case **non-residents and residents are in comparable situations** and, consequently, the different treatment constituted discrimination.

156   Another example is the *Bouanich* case[157] in which the Court – from the perspective of the **host state** – decided that it is discriminatory where non-residents are not allowed, on the occasion of a share repurchase, to deduct the cost of acquisition of the shares whereas residents are allowed to do so. The Court reasoned that the **cost of acquisition is directly linked to the payment made** and, consequently, there is **no objective difference between non-residents and residents**.

157   The ECJ referred as well to the *Gerritse* case[158] in which the Court assumed that **residents and non-residents were in comparable situations** as regards

---

[154] ECJ 25 February 2010, C-337/08, *X Holding* [2010] ECR I-1215.
[155] ECJ 27 January 2009, C-318/07, *Persche* [2009] ECR I-359.
[156] ECJ 8 May 1990, C-175/88, *Biehl* [1990] ECR I-1779, para. 14.
[157] ECJ 19 January 2006, C-265/04, *Bouanich* [2006] ECR I-923.
[158] ECJ 12 June 2003, C-234/01, *Gerritse* [2003] ECR I-5933.

their **business expenses** incurred in generating their income. Consequently, non-residents who exercise an employment in the host state have to be granted in the host state the same deduction of business expenses related to their income as the host state is prepared to grant for its residents who carry out the same activities as the non-residents. Another example is the *Denkavit* case[159] in which the Court had to decide on the taxation of dividend payments. The Court concluded that dividends distributed to a parent company situated in the same state are comparable to dividends distributed to a parent company situated in another Member State. If the former are exempt from taxes, the latter have to be exempt as well. Different treatment merely by reason of the fact that the **registered office** of the parent company is **situated in another Member State** would deprive Art. 49 TFEU (ex Art. 43 EC) of all meaning.

The ECJ in the *Gielen* case[160] decided that a national law provision which **158** puts a non-resident taxpayer in a less attractive situation with regard to a self-employed person's deduction than a national taxpayer remains discriminatory even though the non-resident taxpayer has the **option** to apply the regime for resident taxpayers in order to benefit from the same tax advantage. The Court argued that if such an option were to be accepted in order to bring the national legislation in line with the fundamental freedoms, the consequence would be to validate a tax regime which, in itself, remains contrary to the fundamental freedoms.

In a case similar to the *Denkavit* case, the ECJ had to decide again on the **159** withholding taxation on dividend payments made to a foreign parent company. The difference in the *Aberdeen Property* case[161] was that the foreign company was a Luxembourg SICAV and the ECJ had to decide whether the SICAV which is a fund is comparable to a Finnish company or a Finnish fund. In the affirmative, the Finnish withholding tax were an infringement of the fundamental freedoms as dividend distributions to a Finnish parent company were exempt from tax. The ECJ applied a '*type comparison test*' between a Finnish company and the Luxembourg SICAV. Thereby the Court concluded that the circumstance that in Finnish law there is no type of company with a legal form identical to that of a Luxembourg SICAV cannot itself lead to the result that the two are not comparable. This reasoning is based on the fact that the company law of the Member States has not been fully harmonized at EU level and, consequently, many different company forms may exist within the Member States and which are not identical. Furthermore, the fact that the Luxembourg SICAV is not taxed in Luxembourg whereas a Finnish company is taxed in Luxembourg on its income (except the dividend payments received) was also not a ground for the ECJ to deny the comparability: in the specific case of the dividend taxation the Finnish

---

[159] ECJ 14 December 2006, C-170/05, *Denkavit* [2006] ECR I-11949; see as well ECJ 20 October 2011, C-284/09, *Commission vs. Germany* (not yet published).

[160] ECJ 18 March 2010, C-440/08, *Gielen* [2006] ECR I-2323, paras. 49 et seq.

[161] ECJ 18 June 2009, C-303/07, *Aberdeen Property* [2009] ECR I-5145.

company was exempt from tax as well. Whenever the taxation of a foreign company is concerned, such a 'type comparison test' has to be applied under which the main criteria of the domestic company are compared with the foreign company.

160   One case in which the ECJ decided that **resident and non-resident companies are not in comparable situations** was the *Truck Center SA* case.[162] In this case the ECJ had to deal with the Belgian **withholding tax on interest payments**, which was only levied if payments were made to non-resident companies but not if payments were made to another Belgian company. A Belgian company receiving the interest was taxed on this income but the paying company did not have to withhold taxes at source. The Court decided that the withholding tax on the interest paid to the non-resident company was in line with the fundamental freedoms. The Court held that resident recipient companies are directly subject to the supervision of the Belgian tax authorities, which can ensure the compulsory recovery of taxes. This is not the case with regard to non-resident recipient companies inasmuch as, in their case, recovery of the tax requires the assistance of the tax authorities of the other Member State. Therefore, the two situations are not comparable and, consequently, the **different procedure for charging taxes** is in line with the fundamental freedoms because different situations are treated differently.[163] In the *X NV* case[164] the Court held again that withholding taxes are in line with the fundamental freedoms but this time decided on the level of justification. It held that the retention at source constitutes an appropriate means of ensuring the effective collection of tax claims.

161   With respect to withholding taxes the Court decided that **business expenses which were reported** to the person liable to withhold the source taxes and **which are directly linked** to the activities performed in the source state have to be deducted from the taxable base for withholding tax purposes by the person liable to withhold the source taxes, if a resident taxpayer who performs the same activities is taxed on the net income. Taxation of non-resident taxpayers on gross income, whereas resident taxpayers are taxed on net income is an impediment of the fundamental freedoms even though the non-resident has the option of subsequently taking the business expenses into account in a refund procedure.[165]

162   In which cases the Court decides whether residents and non-residents are in comparable situation cannot be given a generalized answer. This question has to be answered **case-by-case**, taking into consideration the **aim and purpose** of the respective national provisions.

---

[162] ECJ 22 December 2008, C-282/07, *Truck Center SA* [2008] ECR I-10767.
[163] See as well ECJ 3 October 2006, C-290/04, *Scorpio* [2006] ECR I-9461, paras. 35 et seq.
[164] ECJ 18 October 2012, C-498/10, *X NV* (not yet published).
[165] ECJ 3 October 2006, C-290/04, *Scorpio* [2006] ECR I-9461, paras. 46 et seq; ECJ 15 February 2007, C-345/04, *Centro Equestre* [2007] ECR I-1425.

ii. Permanent Establishment in the Host State

In one of the first cases that concerned direct taxation the ECJ had to deal with **163** the French *avoir fiscal*.[166] The French national provision did not grant the **benefit of shareholders' tax credits to a permanent establishment** in France of a company established in another Member State whereas such benefits were granted to French companies.

The Court came to the conclusion that the **permanent establishment and a** **164** **French company are in comparable situations** as the French tax law does not distinguish, for the purpose of determining the income liable to corporate tax, between resident companies and permanent establishments of non-resident companies situated in France. Both are liable to tax on profits generated in France and, consequently, the national law put both on the same footing for the purposes of taxing their profits. The different treatment of the two comparable situations, therefore, constituted discrimination.

In this case the Court compared the taxation of the permanent establishment **165** with that of domestic corporations and explicitly mentioned that a national provision which applies a different treatment to a company seeking to establish itself in that state solely by reason of the fact that it is a non-resident company would **deprive the freedom of establishment** of all meaning.

The ECJ reached the same result in a **triangular case** concerning cross- **166** border dividends attributable to a permanent establishment.[167] In particular, in this case a French company set up a permanent establishment in Germany through which it held shares in other foreign companies and through which it received dividends on such shares. Under German tax law, the permanent establishment was not granted the same tax credit benefits as those granted to German companies. The ECJ again held that the situations are comparable because both the German company and the French company with its profits attributable to the German permanent establishment are taxable in Germany. Consequently, the two comparable situations have to be treated equally.

In these cases the Court again took into consideration the **aim and purpose** **167** of the respective domestic provision to determine whether the factual situation is comparable to the hypothetical one. From these cases the conclusion can be drawn that permanent establishments have to be treated in the same manner as domestic companies.

iii. Personal and Family Allowances

In the *Schumacker* case[168] the ECJ developed a new doctrine that is, however, **168** relevant only to a **limited area within tax law**, namely the deduction of **personal and family allowances**. The ECJ had to decide whether the state of source

---

[166] ECJ 28 January 1986, 270/83, *Commission v France ("Avoir Fiscal")* [1986] ECR 273.
[167] ECJ 21 September 1999, C-307/97, *Saint-Gobain* [1999] ECR I-6161.
[168] ECJ 14 February 1995, C-279/93, *Schumacker* [1995] ECR I-225.

has to grant to non-resident taxpayers the same personal and family deductions as to its own residents.

169   With reference to international tax law, in particular the OECD Model, the Court decided that it is **primarily a matter of the state of residence** to grant personal and family deductions.

170   It reasoned that the income generated by a non-resident in the host state is in most cases **only part of his total income**. The predominant part of the income is usually generated in the residence state. Furthermore, the Court referred to the **ability to pay**, which is determined by reference to the aggregate income and to the personal and family circumstances of the taxpayer and concluded that they are easier to assess at the place where the personal and financial interests are centred.

171   Moreover, that state generally has available all the **information needed to assess** the taxpayer's overall ability to pay, taking account of his personal and family circumstances. Consequently, non-residents and residents are **not in a comparable situation** and the host state does not have to grant to the non-resident taxpayer the same personal and family allowances as it grants to its own residents.

172   The **exception to this general rule** is the situation in which the non-resident receives no significant income in the state of residence and obtains the **major part of his income in the host state**.

173   In this case the state of residence is not in a position to grant the personal and family allowances since the **taxable base is too small**. In such a situation there is no objective difference between the situations of a non-resident and a resident.

174   In the case of a non-resident who receives the major part of his income and almost all his family income in the host state, discrimination arises from the fact that his personal and family circumstances are taken into account **neither in the state of residence nor in the host state**. Consequently, in such a situation the host state has to grant the non-resident the same personal and family deductions as its residents.

175   In its subsequent case law, i.e. *Gschwind*,[169] *Zurstrassen*,[170] *De Groot*,[171] *Gerritse*,[172] *Wallentin*,[173] *D.*,[174] *Conijn*,[175] *Lakebrink*[176] and *Renneberg*[177] the ECJ repeated its doctrine and refined the **area of personal and family allowances**. It comprises, despite the splitting regime for spouses, costs incurred in obtaining

---

[169] ECJ 14 September 1999, C-391/97, *Gschwind* [1999] ECR I-5451.
[170] ECJ 16 May 2000, C-87/99, *Zurstrassen* [2000] ECR I-3337.
[171] ECJ 12 December 2002, C-385/00, *De Groot* [2002] ECR I-11819.
[172] ECJ 12 June 2003, C-234/01, *Gerritse* [2003] ECR I-5933.
[173] ECJ 1 July 2004, C-169/03, *Wallentin* [2004] ECR I-6443.
[174] ECJ 5 July 2005, C-376/03, *D.* [2005] ECR I-5821.
[175] ECJ 6 July 2006, C-346/04, *Conijn* [2006] ECR I-6137.
[176] ECJ 18 July 2007, C-182/06, *Lakebrink* [2007] ECR I-6705.
[177] ECJ 16 October 2008, C-527/06, *Renneberg* [2008] ECR I-7735.

tax advice, contributions to a pension reserve, maintenance payments, tax-free allowances and also losses. **Not within the area of personal and family allowances** are, for example, the application of the tax rate, the deduction of business expenses or other expenses that are inextricably linked to the activities which give rise to the income received.[178]

c) Two Cross-Border Situations

i. General

In recent case law concerning direct taxation the Court has started to compare **176** not only cross-border situations with national situations but also **two cross-border situations** to determine whether the factual situation is comparable to a hypothetical one.

In the *Cadbury Schweppes* case[179] the Court had to deal with the British CFC **177** legislation. Profits of a CFC, namely a foreign company in which the British company owns a holding of more than 50 %, were attributed to the British company and taxed in its hands. The legislation applied if the CFC is subject in its residence country to a **lower level of taxation**; this was the case in which the tax paid by the CFC was less than three quarters of the tax that would have been paid in the United Kingdom. The Court – in addition to the traditional pair of comparison, in which a cross-border situation is compared with a pure domestic situation – compared the situation in which the CFC rules apply to the situation in which the CFC is established in another state in which it is not subject to a lower level of taxation. Inter alia, the Court concluded that the different treatment of the two comparable cross-border situations constitutes discrimination.

As the national provision only **aims** to apply to foreign corporations that may **178** seek to avoid high taxes, it seems to be logical to compare the factual cross-border situation with another hypothetical cross-border situation.

In a recent decision, *Columbus Container*,[180] the ECJ refused to accept the **179** comparison of two cross-border situations. Columbus Container was a Belgian company. Its shareholders were German individuals and a German partnership. From a German perspective Columbus Container was characterized as a partnership and, consequently, according to the transparency concept, the profits of Columbus Container were taxed in the hands of the shareholders resident in Germany. The double taxation convention between Belgium and Germany attributes the taxing rights for the profits of the partnership to Belgium and provides for the exemption method in Germany. But as Columbus Container was taxed in Belgium at a tax rate below 30 %, Germany applied its **Law on External Tax Relations** *(Außensteuergesetz)* under which the credit method was applicable.

---

[178] See ECJ 31 March 2011, C-450/09, *Schröder* (not yet published) paras. 43 et seq.
[179] ECJ 12 September 2006, C-196/04, *Cadbury Schweppes* [2006] ECR I-7995.
[180] ECJ 6 December 2007, C-298/05, *Columbus Container* [2007] ECR I-10451.

Instead of being taxed in Belgium and exempt from tax in Germany, the German partners were taxed at the higher German tax rate whereby the foreign taxes levied on that income were set off against the German tax. Ultimately, the partners are taxed at the same level as partners of a German partnership.

180   In the case at issue the Court compared the cross-border situation with a purely domestic situation. The Court **refrained** from comparing the actual cross-border situation with another hypothetical cross-border situation in which the tax rate in the foreign country reaches a certain level that is not caught by the German **Law on External Tax Relations**.

181   The situation in the ***Cadbury Schweppes*** case described in m.no. 177 is nevertheless different from the ***Columbus Container*** case, since in a purely domestic situation, in the first-mentioned case the profits of the subsidiary, which is a legal entity and a separate taxable person, were never taxed in the hands of the parent company. In the last-mentioned case, the partnership was treated as a transparent entity and profits were taxed in the hands of the partners in a purely domestic situation. Whether the ECJ may bring the diverging decision in line remains to be seen.

182   But, in a very recent decision the ECJ explicitly compared two cross-border situations with each other. In the *Commission v Netherlands* case[181] the ECJ compared, for the purpose of deductions at source, dividend distributions from a Dutch company to beneficiary companies established in a Member State and dividend distributions from a Dutch company to beneficiary companies established in third countries, namely Iceland and Norway, which are EEA states. The Court decided that the **two cross-border situations are comparable** and consequently have to be treated alike. But the Netherlands legislation provided for an exemption of source taxation on dividends distributed to beneficiary companies established in a Member State if a minimum participation of 5 % was held. In contrast, in the case of distributions to Icelandic companies a minimum participation of 10 % was required and in the case of distributions to Norwegian companies a minimum participation of 25 % was required for the exemption according to the respective double taxation agreements. Consequently, the different treatment of the two comparable situations was an impediment to the fundamental freedoms. As all EU cross-border situations were treated in the same manner according to the Netherlands law, the ECJ was able to **compare an EU cross-border situation with a third-country cross-border situation.**

ii. Neutrality of Legal Form

183   In the legal literature the issue of neutrality of legal form is debated. Neutrality *of legal form* addresses the issue whether the **establishment of an agency or branch** compared to the **establishment of a subsidiary** in another Member State must be treated correspondingly.

---

[181] ECJ 11 June 2009, C-521/07, *Commission v Netherlands* [2009] ECR I-4873, para. 43.

In the *CLT-UFA* case[182] the ECJ had to deal with this issue. CLT-UFA was a **184** company that had its seat and central administration in Luxembourg and which established a branch in Germany. The German tax authorities set the tax rate at 42 % for the German branch. For subsidiaries the German tax rate in general is 45 % but could be reduced to 33.5 % (after June 1996: to 30 %) on the condition that the profits had been distributed to the parent company in Luxembourg. Subsidiaries have generally made use of that facility in order to **reduce the tax rate**.

The ECJ held in its decision that the second sentence of the first paragraph of **185** Art. 43 EC (now Art. 49 TFEU) expressly leaves traders free to **choose the appropriate legal form** in which to pursue their activities in another Member State. Therefore, it seems that the freedom of establishment allows companies having their seat in a Member State to open a branch in another Member State under the same conditions as those that apply to subsidiaries.

The Court came to the conclusion that the establishment of a branch in **186** Germany by the Luxembourg company is **comparable** to the establishment of a subsidiary in Germany by that company.

It held that in both cases the **profits were made available** to the Luxembourg **187** company. The only real difference between the two situations is that distribution of the profits of a subsidiary requires a formal decision, whereas the profits of a branch are part of the assets the Luxembourg company even in the absence of a formal decision to that effect. This difference has no impact on the comparability test. Furthermore, both the profits of the subsidiary and the profits of the branch are exempt from tax in Luxembourg under the double taxation convention between Luxembourg and Germany.

According to the special German provision that bases the different treatment **188** of branches and subsidiaries of foreign companies on the fact that branches may not distribute profits as they are not separate legal entities, it seems to be justified to speak of **neutrality of legal form under this specific set of circumstances**.

In the *Marks & Spencer* case[183] the Court could have answered the question **189** of neutrality of legal form in a more general way. The British national provisions allowed the utilization of foreign branch losses at the level of the British company whereas losses of foreign subsidiaries could not been used at the level of the British parent company. Advocate General *Maduro* put forward arguments against the principle of neutrality of legal form. The Court, unfortunately, did not deal with this issue at all in this case.

In the *X Holding* case[184] the Court explicitly decided on the issue and held **190** that foreign permanent establishments and foreign subsidiaries are not in comparable situations with regard to the **allocation of the powers of taxation as provided for in the double taxation conventions**. The foreign subsidiaries are

---

[182] ECJ 23 February 2006, C-253/03, *CLT-UFA* [2006] ECR I-1831.
[183] ECJ 13 December 2005, C-446/03, *Marks & Spencer* [2005] ECR I-10837.
[184] ECJ 25 February 2010, C-337/08, *X Holding* [2010] ECR I-1215, paras. 37 et seq.

independent legal persons and as such subject to tax in the foreign state whereas the foreign permanent establishments remain subject to the fiscal jurisdiction of the state of origin. Therefore, the state of origin may decide to permit the temporary offsetting of losses incurred by the foreign permanent establishment but may deny such a loss set-off of foreign subsidiaries because the foreign subsidiary and the foreign permanent establishment are **not in comparable situations**.

191   Consequently, a **general answer** to the question whether the freedom of establishment under Art. 49 TFEU (ex Art. 43 EC) has to be generally interpreted in favour of the free choice of legal form **cannot be provided**. It is instead dependent on the national law provision and has to be dealt with on a case-by-case basis.

d) Relevance of Double Taxation Conventions

192   Double taxation conventions are part of **international law**. Their status in the respective national tax law system depends on the constitution of the respective state. In some states they automatically become national law whereas in other states they have to be transformed into national law.

193   In its settled case law the ECJ repeats the doctrine that the Member States are competent to determine the criteria for taxation with a view to eliminating double taxation. Member States may do so by concluding international agreements which are based on the OECD MC.

194   In the Swedish case *Bouanich*,[185] to which it refers in m.no. 156, the Court decided that as the convention forms **part of the legal background** to the main proceedings and has been presented as such by the national court, it has to be taken into consideration in interpreting the fundamental freedoms.

195   Although the Court is not competent to interpret national law (i.e. treaties and domestic law),[186] it has to ascertain whether the **legal effects of tax treaties** affect the exercise of fundamental freedoms in respect of the facts that have been presented to it.[187]

196   With regard to the tax treatment under the double taxation convention, Ms Bouanich as non-resident was permitted to deduct the **nominal value** of the shares from the amount payable on the occasion of a repurchase of those shares. The remaining amount was taxed at the rate of **15 %**. Residents were permitted to deduct the **cost of acquisition** of the shares. The remaining amount was taxed at the rate of **30 %**.

197   It should be noted that the tax base for non-residents in most cases may be higher than for residents as the nominal value of the shares is generally lower than the cost of acquisition. As it is up to the national court to find the facts, the

---

[185] ECJ 19 January 2006, C-265/04, *Bouanich* [2006] ECR I-923, para. 51.
[186] ECJ 16 July 2009, C-128/08, *Damseaux* [2009] ECR I-6823, paras. 20 and 22.
[187] ECJ 6 December 2007, C-298/05, *Columbus Container* [2007] ECR I-10451, para. 46 et seq.

ECJ decided that the national court has to find out whether or not the non-resident taxpayer is treated less favourably after the application of the double taxation convention than a resident taxpayer. Consequently, Ms Bouanich is only discriminated against if the reduction in the tax rate according to the double taxation convention does not neutralize the discrimination resulting from the higher tax base. The Court referred in this case to the **effective tax burden** of the taxpayer.

From this case it can be inferred that whenever a national court refers to **198** double taxation conventions as the legal background for the case, the ECJ has to take into account the **effects of the conventions** on national law in answering the question whether or not comparable situations are treated differently or different situations are treated alike.

In the **D. case**[188] the ECJ had to deal with the most-favoured-nation treat- **199** ment. Mr D was a German national and resident. 10 % of his wealth consisted of real property situated in the Netherlands, while the other wealth was held in Germany. The Netherlands refused to grant Mr D the same wealth tax allowance it grants to its own residents. Consequently, Mr D as a **non-resident was treated less favourably than residents** of the Netherlands.

Mr D argued that if he were Belgian, he would have been granted the wealth **200** tax allowances under the **double taxation convention** between Belgium and the Netherlands. Under this specific treaty, non-residents were granted the same wealth tax allowances as residents.

The ECJ did not accept this argument. It held that the fact that the **reciprocal** **201** **rights and obligations** flowing from such a convention apply only to persons resident in one of the two contracting Member States is an inherent consequence of bilateral double taxation conventions. The benefits granted under the double taxation convention between the Netherlands and Belgium, consequently, may not be invoked by a German resident. The German resident may only apply the treaty between Germany and the Netherlands.

Therefore, the ECJ decided that benefits that were granted to non-residents **202** under a specific treaty need not be granted to other non-residents to which **another treaty** is applicable.

e) Equivalence of Exemption and Credit Method

The ECJ was confronted with the question whether the exemption and the credit **203** method to **avoid economic double taxation are equivalent measures**. Economic double taxation is suffered if two different persons are taxable in respect of the same income or capital. The question presented to the ECJ was whether Member States may use the two methods in such a manner that in domestic situations they e.g. apply the exemption method whereas they apply the credit method in

---

[188] ECJ 5 July 2005, C-376/03, *D*. [2005] ECR I-5821.

cross-border situations in order to avoid economic double taxation and to protect the Member States' own tax revenue in the case of low taxation abroad.

204   In the *Test Claimants in the FII Group Litigation* case[189] and the joined cases *Haribo Lakritzen* and *Österreichische Salinen*[190] the ECJ concluded that in domestic situations Member States may apply the exemption method for the taxation of dividends in order to avoid economic double taxation and may apply the indirect credit method in cross-border situations in order to do so. Under the **indirect credit method**, the foreign corporation tax, for which the company that distributes the dividend is liable, is credited against the amount of corporation tax for which the company receiving the dividends is liable.

205   The ECJ clarified that the Member State of the company receiving the dividends is obliged to grant a **credit only up to the amount of taxes for which the company receiving the dividends is liable**. In case the amount of taxes is higher in the State of the company distributing the dividends, the other State is not obliged to repay the difference.

206   Furthermore, the ECJ decided that **additional administrative burdens** on taxpayers under the indirect credit method cannot be regarded as a difference between the two methods. Nevertheless, the administrative burdens under the indirect credit method may not be too excessive.

207   A **tax carry forward** is required for the equivalence of the two methods. In case the taxpayer suffers losses in years in which foreign dividends are received, a credit of foreign corporation taxes is not possible in that year. In that respective year economic double taxation does not arise but it may arise in subsequent years if no carry forward of taxes is provided for under national legislation. Without a carry forward of taxes economic double taxation is suffered in years when the results of the receiving companies are positive because the distributed dividends reduced the losses of the company that received the dividends and which might be set of against the positive result of that company. The reduction of the loss carry forward and the denial of the tax carry forward lead to economic double taxation, which does not arise under the exemption method.

208   Not yet clarified by the ECJ case law is the issue whether both the **statutory and/or the effective** tax rate should be taken into account in determining whether the domestic and the foreign-source dividends are treated equally. Additionally, it remains questionable whether it makes any difference whether the corporation tax is not paid by the foreign company paying the dividends but that it is paid from profits comprising dividends paid by the **direct or indirect subsidiary** resident in a Member State. Furthermore, independent of the application of the tax rate, it remains questionable whether **discrimination remains** and if

---

[189] ECJ 12 December 2006, C-446/04, *Test Claimants in the FII Group Litigation* [2006] ECR I-11753.

[190] ECJ 10 February 2011, C-436/08 and 437/08, *Haribo Lakritzen and Österreichische Salinen* [2011] ECR I-305, paras. 86 et seq.

answered in the affirmative whether it may be **justified**. The ECJ has the opportunity to answer these questions in the second *FII* case, which is still pending.[191]

f) Comparability in Third-Country Situations

The free movement of capital under Art. 63 TFEU (ex Art. 56 EC) is applicable **209** to third states. The third state is not bound by the TFEU and, consequently, a **reciprocal treatment** in these states **cannot be expected**. This fact may have an impact on the interpretation of Art. 63 TFEU (ex Art. 56 EC) and on the question of how far-reaching this fundamental freedom is vis-à-vis third states.

In a third-country situation comparability may be dependent on the **tax rate** **210** of the third state. In the legal literature it is argued that if the foreign tax rate is considerably lower or the foreign state provides for exemption, the cross-border situation may not be comparable to the national situation. Within the internal market this argument was denied by the ECJ but may gain relevance in a third-country situation due to the **lack of reciprocal rights**. As the ECJ is only at the beginning of the road to interpretation of the free movement of capital in third-country situations future decisions of the Court have to be awaited to answer questions of comparability in third-country situations.

In the *A* case[192] the ECJ analysed the scope of the free movement of capital in **211** EU and third country situations in detail and came to the conclusion that in both situations the scope of this freedom has to be the same. Nevertheless, it has to be borne in mind that according to the order of priority of the fundamental freedoms the free movement of capital does not apply if it is merely an unavoidable consequence of another fundamental freedom applicable to the case at issue (see m.nos. 132 et seq.).

Furthermore, in Arts. 64 et seq. TFEU (ex Arts. 57 et seq. EC) there are **special** **212** **rules** for third-country situations which allow EU Member States in special situations to discriminate against capital movements to third countries or allow the Council of the European Union to restrict the scope of the free movement of capital vis-à-vis third countries. Consequently, according to Advocate General *Bot*, the general rule in Art. 64 TFEU (ex Art. 56 EC) must have the same scope in EU and third-country situations.

If the scope of the free movement of capital under Art. 64 TFEU (ex Art. 56 **213** EC) is the same for EU and third-country situations, it is rather likely that the **comparability test will be the same** and that the Court will not use different standards for the comparability test in third-country situations than in EU situations.

---

[191] AG Jääskinen 19 July 2012, C-35/11, *Test Claimants in the FII Group Litigation* (not yet published).
[192] ECJ 18 December 2007, C-101/05, *A* [2007] ECR I-11531.

g) Standstill Clause in Third-Country Situations

214 Art. 64 TFEU (ex Art. 57 EC) contains a special provision applicable in third-country situations allowing Member States to **continue applying discriminatory national provisions** in the area of the free movement of capital under certain conditions:

- The restriction existed on 31 December 1993;
- The restriction concerns the movement of capital to or from third countries, involving:
  1. direct investment (including in real estate);
  2. establishment;
  3. provision of financial services;
  4. the admission of securities to capital markets.

215 The standstill clause on **direct investment** in particular has gained importance in the area of direct taxation. The ECJ thereby defined the term 'direct investment' as investments of any kind undertaken by natural or legal persons and which serve to establish or maintain **lasting and direct links** between the persons providing the capital and the undertakings to which that capital is made available in order to carry out an economic activity.[193]

216 A national measure **adopted after 31 December 1993** does not automatically fall outside the scope of Art. 64 TFEU (ex Art. 57 EC). If the provision is, in substance, **identical** to the previous legislation or is limited to **reducing or eliminating discrimination** under EU law in the earlier legislation, it is still covered by the standstill provision. By contrast, legislation based on an approach which is different from that of the previous law and establishes new law after 31 December 1993 is no longer covered by the standstill clause.[194]

217 It still remains to be seen whether the **scope of Art. 64 TFEU (ex Art. 57 EC) is still of great importance since the development of the priority rule** of the fundamental freedoms by the ECJ. In many cases a 'direct investment' under Art. 64 TFEU (ex Art. 57 EC) is going to fulfil the same criteria as the 'influence test' the Court developed for the primary application of the freedom of establishment (see m.nos. 132 et seq.). Therefore, in many cases, the Court will probably decide that direct investments are primarily covered by the freedom of establishment and that, consequently, the free movement of capital does not apply in third-country situations. This leads to the result that discriminatory provisions concerning direct investments are in line with EU law anyway, because no fundamental freedom is applicable. Only if a discriminatory national legal pro-

---

[193] See ECJ 12 December 2006, C-446/04, *Test Claimants in the FII Group Litigation* [2006] ECR I-11753, para. 185; ECJ 24 May 2007, C-157/05, *Holböck* [2007] ECR I-4051, paras. 32 et seq.

[194] See ECJ 12 December 2006, C-446/04, *Test Claimants in the FII Group Litigation* [2006] ECR I-11753, para. 192; ECJ 1 June 1999, C-302/97, *Konle* [1999] ECR I-03099, para. 52.

vision concerning direct investments is still covered by the free movement of capital because the 'influence test' for the application of the freedom of establishment is not met, may the discriminatory provision fall under the standstill clause and the Member State may still be allowed to apply its discriminatory legislation vis-à-vis third states and does not even need a justification to do so. In the *Haribo and Salinen* case,[195] the Court clarified that holdings of less than 10% of the share capital of the company making the distribution are not characterized as direct investments.

According to Art. 64 para. 3 TFEU (ex Art. 57 para. 3 EC), the Council is in **218** the position to adopt measures which constitute a **step backwards** in EU law as regards the liberalization of the movement of capital to or from third countries. As this provision grants a wide competence to the Council, it is regulated that the Council may only act in accordance with a **special legislative procedure, unanimously** and after **consulting the European Parliament**.

Furthermore, the **Council** and the **Commission** is granted another far-reaching **219** competence under Art. 65 para. 4 TFEU (ex Art. 58 para. 4 EC) with regard to restrictive national legal provisions of Member States concerning third countries. According to this provision, the Commission or, in absence of a Commission decision within three months from the request of a Member State, the Council, may adopt a decision stating that the **restrictive national legal provisions are compatible with the Treaties** in so far as they are justified by one of the objectives of the EU and are compatible with the proper functioning of the internal market. The Council and the Commission may only decide on such a request if no measure is yet taken pursuant to Art. 64 para. 3 TFEU (ex Art. 57 para. 3 EC), see m.no. 218. Furthermore, the Council has to decide unanimously.

7. Justifications

a) Justifications under the TFEU

The TFEU explicitly provides for certain grounds that justify discriminatory **220** national rules. These are **public policy, public security or public health.** In the area of direct taxation these grounds hardly ever serve as justification. In some ECJ decisions these grounds were put forward to justify discrimination but they have never been accepted by the ECJ in the area of direct taxation.

The explicit grounds justify **direct discrimination**. The ECJ has decided, **221** furthermore, that certain grounds may also justify **indirect discrimination**.[196]

Despite the grounds explicitly mentioned in the TFEU, the ECJ decided in its **222** case *Cassis de Dijon*[197] that infringement of the fundamental freedoms may also

---

[195] ECJ 10 February 2011, C-436/08 and 437/08, *Haribo Lakritzen and Österreichische Salinen* [2011] ECR I-305, para. 137.
[196] ECJ 13 November 2003, C-42/02, *Lindman* [2003] ECR I-13519, paras. 24 et seq.
[197] ECJ 20 February 1979, 120/78, *Rewe-Zentral* [1979] ECR 649, para. 8.

be justified by **general grounds of public interest**. Hence, Member States put forward different grounds of public interest as justification with which the Court had to deal in its subsequent case law.

b) Justifications Accepted by the ECJ

i. Cohesion of the Tax System

223 The cohesion of the tax system was **accepted** for the first time as justification in the *Bachmann* case[198] and the *Commission v Belgium* case,[199] which were decided on the same day. In subsequent years the ECJ always dismissed this argument as justification; this changed in the *Wannsee* case.[200]

224 Mr Bachmann was a German national who was employed in Belgium. Belgium **refused to allow deduction** from his total occupational income **contributions** paid in Germany pursuant to sickness and invalidity insurance contracts and a life assurance contract, whereas such contributions paid in Belgium were deductible. The Belgian government argued that payments from the German insurance company were not taxable in Belgium and, consequently, the denial of the deduction of the contributions was justified.

225 The government recognized that if Mr Bachmann moved back to Germany at the end of his active working period and was taxed in Germany on the pensions, the result might be **double taxation**, as the contributions were not deductible in Belgium but the pension payments were taxable in Germany. According to the Belgian government, double taxation is the result of non-harmonized national laws of the Member States.

226 The ECJ did not accept this argument but came to the conclusion that the discrimination can be justified by the cohesion of the Belgium national law system. It held that there is a **connection between the deductibility of contributions and the liability to tax the payments** by the insurers. Consequently, Belgium did not have to grant the deductions of premiums to German institutions as the payables from the German insurance company are not taxable in Belgium.

227 In principle, cohesion is a **concept to avoid double taxation** or to ensure that income is taxed, but only once. Conditions for the application of this grounds of justification are:

- the purpose of the provision has to be to safeguard the fiscal cohesion of the national system;
- there must be a direct correlation between the sums which are deducted from the taxable income and the sums which are subject to tax;
- the deduction and the taxation have to relate to the same tax;
- the deduction and the taxation must concern the same taxpayer;

---

[198] ECJ 28 January 1992, C-204/90, *Bachmann* [1992] ECR I-249.
[199] ECJ 28 January 1992, C-300/90, *Commission v Belgium* [1992] ECR I-305.
[200] ECJ 23 October 2008, C-157/07, *Krankenheim Ruhesitz am Wannsee-Seniorenheimstatt GmbH* [2008] ECR I-8061, paras. 42 et seq.

- the Member State does not avail itself of the cohesion through a double taxation convention.

In the *Danner* case,[201] which was very similar to the *Bachmann* case, the Court **228** denied the cohesion argument as justification. The slightly different Finnish national provision, which **subjected payments from foreign insurance companies to tax** even though contributions to such foreign companies were not deductible, was used by the ECJ to rule that the **direct correlation** between the sums which are deducted from the taxable income and the sums which are subject to tax did not exist (condition (2)).

In the *Wielockx* case[202] the Court denied fiscal cohesion as justification, as a **229** Member State may not rely on the argument that deductions are denied, because payments are not taxable in that state in case the national provision allowed taxation but a **double taxation convention allocated the taxing rights for the payments to the other contracting state**. As double tax treaties restrict national law, the Member State has given up its right to tax the payments. In the *Wielockx* case the Court added this new dimension to the cohesion concept to which it is referred to as condition (5).

In the *Wannsee* case[203] the ECJ again accepted the cohesion argument as justi- **230** fication. Under the German tax system at that time, the German parent company was allowed to take into account losses incurred by a permanent establishment situated in Austria. At the time when that Austrian permanent establishment made profits the German system provided for a tax reintegration of those losses even though those losses may actually not have been utilized by the Austrian permanent establishment; this would lead to a situation of double taxation. The ECJ held that the **reintegration of losses** is the logical complement of the **deduction of losses** previously granted. The principle of cohesion is fulfilled because the German tax legislation did not provide for a reintegration where the German parent company showed that the provisions applicable to it in the foreign country did not in general allow it to benefit from a deduction of losses during years in which profits were generated. But in the case at issue the Austrian tax system, in principle, provided for such a possibility of deducting losses; however, that possibility could not be put into effect in the concrete situation in which the taxpayer found himself. Consequently, the reintegration of losses that lead to the discrimination can be justified by the argument of the cohesion of the German national tax provisions. In the *Commission vs. Hungary* case[204] and the *Commission vs. Belgium* case[205] the Court again accepted the cohesion argument as justification.

---

[201] ECJ 3 October 2002, C-136/00, *Danner* [2002] ECR I-8147.
[202] ECJ 11 August 1995, C-80/94, *Wielockx* [1995] ECR I-2493.
[203] ECJ 23 October 2008, C-157/07, *Krankenheim Ruhesitz am Wannsee-Seniorenheimstatt GmbH* [2008] ECR I-8061, paras. 42 et seq.
[204] ECJ 1 December 2011, C-253/09, *Commission vs. Hungary* (not yet published).
[205] ECJ 1 December 2011, C-250/08, *Commission vs. Belgium* (not yet published).

ii. Territoriality

231   Many countries follow the principle of territoriality in their national tax law system for persons who are **subject to limited tax liability**. This means that a country taxes a person subject to limited tax liability only on income that has a **specific nexus** to this country.

232   As the cohesion argument, the territoriality argument was **only accepted once** (in the *Futura Participations* case[206]) and was regularly rejected as justification in subsequent cases. In the *Futura Participations* case the issue was whether a Luxembourg branch of a French company was able to **take into account losses that were suffered by the head office in France** for the purpose of calculating the basis of assessment for the Luxembourg branch. The Court rejected that option by reasoning that a system is in conformity with the principle of territoriality in which for **non-resident taxpayers** only profits and losses arising from their Luxembourg activities are taken into account in calculating the tax payable by the permanent establishment.

233   The principle of territoriality, consequently, may be used by Member States to **deny the deduction of foreign losses of persons subject to limited tax liability** if foreign profits are not taxed either, whereas persons subject to unlimited tax liability have the option to deduct foreign losses but on the other side are also taxable on their worldwide income.

234   An **exception** to this rule arises if the ***Schumacker* doctrine**[207] applies and almost all of the income of the person is received in the source state and losses are considered to be within the personal and family sphere of the taxpayer. In this situation non-residents have to be granted the right to deduct foreign losses even though foreign profits are not taxable in the source state; otherwise, the losses might not be taken into consideration in the residence state or in the source state. If personal and family allowances are not taken into account in either the source or in the residence state, this leads to discrimination.

235   In the *Manninen* case[208] the Court denied the territoriality argument by holding that this principle does not preclude the granting of a tax credit to a person fully taxable in Finland in respect of dividends paid by companies established in other Member States. Apparently, the Court does not allow the territoriality argument to justify discrimination of **persons subject to unlimited tax liability**.

236   From the case law of the ECJ it can be inferred that the principle of territoriality may only be used to deny benefits to persons **subject to limited tax liability** that are granted to persons subject to unlimited tax liability who are subject to tax on their worldwide income.

---

[206] ECJ 15 May 1997, C-250/95, *Futura Participations* [1997] ECR I-2471.
[207] See m.nos. 168 et seq.
[208] ECJ 7 September 2004, C-319/02, *Manninen* [2004] ECR I-7477, para. 38.

iii. Anti-abuse

Within the European Union direct taxes are not harmonized and, consequently, **237**
Member States are free to decide on their national tax base and on the tax rate
they want to apply to persons who are subject to tax in their country. Some
Member States offer especially **low tax rates to attract foreign investors**. In
order to reduce their tax burden taxpayers try to benefit from such low-tax
countries by using international structures. As such structures may **decrease the
tax revenue** of the other states, most of the Member States have national provisions that deny persons using such structures the same benefits as would be
granted to persons that use international structures based on sound business
reasons.

Not all national provisions that aim to avoid abusive constructions are in line **238**
with the **non-discrimination concept** developed by the ECJ in its case law. In
its case law the Court has shaped an anti-abuse principle, which is often used by
Member States to try to justify discriminatory national provisions.

To justify discriminatory national provisions with the anti-abuse argument, **239**
the **first precondition** is that through the international structure the person may
benefit from a tax advantage which he would not have benefited from in a pure
domestic situation.[209]

The **second precondition** is that the **aim of the national provision** has to be **240**
to counteract abusive or fraudulent conduct. Consequently, a discriminatory national provision may only be justified by this argument if its object and purpose
is to hinder persons from making use of such detrimental constructions.

The **third precondition** is that the national discriminatory provision has to **241**
be designed in such a way as to discriminate against **exclusively abusive behaviour**. A discriminatory national provision that categorically and generally
denies benefits in cross-border situations cannot be justified by the anti-abuse
argument. It is required instead that the national provision allows verifying on a
case-by-case basis whether or not **wholly artificial constructions** are used by
the taxpayer to circumvent the national legislation or to improperly or fraudu-
lently take advantage of provisions of the TFEU.[210] Consequently, a national
discriminatory provision that tackles not only abusive structures but also constructions that are based on sound economic business reasons cannot be justified
by the anti-abuse argument.

In its case law the ECJ has made concrete the term '**wholly artificial arrange- 242
ments**'. If from an **objective perspective** it cannot be seen that the taxpayer's
aim through the behaviour is to escape national tax, the existence of a wholly
artificial arrangement has to be denied. One of these objective criteria may be

---

[209] ECJ 21 November 2002, C-436/00, *X and Y* [2002] ECR I-10829, para. 41; ECJ 12 December 2002, C-324/00, *Lankhorst-Hohorst* [2002] ECR I-11779, para. 37.
[210] ECJ 21 November 2002, C-436/00, *X and Y* [2002] ECR I-10829, para. 42; ECJ 12 September 2006, C-196/04, *Cadbury Schweppes* [2006] ECR I-7995, paras. 51 and 55.

fulfilled if the company that is set up abroad **distributes most of its profits** to the parent company. In this case the foreign profits are repatriated to the residence country of the parent company and may be taxed there. The aim to escape taxation in the residence state of the parent company is, consequently, objectively not fulfilled. The same might apply if a company is set up in a foreign country to exercise **trading activities that require on-site rooms and personnel** and it is, therefore, not just a pure holding company. In such a case, from an objective perspective, a wholly artificial arrangement has to be denied.[211]

243   The Commission in its communication stated that anti-abuse rules "… must not be framed too broadly but be targeted at situations where there is **no genuine establishment** or more generally where there is a lack of commercial underpinning."[212]

iv. Effectiveness of Fiscal Supervision

244   The ECJ held that the effectiveness of fiscal supervision constitutes an overriding requirement of general interest capable of justifying discrimination.[213] One of the cases in which the Court accepted this argument as justification was the *Futura Participations* case. The case concerned a Luxembourg branch of a French company that wanted to carry forward the losses of the Luxembourg branch in Luxembourg. The Luxembourg authorities required the French company to keep accounts for the Luxembourg branch that complied with the domestic Luxembourg tax accounting rules. Consequently, the French company was forced, **in addition to keeping accounts** that complied with the domestic French tax accounting rules, to keep **accounts for the Luxembourg branch** that have to comply with the Luxembourg rules. The Court decided that this requirement discriminates against the foreign company.

245   However, the ECJ decided that this discrimination may be justified by the argument of fiscal supervision. As every Member State has its own rules to determine profits and losses, the separate accounts for the Luxembourg branch are **essential in order to determine the amount of losses** actually incurred by it. Based on the separate accounts, Luxembourg was able to verify the amount of losses that could be carried forward. This would not have been possible if the French company had not prepared separate accounts for the Luxembourg branch.

246   In the *Commission vs. Portugal* case[214] the Court decided that the taxation of dividends received by a non-resident pension fund at a higher rate than the taxation of dividends received by a Portuguese pension fund constitutes discrimination but it accepted the argument of effectiveness of fiscal supervision as justification. The exemption of domestic pension funds is linked to the **fulfilment of**

---

[211] ECJ 12 September 2006, C-196/04, *Cadbury Schweppes* [2006] ECR I-7995, para. 61.
[212] European Commission, MEMO/07/558 of 10 December 2007.
[213] ECJ 20 February 1979, 120/78, *Rewe-Zentral* [1979] ECR 649, para. 8.
[214] ECJ 6 October 2011, C-493/09, *Commission vs. Portugal* (not yet published).

strict requirements enacted under national law in order to ensure the maintenance of the Portuguese pension system. The national law provisions concern issues such as management, operation, capitalization and financial responsibility. Foreign pension funds are not bound by the national law provision and consequently may be treated differently.

Member States are, therefore, able to justify national measures that distinguish between foreign and domestic nationals if these measures are necessary for the effectiveness of fiscal supervision. For the principle of proportionality in the *Futura Participations* case, see m.nos. 287 et seq. and in the *Commission vs. Portugal* case, see m.no. 290. For third-country situations see m.nos. 296 et seq. **247**

v. Neutralization in the Other State

In recent case law the ECJ has launched the idea that discrimination of one Member State may be neutralized by another Member State. This means that if Member States apply discriminatory national provisions which cannot be justified by one of the arguments discussed in the previous sections, there may still be the chance that this Member State may nevertheless apply its national provision. It may do so if the other Member State involved is willing to and, in actual fact does, **neutralize the discrimination by crediting the tax** which was levied in a discriminatory manner. **248**

In the *Denkavit* case[215] a French company distributed dividends to a company established in the Netherlands. According to the French national law, these dividends were subject to **withholding tax**. Dividends distributed to another French company were not subject to tax. Consequently, the cross-border dividend payments were discriminated against. As an intermediary result the Court concluded that the French **domestic rule is discriminatory and cannot be justified** by overriding reasons of public interest. **249**

The analyses of the Court were not finalized at that stage. It furthermore addressed the issue whether the applicable double taxation convention between France and the Netherlands has any influence on the legal situation of the case. The double taxation convention between France and the Netherlands provides for a 5 % withholding tax for the dividends distributed. France was therefore authorized under the double taxation convention to levy its domestic withholding tax on dividends distributed to a Dutch company at a rate of 5 %. The Netherlands pledged itself to credit the tax withheld in France. As the Netherlands is prepared to **credit the French withholding tax against the Dutch taxes, double taxation is prevented**. The Court held that in such a case in which the Netherlands is prepared to give a credit, discrimination in France is neutralized with the result that France is not hindered in levying the 5 % withholding tax on dividends distributed to a treaty partner that credits the foreign withholding tax against its own domestic tax. **250**

---

[215] ECJ 14 December 2006, C-170/05, *Denkavit* [2006] ECR I-11949.

251   But the Court **limited this option of neutralization** of discriminatory legislation. First, the credit of the taxes levied in the source state needs to be credited in the residence state on the legal basis of a **bilateral tax convention**. The unilateral grant of a tax credit under the legislation of the residence state is not sufficient in order to neutralize the discrimination in the source state.[216] Second, the residence state **in fact credits** the foreign withholding tax levied under the treaty. In the *Denkavit* case the Netherlands **exempted the dividends** received by the Dutch company from tax. According to the **limitation of the foreign tax credit,** the amount set off may not exceed the amount of the Netherlands tax payable on these dividends. Consequently, the Netherlands did not in fact set off the French taxes as it did not levy any tax on these dividends. In such a case the source state that applied the discriminatory domestic legislation has to cease applying its legislation as neutralization does not take place in the other contracting state.[217] Furthermore, the requirements for neutralization are not fulfilled either if the other contracting state does not credit the source taxes in the **full amount** but only partly; this may be the case if the amount of taxes levied in the residence state is less than the withheld taxes in the source state.[218]

vi. Balanced Allocation of Taxing Rights

252   In the *Marks & Spencer* case (see m.nos. 153) the ECJ for the first time accepted the need to safeguard the balanced allocation of the power to impose taxes as justification but only in combination with other reasons. In the *X Holding* case[219] the ECJ went a step further and accepted the need to safeguard the balanced allocation of the power to impose taxes by itself as **justification**.

253   In the *X Holding* case the Court had to decide whether the Netherlands **group taxation system** is in line with the freedom of establishment. The group taxation system was limited to domestic companies and did not allow the integration of foreign companies. The ECJ decided that the different treatment of domestic and foreign companies infringes the freedom of establishment but may be justified. The Court held that the integration of foreign companies into the group taxation system allows the group to choose in which state the profits may be taxed or the losses may be deducted. The **free choice of the taxing jurisdiction** would seriously undermine a balanced allocation of the power to impose taxes between the Member States. Consequently, the Netherlands group taxation system can be justified by the above-mentioned reason and is in line with the freedom of establishment.

---

[216] See ECJ 3 June 2010, C-487/08, *Commission vs. Spain* [2010] ECR I-4843, para. 66.
[217] See as well ECJ 8 November 2007, C-379/05, *Amurta* [2007] ECR I-9569; ECJ 19 November 2009, C-540/07, *Commission v Italy* [2009] ECR I-10983; ECJ 20 October 2011, C-284/09, *Commission vs. Germany* (not yet published).
[218] ECJ 3 June 2010, C-487/08, *Commission vs. Spain* [2010] ECR I-4843, paras. 59 et seq.
[219] ECJ 25 February 2010, C-337/08, *X Holding* [2010] ECR I-1215, paras. 31 et seq.

The justification connected with the need to safeguard the balanced allo- **254**
cation of taxing rights between the Member States may consequently be accepted
where the national law provision is designed to prevent structures which are
capable of jeopardizing the right of a Member State to exercise its **taxing
powers in relation to activities carried out in its territory.**

The balanced allocation of taxing right argument **cannot be used as justi- 255
fication** in case economic activities are carried out in a country by a foreign
taxpayer if the foreign taxpayer is taxed in that country, whereas the **domestic
taxpayer pursuing the same economic activities is not taxed** there. The argument that otherwise a foreign taxpayer may carry out economic activities in the
respective country without being taxed is no longer valid if this country decided
to not tax comparable domestic taxpayers.[220]

vii. Promotion of National Education and Training

In the *Commission vs. Austria* case[221] the ECJ held that the objective of pro- **256**
moting national education and training could constitute a justification. In the
case at issue the Austrian national law provision did not allow the deduction
from tax of gifts made to teaching institutions established outside the territory of
Austria whereas such gifts were deductible if they were made to such institutions
established in Austria. Nevertheless, the Court concluded in that case that the
national law provision did not comply with the principle of proportionality.

c) Justifications Not Accepted by the ECJ

i. Non-Harmonization in the Area of Direct Taxation

Direct taxation within the European Union has **not yet been harmonized com- 257
prehensively** as it has in the area of indirect taxes. Direct taxation has been
harmonized in only a few selected areas as described in Chapters IV (m.nos. 429
et seq.). As a consequence, the tax systems of the Member States differ quite extensively. Therefore, Member States have tried to argue that different measures
are necessary for persons exercising their fundamental rights under the TFEU in
order to **take account of the differences** between the tax systems. They tried to
justify discriminatory measures by the argument that the area of direct taxation
is not harmonized.

The Court **did not accept this argument.** The Court held that even in the **258**
absence of harmonization, Member States are not allowed to apply measures to-
foreign nationals exercising their fundamental rights that differ from those
which apply to their own nationals, unless these measures are justified and proportionate.

---

[220] See ECJ 20 October 2011, C-284/09, *Commission vs. Germany* (not yet published).
[221] ECJ 16 June 2011, C-10/10, *Commission vs. Austria* (not yet published), para. 38.

259   On the other hand, Member States can limit deductible expenses, e.g. for university tuition fees paid to institutions in other Member States, up to a **maximum amount** which is set for the corresponding costs of attending similar courses at a national university. The state of residence is not obliged to deduct a greater amount of tuition fees if the foreign fees exceed those at the national level.

ii. Difficulties in Obtaining Information

260   In cross-border situations the issue often arises that authorities need information from the foreign state in order to enable them to effect a correct assessment of taxes. Such information is often difficult to obtain from a foreign state. Within the European Union a Directive on **mutual assistance in the exchange of information, 77/799/EEC,** has been enacted and was repealed by Directive 2011/16/EU. This Directive is applicable in all Member States and obliges the Member States to cooperate with each other. In principle, the Member States may obtain the required information through this Directive. Consequently, whenever a Member State tried to justify a discriminatory provision with the argument that difficulties in obtaining information exist, the ECJ always denies this justification by referring to Directive 77/799/EEC, repealed by Directive 2011/16/EU.

261   Even though the Member States argue that this instrument is not effective as it is quite **difficult to obtain the required information** from certain Member States, the Court was not impressed by this argument. The Court held that it is up to the Member State to make this instrument effective. The Court has never accepted **practical difficulties** as a justification.[222] Directive 77/799/EEC, repealed by Directive 2011/16/EU, serves as a legal basis that enables the Member States to exchange information, which means that the argument of difficulties in obtaining information is not one that is of an overriding public interest.

262   There are **limits to the exchange of information** under Directive 77/799/EEC. Art. 8 of the Directive lists these limits. Member States are therefore not obliged to exchange information if they are prevented by their laws or administrative practices from carrying out the requested enquiries or from collecting or using the requested information for their own purposes. Furthermore, Member States may refuse the provision of information where it would lead to the disclosure of a commercial, industrial or professional secret or of a commercial process, or of information whose disclosure would be contrary to public policy. No information has to be provided either, if the requesting state is unable for practical or legal reasons to provide similar information. Under Directive 2011/16/EU, the exceptions to the provision of information are very similar but are limited on one considerable point. According to Art. 18 para. 2 of the Directive,

---

[222] See ECJ 14 September 2006, C-386/04, *Stauffer* [2006] ECR I-8203, para. 48; ECJ 27 November 2008, C-418/07, *Papillon* [2008] ECR I-8947, para, 54; ECJ 1 July 2010, *Dijkman* [2010] ECR I-6649, para 43.

Member States may no longer rely on national bank secrecy legislation in order to deny the provision of information. Hence, the Directive follows the international trend in combating harmful tax evasion.

If one of the **exceptions to the requirement of providing information is applicable**, Member States may rely on the argument that difficulties in obtaining information exist in order to **justify** discrimination.[223] For the principle of proportionality in this context, see m.no. 289. For the application in third-country situations see m.nos. 280 et seq. **263**

iii. Loss of Tax Revenue

In many cases in which Member States apply discriminatory national provisions, the Member States do so in order to avoid a loss in their own tax revenue. But a reduction in tax revenue has **never been accepted** by the Court as an overriding reason in the public interest that may justify a discriminatory national provision. When Member States have tried to justify discriminatory national provisions on these grounds, the Court has not accepted this argument. **264**

It seems that the Court does accept the fact that within the internal market the fact that one Member State's tax revenue is **reduced** in a cross-border situation does not play a role even though **another Member State does not have to suffer a reduction in its tax revenue**. This principle was eminently demonstrated by the Court in the *Manninen* case.[224] This case concerned the Finnish imputation tax system for dividends. Dividends received by a natural person were taxed at the full income tax rate. To avoid economic double taxation which would arise because the company distributing the dividends had to pay corporate tax on its profits before these profits could be distributed to its shareholders, the Finnish dividend taxation system provided for a credit of the corporate tax against the tax paid by the individual shareholder. If a shareholder received dividends from a foreign corporation, Finland wanted to deny the credit of the underlying foreign corporate tax against the Finnish individual income tax levied on the dividends in the hands of the receiving individual shareholder. The Finnish government argued that the foreign corporation had to pay foreign corporate tax and, consequently, it would be justified if it were to deny the credit of the foreign tax as the corporate tax was not levied by Finland but by the foreign state. The **credit would lead to a reduction in the Finnish tax revenue** because Finland may only levy tax on the difference between the individual income tax of the Finnish shareholder and the foreign corporate tax if there is such a difference. By referring to former case law, the ECJ denied this argument and obliged Finland to give a credit for the foreign corporation tax. **265**

---

[223] ECJ 11 October 2007, C-451/05, *Elisa* [2007] ECR I-8251.
[224] ECJ 7 September 2004, C-319/02, *Manninen* [2004] ECR I-7477.

iv. Compensation of Unfavourable Tax Treatment by Other Tax Advantages

266   In some cases governments have argued that discrimination may be justified by the fact that the taxpayer is granted a **tax advantage which is not related to the discriminatory measure**. They try to compensate a discriminatory tax treatment by other tax advantages. This argument has never been accepted by the ECJ as justification. In one of the first direct tax cases, *Commission v France ("Avoir Fiscal")*,[225] the Court held that difference in treatment cannot be justified by any other advantages, even if such advantages actually exist. The Court completed its reasoning by holding that discrimination is prohibited even if it is **only of a limited nature**.

267   The case concerned the French *avoir fiscal*, which was a tax credit in order to avoid economic double taxation caused by the fact that profits are subject to corporate tax in the hands of the company distributing dividends and then to income tax in the hands of the recipient of those dividends. To avoid the negative effect of economic double taxation, the recipient of the dividends was able to credit an amount which was equal to half the amount actually paid by the distributing company. This credit was granted to French shareholders who received dividends from French companies but was not granted to French branches of foreign companies. This different treatment was characterized by the ECJ as discrimination, as foreign companies that pursue their activities in France through branches are not treated in the same way as French companies. The French government argued that French **branches of foreign companies enjoy various advantages over French companies** and that these advantages **balance out any disadvantages** suffered by the foreign company due to the denial of the shareholders' tax credit. The Court was not impressed by this argument and denied this argument as justification.

268   In the *Dijkman* case[226] the Court again denied the compensation argument. The case concerned the Belgian national law provision on the taxation of income from investments made in another Member State. Such income is subject to **supplementary municipal tax** whereas income from investments made in Belgium is not subject to such a supplementary municipal tax. The Belgian Government argued that this unfavourable tax treatment in the cross-border situation could be compensated by the **cash-flow advantage** that would result to taxpayers with income from investments made in other Member States because income from investments made in Belgium is subject to a withholding tax.

---

[225] ECJ 28 January 1986, 270/83, *Commission v France ("Avoir Fiscal")* [1986] ECR 273, para. 21.

[226] ECJ 1 July 2010, *Dijkman* [2010] ECR I-6649, para 43.

v. Double Taxation

In the *Block* case[227] the ECJ had to decide on the double taxation of an inherit- **269** ance which occurred because Germany and Spain applied different connecting factors for levying inheritance tax. The Court clarified in its decision that EU law, in the current stage of its development, does not lay down any general criteria for the attribution of areas of competence between the Member States in relation to the elimination of double taxation within the European Union. Consequently, apart from the Parent-Subsidiary Directive, the Interest and Royalty Directive and the EU Arbitration Convention, no uniform measure or harmonization measure designed to eliminate double taxation has as yet been adopted at EU law level.[228] Consequently, the Court held that **at the current stage of the development of EU law**, the Member States enjoy a certain autonomy in this area, provided they comply with EU law, and **are not obliged** therefore to adapt their own tax systems to the different systems of tax of the other Member States in order, inter alia, **to eliminate the double taxation** arising from the exercise in parallel by those Member States of their fiscal sovereignty. Recently, the Court again confirmed its findings in the *Banco Bilbao* case[229] by holding that the parallel exercise of tax competences does not constitute discrimination under the condition that such an exercise is not discriminatory.

To summarize, the ECJ decided that in so far as EU law does not lay down **270** any general criteria for the attribution of areas of competence between the Member States relating to the elimination of double taxation within the EU a situation of double taxation does not lead to discrimination if both states involved apply their national provisions in a non-discriminatory manner.[230]

vi. Promotion of National Research and Development

In the *Laboratoires Fournier* case[231] the ECJ held that the promotion of research **271** and development **may be accepted** as justification. Nevertheless, a national law provision that grants a tax credit only for research and development carried out in the Member State concerned but refuses the benefit of such a tax credit if the research and development is carried out abroad cannot be justified with this argument. The Court referred to the **Community policy on research and technological development** enacted under Art. 179 TFEU (ex Art. 163 EC) and held that such legislation is directly contrary to that objective and therefore cannot be justified with the argument of promoting research and development.

---

[227] ECJ 12 February 2009, C-67/08, *Block* [2009] ECR I-883.
[228] See as well ECJ 14 November 2006, C-513/04, *Kerckhaert-Morres* [2006] ECR I-10967, para. 22; ECJ 6 December 2007, C-298/05, *Columbus Container* [2007] ECR I-10451, para. 45.
[229] ECJ 8 December 2011, C-157/10, *Banco Bilbao* (not yet published).
[230] See ECJ 16 July 2009, C-128/08, *Damseaux* [2009] ECR I-6823.
[231] ECJ 10 March 2005, C-39/04, *Laboratoires Fournier* [2005] ECR I-2057, para. 23.

vii. Adequate Special Qualification through Domestic Presence

272 In the *Commission vs. Austria* case[232] the ECJ decided that the Austrian national law provision, which requires the appointment of a **domestic tax representative** who has to disclose the amount of distributions of investment funds or real estate funds is discriminatory and cannot be justified. The Court did not accept the argument that only a domestic tax representative is in the position to provide adequate information. It argued that the presence of a tax representative in Austria does not guarantee that the tax representative has special competences in the Austrian tax law. In addition, the domestic law provision foresees that the taxpayer himself may calculate and disclose the taxable amount of the deemed distributions. Consequently, the domestic presence of the tax representative violates the freedom to provide services.

viii. Lack of Reciprocity in Third-Country Situations

273 In the *Haribo and Salinen* case[233] the Court decided that the lack of reciprocity in relations between Member States and third countries does not serve as a justification. It held that when the principle of free movement of capital was extended to third countries, the Member States chose to enshrine this principle in the **same article and terms** for intra-Community situations and third-country situations.

d) Combination of Justifications by the ECJ

274 **One isolated reason** that a Member State presents in order to justify discriminatory domestic legislation is in certain constellations **not sufficient**. Some reasons are, by themselves, not convincing enough for the Court to accept them as justification. But if more than one of such reasons is presented together by the Member State, the Court might accept them as justification. Furthermore, the Court is willing to accept a reason which it would, **in general, deny as justification** if it is combined with other reasons that do not serve as justification by themselves. The combination of justifications that are generally not accepted has been upheld by the ECJ in recent case law in particular.

275 In the *Marks & Spencer* case[234] the Court accepted a combination of reasons as justification for the first time. It accepted the **need to safeguard the balanced allocation of the power to impose taxes** between Member States in conjunction with the **need to prevent a double utilization of losses** and the **need to prevent tax avoidance**. In subsequent case law the Court again accepted a combination of grounds of justification.[235]

---

[232] ECJ 29 September 2011, C-387/10, *Commission vs. Austria* (not yet published), paras. 27 et seq.

[233] ECJ 10 February 2011, C-436/08 and 437/08, *Haribo Lakritzen and Österreichische Salinen* [2011] ECR I-305, paras. 127 et seq.

[234] ECJ 13 December 2005, C-446/03, *Marks & Spencer* [2005] ECR I-10837.

[235] See ECJ 29 March 2007, C-347/04, *Rewe Zentralfinanz* [2007] ECR I-2647; ECJ 18 July 2007, C-231/05, *Oy AA* [2007] ECR I-6373.

In the *Lidl Belgium* case[236] the Court clarified that the three reasons accepted **276** as justification in the *Marks & Spencer* case **must not necessarily be understood as being cumulative**. The existence of two of the three justifications may already serve as justification.[237]

In the *National Grid Indus* case[238] the ECJ referred to the principle of fiscal **277** **territoriality** linked to a temporal component and the **balanced allocation of the power to impose taxes** and accepted these grounds as justifications. In the *SGI* case[239] the Court accepted the **need to safeguard the balanced allocation of the power to impose taxes** between Member States in conjunction with the **need to prevent tax avoidance**.

e) Justifications in Third-Country Situations

As the underlying principle of the **cohesion argument** is the **avoidance of double** **278** **taxation**, which is a desirable political aim within the internal market, avoidance of double taxation could be interpreted differently in a third-country situation. The willingness to avoid double taxation if a third country is involved might be **lower** than in a pure EU situation.

In a pure EU situation both states that might create a situation of double tax- **279** ation are bound by EU law and are at least prohibited from discriminatory behaviour. Many situations of double taxation are therefore **already eliminated through the non-discrimination principle**. In contrast, a third country is not bound by EU law and, consequently, many more situations of double taxation may arise in third-country situations than in EU situations. Therefore, it might be argued that the principle of avoidance of double taxation is different in third-country situations than in EU situations; this may also affect the justifications that are based on this principle. Consequently, the cohesion argument may possibly be **easier to use to justify discrimination in third-country situations**.

In the *A* case[240] the issue was whether discrimination vis-à-vis third states **280** may be justified by the argument that there are **difficulties in obtaining information**. Third countries are in general not bound by the directives of the European Union. **Directive 77/799/EEC** on mutual assistance for the exchange of information, repealed by Directive 2011/16/EU, is only applicable within the European Union.[241] In cases concerning discrimination within the European Union, the ECJ does not accept the argument of national governments that there are difficulties in obtaining information to justify discrimination. The Court held that Member States may gain the information needed to exercise their taxing rights via the Directive, see m.nos. 260 et seq.

---

[236] ECJ 15 May 2008, *Lidl Belgium* [2008] ECR I-3601, paras. 39 et seq.
[237] See ECJ 18 July 2007, C-231/05, *Oy AA* [2007] ECR I-6373, para. 60.
[238] ECJ 29 November 2011, C-371/10, *National Grid Indus* (not yet published), para. 46.
[239] ECJ 21 January 2010, C-311/08, *Société de Gestion Industrielle* [2010] ECR I-487, para. 69.
[240] ECJ 18 December 2007, C-101/05, *A* [2007] ECR I-11531.
[241] See Chapter VIII (m.nos. 562 et seq.).

281   In relation to third states, mutual assistance in the exchange of information can be agreed upon in **double taxation conventions or tax information exchange agreements (TIEA)**. The OECD Model provides in **Art. 26** for the exchange of information by the contracting states. Consequently, based on the double tax convention a Member State may ask the third country to provide information needed to exercise its taxing rights. Nevertheless, it has to be considered that such double taxation conventions have not been concluded with all third countries. With low-tax countries in particular Member States are rather reluctant to conclude agreements to avoid double taxation.

282   Recently, low-tax jurisdictions tend to conclude **TIEA agreements** in order to be not stigmatized by the OECD and its classifications of states as states which have implemented the internationally agreed tax standard (white list), states which have committed to the standard but have not yet substantially implemented it (gray list) and states which have not committed to the standard at all (black list).[242] Furthermore, some states have started to implement discriminatory provisions which apply to states listed on the black list. The list may vary from country to country according to the definition of un-cooperative foreign states.

283   In the *A* case a Swedish national provision was at stake that granted an exemption from income tax in respect of dividends distributed in the form of shares in a subsidiary if the distributing company was established in the EU or the EEA or in a country with which a double tax convention with an exchange of information article had been concluded. In the *A* case the distributing company was established in Switzerland. As Switzerland is not a member of the European Union, Directive 77/799/EEC did not apply. Furthermore, no article on the exchange of information had been agreed upon in the double tax convention between Sweden and Switzerland. Consequently, the Court decided that Sweden may **justify** its discrimination and that, therefore, it is not hindered from continuing to apply its discriminatory domestic provisions in relation to Switzerland where that exemption is subject to compliance conditions which can be verified by the competent authorities of Sweden only by obtaining information from Switzerland. Nevertheless, the Court has explicitly held that the case-law concerning **restrictions** on the exercise of freedom of movement **within the European Union cannot be transposed in its entirety** to movements of capital between Member States and third countries since such movements take place in a different legal context.[243]

---

[242] See the Progress Report on the Jurisdictions surveyed by the OECD Global Forum in Implementing the Internationally Agreed Tax Standards, 29 January 2010: http://www.oecd.org/dataoecd/50/0/43606256.pdf.

[243] See ECJ 19 November 2009, C-540/07, *Commission v Italy* [2009] ECR I-10983, para. 69; ECJ 28 October 2010, C-72/09, *Établissements Rimbaud* [2010] ECR I-10659, para. 46; ECJ 10 February 2011, C-436/08 and 437/08, *Haribo Lakritzen and Österreichische Salinen* [2011] ECR I-305, para. 65.

In the *Commission v Netherlands* case[244] the Court again had to deal with a **284** third-country situation, namely the retention at source on dividend distributions made to Icelandic and Norwegian beneficiary companies. The national provision constituted an infringement of the EEA Agreement because the minimum holding requirement for EU beneficiary companies in order to benefit from the exemption of the withholding tax was lower than for the Icelandic and Norwegian beneficiary companies. The Netherlands took the position that the discrimination was justified by arguing that there are difficulties in obtaining information. Iceland and Norway are EEA states but are not EU Member states and, consequently, Directive 77/799/EEC on mutual assistance in the exchange of information does not apply. The double taxation agreements did not provide for an adequate exchange of information, either. The Netherlands argued that such an exchange of information is required in order to verify whether the Icelandic and Norwegian beneficiary companies fulfil the requirements imposed on EU beneficiary companies, i.e. whether these companies take one of the legal forms set out in the annex of the Parent-Subsidiary Directive or in the ministerial decree; secondly, whether these companies are subject to tax on profits and thirdly, whether these companies are the final beneficiaries. The **ECJ dismissed this justification** by holding that in principle this ground serves as justification but it does not justify the legislation at stake which **makes the exemption subject to a higher participation** in the case of distributions made to Icelandic and Norwegian beneficiary companies than in the case of distributions made to EU beneficiary companies. The Court concluded that the higher participation requirement bears **no relation** to the conditions otherwise required from all companies in order to be entitled to the exemption.

In the *Commission v Italy* case[245] the ECJ had to decide on the Italian pro- **285** visions for withholding taxes on dividends distributed to third-country beneficiary companies. In contrast to the *Commission v Netherlands* case, the Italian provisions in **general provided for a withholding tax at source for dividends distributed to third-country beneficiary companies** without making a differentiation between a substantial or minority shareholding as the Dutch provisions did. Dividend distributions to resident beneficiary companies were exempt from tax. The ECJ decided that the different treatment of domestic and cross-border dividends is discrimination but this discrimination can be justified with the **anti-abuse argument**. The ECJ thereby applies **a different standard** for this justification than for an intra-Union situation. In the third-country situation the ECJ did not require that the national provision be designed in such a way as to discriminate against exclusively abusive behaviour as it requires in a EU situation, see mo.no. 238. The ECJ based its decision on the fact that in the respect-

---

[244] ECJ 11 June 2009, C-521/07, *Commission v Netherlands* [2009] ECR I-4873, paras. 43 et seq; see m.no. 182.

[245] ECJ 19 November 2009, C-540/07, *Commission v Italy* [2009] ECR I-10983.

ive third-country situations **no mutual assistance in the exchange of infor-mation** existed. The ECJ case law is misleading because Italy concluded double taxation agreements with both states which provide for an extensive exchange of information in Art. 27. On this legal basis, Italy is in a position to obtain the in-formation from Iceland and Norway which is necessary for the carrying out of its domestic law. Furthermore, the ECJ did not provide any information on which abusive situations may be prevented by the withholding at source. But the ECJ confirmed its decision on the different standard of the anti-abuse argument in its subsequent case law.[246]

8. Principle of Proportionality in EU Situations

286 National measures that are an impediment to the fundamental freedoms may be justified by overriding reasons of public interest as described in m.no. 222. Nevertheless, the principle of proportionality must still be complied with. This means that even though a discriminatory national provision is justified, it may **not go beyond what is necessary to achieve its purpose and aim**. Therefore, Member States are obliged to apply the least discriminatory measure that is necessary **to achieve the aim of the provision**.

287 In m.nos. 244 et seq. the *Futura Participations* case was described and it was concluded that Luxembourg was able to justify its discriminatory domestic legislation with the argument of effectiveness of fiscal supervision. Luxembourg asked the French company to keep separate accounts for its Dutch branch in order to determine the amount of losses which was asked to carry forward to a subsequent taxable year. Even though this domestic legislation is justified, the Court decided that it is not proportionate to ask the French company to **keep separate accounts**.

288 The aim of the Luxembourg provision is to ascertain clearly and precisely that the amount of losses to be carried forward correspond, under the Luxem-bourg domestic tax accounting rules, to the amount of losses actually incurred in Luxembourg. As Luxembourg **refrained from obliging non-residents in gene-ral to keep separate accounts** for their Luxembourg activities and only did so if they asked to carry forward losses incurred in Luxembourg, the Court held that Luxembourg in principle had given up of its right to inspect their accounts. Con-sequently, the Court decided that there are **less restrictive measures** to preserve Luxembourg's effective fiscal supervision than asking the non-resident company to keep separate books for the Luxembourg branch in Luxembourg. Luxembourg therefore had to accept **other evidence** of the non-resident company that the amount of losses to be carried forward corresponded, under the Luxembourg

---

[246] ECJ 5 May 2011, C-267/09, *Commission vs. Portugal* (not yet published) paras. 55 et seq; ECJ 10 February 2011, C-436/08 and 437/08, *Haribo Lakritzen and Österreichische Salinen* [2011] ECR I-305, para. 69.

domestic tax accounting rules, to the amount of losses actually incurred in Luxembourg.

Another example of the principle of proportionality relates to **difficulties in** **289** **obtaining information** as a justification for discrimination, which was described in m.nos. 260 et seq. If Member States are not able to obtain information due to the limitations under Directive 77/799/EEC, repealed by Directive 2011/16/EU, they may use the argument that difficulties in obtaining information exist in order to justify discriminatory national provisions. Nevertheless, Member States have to respect the principle of proportionality. Even though Member States may not obtain the required information through the Directive, a less restrictive measure than denying the benefits to the non-resident person is to **request the taxpayer himself** to provide the required information for the correct assessment of the taxes. If the taxpayer is precluded *a priori* from providing the relevant documentary evidence, the principle of proportionality is not complied with. Consequently, Member States may not *a priori* deny the application of the same national provision to a non-resident that is applicable to residents without giving him the option to provide evidence himself.[247] Thereby, the form required for providing evidence **must not be too formalistic**. The provision of documentary evidence shall enable the tax authorities to ascertain clearly and precisely whether the conditions of the tax benefits are met.[248] If the taxpayer does not provide documentary evidence due to e.g. practical reasons or to difficulties in obtaining the required information, the Member States are not obliged to grant the tax benefits to the taxpayer.[249]

In the *Commission vs. Portugal* case,[250] as described under m.no. 246, the **290** Court accepted a higher taxation of foreign pension funds than of domestic pension funds but concluded that the national law provision **excluding a priori foreign pension funds** from the exemption of taxation even if they fulfil the national law requirements is not proportionate. Again, the Court decided that the taxpayer must have the opportunity to provide relevant documentary evidence, enabling the tax authority to ascertain whether the taxpayer meets equivalent requirements to those under national law. Furthermore, the Court referred to Directive 77/799/EEC and Directive 2008/55/EC on mutual assistance for the recovery of tax claims and concluded that these two legal instruments provide the tax authority with a **legal framework enabling them to obtain the required information and the opportunity to recover possible tax debts** from the foreign taxpayer.

---

[247] ECJ 11 October 2007, C-451/05, *Elisa* [2007] ECR I-8251; see as well ECJ 30 June 2011, C-262/09, *Meilicke/Weyde/Stöffler* (not yet published) para. 43.

[248] ECJ 30 June 2011, C-262/09, *Meilicke/Weyde/Stöffler* (not yet published) paras. 45 et seq.

[249] ECJ 10 February 2011, C-436/08 and 437/08, *Haribo Lakritzen and Österreichische Salinen* [2011] ECR I-305, para. 98; ECJ 30 June 2011, C-262/09, *Meilicke/Weyde/Stöffler* (not yet published) para. 48.

[250] ECJ 6 October 2011, C-493/09, *Commission vs. Portugal* (not yet published).

291   Directive 77/799/EEC, repealed by Directive 2011/16/EU, provides the **option** for national tax authorities **to request information** from tax authorities of other Member States. The ECJ in recent case law decided that the primary obligation to request relevant information for the application of domestic legislation does not lie in the hands of the competent authorities of the Member States but rather in the hands of the taxpayer. The Court thereby stressed that the wording of Directive 77/799/EEC provides the competent authorities of the Member States the possibility of requesting information but does not constitute an obligation on them. The Court followed a literal interpretation and referred to Art. 2 para. 1 of the Directive, which states that the competent authorities of the Member States **'may' request information** and deducted therefrom that the **competent authorities are not obliged** to do so.[251] Directive 2011/16/EU does not contain an obligation for the competent authorities of the Member States to use the Directive in order to request information relevant for the application of domestic legislation either. Consequently, the taxpayer may be asked by the competent authority of its Member State to provide the evidence necessary in order to benefit from the national legislation.

292   In the *Halley* case[252] the ECJ had to decide whether the Belgian provision on the limitation period for the valuation of registered shares for the purpose of inheritance tax is proportionate. Under national law, the limitation period for foreign shares was ten years, whereas the limitation period for domestic shares was only two years. The Court accepted the need to guarantee the effectiveness of fiscal supervision and the prevention of tax evasion as justification but concluded that the provision is not proportionate. The Court argued that in case the **national tax authority have evidence** concerning the taxable income the **longer recovery period** for foreign shares in **not proportionate**. This was the case at issue because the foreign shares were mentioned in the inheritance declaration. Consequently, the tax authorities had the opportunity to request the information necessary via the Directive 77/799/EEC, repealed by Directive 2011/16/EU, or bilateral conventions. On the other hand, the ECJ decided that a longer recovery period for foreign taxable items than for national taxable items is proportionate if the foreign taxable items were concealed from the tax authorities.[253] It is interesting to note that in the *Halley* case the Court obviously assumed that **administrative assistance** under Directive 77/799/EEC, repealed by Directive 2011/16/EU, **and under bilateral tax conventions is in principle equivalent.**

---

[251] ECJ 27 January 2009, C-318/07, *Persche* [2008] ECR I-359, para. 65; ECJ 10 February 2011, C-436/08 and 437/08, *Haribo Lakritzen and Österreichische Salinen* [2011] ECR I-305, para. 101; ECJ 30 June 2011, C-262/09, *Meilicke and Others* [2011] not yet published, paras. 50 et seq; ECJ 15 September 2011, C-310/09, *Accor* (not yet published), para. 98; ECJ 30 June 2011, C-262/09, *Meilicke/Weyde/Stöffler* (not yet published) paras. 50 et seq.

[252] ECJ 15 September 2011, C-132/10, *Halley* (not yet published) para. 36.

[253] See ECJ 11 June 2009, C-155/08 and C-157/08, *X and Passenheim-van Schoot* [2009] ECR I-5093, paras. 69 et seq.

The *National Grid Indus* case[254] is an example of a case in which the ECJ **293** concluded that the national **exit tax provision** is justified[255] and proportionate. The case concerned the Dutch legislation on the taxation of unrealized capital gains in relation to the assets of a company on the occasion of the transfer of its place of management to another country. The Court concluded that the establishment of the amount of tax at the time of the transfer of the place of management without considering decreases in value that occur after the transfer of the place of management is proportionate. It argued that after the transfer of the place of management the **host state has the exclusive taxing right** for the profits of the company and consequently this state may also **consider losses** that are suffered by depreciation of the asset concerned and which occurred after the transfer of seat. In contrast, the ECJ decided in the *N*. case[256] concerning the national legislation under which a private individual was subject to tax on unrealized capital gains relating to a substantial shareholding in a company at the time of the transfer of his residence. In this case the ECJ decided that the home state has to take into account the full decrease in value that may arise after the transfer of residence unless such a decrease have been taken into account in the host state in order to be proportionate. It remains questionable whether the **Court decided differently due to the fact that business property** was at stake in the *National Grid Indus* case and **private property** was at issue in the *N*. case or whether other factors were of relevance as well.

In the *National Grid Indus* case[257] the ECJ furthermore clarified that an im- **294** mediate recovery of taxes at the time of the transfer of the place of management is not proportionate. The taxpayer must at least have the **choice** between an **immediate recovery of taxes or a deferred payment of taxes at the time of the actual realization** of the hidden reserves. An immediate recovery of taxes may create a cash-flow disadvantage for the taxpayer but it frees him from subsequent administrative burdens that may occur in the case of deferred payment because a deferred payment requires to trace the transferred assets.

The **ECJ was criticized** on its decision in the *X Holding* case, see m.no. 253, **295** in particular on the issue that the Court accepted the national law provision as being proportionate. Instead of denying the integration of foreign subsidiaries into the Dutch group taxation system, a less restrictive measure would be to implement a **minimum time period for the group election** in order to limit the free choice of the taxing jurisdictions that undermines a balanced allocation of the power to impose taxes between the Member States. Furthermore, a **recapture mechanism**, which ensures that the set-off of losses is merely temporary, would also be a less restrictive measure, all the more as the Netherlands applies such a mechanism to foreign permanent establishments.

---

[254] ECJ 29 November 2011, C-371/10, *National Grid Indus* (not yet published) para. 58.
[255] See m.no. 277.
[256] ECJ 7 September 2006, C-470/04, *N* [2006] ECR I-7409.
[257] ECJ 29 November 2011, C-371/10, *National Grid Indus* (not yet published) para. 73.

9. Principle of Proportionality in Third-Country Situations

296   In a **third-country situation** the principle of proportionality is **applied differently** by the ECJ. If no equivalent legal basis for the exchange of information under Directive 77/799/EEC, repealed by Directive 2011/16/EU, exists, the Member States are in the position to justify their national discriminatory provisions with the argument that difficulties in obtaining information exist, see m.nos. 280. However, the Member States are **not required to request the taxpayer himself** to provide the required information for the correct assessment of the taxes as the tax authorities have no possibility to verify the information provided.[258]

297   In contrast, with regard to the missing legal instrument for the **recovery of tax claims** in third-country situations, the Court decided that this is not an argument for Member States to neglect tax benefits for foreign taxpayers. It held that a **less restrictive measure** would be e.g. the obligation to provide the necessary financial guarantees.[259] Furthermore, the argument of recovery of tax claim may only be accepted as a justification in a proportionate manner if the recovery of tax claim proves necessary for the purpose of attaining the objective of the national law provision. The ECJ neglected the necessity thereof in the *Haribo and Salinen* case[260] in which the Court had to decide on the Austrian national law provision under which portfolio dividends from companies established in non-Member States are only exempt if, inter alia, an agreement for mutual assistance exists with regard to the enforcement of taxes whereas domestic dividends are exempt from tax without any further preconditions. The Court held that the recipient of the income is resident in Austria and therefore the assistance of a non-Member State's authority cannot be required in order to benefit from the tax exemption.

298   In the *Commission v Italy* case, see m.no. 285, the Court accepted the anti-abuse argument as justification in third-country situations even though the national provisions were not designed in such a way as to discriminate against exclusively abusive behaviour. In addition, the Court decided that this provision corresponded with the principle of proportionality.[261]

---

[258] See ECJ 28 October 2010, C-72/09, *Établissements Rimbaud* [2010] ECR I-10659, para. 50.

[259] ECJ 6 October 2011, C-493/09, *Commission vs. Portugal* (not yet published) para. 50.

[260] ECJ 10 February 2011, C-436/08 and 437/08, *Haribo Lakritzen and Österreichische Salinen* (not yet published) para. 73.

[261] ECJ 19 November 2009, C-540/07, *Commission v Italy* [2009] ECR I-10983, para. 71; see as well ECJ 18 December 2007, C-101/05, *A* [2007] ECR I-11531.

III. The State Aid Provisions of the TFEU in Tax Matters

Marie-Ann Kronthaler[262] & Yinon Tzubery[263]

Literature: Easson, Harmful Tax Competition: The EU and the OECD Responses compared, *EC Tax Journal* 1998, p. 1; Schön, Taxation and State aid law in the European Union, *CMLR* 1999, p. 911; Santos, Point J of the Code of Conduct or the Primacy of Politics over Administration, *ET* 2000, p. 417; Sutter, The Adria Wien Pipeline Case and the State Aid Provisions of the EC Treaty in Tax Matters, *ET* 2001, p. 239; Vajda, Unlawful State Aid: What is it and what are its legal consequences?, *EC Tax Journal* 2001, p. 77; Schön, Tax Competition in Europe – The National Perspective, *ET* 2002, p. 490; Pinto, *Tax Competition and EU Law* (2003); Krugman, Obstfeld, *International Economics: Theory and Policy* (2003); Schön, Tax Competition in Europe – General Report, in Schön (ed.) *Tax Competition in Europe* (2003) p. 1; Rossi-Maccanico, State Aid Review of Member States' Measures relating to Direct Business Taxation, *EStAL* 2004, p. 229; Sutter, Art 88, 89 EGV, in Mayer (ed.) *Kommentar zu EU- und EG-Vertrag* (2005); Sutter, *Das EG-Beihilfenverbot und sein Durchführungsverbot in Steuersachen* (2005); Nicolaides/Kekelekis/Buyskes, *State aid policy in the European Community: a guide for practitioners* (2005); Luja, State Aid Reform 2005/09: Regional Fiscal Autonomy and Effective Recovery, *ET* 2005, p. 566; Jaeger, *Beihilfen durch Steuern und parafiskalische Abgaben* (2006); Schön, State Aid in the Area of Taxation, in Hancher/Ottervanger/Slot (eds.) *EC State Aids* (2006) p. 241; Mamut/Paterno, The Wienstrom Judgment: Some Further Reflections on the Standstill Obligation, *EStAL* 2009, p. 343; Rossi-Maccanico, The Gibraltar Judgment and the Point on Selectivity in Fiscal Aids, *EC Tax Review* 2009, p. 67; Mamut, *Konkurrentenschutz im Abgabenrecht* (2010); Pistone, Smart Tax Competition and the Geographical Boundaries of Taxing Jurisdictions: Countering Selective Advantages Amidst Disparities, *Intertax* 2012, p. 85; Micheau, Fundamental Freedoms and State Aid Rules under EU Law: The Example of Taxation, *ET* 2012, p. 210; Lang, State Aid and Taxation: Recent Trends in the Case Law of the ECJ, *EStAL* 2012, p. 411.

---

[262] Marie-Ann Kronthaler has authored the chapter in the first two editions of the book.
[263] Yinon Tzubery has revised and updated the chapter in this edition of the book.

1. Background to the EU Prohibition on State Aid

299 The competition policy of the European Union was developed to ensure **fair competition, functioning markets and a competitive economy** within the common market. The State aid control is part of the **rules on competition** in the European Union, and accordingly located in section 2, chapter 1, title VII of the TFEU.

300 The main pillar of these rules is **Art. 107(1) TFEU (ex Art. 87(1) EC)**, which provides: "Save as otherwise provided in the Treaties, any aid granted by a Member State or through State resources in any form whatsoever which distorts or threatens to distort competition by favouring certain undertakings or the production of certain goods shall, in so far as it affects trade between Member States, be incompatible with the internal market." It prohibits the provision of **advantages**, in any form, by national **public authorities** to **undertakings** on a **selective basis**.

301 In general, according to the Commission and the ECJ, prohibited State aid exists if **four cumulative conditions** are fulfilled: First, the measure confers an **advantage** on its recipients which relieves them from charges that are normally borne from their budgets. Second, the advantage is granted by the state or through **state resources**. Third, the measure **affects competition and trade** between

Member States. Lastly, the advantage conferred is **specific or selective** in that if favours 'certain undertakings or the production of certain goods'.[264]

The prohibition on State aid serves a **double purpose**:   **302**
- It **prevents waste** of public resources via inefficient subsidies, therefore help-ing Member States to manage their budgets more wisely and keep the right priorities.[265] In a democratic system, where demand for public support is abundant and political compromises are frequent, governments may very well need such help.
- It **prevents the crowding out of efficient private investments**[266] by pre-serving competitive and open internal market.[267] This, in turn, contributes to spurring more growth in the internal market, for which a necessary condition is developing competition.[268]

Nevertheless, state subsidies are **not always** a negative phenomenon. Public in-   **303** tervention is **fully justified** – and in fact needed – where it is put in place in or-der to target **market failures** and thereby complement, not replace, private spending.[269] Therefore, State aid may be required in order **to give people goods and services that the market would not deliver** on fair and equal terms or would not deliver at all. Apart from targeting market failures, **'good aid' induces its beneficiaries** to undertake economic activities they would not have taken ab-sent the aid, is designed in a way that **avoid waste of public money** and **has no better market alternative**.[270]

Economic studies have identified two kinds of **market failures that seem to**   **304** **be relevant for State aid policies** of advanced countries:[271]

- The **inability** of firms in high-technology industries to capture the benefits of that part of their contribution to knowledge that **spills over** to other firms. While firms can appropriate some of the benefits of their investment in

---

[264] Commission notice on the application of the State aid rules to measures relating to direct business taxation (hereinafter: Notice on Business Taxation), OJ C 384 of 10 December 1998, pp. 3–9, paras. 9–12.

[265] Almunia, The State Aid Modernization Initiative, Brussels, of 7 June 2012, Speech/12/424, p. 8.

[266] Almunia, Priming Europe for Growth, Brussels, of 2 February 2012, Speech/12/59, p. 4; Almunia, The State Aid Modernization Initiative, Brussels, of 7 June 2012, Speech/12/424, p. 3.

[267] Communication from the Commission to the European Parliament, the Council, the Euro-pean Economic and Social Committee and the Committee of the Regions – EU State aid Modernisation (SAM) (hereinafter: Communication on SAM), Brussels, of 8 May 2012, COM(2012) 209 final, para. 5.

[268] Communication on SAM, Brussels, of 8 May 2012, COM(2012) 209 final, para. 12.

[269] Communication on SAM, Brussels, of 8 May 2012, COM(2012) 209 final, para. 12.

[270] Almunia, The State Aid Modernization Initiative, Brussels, of 7 June 2012, Speech/12/424, p. 3.

[271] Krugman, Obstfeld, *International Economics: Theory and Policy* (2003), chapter 11.

knowledge, they usually cannot appropriate them fully. Some of the benefits accrue to **other firms** that can **imitate the technology** of the innovative firm. In electronics, for example, it is not uncommon for firms to **"reverse engineer"** their rivals' designs, taking their product apart to figure out how they work and how they were made. Because **patent laws** provide only **partial protection** for innovators, there is a reasonable presumption that high technology firms do not receive **as strong an incentive to innovate** as they should. This market failure justifies the granting of **subsidies for research and development activities (R&D)**.

- The presence of **monopoly profits** in highly concentrated oligopolistic industries due to the **lack of perfect competition**. In some industries there are **only a few firms** in effective competition. Because of the small number of firms, the assumptions of **perfect competition** do not apply. In particular, there will typically be **excess returns** for investment in such markets, i.e. firms will make profits above what equally risky investments elsewhere in the economy can earn. In such circumstances it is possible in principle for a government to **shift the excess returns** from foreign to domestic firms using **subsidies**. Subsidies will **stimulate domestic firms** to invest and **deter** investment by the **foreign competitor**, and therefore can **raise the profits of domestic firms** by more than the amount of the subsidy.

  Critics of this strategic justification argue that it requires more **information** about the expected returns from the investment than is likely to be available. Moreover, such **beggar-thy-neighbour policies,** which increase the welfare of one country at other countries' expense, risk foreign relations, may lead to **trade war** that would leave everyone worse off.

305 For this reason, the ban on State aid is not absolute, and provides for **exemptions under Art. 107(2) and (3) TFEU (ex Art. 87(2) and (3) EC)**. The Treaty gives the **Commission** the responsibility, under a system of **prior authorization**, to make sure that Member States conceive and design only aid measures to help firms produce goods and services that would **otherwise not be provided in the internal market**, and not measures that **distort competition** by strengthening the particular interests of a region or sector to the detriment of the economy as a whole.[272] Member States **may not** put their proposed aid measures **into effect** until the Commission has **approved** them.[273] The Commission decision is subject to a two-tier judicial review by the ECJ.[274]

---

[272] Almunia, The State Aid Modernization Initiative, Brussels, of 7 June 2012, Speech/12/424, p. 7–8.
[273] Notice on Business Taxation, OJ C 384 of 10 December 1998, pp. 3–9, para. 7.
[274] Art. 256 (1) TFEU (ex Art. 225 (1) EC).

2. The Role of the Prohibition on State Aid in the Commission Policy Making

As of 1998 the prohibition on State aid is being used by the Commission in order **306** to **tackle harmful tax competition** within the EU and **promote good governance**. This change in policy was accompanied by a Commission campaign to increase awareness among Member States. The campaign includes an array of **'soft law'** instruments such as **communications, notices** and **other non-binding instruments**. The following chapter will review the **considerations** which **underpin this policy change**, and which are necessary in order to understand the **developments** in the application of the State aid prohibition to direct business taxation.

The **Ruding Report**, released in 1992, was the first study to deal with the **307** effects of **tax competition** on the development of the common market.[275] The report found differences in Member States' corporate tax regimes to cause **significant distortions** to the internal market, as such differences **influence choices** of companies' location and investments. It offered to eliminate these distortions, by among other things, **approximating** Member States' corporate tax rates and **harmonizing** their corporate tax basis. Those recommendations were **rejected**, both by the Member States and the Commission, in view of the Member States' reluctance to give up their **sovereignty** in the field of direct taxation.[276]

Following a latter Commission report on the **harmful implications** of tax **308** competition within the EU on the development of the internal market,[277] the Commission took a **different approach**. With no support for more **positive integration** in the field of direct taxation in sight, the Commission conceded that some degree of tax competition within the EU may have **beneficial effects**. Nevertheless, the Commission considered it necessary to adopt measures to curb what it recognized as the **harmful effects of tax competition**. To that end, the Commission offered to adopt a **'tax package'**, comprising a set of measures designed to combat harmful tax competition in the EU.[278] Within this package a **Code of Conduct for Business Taxation** was adopted by the Council of Economics and Finance Ministers (ECOFIN)[279] which was to be **complemented** by the publication of a **Commission notice on the application of the State aid rules to measures relating to direct business taxation**.[280]

---

[275] Ruding, Onno, *Report of the Committee of Independent Experts on Company Taxation* (1992).
[276] Pinto, Carlo, *Tax Competition and EU Law* (2003), p. 32.
[277] Taxation in the European Union Report on the development of tax systems, Brussels, of 22 October 1996, COM(96) 546 final.
[278] Towards Tax Coordination in the European Union: a Package to Tackle Harmful Tax Competition, Brussels, of 1 October 1997, COM(97) 459 final.
[279] Resolution of the Council and the representatives of the governments of the Member States, meeting within the Council of 1 December 1997 on the code of conduct for business taxation (hereinafter: Code of Conduct) OJ C 2/2 of 6 January 1998, pp. 2–5.
[280] Notice on Business Taxation, OJ C 384 of 10 December 1998, pp. 3–9.

a) The Code of Conduct

309 The Code of Conduct is **not a legally binding** instrument but rather a **political commitment** made by Member States to respect principles of fair competition and to refrain from tax measures that are harmful. The Code concerns those measures, whether in the form of laws, regulations or administrative practices, which **affect or may affect** in a significant way the **location of business activity** in the Community. Business activity in this respect includes activities carried out within a group of companies.[281] Tax measures which provide for a **significantly lower** effective level of taxation than those levels which generally apply in the Member States in question, **including zero taxation**, are to be regarded as **potentially harmful** and therefore covered by the Code of Conduct.

310 When assessing whether tax measures are harmful, account could be taken of, *inter alia*:[282]

1. Whether advantages are accorded **only to non-residents** or in respect of transactions carried out with non-residents, or
2. Whether advantages are **ring-fenced from the domestic market**, so they do not affect the national tax base, or
3. Whether advantages are **granted even without any real economic activity** or substantial economic presence within the Member State offering such tax advantages, or
4. Whether the rules for profit determination in respect of activities within a multinational group of companies **depart from internationally accepted principles**, notably the rules agreed upon within the OECD, or
5. Whether the tax measures **lack transparency**, including where legal provisions are relaxed at the administrative level in a non-transparent way.

311 The Member States undertook in the Code of Conduct **not to introduce new tax measures which are harmful** within its meaning (the **standstill obligation**)[283] and to **re-examine their existing laws** and established practices in order to eliminate harmful measures as soon as possible (the **rollback obligation**).[284]

312 The Code of Conduct anticipates the establishment of a group to assess tax measures of Member States that may fall within its scope and to oversee the provision of information on those measures.[285] The Council confirmed the establishment of the Code of Conduct Group on 9 March 1998. In a report of 23 November 1999 the Code of Conduct Group identified 66 tax measures as harmful, dividing the list into the following six broad groups in which the activities are potentially highly mobile: Financial services, group financing and royalty pay-

---

[281] Code of Conduct, OJ C 2/2 of 6 January 1998, pp. 2–5, para. A.
[282] Code of Conduct, OJ C 2/2 of 6 January 1998, pp. 2–5, para. B.
[283] Code of Conduct, OJ C 2/2 of 6 January 1998, pp. 2–5, para. C.
[284] Code of Conduct, OJ C 2/2 of 6 January 1998, pp. 2–5, para. D.
[285] Code of Conduct, OJ C 2/2 of 6 January 1998, pp. 2–5, para. H.

ments; Insurance, reinsurance and captive insurance; Intra group service; Holding companies; Exempt and Offshore Companies; and Miscellaneous measures.[286] The Code of Conduct Group is further monitoring the implementation of the standstill and rollback obligations, and reports regularly to the Council.

b) Commission Notice on the Application of the State Aid Rules to Measures Relating to Direct Business Taxation

Nevertheless, the Commission **was not ready** to leave the tackling of harmful intra-EU tax competition only to the good will of Member States. It therefore resorted to the **only binding instrument** available to it for preventing the harmful effects of tax competition, and stated that as **a matching mechanism to the political agreement** of the Member State on the Code of Conduct it will **re-examine its policy in the field of fiscal State aid** in order to make full use of its power under the Treaty rules in order to **help combat tax competition.** 313

In order to ensure that its decisions are **predictable** and that **equal treatment** is guaranteed, the Commission announced that it will associate itself with the commitment entered by the Member States in the Code of Conduct by **publishing guidelines** to the **application of the State aid rules to measures relating to direct business taxation.**[287] And indeed, the notice on the application of the State aid rules to measures relating to direct business taxation were published soon after, on 11 November 1998.[288] 314

As a result of the Commission Notice the Commission **initiated a stricter approach** to the **application of the State aid rules** to **direct business taxation measures**, examining and **re-examining tax arrangements** and **proposed new legislation**, despite the fact that **prior** to the Commission Notice **not much attention** had been dedicated to such measures in the enforcement of the prohibition on State aid.[289] 315

Between **'harmful tax competition'** as interpreted in the Code of Conduct and **the scope of the prohibition on State aid** as implemented to direct business taxation measures **a gap exists**, which is **not disputed by the Commission.**[290] With regard to the relations between the Code of Conduct and the prohibition 316

---

[286] Report from the Code of Conduct Group (Business Taxation) to ECOFIN Council on 29 November 1999, Brussels, of 23 November 1999, SN 4901/99.

[287] Towards Tax Coordination in the European Union: a Package to Tackle Harmful Tax Competition, Brussels, of 1 October 1997, COM(97) 459 final, para. 17; Code of Conduct, OJ C 2/2 of 6 January 1998, pp. 2–5, para. J.

[288] Notice on Business Taxation, OJ C 384 of 10 December 1998, pp. 3–9.

[289] Pinto, Carlo, *Tax Competition and EU Law* (2003), p. 137.

[290] Report on the implementation of the Commission notice on the application of the State aid rules to measures relating to direct business taxation (hereinafter: Report on Implementation), Brussels, of 9 February 2004, C(2004) 434, Box no. 13; Code of Conduct, OJ C 2/2 of 6 January 1998, pp. 2–5, para. J.

on State aid, the Commission Notice provides:[291] "The **qualification of a tax measure as harmful** under the code of conduct **does not affect** its **possible qualification as a State aid**. However the **assessment of the compatibility** of fiscal aid **with the common market** will have to be made, taking into account, *inter alia*, **the effects of aid** that are brought to light in the application of the code of conduct". Nevertheless, it seems that some of the recent **controversial decisions** of the Commission and the ECJ (e.g., *Adria-Wien Pipeline*,[292] *Gibraltar*)[293] can be understood as **attempts to bridge the gap** between the **application of the prohibition on State aid** in the field of direct business taxation and the **Code of Conduct** by means of interpretation (**negative integration**).[294]

317 The Commission Notice was followed up by a **Commission report** of 9 February 2004 on the **implementation of the Commission Notice**.[295] The Report furthers **refines and clarifies the Commission practice** in the application of the prohibition on State aid to measures relating to direct business taxation based on the **experience gained** by the Commission in the application Commission Notice.

c) Promoting Good Governance in Tax Matters

318 On 28 April 2009 the Commission marked the **next target** for its development of the State aid prohibition enforcement in the field of tax, in a **Communication on promoting good governance in tax matters**.[296] Good governance in the tax area is defined by the Communication as **international tax cooperation to promote common standards** of **transparency, exchange of information** and **fair tax competition**.[297] In the Communication the Commission describes the measures taken by the EU, both within the Union and internationally, **in order to promote good governance in the tax area**. It also **questions how to strengthen** the principle of good governance in the tax area within the EU and internationally. Among the **measures of existing tax cooperation** designed to promote better governance within the EU the Communication mentions the **Code of Conduct** and the **State aid prohibition**. What influence this Communication will have on the Commission policy with regard to the application of the State aid prohibition is yet to be seen.

---

[291] Notice on Business Taxation, OJ C 384 of 10 December 1998, pp. 3–9, para. 30.

[292] ECJ 8 November 2001, C-143/99, *Adria-Wien Pipeline* [2001] ECR I-8365.

[293] ECJ 15 November 2011, joined cases C-106/09 P and C-107/09 P, *Commission v Gibraltar* [2011] ECR I-0.

[294] Pistone, *Intertax* 2012, p. 87.

[295] Report on Implementation, Brussels, of 9 February 2004, C(2004) 434.

[296] Communication from the Commission to the Council, the European Parliament and the European Economic and Social Committee, Promoting Good Governance in Tax Matters, Brussels, of 28 April 2009, COM(2009) 201 final.

[297] Communication from the Commission to the council, the European parliament and the European economic and social committee, Promoting Good Governance in Tax Matters, Brussels, of 28 April 2009, COM(2009) 201 final, p. 4.

3. General Issues Raised by State Aid in Tax Matters

a) The prohibition on State Aid and the fundamental freedoms

The prohibition on State aid, like the prohibition of discrimination,[298] the free- **319**
dom of establishment,[299] and the free movement of services,[300] capital[301] and
workers,[302] has been designed in order ensure that **free competition in the internal market is not distorted**. While the State aid rules aim at ensuring that
Member States do not provide selective advantages to certain undertakings to
the detriment of others, the fundamental freedoms are designed to remove
barriers to the free movement of services, goods, capital and persons.[303]

It is important to stress that **the scope of the prohibition on State aid is** **320**
much broader than that of the fundamental freedoms. On the one hand, while
the fundamental freedoms only apply to cross-border situations, State aid is also
prohibited in purely domestic situations. On the other hand, while the fundamental freedoms prohibit only discrimination of non-residents, Art. 107(1) TFEU
(ex Art. 87(1) EC) prohibits any form of discrimination that involves the granting
of an advantage to a certain group of undertakings.[304]

A tax measure may be the cause of a **parallel infringement** of both the State **321**
aid prohibition and the prohibition on discrimination or one of the protected freedoms in the TFEU.[305] The ECJ has consistently held that where an aid measure
violates another provision of the Treaty, the Commission cannot find it to be
compatible with the internal market under the procedure provided for in Art. 108
TFEU (ex Art. 88 EC).[306] However, the mere fact that a national measure may
possibly be defined as aid within the meaning of Art. 107(1) TFEU (ex Art. 87(1)
EC) is not an adequate reason for exempting it from the scope of the fundamental
freedoms.[307]

The result of such a dual infringement could be problematic when it comes **322**
to remedies. As will be presented later in this chapter, the consequence of infringement of the State aid prohibition is that the **aid should be recovered with**

---

[298] Art. 18 TFEU (ex Art. 12 EC).
[299] Art. 49 TFEU (ex Art. 43 EC).
[300] Art. 56 TFEU (ex Art. 49 EC).
[301] Art. 63 TFEU (ex Art. 56 EC).
[302] Art. 45 TFEU (ex Art. 39 EC).
[303] Micheau, *ET* 2012, p. 213.
[304] Schön, in Hancher/Ottervanger/Slot (eds.) *EC State Aids* (2006) p. 245 et seq.; Rossi-
Maccanico, *EStAL* 2007, p. 227.
[305] ECJ 22 March 1977, Case 74/76, *Iannelli & Volpi SpA* [1997] ECR 557, para. 9; ECJ
17 November 2009, Case C-169/08, *Regione Sardegna* [2009] ECR I-10821.
[306] ECJ 19 September 2000, C-156/98, *Germany v Commission* [2000] ECR I-6857, para. 78.
[307] ECJ 7 May 1985, 18/84, *Commission v France* [1985] ECR I-1339, para. 14; ECJ 20 March
1990, C-21/88, *Du Pont de Nemours Italiana SpA* [1990] ECR I-889, para. 20.

interest at a rate fixed by the Commission.[308] By contrast, a breach of the fundamental freedoms allows undertakings which have paid the tax at issue to be **reimbursed**. Even though both remedies are designed to **restore the situation that existed before the infringement took place**, if implemented simultaneously, such result would not be achieved but rather **the discrimination would be reversed**. The issue of the application of remedies in a situation of cumulative application of both the State aid rules and the fundamental freedom provisions is yet to be resolved by the ECJ.[309] Nevertheless, it seems that from an economic point of view it does not matter which of the remedies is applied, as long as they are not applied simultaneously.

b) The prohibition on State Aid and indirect taxation

323　The Commission Notice concerns only **direct business taxation**. Nevertheless, the principles it contains seem largely applicable for analysing certain cases in the field of **indirect taxation** as well. The Commission therefore has referred to the notice in a number of decisions relating to indirect taxation measures.[310]

324　It should be noted that since **VAT** reductions are subject to strict Community rules, such reductions are not usually caught by Art. 107(1) (ex Art. 87(1) EC) that is relevant only to intra-EU competition. The same is not true for **excise taxation**, which allows Member States to unilaterally grant specific exemptions. A reduction in such duties, which favour certain undertakings, may constitute State aid.[311]

c) Pros & Cons of the EU's Prohibition on State Aid

325　From a competition point of view, the application of Arts. 107 et seq. TFEU (ex Arts. 87 et seq. EC) provides for a **level playing field** within the common market. **Fair and just competition** without state interference can be ensured.

326　Otherwise, the extensive interpretation of the criteria laid down in Art. 107(1) TFEU (ex Art. 87(1) EC) and the application of the ban on State aid by the Commission and the ECJ makes it more difficult for the Member States to **assess the consequences** of their legislative acts. This is particularly true for State aid in tax matters. Nevertheless, the Commission's practice in tackling State aid that is granted in the form of tax incentives is a necessary approach in the struggle against harmful tax competition in the European Union.[312]

---

[308] See Art. 14 of Regulation No. 659/1999.

[309] Micheau, *ET* 2012, p. 213.

[310] Report on Implementation, Brussels, of 9 February 2004, C(2004) 434, para. 71, Box No. 15.

[311] Report on Implementation, Brussels, of 9 February 2004, C(2004) 434, para 72.

[312] See e.g. Easson, *EC Tax Journal* 1998, p. 1 et seq.; Santos, *ET* 2000, p. 417 et seq.; Schön, *ET* 2002, p. 490 et seq.; Schön, in Schön (ed.) *Tax Competition in Europe* (2003) p. 1 et seq.; Rossi-Maccanico, *EStAL* 2004, p. 229 et seq.

In any case, it can be seen as the Commission's task to take into account the **327** different aspects and situations and to ensure a coherent application of the EU provisions on State aid in the Member States.

4. The Prohibition of State Aid under Art. 107(1) TFEU (ex Art. 87(1) EC)

a) "Any Aid ... in Any Form Whatsoever"

Aid is an **advantage** or **benefit** that improves the beneficiary financial or other **328** situation. The forms of aid covered by Art. 107(1) TFEU (ex Art. 87(1) EC) are very **broad**.

Indeed, the simple situations which are covered by the State aid prohibition **329** are positive benefits given to some undertakings by a Member State while withheld from other undertakings in the same situation, e.g. **direct payments, state guarantees** or **benefits in kind (positive aid)**. However, **exemption** or **mitigation of charges (negative aid)** has the same budgetary effect as direct grants, since in both cases **the recipient's financial position improves** in comparison to others.[313]

For this reason, the definition of aid in Art. 107 (1) TFEU (ex Art. 87(1) EC) **330** provides for "**form neutrality**", meaning that the Commission and the ECJ examine the compatibility of aid with the internal market not in terms of the form which it may take, but in terms of **its effect**.[314] The State aid prohibition therefore applies **not only to subsidies** but also to measures by which the public authorities grant certain undertakings tax alleviations so that the tax normally payable by the beneficiary is reduced (also known as "**tax expenditures**").[315] Hence, State measures which, in various forms, confers on recipients an **advantage** or **relieves them of charges** that are normally included in their budgets, are considered aid within the meaning of Art. 107 (1) TFEU (ex Art. 87(1) EC).[316]

---

[313] ECJ 15 March 1994, C-387/92, *Banco Exterior de España* [1994] ECR I-877, para. 14; ECJ 8 September 2011, joined cases C-78/08 to C-80/08, *Paint Graphos* [2011] ECR I-0, para. 46; ECJ 15 November 2011, joined cases C-106/09 P and C-107/09 P, *Commission v Gibraltar* [2011] ECR I-0, para. 72.

[314] Notice on Business Taxation, OJ C 384 of 10 December 1998, pp. 3–9, para. 7.

[315] EC Commission Report of 9 February 2004 on the implementation of the Commission Notice on the application of the State Aid rules, para. 18; ECJ 23 February 1961, 30/59, *De Gezamenlijke Steenkolenmijnen* [1961] ECR English Special Edition 1, para. 42; ECJ 2 July 1974, Case 173/73, *Italy v Commission* [1974] ECR 709, paras. 36-39; ECJ 15 March 1994, C-387/92, *Banco Exterior de España* [1994] ECR I-877, para. 13.

[316] ECJ 8 November 2001, C-143/99, *Adria-Wien Pipeline* [2001] ECR I-8365, para. 38; ECJ 8 September 2011, joined cases C-78/08 to C-80/08, *Paint Graphos* [2011] ECR I-0, para. 45; ECJ 15 November 2011, joined cases C-106/09 P and C-107/09 P, *Commission v Gibraltar* [2011] ECR I-0, para. 71.

331   Therefore, in order to determine whether a **derogating tax scheme** may constitute State aid, it must be established whether the resulting tax burden is **lower** than that which would have resulted from the application of the relevant Member State's **normal taxation** method.[317]

332   **"Tax expenditure"** may provide for a reduction in a firm's tax burden in various ways, including:[318]

- A reduction in the **tax base** (such as special deductions, special or accelerated depreciation arrangements or the entering of reserves on the balance sheet),
- A total or partial reduction in the **amount of tax** (such as exemption or a tax credit),
- **Deferment, cancellation** of even special **rescheduling** of tax debt.

333   Some instances of seeming tax alleviations are **not considered to be aid** within the meaning of Art. 107 (1) TFEU (ex Art. 87(1) EC):

- **Refund of taxes** unduly collected does not constitute State aid because it does not involve the transfer of public funds or the waiver of revenue.[319]
- If the recipient gives an **adequate compensation** for the benefits it received, the requirements of the prohibition on State aid are not met, as those undertakings do not enjoy beneficial treatment.[320] However, the fulfilment of **general macroeconomic expectations** of the Member States, such as reducing the unemployment rate or the fostering of underdeveloped areas, cannot be seen as such a "market equivalent" compensation for benefits granted. In order to **discern** adequate compensation from prohibited State aid, and to ensure that there is no "overcompensation", the ECJ requires the fulfilment of certain conditions. The recipient undertaking must have clearly defined **public service obligations** to discharge, the **parameters** on the basis of which the compensation is **calculated** must be **established in advance** in an objective and **transparent manner**, the compensation may not exceed **what is necessary** to cover all or part of the costs incurred in the discharge of public service obligations and the enterprise that is to render the public services must be chosen pursuant to an **objective public procurement procedure.**[321]
- **Consequential tax alleviations** that are the result of a reform in general law (e.g., degradation in tax collection due to deregulation of labour law that leads to a reduction in wages)[322] are not considered State aid due to its **remoteness.**[323]

---

[317] Report on Implementation, Brussels, of 9 February 2004, C(2004) 434, Box No. 1.

[318] Notice on Business Taxation, OJ C 384 of 10 December 1998, pp. 3–9, para. 9.

[319] Schön, *CMLR* 1999, pp. 911–936, 921.

[320] ECJ 22 November 2001, C-53/00, *Ferring* [2001] ECR I-9067, para. 26 et seq.

[321] ECJ 24 July 2003, C-280/00, *Altmark* [2003] ECR I-7747, para. 87 et seq.

[322] ECJ 17 March 1993, joined cases C-72/91 and C-73/91, *Sloman Neptun Schiffahrts AG* [1993] ECR I-887, para. 21.

[323] Schön, *CMLR* 1999, p. 920.

The form neutrality provides that Art. 107(1) TFEU (ex Art. 87(1) EC) prohibits **334** **both direct** and **indirect State aid**. For this reason, the recipients of aid are not necessarily only the ones directly enjoying from the beneficial tax measure, but rather, account must be taken of the **actual effects** of the aid, with a view to classifying as the aid recipients all firms which have **actually benefited** from it. In this respect, the ECJ held tax-free grants to coal mine workers to be State aid favouring the coal industry because it helped the coal mining enterprises to more easily recruit employees, and thus put them in a better position than their competitors.[324] In another case, the Court held that a tax allowance for private savings in a certain fund which granted loans to specific undertakings at preferential rates constitutes an aid to the benefit of the borrowers.[325]

Furthermore, a tax measure cannot be saved from categorization as aid where **335** the aid beneficiary is subject to a specific charge which is **different from** and **unconnected** with the aid in question.[326]

It should be noted that the existence of aid in the form of "tax expenditure" is **336** **closely related** to the fulfilment of the selectivity requirement of Art. 107(1) (ex Art. 87(1) EC), which will be further discussed later on in this chapter. In fact, on the one hand, only when a tax measure is considered selective will it be aid in the form of "tax expenditure", and on the other, whenever a tax measure is considered selective it will consequently also be "tax expenditure". This **causal connection** is due to the fact that **the notion "tax expenditure" inherently assumes selectivity**. In other words, in order for a tax measure to be aid within the meaning of Art. 107(1) (ex Art. 87(1) EC) it must put a taxpayer in an advantageous position in comparison to other taxable persons in a comparable legal and factual situation in light of the objective pursued by the tax system in the relevant Member State.[327]

b) "Granted by a Member State or Through State Resources"

Furthermore, Art. 107(1) TFEU (ex Art. 87(1) EC) requires that the advantage **337** granted is attributable to the **Member State resources**. The benefit must thus be a burden to the **public budget**. This criterion applies not only with regard to aid granted by **central government institutions** but also with regard to aid provided by **regional or local bodies** in the Member States.[328] The same holds for aid provided by **private companies that are controlled by the state**.[329]

---

[324] ECJ 23 February 1961, 30/59, *De Gezamenlijke Steenkolenmijnen* [1961] ECR English Special Edition 1.

[325] ECJ 13 July 1988, C-102/87, *Commission v France* [1988] ECR 4067, para. 5.

[326] ECJ 8 December 2011, C-81/10 P, *France Télécom SA* [2011] ECR I-0, para. 43.

[327] ECJ 8 November 2001, C-143/99, *Adria-Wien Pipeline* [2001] ECR I-8365, para. 41.

[328] Notice on Business Taxation, OJ C 384 of 10 December 1998, pp. 3–9, para. 10.

[329] ECJ 2 February 1988, joined cases 68/85, 69/85 and 70/85, *Kwekerij Gebroeders van der Kooy and others* [1988] ECR 219, para. 35 et seq.

338   A **loss of tax revenue is equivalent to consumption of state resources** in the form of fiscal expenditure.[330] Granting a tax concession entails a loss of resources for the State in that it forgoes revenue. Therefore, **any tax relief creates a burden on the public budget**. For this reason, it appears to be clear that **tax benefits are always granted from "state resources"**.[331] From an economic point of view, it does not make a difference whether the state levies taxes and then grants the resources to certain undertakings or whether the state abstains from levying taxes with regard to certain undertakings in the first place.[332]

339   State support may be provided just as much through tax provisions of a **legislative**, **regulatory** or **administrative** nature as through the **practices of the tax authorities**.[333] Nevertheless, only a practice of deliberate **misapplication of a tax provision** by the tax authorities to the advantage of a taxpayer may constitute State aid. This approach has been criticized since it takes into account the causes and aims of an aid, in comparison to form neutrality.[334]

340   The state resources criterion must be assessed at the level of **individual recipients** in the light of the aid recipient's situation, without reference to the induced effect of the measure in economic or budgetary terms.[335] Therefore, the fact that a tax aid scheme has a **positive overall effect on budget revenue** is not sufficient to rule out the presence of state resources.[336]

c) "Which Distorts or Threatens to Distort Competition ... in so far as it Affects Trade between Member States"

341   A tax measure is considered State aid in accordance to Art. 107(1) TFEU (ex Art. 87(1) EC) only if it is a **cause for distortion of competition** that **affects trade between Member States**. These criteria are inextricably linked to one another.[337]

342   Not only actual but also **potential distortions to competition** that are **liable to affect trade** are caught under Art. 107 (1) (ex Art. 87(1) EC).[338] This is due to the fact that according to the procedure laid down in Art. 108(3) TFEU (ex Art. 88(3) EC) Member States have to inform the Commission **in advance** of any

---

[330] Notice on Business Taxation, OJ C 384 of 10 December 1998, pp. 3–9, para. 10.

[331] Lang, *EStAL 2012*, p. 2.

[332] Sutter, *Das EG-Beihilfenverbot und sein Durchführungsverbot in Steuersachen* (2005), p. 72.

[333] Notice on Business Taxation, OJ C 384 of 10 December 1998, pp. 3–9, para. 10.

[334] See Schön, *CMLR* 1999, p. 921; Schön, in Hancher/Ottervanger/Slot (eds.) *EC State Aids* (2006) p. 254.

[335] Report on Implementation, Brussels, of 9 February 2004, C(2004) 434, para. 20, Box No. 3.

[336] Report on Implementation, Brussels, of 9 February 2004, C(2004) 434, para. 19.

[337] See Nicolaides/Kekelekis/Buyskes, *State aid policy in the European Community: a guide for practitioners* (2005) p. 26 et seq.

[338] ECJ 10 January 2006, C-222/04, *Cassa di Risparmio di Firenze SpA* [2006] ECR I-289, para. 140.

plans to grant or alter State aid, which requires the Commission to make a decision **before** the real effects of an aid measure on the market can be determined. It is therefore sufficient that aid is **capable of distorting competition** or **affecting trade**.

Competition is considered distorted and intra-Community trade is considered **343** affected if the aid in question **strengthens the competitiveness of the recipient**, for instance by reducing its operating costs, in comparison with its competitors in the intra-Community trade. Neither the fact that aid is relatively small in amount, nor the fact that the recipient is moderate in size or that its share of the Community market is very small, and not even the fact that the recipient does not carry out exports or exports virtually all its production outside the Community can do anything to alter this conclusion.[339]

The reason for including programmes that strengthen the position of under- **344** takings with no intra-Community trade within the scope of Art. 107(1) TFEU (ex Art. 87(1) EC) is that such aid may still influence trade between Member States by **reducing the opportunities** for undertakings from other Member States to **penetrate that domestic market**. Furthermore, fortifying the domestic market position of an undertaking which is not involved in intra-Community trade may enable that undertaking to **penetrate the markets of other Member States**.[340]

The wide scope of potential causes for distortion of competition that affects **345** trade between Member States leads to the result that **whenever an aid is granted by a Member State to certain undertakings, these criteria are fulfilled**. For this reason, these criteria are usually not examined thoroughly by the Commission and the ECJ with regard to measures suspected to be State aid and are simply **assumed to be fulfilled**.[341]

The existence of **comparable or rival tax rules in other Member States**, so **346** that the tax measure concerned could be perceived as bringing charges in the relevant sector more into line with those of its competitors in other Member States **is not relevant for the assessment of State aid**. Each scheme must be assessed in the context of the tax system in the Member State concerned.[342]

d) Undertaking

The criteria **cause for distortion of competition** that **affects trade between** **347** **Member States** presuppose that the beneficiary of the measure **exercises an economic activity**. An economic activity, in that regard, is **any activity consist-**

---

[339] Notice on Business Taxation, OJ C 384 of 10 December 1998, pp. 3–9, para. 11; ECJ 17 September 1980, 730/79, *Philip Morris v Commission* [1980] ECR 2671, para. 11.

[340] ECJ 10 January 2006, C-222/04, *Cassa di Risparmio di Firenze SpA* [2006] ECR I-289, para. 143; ECJ 8 September 2011, joined cases C-78/08 to C-80/08, *Paint Graphos* [2011] ECR I-0, para. 80.

[341] Report on Implementation, Brussels, of 9 February 2004, C(2004) 434, para. 22.

[342] Notice on Business Taxation, OJ C 384 of 10 December 1998, pp. 3–9, para. 15; Report on Implementation, Brussels, of 9 February 2004, C(2004) 434, para. 24, Box No. 4.

ing in offering goods and services on a given market.[343] Thus, the prohibition on State aid applies only when the beneficiary, regardless of its legal form of organization or means of financing, is engaged in offering goods and services on a given market.[344] The notion **"undertaking"** in Art. 107(1) TFEU (ex Art. 87(1) EC) must therefore be interpreted accordingly.

348 Usually the economic activity is carried out **directly** on the market. However, economic activities could also be carried out **indirectly** by an entity controlling an operator in direct contact with the market. In that regard, the mere holding of shares, even controlling shareholdings, is insufficient to characterize as economic the activity of the entity holding those shares. However, if the controlling entity actually **exercises its control** by involving itself directly or indirectly in the management of the controlled undertaking it must be regarded as taking part in the economic activity carried on by the latter. In such cases, the controlling entity must be regarded, for itself, as an undertaking within the meaning of Art. 107(1) TFEU (ex Art. 87(1) EC).[345]

349 The wide definition above provides that **non-profit-making organizations** or **public enterprises** may also fall within the scope of Art. 107(1) TFEU (ex Art. 87(1) EC) as far as they take part in economic life. This result is required since such activity may be in competition with private profit-making operators.[346]

350 With regard to the application of the State aid prohibition to public enterprises Art. 106(2) TFEU (ex Art. 86(2) EC) provides some special conditions. According to it, undertakings entrusted by a Member State with the operation of **services of general economic interest** or **having the character of a revenue-producing monopoly** are subject to the prohibition on State aid. However, in order to secure their proper function, Art. 106(2) TFEU (ex Art. 86(2) EC) provides for a limitation on the applicability of the State aid prohibition with regard to public undertakings in so far as its application hinders the performance, in law or in fact, of the particular tasks assigned to them. This limitation must not affect the development of trade to such an extent that would be contrary to the interests of the Union.

351 Consequently, tax privileges or other benefits granted to **private persons, non-profit organizations and public authorities that do not engage in economic activity** are not covered by Art. 107(1) TFEU (ex Art. 87(1) EC). It should be noted that for the purpose of applying Art. 107 (1) (ex Art. 87(1) EC) to an aid scheme, it is sufficient that the scheme benefits certain undertakings, a finding

---

[343] ECJ 12 September 2000, joined cases C-180/98 to C-184/98, *Pavlov and others* [2000] ECR I-6451, para. 74 et seq.; ECJ 1 July 2008, C-49/07, *MOTOE* [2008] ECR I-4863, para. 22.

[344] Notice on Business Taxation, OJ C 384 of 10 December 1998, pp. 3–9, para. 11.

[345] ECJ 10 January 2006, C-222/04, *Cassa di Risparmio di Firenze SpA* [2006] ECR I-289, para. 109 et seq.

[346] ECJ 10 January 2006, C-222/04, *Cassa di Risparmio di Firenze SpA* [2006] ECR I-289, para. 123.

not called into question by the fact that it may also benefit entities which are not undertakings.[347]

e) "Favouring Certain Undertakings or the Production of Certain Goods" (Specificity or Selectivity)

The **main criterion**, and the **constituent factor**,[348] in applying Art. 107 (1) (ex Art. 87(1) EC) is that the measure must be **specific or selective** in that it favours "certain undertakings or the production of certain goods". In other words, it has to be determined whether there is a specific "**target group**" that benefits from the measure whilst other economic agents do not. Otherwise, if a measure is general in nature, it usually falls within the competence of the Member State. **352**

The wording "**production of certain goods**" may be misleading, since it seems to restrict the application of Art. 107 (1) (ex Art. 87(1) EC) only to production branches in manufacturing industry. However, the wording "**certain undertakings**" allows for a measure to be regarded as selective whenever its eligibility criteria **set a group of beneficiaries apart** from the rest of the economic agents based on **common features,** excluding other undertakings from becoming beneficiaries.[349] Nevertheless, where the distinction between undertakings is merely the consequence of a random event, for example unexpected under or over-profitability, those effects are not considered to favour 'certain undertakings' or 'the production of certain goods' within the meaning of Art. 107 (1) (ex Art. 87(1) EC).[350] A tax incentive that deviates from a Member State's "benchmark" tax system is therefore considered to be selective if it is **limited to certain taxpayers or to certain categories of taxpayers based on common features**. **353**

Such categories could be, for example, certain sectors of the economy (**sectorial aid**),[351] certain business activity within a branch (**horizontal aid**), certain geographic areas (**regional aid**),[352] **public undertakings** carrying out an economic activity,[353] **large companies, multinational companies,**[354] **exporters**, sectors that are subject to **international competition**,[355] **offshore companies**,[356] or **354**

---

[347] ECJ 15 December 2005, C-66/02, *Italy v Commission* [2005] ECR I-10901, paras. 91–92.

[348] ECJ 6 September 2006, C-88/03, *Portugal vs. Commission* [2006] ECR I-7115, para. 54.

[349] Report on Implementation, Brussels, of 9 February 2004, C(2004) 434, Box No. 5; ECJ 6 September 2006, C-88/03, *Portugal v Commission* [2006] ECR I-7115, para. 56; Lang, *EStAL 2012*, p. 420.

[350] ECJ 15 November 2011, joined cases C-106/09 P and C-107/09 P, *Commission v Gibraltar* [2011] ECR I-0, para. 83.

[351] Notice on Business Taxation, OJ C 384 of 10 December 1998, pp. 3–9, para. 18.

[352] Notice on Business Taxation, OJ C 384 of 10 December 1998, pp. 3–9, para. 17.

[353] Notice on Business Taxation, OJ C 384 of 10 December 1998, pp. 3–9, para. 19.

[354] Report on Implementation, Brussels, of 9 February 2004, C(2004) 434, Box No. 5.

[355] Notice on Business Taxation, OJ C 384 of 10 December 1998, pp. 3–9, para. 18.

[356] ECJ 15 November 2011, joined cases C-106/09 P and C-107/09 P, *Commission v Gibraltar* [2011] ECR I-0, para. 107.

non-resident companies providing certain services (for example, financial services) within a group.[357] The same is true for measures that apply only to firms that were **set up after a certain date**, in that existing companies are excluded from receiving such aid.[358]

355 A selective advantage may arise from a beneficial exception to the tax provision of a **legislative, regulatory** or **administrative** nature or from a **discretionary practice** on the part of the tax authorities.[359] In order to distinguish between *general* economic measures and *selective* measures a "**selectivity test**" is performed.

356 The "selectivity test" is composed of **three steps**. In the first step, the Member State's "**common**" or "**normal**" tax system must be recognized.[360] Secondly, it must be determined whether the tax measure at issue grants an **advantageous deviation** from the "normal" tax system, so that it differentiates between economic operators in a comparable factual and legal situation in the light of the objectives assigned to the tax system in the Member State concerned.[361] This comparability examination[362] is **subjective** in the sense that its results depends on the **nature or the general scheme** of the relevant Member State's tax system. At the last step, it must be examined whether the exception to the system or differentiation within that system may be **justified by the 'nature or general scheme of the tax system'**, that is to say, whether it "results directly from the basic or guiding principles of the tax system in the Member States concerned".[363] If so, the measure is not considered to be aid within the meaning of Art. 107 (1) TFEU (ex Art. 87(1) EC).[364] If this is not the case, than State aid is involved.[365]

357 The distinction between the first and second steps of the selectivity test is artificial and made only for simplification reasons. In practice, these stages are examined simultaneously. It involves the recognition of at least two tax treat-

---

[357] Notice on Business Taxation, OJ C 384 of 10 December 1998, pp. 3–9, para. 26.

[358] Report on Implementation, Brussels, of 9 February 2004, C(2004) 434, Box No. 5.

[359] Notice on Business Taxation, OJ C 384 of 10 December 1998, pp. 3–9, para. 12.

[360] Notice on Business Taxation, OJ C 384 of 10 December 1998, pp. 3–9, para. 16.

[361] ECJ 8 November 2001, C-143/99, *Adria-Wien Pipeline* [2001] ECR I-8365, para. 41; ECJ 22 December 2008, C-487/06 P *British Aggregates v Commission* [2008] ECR I-10515, para. 82; ECJ 8 September 2011, joined cases C-78/08 to C-80/08, *Paint Graphos* [2011] ECR I-0, para. 49; ECJ 15 November 2011, joined cases C-106/09 P and C-107/09 P, *Commission v Gibraltar* [2011] ECR I-0, para. 75.

[362] Lang, *EStAL 2012*, p. 418.

[363] ECJ 6 September 2006, C-88/03, *Portugal v Commission* [2006] ECR I-7115, para.81.

[364] Notice on Business Taxation, OJ C 384 of 10 December 1998, pp. 3–9, para. 13; ECJ 8 November 2001, C-143/99, *Adria-Wien Pipeline* [2001] ECR I-8365, para. 42; ECJ 22 December 2012, C-487/06 P *British Aggregates v Commission* [2008] ECR I-10515, para. 83; ECJ 15 November 2011, cases C-106/09 P and C-107/09 P, *Commission v Gibraltar* [2011] ECR I-0, para. 145.

[365] Notice on Business Taxation, OJ C 384 of 10 December 1998, pp. 3–9, para. 16.

ments, a beneficial and a less beneficial one. The less beneficial tax treatment is considered to be the "normal" tax system, whereas the more beneficial tax treatment the deviation. It does not matter in this regard which of the provisions applies to the larger number of undertakings and which to the smaller number.[366]

The implementation of the selectivity test to tax measures providing **regional** **358** **preferential treatment** may seem somewhat unique, but in fact applies the principles described above. In general, a tax benefit that is relevant only to undertakings in a specific region is considered selective, as it deviates from the national "common" or "normal" tax system. However, with regard to tax benefits implemented by legislative or administrative bodies at subnational levels, the regional tax system may be considered to be the **correct reference point** rather than the national system. This will be the case when an infra-State body, such as federal states or municipalities, enjoys **sufficient institutional, procedural and economic autonomy** to be able to determine its own tax system,[367] as part of defining the political and economic environment in which undertakings operate.[368] In such circumstances, a tax benefit implemented by the regional authority will not be considered selective if benefiting only economic operators in the specific region since such undertakings are **not in a comparable factual and legal situation** to other economic operators in the State.

Three conditions must be fulfilled in order for regional autonomy to be **359** recognized by the ECJ.[369] First, the regional authority needs to have, from a constitutional point of view, a **separate political and administrative status** from the national government **(institutional autonomy)**. Second, the measure must be adopted with **no central government being authorized to directly intervene** in the decision **(procedural autonomy)**. This does not preclude the establishment of a conciliation procedure in order to avoid conflicts with the central government, provided that the final decision is taken by the regional authority and not by the central government.[370] Finally, the financial consequences of the beneficial treatment given to undertakings in the region must **not be offset** by aid or subsidies from other regions or the central government **(economic and financial autonomy)**. The regional authority must assume the responsibility for the political and financial consequences of the tax reduction measures it implements.

---

[366] Lang, *EStAL 2012*, p. 420.

[367] ECJ 6 September 2006, C-88/03, *Portugal v Commission* [2006] ECR I-7115, para 67.

[368] ECJ 11 September 2008, joined cases C-428/06 to C-434/06, *Unión General de Trabajadore de La Rioja (UGT-Rioja) v Juntas Generales del Territorio Histórico de Vizcaya* [2008] ECR I-6747, paras. 54–55.

[369] Report on Implementation, Brussels, of 9 February 2004, C(2004) 434, Box No. 6; ECJ 6 September 2006, C-88/03, *Portugal v Commission* [2006] ECR I-7115, para 67.

[370] ECJ 11 September 2008, joined cases C-428/06 to C-434/06, *Unión General de Trabajadore de La Rioja (UGT-Rioja) v Juntas Generales del Territorio Histórico de Vizcaya* [2008] ECR I-6747, para. 96.

That cannot be the case where the infra-State body is not responsible of both its revenue and expenditure.[371]

360   As mentioned above, an allegedly selective tax measure may be justified by the **nature or general scheme of the tax system** if it serves to fulfil the basic logic or guiding principles of the respective Member State's tax system.[372] This is the case with measures whose economic rational makes them **necessary to the functioning and effectiveness of the tax system.**[373] In that context, a distinction must be made between, on the one hand, **external objectives** to the tax system which are assigned to a particular tax scheme (e.g., social or regional objectives) and, on the other hand, the objectives which are inherent in the tax system.[374] The tax system's **internal objectives** may entail that different taxpayers are considered to be in different factual and legal situations, and therefore treated differently without this being considered prohibited State aid. As opposed to objectives which are inherent in the tax system, **external objectives cannot justify a selective tax measure.** The fact that a selective tax measure is based on objective criteria does not suffice to prove that the measure is consistent with the logic of the system concerned.[375]

361   In the absence of European Union rules governing direct taxation matters, it falls within the competence of the Member States, or infra-state bodies having fiscal autonomy, to decide on the economic policy which they consider most appropriate, to designate bases of assessment and, in particular, to spread the tax burden as they see fit across the different factors of production and economic sectors.[376] In other words, **Member States hold the sovereignty to set their tax system's internal objectives.**[377] The basis of assessment that is implemented in a tax system could be an indication of its nature or general scheme, nevertheless, it is not conclusive and reference could be made to other indications.[378]

---

[371] ECJ 11 September 2008, joined cases C-428/06 to C-434/06, *Unión General de Trabajadore de La Rioja (UGT-Rioja) v Juntas Generales del Territorio Histórico de Vizcaya* [2008] ECR I-6747, para. 67.

[372] Notice on Business Taxation, OJ C 384 of 10 December 1998, pp. 3–9, paras. 16, 26; ECJ 6 September 2006, C-88/03, *Portugal v Commission* [2006] ECR I-7115, para. 83.

[373] Notice on Business Taxation, OJ C 384 of 10 December 1998, pp. 3–9, para. 23.

[374] Notice on Business Taxation, OJ C 384 of 10 December 1998, pp. 3–9, para. 26; ECJ 6 September 2006, C-88/03, *Portugal v Commission* [2006] ECR I-7115, para. 52, 81.

[375] Report on Implementation, Brussels, of 9 February 2004, C(2004) 434, Box. No. 8.

[376] Notice on Business Taxation, OJ C 384 of 10 December 1998, pp. 3–9, para. 13; ECJ 15 November 2011, joined cases C-106/09 P and C-107/09 P, *Commission v Gibraltar* [2011] ECR I-0, para. 97.

[377] Notice on Business Taxation, OJ C 384 of 10 December 1998, pp. 3–9, paras. 24, 26 and 27.

[378] ECJ 8 November 2001, C-143/99, *Adria-Wien Pipeline* [2001] ECR I-8365, para. 54; ECJ 15 November 2011, joined cases C-106/09 P and C-107/09 P, *Commission v Gibraltar* [2011] ECR I-0, para. 101.

The internal objectives must be **consistent** in the manner in which the tax **362** system is implemented in order to be recognized by the Commission and the ECJ.[379] It is therefore for the Member State concerned to introduce and apply **appropriate control and monitoring procedures** in order to ensure that specific tax measures are consistent with the logic and general scheme of the tax system and to prevent economic entities from taking actions for the sole purpose of taking advantage of the tax benefits provided by the tax system.

Moreover, in order for tax exemptions to be justified by the nature or general **363** scheme of the tax system, it is also necessary to ensure that those exemptions are consistent with the **principle of proportionality** and do not go beyond what is necessary, in that the legitimate objective being pursued could not be attained by less far-reaching measures.[380]

The Commission and the ECJ listed some **examples** of differential tax **364** measures that may be justified by the nature or general scheme of a tax system: the **progression of income tax rates** and **specific provisions on the taxation of small and medium-sized enterprises** (including small agricultural enterprises), because they may fulfil the redistributive purposes of a tax system; calculation of **asset depreciation** and **stock valuation methods**, because they may be inherent in the tax system to which they belong; in the same way, the **arrangements for the collection of fiscal debts** can differ from one Member State to the other; **tax exemption for non-profit-making undertakings**, such as foundations or associations, because profit tax cannot be levied if no profit is earned; **tax exemption for cooperatives** which distribute all their profits to their members, when tax is levied at the level of their members; provisions allowing for tax to be determined on a **fixed basis** (for example, in the agriculture or fisheries sectors), because of specific accounting requirements or the importance of land in assets which are specific to certain sectors; some tax measures may be justified by **objective differences** between taxpayers, certain sectors or certain types of transaction where there is a direct link between the alleged specific features and the tax concessions granted.

In seems that in order to determine both whether undertakings are in a com- **365** parable legal and factual situation, as part of the first and second steps of the selectivity test, and in order to determine whether an ostensibly selective tax measure may be justified, as part of the final step of the selectivity test, the nature or general scheme of the tax system must be examined. The distinction between these two stages is **procedural** and concerns **shifting the burden of proof**. While the Commission examines the nature or general scheme of the tax system independently as part of the first and second steps of the selectivity test, it is up to the Member State concerned to show that an ostensibly selective

---

[379] Rossi-Maccanico, *EC Tax Review* 2009, p. 74.
[380] ECJ 8 September 2011, joined cases C-78/08 to C-80/08, *Paint Graphos* [2011] ECR I-0, paras. 73–75.

measure is actually justified by the nature or general scheme of its tax system as part of the third step of the selectivity test.[381]

366 It should be made clear that the fact that a measure is alien to the inherent logic of a tax system does not mean, of itself, that that measure becomes selective. Such measure could be general in nature.[382]

367 **A general measure** is the opposite of a selective measure. A tax benefit will not be considered selective if it is open without distinction to **every undertaking** in a comparable legal and factual situation **operating within the territory of the respective Member State,** as such a benefit does not favour certain undertakings or the production of goods. It will therefore not be considered prohibited State aid under Art. 107(1) TFEU (ex Art. 87(1) EC).[383] In order to be considered as such, a general measure must be effectively **open to all firms on an equal access basis**, and may not *de facto* be reduced in scope through, for example, the discretionary power of the State to grant it or through other factors that restrict its practical effect.[384]

368 Therefore, the selectivity requirement may also be fulfilled if a tax provision leaves the tax administration with **discretion** to grant tax incentives as it sees fit.[385] The ECJ acknowledged that treating economic agents on a discretionary basis may mean that the individual application of a general measure takes on the features of a selective measure, in particular where the exercise of the discretionary power goes beyond the simple management of tax revenue by reference to objective criteria.[386]

369 Provided that they apply without distinction to all firms and to the production of all goods, tax measures of **a purely technical nature** (for example, setting the rate of taxation; depreciation rules on loss carry-overs; provisions to prevent double taxation or tax avoidance) and tax measures pursuing general economic

---

[381] See Notice on Business Taxation, OJ C 384 of 10 December 1998, pp. 3-9, para. 23; Report on Implementation, Brussels, of 9 February 2004, C(2004) 434, para. 35, Box no. 7; ECJ 24 April 2004, C-159/01, *Netherlands v Commission* [2004] ECR I-4461, paras. 43, 77; ECJ 15 November 2011, joined cases C-106/09 P and C-107/09 P, *Commission v Gibraltar* [2011] ECR I-0, paras. 146, 151.

[382] ECJ 15 November 2011, joined cases C-106/09 P and C-107/09 P, *Commission v Gibraltar* [2011] ECR I-0, para. 81.

[383] Case C-156/98 *Germany vs. Commission* [2000] ECR I-6857, para. 22; joined Cases C-393/04 and 41/05 *Air Liquide Industriea Belgium* [2006] ECR I-5293, para. 31; ECJ 8 November 2001, C-143/99, *Adria-Wien Pipeline* [2001] ECR I-8365, para. 35 et seq.; ECJ 15 November 2011, joined cases C-106/09 P and C-107/09 P, *Commission v Gibraltar* [2011] ECR I-0, para. 79.

[384] Notice on Business Taxation, OJ C 384 of 10 December 1998, pp. 3–9, para. 13; ECJ 15 November 2011, joined cases C-106/09 P and C-107/09 P, *Commission v Gibraltar* [2011] ECR I-0, paras. 130, 132.

[385] Notice on Business Taxation, OJ C 384 of 10 December 1998, pp. 3–9, para. 21.

[386] ECJ 26 September 1996, Case C-241/94, *France vs. Commission* [1996] ECR I-4551, paras. 23–24.

policy objectives through a reduction of the tax burden related to **certain production costs** (for example, research and development (R&D), the environment, training, employment) are not considered an aid within the meaning of Art. 107 (1) TFEU (ex Art. 87(1) EC).[387] Consequently, a preferential tax treatment for an **incorporated business** (i.e., a reduction of the corporate tax which does not affect partnerships or self-employed traders) is not selective. It only concerns a legal form, which is open to everyone carrying on trade or business, and therefore is of a purely technical nature.

A tax measure's character as general is **qualitative rather than quantitative**. 370 Therefore, on the one hand, it is not necessary that all economic agents enjoy a tax incentive equally in order for it to be considered general[388] and, on the other hand, the fact that a tax incentive benefits important, diverse and large economic sectors does not make it general in the respective Member State.[389]

The Commission and the ECJ follow a **functional approach** when determin- 371 ing the character of a tax measure to be selective or general, taking into account only the effects of the measure, without considering relevant the nature of the objectives pursued by the measure or their grounds of justification.[390] This approach does not allow for a distinction to be made among aid effects based on the regulatory technique used to achieve them.[391] Hence, the reason why a Member State implemented an aid measure, what goals the Member State wished to achieve or how the Member State planned to achieve these goals does not matter. Any state intervention that brings about the effects of illegal State aid is prohibited under Art. 107(1) TFEU (ex Art. 87(1) EC).

For this reason, where **the criteria forming the basis of assessment** which a 372 tax system adopts are such that characterise only some undertakings as **privileged by virtue of properties which are specific to them**, without such privilege being justified by the nature or general scheme of the tax system, such a regime will not be considered to apply general measures but rather as conferring a selective advantage.[392] This distinction is required in order to prevent Member States from applying "**disguised State aid**",[393] achieving the results of selectivity by adjusting their tax systems' basis of assessment in such a way that its **very**

---

[387] Notice on Business Taxation, OJ C 384 of 10 December 1998, pp. 3–9, para. 13.

[388] Notice on Business Taxation, OJ C 384 of 10 December 1998, pp. 3–9, para. 14.

[389] ECJ 8 November 2001, C-143/99, *Adria-Wien Pipeline* [2001] ECR I-8365, para. 48; ECJ 17 June 1999, C-75/97, *Belgium v Commission ("Maribel")* [1999] ECR I-3671, para. 32.

[390] Notice on Business Taxation, OJ C 384 of 10 December 1998, pp. 3–9, para. 15; ECJ 8 December 2011, C-81/10 P, *France Télécom SA* [2011] ECR I-0, para. 17.

[391] ECJ 15 November 2011, joined cases C-106/09 P and C-107/09 P, *Commission v Gibraltar* [2011] ECR I-0, para. 87–88.

[392] ECJ 8 November 2001, C-143/99, *Adria-Wien Pipeline* [2001] ECR I-8365, para. 40 et seq.; ECJ 15 November 2011, joined cases C-106/09 P and C-107/09 P, *Commission v Gibraltar* [2011] ECR I-0, paras. 91–93, 104.

[393] See Sutter, *Das EG-Beihilfenverbot und sein Durchführungsverbot in Steuersachen* (2005) p. 92.

application results in a different tax burden for different undertakings.[394] One example of a legislative technique used by Member States in order to disguise State aid in such way is to adopt a tax system that does not apply a general basis of assessment but rather specific bases of assessment, which in practice allows from the outset the exclusion of some undertakings from paying taxes.[395]

f) *De minimis* Limitation

373　As has been shown above, the Commission and the ECJ regard the requirements of distortion of competition and effects on trade as easily fulfilled. Nonetheless, there is a limit to the scope of Art. 107(1) TFEU (ex Art. 87(1) EC). In this respect, State aid is only deemed to have harmful implications if it reaches a **certain quantity**.

374　In order to determine the acceptable amount of State aid, the Commission has (on the basis of the authorization by the Council) adopted a **Regulation on the application of Art. 107 and Art. 108 TFEU (ex Art. 87 and 88 EC) to *de minimis* aid**.[396] This Regulation sets out a threshold under which aid measures are deemed not to meet all the criteria of Art. 107(1) TFEU (ex Art. 87(1) EC) and therefore do not constitute State aid nor fall under the notification procedure provided for in Art. 108(3) TFEU (ex Art. 88(3) EC).

375　The underlying assumption is that below a certain amount of aid, no distortion of competition or effect on trade between Member States occurs. In general, the *de minimis* ceiling is **EUR 200,000 over any period of three fiscal years**.[397]

376　Some aid measures in sensitive sectors are exempted from the application of the *de minimis* rule, for example aid granted to certain sectors of primary production, aid granted to export-related activities towards third countries or aid granted to undertakings in difficulty.[398] Furthermore, the *de minimis* provision only applies to aid that is granted in the form of a **cash grant** or in respect of which it is possible to calculate precisely the gross grant equivalent *ex ante* without any need to undertake a risk assessment (this includes, for instance, capped tax exemptions).[399] The Member States also have monitoring obligations to ensure that the total amount of aid granted to the same undertaking does not exceed the *de minimis* limitation.

---

[394] ECJ 15 November 2011, joined cases C-106/09 P and C-107/09 P, *Commission v Gibraltar* [2011] ECR I-0, para. 93.

[395] ECJ 15 November 2011, joined cases C-106/09 P and C-107/09 P, *Commission v Gibraltar* [2011] ECR I-0, paras. 100-102.

[396] Commission Regulation (EC) No. 1998/2006 of 15 December 2006 on the application of Articles 87 and 88 of the Treaty to *de minimis* aid, OJ L 379 of 28 December 2006, pp. 5–10 (replacing the Commission Regulation (EC) No. 69/2001 of 12 January 2001, OJ L 10 of 13 January 2001, pp. 30-32.

[397] Art. 2(2) of the *de minimis* Regulation No. 1998/2006.

[398] Art. 1(1) of the *de minimis* Regulation No. 1998/2006.

[399] Art. 2(3) and (4) of the *de minimis* Regulation No. 1998/2006.

5. Exemptions from the Prohibition on State Aid under Art. 107(2) and (3) TFEU (ex Art. 87(2) and (3) EC)

According to Art. 107(1) TFEU (ex Art. 87(1) EC), State aid is generally incompatible with the common market and therefore prohibited. However, this prohibition is neither absolute nor unconditional. Art. 107(2) and (3) (ex Art. 87(2) and (3) EC) TFEU and the ensue Regulations provides for a number of cases in which State aid *must be* or *might be* **considered compatible** with the common market. Consequently, the granting of aid cannot be regarded as being automatically contrary to the TFEU.   **377**

A Member State which seeks to be allowed to grant aid by way of derogation from the prohibition on State aid has a duty to collaborate with the Commission. In pursuance of that duty, it must in particular provide all the information necessary to enable the Commission to verify that the conditions for the derogations sought are fulfilled.[400]   **378**

a) Legal Exemptions under Art. 107(2) TFEU (ex Art. 87(2) EC)

Art. 107(2) TFEU (ex Art. 87(2) EC) defines in three instances that certain aid is **automatically compatible** with the common market (**legal exemption**). Hence,   **379**

1. Aid having a **social character**, granted to individual customers, provided that such aid is granted without discrimination to the origin of the products concerned;
2. Aid to make good the damage caused by **natural disasters or exceptional occurrences**;
3. Aid granted to the economy of certain areas of the **Federal Republic of Germany** affected by the division of Germany, insofar as such aid is required in order to compensate for the economic disadvantages caused by that division,

is *ex lege* seen as compatible with the common market.

With regard to the **social character of the aid**, the beneficiaries usually are lower income groups that need financial support, such as elderly people, children and handicapped persons. According to Art. 107(1) TFEU (ex Art. 87(1) EC), aid given to individuals does not fall under the scope of the prohibition of State aid in any case. Nevertheless, Art. 107(2) TFEU (ex Art. 87(2) EC) ensures that the beneficial effect indirectly granted to the undertakings when favouring certain customer groups does not undermine the exemption.   **380**

Concerning aid granted for **natural disasters or exceptional occurrences**, it is necessary that there are substantial and unpredictable circumstances that are   **381**

---

[400] ECJ 28 April 1993, C-364/90, *Italy vs. Commission* [1993] ECR I-2097, para. 20; ECJ 29 April 2004, C-372/97, *Italy v Commission* [2004] ECR I-3679, para. 81; ECJ 15 November 2011, joined cases C-106/09 P and C-107/09 P, *Commission v Gibraltar* [2011] ECR I-0, para. 147.

out of the ordinary (e.g. tornadoes, floods, droughts, earthquakes, wars, major nuclear industrial accidents). During the last couple of years, Art. 107(2)(b) (ex Art. 87(2)(b) EC) has been the basis for the authorization of aid to businesses affected by marine pollution caused by the sinking of oil tankers and to airlines to compensate them for the losses caused by the closing of the United States airspace and the increasing of the insurance premiums in the aftermath of the terrorist attacks on New York in September 2001.[401]

382   Aid in relation to the **division of Germany** has not been authorized during the past decade and is thus of little practical relevance. In the past, it affected the authorization of aid granted for poorer communication systems or extra transport costs caused by the former physical division of the Federal Republic of Germany.

383   If an aid measure is covered by one of these events, it is definitely compatible with the common market and automatically exempted from the prohibition of State aid. This does **not exclude the Member States from their obligation to notify** their plans to the Commission prior to being put into effect. The Commission only has to examine whether the aid measure in question falls within the scope of Art. 107(2) TFEU (ex Art. 87(2) EC). In practice, only very few cases of aid are authorized every year under Art. 107(2) TFEU (ex Art. 87(2) EC).

b) Discretionary Exemptions under Art. 107(3) TFEU (ex Art. 87(3) EC)

384   Art. 107(3) TFEU (ex Art. 87(3) EC) defines five instances in which State aid *may be* compatible with the common market. In this regard, State aid is not automatically exempted but **may be declared acceptable by the Commission**.

385   Whenever the Commission examines aid schemes notified by Member States, it is bound by EU law to authorize only those measures which fall within the exemption categories of Art. 107(3) TFEU (ex Art. 87(3) EC). Any other kind of aid must be rejected. Therefore,

1. Aid to promote the **economic development of areas** where the standard of living is abnormally low or where there is serious underemployment;
2. Aid to promote the execution of an **important project** of common European interest or to **remedy a serious disturbance** in the economy of a Member State;
3. Aid to facilitate the **development of certain economic activities or of certain economic areas,** where such aid does not adversely affect trading conditions to an extent contrary to the common interest;
4. Aid to promote **culture and heritage conservation** where such aid does not affect trading conditions and competition in the EU to an extent that is contrary to the common interest and
5. Such other categories of aid as may be specified by **decision of the Council** acting by a qualified majority on a proposal from the Commission,

may be considered compatible with the common market.

---

[401] See Nicolaides/Kekelekis/Buyskes, *State aid policy in the European Community: a guide for practitioners* (2005) p. 33.

The categories of aid that are of major interest are the first (**regional aid**) and **386** above all the third one (**aid for certain economic activities or areas**). Both events cover aid granted to underdeveloped regions within the Member States. As to the acceptance of aid granted for the execution of an important project of common European interest or aid as a remedy for a serious disturbance in the economy of a Member State, the Commission takes a very restrictive approach. The provisions on aid for cultural purposes and aid otherwise defined by the Council are used very infrequently, too.[402]

The **Commission** as the competent authority in EU State aid matters has wide **387** discretion to decide on the compatibility of the aid with the common market, since it is exclusively its responsibility to make the determination of compatible State aid. The exercise of the Commission's discretion involves an economic and social assessment in an EU context.[403] The Commission has to investigate further whether the aid measure in question infringes other provisions of the TFEU, including the fundamental freedoms and Art. 110 TFEU (ex Art. 90 EC), and whether the aid measure contradicts provisions of secondary law, for example provisions on taxation. Additionally, the Commission has to respect its own authorization practice in order to ensure equal treatment of the Member States. The decisions of the Commission are **subject to review by the ECJ**. However, the Court must restrict itself to examining whether the assessment of the Commission is not based on a manifest error or misuse of powers.[404]

To make the exercise of the discretionary power more transparent and pre- **388** dictable and to ensure **legal certainty** for undertakings and authorities, the Commission has issued a number of guidelines, communications, notices and frameworks. These publications include the criteria that the Commission uses when deciding on the compatibility with the common market under Art. 107(3) TFEU (ex Art. 87(3) EC). However, these acts do not have a binding legal character but only show the Commission's view on the application of its discretion.

Furthermore, on the basis of a Council Directive, the Commission has the **389** power to adopt **group exemption regulations** which can be directly applied by national courts.[405] By means of such regulations, the Commission may declare certain categories of aid compatible with the common market pursuant to the

---

[402] See Sutter, in Mayer (ed.) *Kommentar zu EU- und EG-Vertrag* (2005) Art. 87, m.nos. 97 et seq.

[403] See ECJ 17 September 1980, 730/79, *Philip Morris v Commission* [1980] ECR 2671, para. 24.

[404] ECJ 14 March 1973, 57/72, *Westzucker* [1973] ECR 321, para. 14; ECJ 14 January 1997, C-169/95, *Spain v Commission* [1997] ECR I-135, para. 34; ECJ 12 December 2002, C-456/00, *France v Commission* [2002] ECR I-11949, para. 41; ECJ 23 February 2006, joined cases C-346/03 and C-529/03, *Atzeni and others* [2006] ECR I-1875, para. 84.

[405] Council Regulation (EC) of 7 May 1998 No. 994/98 on the application of Articles 92 and 93 of the Treaty establishing the European Community to certain categories of horizontal State aid, OJ L 142 of 14 May 1998, pp. 1–4.

provisions of Art. 107(2) and (3) TFEU (ex Art. 87(2) and (3) EC) (e.g. aid to small and medium-sized enterprises, aid for employment, aid for training and regional aid). In this way the Commission should be relieved of investigating a large number of routine cases.

390 Finally, it is important to note that the prohibition of State aid under Art. 107(1) TFEU (ex Art. 87(1) EC) is addressed to the **Member States** only and thus does not have direct effect. Therefore, it does not confer any rights or obligations on individuals. Consequently, it is not possible to challenge the compatibility of an aid with EU law before national courts just on the basis of this provision. However, a national court may **refer a preliminary question to the ECJ** based on Art. 267 TFEU (ex Art. 234 EC) and request the interpretation of Art. 107(1) TFEU (ex Art. 87(1) EC) if it is of the opinion that a decision thereon is necessary to enable it to give judgment.

6. The State Aid Control System under Art. 108 TFEU (ex Art. 88 EC)

a) Overview of the Procedural Aspects of State Aid in Art. 108 TFEU (ex Art. 88 EC)

391 Art. 108 TFEU (ex Art. 88 EC) provides for the procedural rules of the EU State aid control system. In 1999 detailed rules for the application of Art. 88 EC (now Art. 108 TFEU) were laid down in Regulation 659/1999.[406] Under this system, a clear distinction has to be made between **existing aid and new aid**. This differentiation is of great relevance as Art. 108 TFEU (ex Art. 88 EC) provides for completely different review systems on that basis.

392 **Existing aid** is aid that was in operation before the establishment of the European Union in 1958 or before a Member States acceded to the European Union (**accession date**). Other forms of existing aid are:[407]

- Aid that has been authorized by the Commission or by the Council, i.e. new aid that has been accepted.
- Aid that is deemed to have been authorized because it has been notified to the Commission and the Commission has not taken a decision regarding its compatibility with the common market within two months.
- Aid that is deemed to be existing aid because with regard to the unlawful aid the limitation period of ten years to recover has expired.
- Aid that is deemed to be existing aid because it can be established that at the time it was put into effect it did not constitute an aid, and subsequently became an aid due to the **evolution of the common market** without having

---

[406] Council Regulation (EC) No. 659/1999 of 22 March 1999 laying down detailed rules for the application of Article 93 of the EC Treaty, OJ L 83 of 27 March 1999, pp. 1–9.
[407] See Art. 1(b) of Regulation No. 659/1999.

been altered by the Member State. The provision takes into consideration the dynamic nature of State aid law.

In the case of existing State aid, only a *pro futuro* monitoring procedure of the **393** Commission under Art. 108(3) TFEU (ex Art. 88(1) EC) takes place. Existing State aid is considered to be lawful and may be granted as long as the Commission does not find it incompatible with the common market, after having performed the formal investigation procedure under Art. 108(2) TFEU (ex Art. 88(2) EC).

New aid means all aid that is not existing aid. Therefore, all aid that is intro- **394** duced *after* a Member State's accession to the European Union is new aid. The same holds for any alterations of existing aid. In the case of new State aid, a "stricter" State aid procedure applies: the Member States must first notify the Commission of their proposed State aid plans and obtain its authorization before they implement them. Thus, Art. 108(3) TFEU (ex Art. 88(3) EC) provides for the **direct blocking effect or the prohibition of implementation**, meaning that the Member State may not implement the intended measures (the new State aid) prior to the Commission issuing a final decision.

The **purpose of this preventive review procedure** for new State aid is to en- **395** able the Commission to evaluate planned State measures before they are implemented in order to prevent new undesirable burdens on the common market from the beginning. Even if the unlawfully granted measure comes to light and can be tackled, it can be very difficult to restore the *ex ante* competitive situation and undo the negative effects caused by the measure even if the aid is eventually recovered from the beneficiary.

Therefore, Art. 108(2) TFEU (ex Art. 88(2) EC) and Regulation 659/1999 pro- **396** vide for a **formal investigation procedure** which is to be started if the suspicion of State aid exists after a preliminary investigation of the measure. First, the different procedural aspects of existing aid and new aid are examined. In a next step, the formal investigation procedure and other procedural questions are taken into account.

b) The Procedural Treatment of Existing Aid

According to Art. 108(3) TFEU (ex Art. 88(1) EC), "the Commission shall, in **397** cooperation with the Member States, keep under **constant review all systems of aid existing** in those States. It shall propose to the latter any appropriate measure required by the progressive development or by the functioning of the common market." Therefore, existing State aid falls under the regime of constant review by the Commission. Hence, Member States have to submit **annual reports** on all existing aid schemes.[408] In the case of tax relief or full or partial tax exemption, this includes an estimation of the budgetary revenue lost. Existing aid may be implemented as long as the Commission has not found it to be incompatible with

---

[408] See Art. 21(1) of Regulation No. 659/1999.

the common market (**"repressive monitoring system"**).[409]As long as the Commission does not raise any objections to all these existing aid measures, they are permissible and may be granted by the Member State. As a first step, the Commission may propose to the Member State any **appropriate measure** required by the progressive development or by the functioning of the common market, e.g. a substantial change or the abolition of the aid. Although the suggestion of appropriate measures is a recommendation and thus not legally binding for the Member State, it may be seen as a kind of pre-stage to the formal investigation procedure. If the Member State is not willing to comply with the Commission's suggested measures within a certain period of time, then the Commission starts the formal investigation procedure under Art. 108(2) TFEU (ex Art. 88(2) EC).

398 **Individuals** who have concerns about an existing State aid may only give notice to the Commission and propose the initiation of an investigation procedure. However, they have no right to have the formal investigation procedure under Art. 108(2) TFEU (ex Art. 88(2) EC) started.

399 If the Commission initiates an investigation procedure and finds that an existing aid measure is not, or is no longer, in line with the common market, this negative decision only has **effect for the future (*ex nunc*)**. Only if the Member State keeps applying the incompatible State aid measure is a request for recovery possible.[410]

c) The Procedural Treatment of New Aid

400 As to new aid, the procedural demands are higher. Art. 108(3) first sentence TFEU (ex Art. 88(3) first sentence EC) provides that the Member States must inform the Commission of any plans to grant or alter new aid (**notification requirement**). The notification obligation is quite far-reaching: the Member States have to notify any measure that arouses the suspicion of State aid.

401 The notification has to take place in time so that the Commission can comment on the measure before it is implemented. Hence, there is a **prohibition of implementation** of the notified measure as long as it is not declared compatible with the common market by the Commission, or is deemed to have been declared compatible. This **direct blocking effect** is provided for in **Art. 108(3) third sentence TFEU (ex Art. 88(3) third sentence EC)**. The prohibition of implementation is effective during the whole investigation procedure until the final decision is made.

402 The question that arises in this context is: when is aid implemented? If aid is implemented, it is too late for notification and the aid is at least formally illegal. It is not necessary that aid be paid; if the aid may be granted without further for-

---

[409] ECJ 30 June 1992, C-47/91, *Italy v Commission ("Italgrani")* [1992] ECR I-4145, para. 25; ECJ 15 March 1994, C-387/92, *Banco Exterior de España* [1994] ECR I-877, para. 20; ECJ 29 April 2004, C-372/97, *Italy v Commission* [2004] ECR I-3679, para. 42.

[410] See Sutter, in Mayer (ed.) *Kommentar zu EU- und EG-Vertrag* (2005) Art. 88, m.no. 27; ECJ 15 March 1994, C-387/92, *Banco Exterior de España* [1994] ECR I-877, para. 20.

mality, it can be seen as "implemented". Therefore, the measures (potentially) constituting State aid should be notified to the Commission before their **legal adoption** in the respective Member State. In this respect, the Commission has recommended that Member State authorities write a reserve clause into legislation whereby the implementation of the measure takes place only after the Commission has decided on the character of the measure.

However, there are a number of **exceptions** to the notification requirement. **403** Firstly, notification is not necessary in the case of *de minimis* aid. Secondly, there is no notification requirement if the aid is covered by an authorized aid scheme. Finally, aid covered by group exemption regulations does not need to be notified (e.g. aid for small and medium-sized enterprises, research and development, environmental protection, employment and training). These exceptions save the Commission from dealing with a high number of routine State aid cases.

According to the case law of the ECJ, the prohibition of implementation in **404** Art. 108(3) third sentence TFEU (ex Art. 88(3) third sentence EC) is **directly applicable in the Member States** and confers rights on **individuals** that the national courts are bound to safeguard.[411] In contrast, Art. 107(1) TFEU (ex Art. 87(1) EC) does not provide for such a direct effect.

The direct effect of the prohibition on implementation requires all **national** **405** **authorities** to apply it. Thus, the addressees of Art. 108(3) TFEU (ex Art. 88(3) EC) may be the legislator as well as the tax authorities and the national courts. None of them may apply a national provision suspected to be State aid. Therefore, a court may not grant such aid even if others have already received it.

If the national court has doubts whether a measure fulfils all the criteria of **406** Art. 107(1) TFEU (ex Art. 87(1) EC), it may request the **ECJ to give a preliminary ruling** on the subject under Art. 267 TFEU (ex Art. 234 EC). In the case of a decision of a court of last instance, the question *has* to be referred to the ECJ for a preliminary ruling. The Commission points out that Member States must also request assistance from the Commission by asking it for legal or economic information, especially where the application of Art. 107(1) TFEU (ex Art. 87(1) EC) raises particular difficulties.[412]

Hence, concerning the control system of new State aid, there is a "**triangle of** **407** **power**" consisting of the European Commission, the ECJ and the national courts:[413] While the supervision of new State aid (and existing aid) lies in the hands of the Commission, which therefore plays an integral part in any State aid procedure, its decisions are subject to review by the ECJ. National courts, on the other hand, have to ensure the effectiveness of the notification obligation and safeguard the rights that individuals enjoy as a result of the direct effect of the

---

[411] ECJ 15 July 1964, 6/64, *Costa v E.N.E.L.* [1964] ECR 1141, p. 1273; ECJ 11 December 1973, 120/73, *Lorenz* [1973] ECR 1471, para. 8.

[412] Notice on cooperation between national courts and the Commission in the State aid field, OJ C 312 of 23 November 1995, pp. 18–23, para. 29.

[413] Sutter, *ET* 2001, p. 249.

prohibition of implementation. However, neither the ECJ nor the national courts can ultimately decide on the compatibility of State aid with the common market. This lies within the exclusive power of the Commission.

408   After receiving the notification of a new aid measure, the Commission initiates a **preliminary examination procedure** that has to result in a decision within a period of two months (also known as the *Lorenz*-period).[414] The period may only be extended with the consent of the Member State concerned. If after the preliminary examination the Commission comes to the conclusion that the notified measure does not constitute aid or that the measure is aid but falls under an exception provided for by the TFEU and is therefore compatible with the common market, it gives a decision thereon. Otherwise, the Commission decides to initiate the formal investigation procedure pursuant to Art. 108(2) TFEU (ex Art. 88(2) EC).[415]

409   If the Commission does **not reach a decision within two months from opening a preliminary examination**, the aid is deemed to have been authorized by the Commission. The Member State concerned may thus implement the aid, unless the Commission takes a decision within a period of 15 working days to open the formal investigation procedure under Art. 108(2) TFEU (ex Art. 88(2) EC).[416]

d) The Formal Investigation Procedure under Art. 108(2) TFEU (ex Art. 88(2) EC)

410   The formal investigation procedure applies to both the existing State aid regime and the new aid regime.

411   The decision to open the formal investigation procedure is communicated to the respective Member State by letter. The other Member States and interested parties are informed by note in the Official Journal. The Commission provides for a **notification period of one month** in which the Member States and all parties (e.g. other Member States, individuals, undertakings, the recipient of the aid, his competitors) may submit their comments.

412   The formal investigation procedure ends with a **final decision** by the Commission. It may either decide that the proposed measure is incompatible with the common market (**negative decision**) or compatible with the common market (**positive decision**) or the aid that has to be modified in order to be regarded as compatible (**conditional decision**). On average, only about 2.7 % of all cases of correctly notified State aids are held incompatible with the common market. On the other hand, the need for the Commission to intervene in the granting of aid with a negative decision or, in some cases, a conditional decision with regard

---

[414] ECJ 11 December 1973, 120/73, *Lorenz* [1973] ECR 1471, para. 4; Art. 4(5) of Regulation No. 659/1999.

[415] See Art. 4(2) and (3) of Regulation No. 659/1999.

[416] See Art. 4(6) of Regulation No. 659/1999.

to aid unlawfully implemented by a Member State is almost ten times higher (25.6 %).[417]

With regard to the time limit of the investigation procedure, the Regulation provides for a benchmark **time period of 18 months**. The length of the investigation depends on whether the Commission initiates a more detailed investigation, invites interested parties to express their views and receives their comments in due time.   413

In order to challenge the final decision of the Commission, the respective parties must make clear that they are **directly and individually concerned** in terms of Art. 263(4) TFEU (ex Art. 230(4) EC) by the Commission's decision. The Member States are privileged under Art. 263(2) TFEU (ex Art. 230(2) EC). Hence, competitors of the recipient of the aid must demonstrate that they have played a significant role in the State aid procedure and that their position on the market is significantly affected by the aid.[418] Therefore, challenging the final decision of the Commission is made difficult. On the other hand, the potential recipient of an aid may also challenge a negative or conditional decision.[419]   414

e) The Consequences of Unlawful Aid

With regard to the **treatment of unlawful aid**, there are several distinctions to be made. First, one has to take a look at the procedural effects at the level of both the Member States and the Commission. Secondly, another crucial question is whether the aid is only formally unlawful because it is in breach of the notification obligation but substantially compatible with the common market or whether the aid is formally unlawful *and* incompatible with the common market.   415

Subsequently, when dealing with unlawful aid, there are **two levels** that have to be taken into regard. On the one hand, there is the procedure on the level of the Commission for deciding upon the compatibility of the aid with the common market. On the other hand, the consequence of unlawful aid in the Member States, that is to say the enforcement by the national authorities, has to be taken into account.   416

Unlawful aid is aid that is granted without notification to the Commission or notified aid that is granted before the Commission has made its final decision. In the case of formally unlawful aid the **Commission** starts the procedure against the Member State *ex officio* or following a **complaint from a third party** (e.g., competitors).[420] At first, the Commission charges the Member State with pro-   417

---

[417] See the spring edition 2007 State Aid Scoreboard, p. 13, at: http://ec.europa.eu/comm/competition/state_aid/studies_reports/2007_spring_de.pdf.

[418] ECJ 28 January 1986, 169/84, *Cofaz* [1986] ECR 391, para. 25; ECJ 23 May 2000, C-106/98 P, *Comité d'entreprise de la Société française de production and others* [2000] ECR I-3659, para. 40. However, the requirement of the active participation and the effect on the market position is not yet fully clear; see Mamut, *Konkurrentenschutz im Abgabenrecht* (2010) p. 232 et seq.

[419] ECJ 14 November 1984, 323/83, *Intermills* [1984] ECR 3809, para. 16.

[420] See Art. 20(2) of Regulation No. 659/1999.

viding **complete information** on the aid at hand. Moreover, in order to ensure the effectiveness of the prohibition of implementation, the Commission may also issue an interim **suspension order** requiring the Member State to suspend any unlawful aid until the Commission has taken its decision on the compatibility of the aid with the common market. Additionally, under certain qualifying circumstances, the Commission may also adopt a decision to **provisionally recover** any unlawful aid from the Member State until it has come to its final decision.[421]

418   The mere fact that the aid measure was not notified does not automatically mean that it is also incompatible with the common market.[422] On the contrary, the Commission is obliged to examine the compatibility of the aid with the common market, in accordance with the procedure laid down in Art. 108(2) and (3) TFEU (ex Art. 88(2) and (3) EC).[423] Just as in the case of notified (and therefore *lawful)* aid, the Commission may issue the following decisions regarding unlawful aid: On the one hand, it may find that the measure does not fulfil the criteria of Art. 107(1) TFEU (ex Art. 87(1) EC) or that the measure is compatible with the common market (**unnotified (= unlawful) *but* compatible aid**). On the other hand, it may come to the conclusion that the aid is not compatible with the common market and must therefore be banned (**unnotified (= unlawful) incompatible aid**). The differentiation between these two types of illegal aid is of material importance, since the ultimate consequences – the recovery of aid – are dependent on the type of unlawful aid.

419   The **Commission** may only provide for recovery of **unnotified incompatible aid**.[424] On the other hand, since **national courts** are not authorized to conclude that a measure is compatible with the common market, they must provide for the **recovery of any unnotified aid**.[425] The fact that only national courts and not the Commission are obliged to recover the formally unnotified aid puts the effectiveness of the prohibition of implementation at risk.

420   When enforcing EU law, the Member States must, in the absence of relevant provisions under EU law, follow the **procedural and substantive provisions of their national law**.[426] In doing so, they must comply with the requirements of the effectiveness imperative and the equivalence imperative, which are general principles of EU law, in order not to undermine the effectiveness of protection. The **effectiveness imperative** means that national proceedings may not render practically impossible, or disproportionately aggravate, the exercising of rights conferred on the basis of EU legislation. The **equivalence imperative** requires that

---

[421] See Art. 11 of Regulation No. 659/1999.
[422] ECJ 5 October 1994, C-47/91, *Italy v Commission ("Italgrani")/*[1994] ECR I-4635, para. 26.
[423] ECJ 14 February 1990, C-301/87, *France v Commission ("Boussac")* [1990] ECR I-307, para. 11.
[424] ECJ 14 February 1990, C-301/87, *France v Commission ("Boussac")* [1990] ECR I-307, para. 11.
[425] ECJ 11 July 1996, C-39/94, *SFEI and others* [1996] ECR I-3547, para. 67 et seq.; ECJ 21 November 1991, C-354/90, *Fédération Nationale du Commerce Extérieur des Produits Alimentaires (FNCE) and* others [1991] ECR I-5505, para. 12.
[426] See also Art. 14(3) of Regulation No. 659/99.

national proceedings for the enforcement of claims under EU law may not be less favourable than proceedings in purely national matters. This way, **minimum standards** concerning the effective enforcement of claims based on Art. 108(3) TFEU (ex Art. 88(3) EC) are set for the procedural laws of the Member States.

Therefore, the application of the prohibition of implementation and the en- 421
suing recovery depends on the procedural rules and remedies in the respective Member State's legal order.[427] Nevertheless, effective protection of the direct effect of Art. 108(3) third sentence TFEU (ex Art. 88(3) third sentence EC) requires national courts to apply the prohibition of implementation "... without any possibility of its being excluded by rules of national law of any kind whatsoever ...".

The same holds for claims of individuals such as the **competitors** of the re- 422
cipient of State aid. According to the ECJ, the "national courts must offer to individuals in a position to rely on such breach [of the prohibition of implementation] the certain prospect that all the necessary inferences will be drawn, in accordance with their national law, as regards the validity of measures giving effect to the aid, the recovery of financial support granted in disregard of that provision and possible interim measures."[428] Thus, a competitor who is put in a worse position in comparison to the recipient of unlawful aid must be given the possibility to defend his rights conferred to him by the direct application of the prohibition of implementation. He should therefore be enabled under the national law of the respective Member State to enforce his claim and invoke the breach of Art. 108(3) TFEU (ex Art. 88(3) EC). Most Member States do not provide for such a competitor's claim. However, this cannot be used as an excuse not to grant the competitor his rights conferred to him by directly applicable EU law, given that EU law overrides conflicting national laws of the Member States.

This leads to the difficult question of the **relation between EU law and** 423
national procedural law. If national procedural laws do not provide for a basis for recovery or a competitor's claim at all or if they set special limitation periods for recovery, what influence does EU law have? Since the TFEU does not lay down specific rules for the procedural treatment of claims based on EU law, there are no detailed specifications for the Member States to take into account. As a general rule, one could say that national provisions may restrict recovery insofar as they still respect the effectiveness and equivalence imperative and do not render EU law practically impossible. However, at present, the situation is not entirely clear and is still being discussed among scholars.[429]

---

[427] ECJ 11 December 1973, 120/73, *Lorenz* [1973] ECR 1471, para. 8 et seq.

[428] ECJ 21 November 1991, C-354/90, *Fédération Nationale du Commerce Extérieur des Produits Alimentaires (FNCE) and others* [1991] ECR I-5505, para. 12.

[429] See Borgsmidt, *EC Tax Journal* 2001, p. 11 et seq.; Luja, *ET* 2005, p. 568 et seq.; Nicolaides/ Kekelekis/Buyskes, *State aid policy in the European Community: a guide for practitioners* (2005) p. 71 et seq.; Sutter, *Das EG-Beihilfenverbot und sein Durchführungsverbot in Steuersachen* (2005) p. 281 et seq.; Staringer, in Holoubek/Lang (eds.) *Abgabenverfahrensrecht und Gemeinschaftsrecht* (2006) p. 362 et seq.

424   Another question is whether already implemented measures that are later declared compatible with the common market by the Commission may be healed by its retroactive approval. If such a breach of the prohibition of the implementation can be healed by a positive final decision of the Commission, then the infringement of the notification procedure does not have any consequences. However, the ECJ has held that the implementation of unlawful State aid can **never be validated retroactively by a positive decision** of the Commission. The positive decision of the Commission on the compatibility of unnotified aid under Art. 108(3) TFEU (ex Art. 88(3) EC) is only applicable *pro futuro* ("deactivation of the prohibition of implementation") but cannot heal the illegality of the past.[430] In any case, the **details of the consequences of a** retroactive positive decision by the Commission are still heavily disputed among legal scholars in all Member States.[431]

425   In the *CELF* case, the ECJ made clear that the national court must in any case order the aid recipient to **pay interest** in respect of the period of unlawfulness. This way, the advantage gained by the premature receipt of the aid is neutralized.[432]

426   To summarize, only in the case of unlawful incompatible aid is the Commission obliged to provide for recovery from the Member State concerned. The **recovery decision** directly addresses the Member States, which have to ensure full recovery under their domestic procedural laws. When ordering the recovery of aid declared incompatible with the common market the Commission is not required to provide the exact amount that is to be recovered. It is sufficient for the decision to include enough information to enable the recipient to calculate the amount without too much difficulty.[433] In general, the recovery of aid also includes interest.

427   Nonetheless, there are **limitations to the recovery** of State aid. First, Art. 15 of Regulation 659/1999 provides that the Commission can only require recovery of unlawful and incompatible aid granted within a period of **ten years**. It is apparent from Art. 15(2) of Regulation 659/1999 that the limitation period does not begin to run until the day on which the unlawful aid is awarded to the beneficiary rather than the date on which the aid scheme was adopted.[434] However, any action taken by the Commission interrupts the limitation period, which then starts running afresh. Secondly, Art. 14 of Regulation 659/1999 provides that recovery does not have to take place if general principles of EU law, such as the **legitimate expectations** of the beneficiaries or the **legal certainty**, are con-

---

[430] ECJ 21 November 1991, C-354/90, *Fédération Nationale du Commerce Extérieur des Produits Alimentaires (FNCE) and others* [1991] ECR I-5505, para. 16; ECJ 21 October 2003, C-261/01, *van Calster* [2003] ECR I-12249, para. 63; ECJ 5 October 2006, C-368/04, *Transalpine Ölleitung* [2006] ECR I-9957, para. 41 et seq. and 54 et seq.

[431] See e.g. Vajda, *EC Tax Journal* 2001, p. 77 et seq.; Mamut/Paterno, *EStAL* 2009, p. 343 et seq.

[432] ECJ 12 February 2008, C-199/06, *CELF* [2008] ECR I-469, para. 55.

[433] ECJ 8 December 2011, C-81/10 P, *France Télécom SA* [2011] ECR I-0, para. 102.

[434] ECJ 8 December 2011, C-81/10 P, *France Télécom SA* [2011] ECR I-0, paras. 80–81.

cerned. Moreover, this is also the case if it is objectively **absolutely impossible** to recover the aid.[435] It should be noted that according to the ECJ undertakings to which aid has been granted may not entertain a legitimate expectation that the aid is lawful unless it has been granted in compliance with the procedure laid down in Art. 108 TFEU (ex Arts. 87 et seq. EC), since a diligent business operator should normally be able to determine whether that procedure has been followed.[436]

7. Overview of the Procedural Treatment of State Aid   428

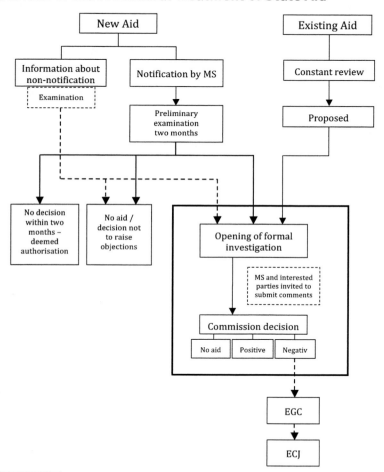

---

[435] ECJ 23 February 1995, C-349/93, *Italy v Commission* [1995] ECR I-343, para. 12; ECJ 4 April 1995, C-348/93, *Italy v Commission* [1995] ECR I-673, para. 16.

[436] Joined cases C-183/02 P and C-187/02 P Demesa and Territorio Historico de Alava [2004] ECR I-10609, paras 44–45; ECJ 8 December 2011, C-81/10 P, *France Télécom SA* [2011] ECR I-0, para. 59.

IV. The Parent-Subsidiary Directive

Mario Tenore

Legal Basis: Council Directive 2011/96/EU of 30 November 2011 on common system of taxation applicable in the case of parent companies and subsidiaries of Member States, *OJ L 225 of 20 August 1990, pp. 6–9.*

Literature: Schonewille, Some questions on the Parent-Subsidiary Directive and the Merger Directive, *Intertax* 1992, p. 14; Garcia Prats, Application of the Parent-Subsidiary to Permanent Establishment, *ET* 1995, p. 181; Helminen, *The Dividend Concept in International Tax Law* (1999); Brokelind, *Une interprétation de la directive sociétés mères et filiales du 23 juillet 1990* (2000); Da Camara, Parent-Subsidiary Directive: The Epson case, *ET* 2001, p. 307; Stavropoulos, ECJ: Greek Income Tax Provision is a Withholding Tax within the Meaning of the Parent-Subsidiary Directive, *ET* 2002, p. 94; Brokelind, The Proposed Amendments to the Parent-Subsidiary Directive: Some progress, *ET* 2003, p. 451; European Team of the IBFD, The Océ Van Der Grinten Case: Implications for other EU Member States, A critical assessment, *ET* 2003 p. 394; Maisto, The 2003 amendments to the EC Parent-Subsidiary Directive: What's next?, *EC Tax Review* 2004, p. 164; Zanotti, Taxation of Inter-Company Dividends in the Presence of a PE: The impact of EC Fundamental Freedoms (Part One), *ET* 2004, p. 493; Hausner, Source and Residence aspects in the amended parent subsidiary directive, in Aigner/Loukota (eds.) *Source Versus Residence in International Tax Law* (2005); Thömmes/Nakhai, Commentary on the Parent-Subsidiary Directive, in Thömmes/Fuks (eds.) *EC Corporate Tax Law* (loose leaf); Terra/Wattel, *European Tax Law* (2008); Tenore, Taxation of dividends: a comparison of selected issues under Article 10 OECD MC and the Parent-Subsidiary Directive, *Intertax* 2009, p. 222.

1. Aims of the Directive

429 Council Directive 2011/96/EU of 30 November 2011 (recast)[437] on the common system of taxation applicable in the case of parent companies and subsidiaries of Member States (hereinafter "the Directive") deals with the elimination of economic double taxation arising within a group of companies from **cross-border distributions of profits**.

430 The first preamble of the Directive affirms the need to create within the EU "conditions analogous to those of an internal market" and to "ensure the establishment and effective functioning of the common market ...". The third preamble recognizes the fact that – from a tax viewpoint – the **grouping of companies from different Member States** is often put at a disadvantage as compared to the grouping of companies resident in the same Member State. In most states, economic double taxation of dividends distributions was only relieved in purely domestic situations.

431 It follows therefore that its elimination was a necessary condition to achieve **neutral conditions** between internal groupings of companies, on the one hand, and cross-border groupings of companies, on the other hand.

432 The Directive provides – under certain conditions – an exemption from the withholding tax in the state of the subsidiary, as well as the obligation for the state of the parent company to **eliminate economic double taxation**. In particular, it relieves the two layers of tax levied in the hands of the parent company upon the distribution of profits, i.e. the withholding tax in the state of the subsidiary and the corporate tax levied in the hands of the parent company upon the profits so received in its state of residence.[438]

433 The first draft proposal of the Directive was delivered in 1969 and was afterwards subject to a number of amendments prior to the final approval. The Directive was finally **adopted in 1990**, together with the Merger Directive[439] and the Arbitration Convention.[440] The final version of the Directive departed from the

---

[437] The Directive recast Council Directive 90/435/EEC of 23 July 1990 without entailing any material amendment of the rules contained in this directive. The recast was necessary since Directive 90/435/EEC has been amended several times and further amendments may possibly be made in the future. The recast was also necessary (i) to update the Annexes to Directive 90/435/EEC and (ii) to redraft the wording of the second subparagraph of Article 4(3) of Directive 90/435/EEC, for the purpose of clarifying that the rules referred to therein are adopted by the Council acting in accordance with the procedure provided for in the TFUE.

[438] It follows that the income remains taxed only once in the hands of the subsidiary in its state of residence.

[439] Council Directive 90/434/EEC of 23 July 1990 on the Common system taxation applicable of mergers, divisions, partial divisions, transfers of assets and exchange of shares concerning companies of different Member States and to the transfer of the registered office, of an SE or SCE, between Member States.

[440] Convention 90/436 of 23 July 1990 on the elimination of double taxation in connection with the adjustment of profits of associated enterprises.

1969 draft proposal in at least two respects. First, whilst the 1969 Draft proposal envisaged the exemption method exclusively, the final version of the Directive left the Member States free to decide between the exemption and the indirect credit method in order to relieve economic double taxation. Second, the final version of the Directive contained no option for the parent company to consolidate the profits of the foreign subsidiary, with a view to making such a company comparable to a foreign permanent establishment.

In 2003 the Directive was substantially revised by the **amending Directive** **2003/123/EC** (hereinafter "the amending Directive") in order to deal with the practical problems that had meanwhile arisen since the early 1990s.[441] The amending Directive, which had to be implemented by 1 January 2005, has broadened *inter alia* the scope of the Directive by extending it to permanent establishments as well as to the SE.[442] There are no transitional rules that deal with the distribution of profits derived before the amendments became effective and distributed after 1 January 2005. However, the Directive should still apply due to the fact that its wording seems to give relevance exclusively to the time of the distribution. **434**

2. Subjective Scope

a) Definition of "Company of a Member State"

Art. 2 of the Directive provides for a definition of the terms "**company of a** **Member State**". The terms "company of a Member State" include any company that meets the following cumulative requirements: **435**

  (i) it takes one of the forms listed in the annex of the Directive;
 (ii) it resides for domestic tax purposes in a Member State; furthermore, under any double taxation convention concluded with non-EU Member States, such a company may not be regarded as resident in any of those states;
(iii) it is subject to one of the corporate taxes listed in Art. 2, without the possibility of an option or of being exempt.

Under (i) and (iii) the Directive adopts a **list-based approach**. The Annex to the Directive lists the legal forms; in respect of certain states the list includes, however, a residual entity clause that allows the application of the Directive to any company constituted under the law of such countries and is subject to corporate **436**

---

[441] The amendment of the Directive was also envisaged by the Commission in its Communication "Company Taxation in the Internal Market", COM(2001) 582 final, SEC (2001) 1681.

[442] The amending Directive also introduced other substantive changes in the 1990 version of the Directive, namely the gradual reduction to 10 % of the minimum holding threshold, the treatment of profits derived by subsidiary companies that are regarded as transparent for tax purposes in the state of the parent, and finally the abolition of transitional and special regimes.

tax therein.[443] Investment funds and pension funds are not listed, save a few exceptions.[444] In respect of certain states, the list also includes public and private entities that are subject to corporate tax and carry on business activities. In the *Gaz de France* case the Court pointed out the exhaustive nature of the list; accordingly, the application of the Directive may not be extended by analogy to other forms of company, even if these companies were later included by virtue of Directive 2003/123/EC of 22 December 2003.[445]

437   Art. 2 of the Directive lists the **types of corporate tax**. Such article also includes a residual clause, which refers "to any other tax which may be substituted for any of the above taxes". The condition under (ii) above requires the company to be resident in a Member State both under domestic and tax treaty law. Such a requirement prevents the application of the Directive even if a company is resident for domestic law purposes in a Member State but is considered to be a resident of a non-EU Member State under the tie-breaker rule contained in the double taxation convention concluded with such non-EU Member State.[446] It is not compulsory for a company to meet the three requirements in the same Member State.[447] The Directive also applies to companies that are constituted under the law of a certain Member State and are subject to corporate tax in a different Member State. The residual entity clauses provided in the Annex to the Directive, however, seem to support a more restrictive interpretation, according to which the company must be constituted under the law of a Member State and must be subject to corporate tax in that same state.

b) Definition of "Parent Company"

438   Art. 3(1)(a) defines the term "**parent company**" as a company that holds at least a 15 % stake in the capital of a company of another Member State; both companies must fulfil the requirement provided for in Art. 2. The participation in the latter company may also be held wholly or partially through a permanent establishment.[448]

439   The ECJ held in the *Les Vergers du Vieux Tauves SA* case that the concept of a holding in the capital of a company of another Member State does not include

---

[443] See the annex to Directive 90/435 and namely, letters a), b), c), d), e), f), i), j) and k).

[444] See letters p) and s) listing respectively the Netherlands "Fonds voor gemene rekening" and the Luxembourg "Association d'épargne pension". See Maisto, *EC Tax Review* 2004, p. 172.

[445] ECJ 1 October 2009, C-247/08, *Gaz de France* (not yet published).

[446] Art. 4(3) OECD MC provides for a tie-breaker rule that applies when a company is considered resident under domestic law of both Contracting States. In such a case, the provision states that the company must be regarded as resident only in the state in which its place of effective management is located.

[447] Terra/Wattel, *European Tax Law* (2008) p. 480.

[448] The scenario in which the participation is held through a permanent establishment will be dealt with in m.nos. 480 et seq.

the **holding of shares in usufruct**. The usufruct arrangement is not such as to endow the company receiving the dividends with the "status of shareholder", even if the usufruct holder were to be attributed the voting powers and would *de facto* not differ from a shareholder in this respect.[449]

As from 1 January 2009 such percentage will be further lowered to 10 %. It is **440** unclear whether the holding stake may be held indirectly, i.e. through an intermediate company.[450]

Art. 3(2) gives the Member States the opportunity to derogate twice to **441** Art. 3(1)(a). First, Member States may replace – by means of a bilateral agreement – the criterion of the 15 % holding in the capital of the subsidiary with that of the voting rights. Second, Member States may also render the application of the Directive subject to an **uninterrupted holding period** requirement of at least two years.

The first derogation takes into account the fact that many Member States do **442** make reference in their domestic law to the **voting rights requirement** whereas the second derogation is meant to prevent abusive constructions, such as securities lending schemes, aimed at obtaining the more favourable tax regime provided for in the Directive.

The **holding period requirement** may be relevant for both outgoing and in- **443** going flows of dividends, i.e. respectively for profits distributed to foreign parent companies and for profits received by domestic parent companies. Vice versa, it is possible for a Member State to set a holding period requirement exclusively for outgoing flows of profits or – alternatively – exclusively for ingoing flows of profits. Finally, it is even possible that a Member State may provide for different holding periods for outbound and for inbound distributions.[451]

The ECJ has clarified the application of the holding period requirement in **444** joined case **Denkavit-Vitic-Voormer**,[452] which involved cross-border dividend distributions from German subsidiaries to the Netherlands parent companies. In particular, the Netherlands parent companies were denied in Germany the ex-

---

[449] ECJ 22 December 2008, C-48/07, *Les Vergers du Vieux Tauves SA* [2008] ECR I-10627, para. 41.

[450] See Maisto, *EC Tax Review,* 2004, p. 176, according to whom indirect holdings should not be covered "due to the fact that the lowering of the minimum holding satisfied by itself the desire to broaden the scope of the Directive". A statement that seems to accept the relevance of indirect holdings can be found in the Commission Communication COM 2011(714) Final, Proposal for a Council Directive on a common system of taxation applicable to interest and royalty payments made between associated companies of different Member States, p. 8.

[451] It is, however, possible that, due to the existence of different holding requirements as well as different holding periods in the Member States, the Directive regime may be applicable solely in one state, e.g. the state of the subsidiary, and not in another state, i.e. the state of the parent. See Terra/Wattel, *European Tax Law* (2008) p. 484.

[452] ECJ 17 October 1996, joined cases C-283/94, C-291/94 and C-292/94, *Denkavit, VITIC and Voormer* [1996] ECR I-5063.

emption from withholding tax – provided for in Art. 5 – on the grounds that the dividends were paid before the 12-month holding period had expired.[453] According to the German tax authorities, a strict interpretation of the derogation provided in Art. 3(2) was supported by Art. 1(2), which safeguards the application of domestic or agreement-based provisions aimed at preventing fraud or abuse. The ECJ held, however, that such procedural issues were to be dealt with in domestic law and that, in addition, Member States could not be obliged to grant the exemption upon a unilateral undertaking of parent companies to observe the minimum holding requirement. However, the ECJ also held that a restrictive interpretation of Art. 3(2) would not be in line with both the wording and the legislative intention of the Directive. As a result, the ECJ concluded that the exemption from withholding tax had be granted in respect of profits distributed before the expiration of the 12-month period and that Member States were – among various options – allowed to grant such benefits retroactively.

c) Definition of "Subsidiary Company"

445 Art. 3(2)(b) defines the term "**subsidiary company**" having reference to the company the capital of which the holding of the "parent" as defined in Art. 3(2) (a) is included. The amending Directive has introduced Art. 4(1)(a) in order to clarify that when the state of the parent company considers the subsidiary transparent for tax purposes "on the basis of that State's assessment of the legal characteristics of that subsidiary arising from the law under which it is constituted ...", this state is nevertheless obliged to eliminate economic double taxation when taxing the profits when they arise and to regard as irrelevant for tax purposes the subsequent distribution of profits.

446 Art. 4(1)(a) eliminates therefore any possibility of economic double taxation, which could **temporarily** persist due to the fact that taxation of profits when they arise occurs prior to the time of the actual distribution of dividends.[454] The Directive does not provide any rule concerning the case in which the parent company is regarded as transparent under the domestic law of the subsidiary.

d) Definition of "Permanent Establishment"

447 The amending Directive included a definition of the term "**permanent establishment**", which was needed in the light of the broader scope of the Directive. The term "permanent establishment" is defined in Art. 2(2) as "a fixed place of business situated in a Member State through which the business of a company of another Member State is wholly or partly carried on ...".

---

[453] At that time, most Member States, except for Austria and the Netherlands, granted the benefits of the Directive as from the expiration of the 12-month period.

[454] This result was achieved by the domestic law of most states even prior to the addition of Art. 4(1)(a) in the Directive. See Maisto, *EC Tax Review,* 2004, p. 175.

The definition of Art. 2(2) does refer to what is known as the **material permanent establishment**, defined in Art. 5(1) OECD MC. Moreover, such a definition requires the profits of permanent establishment to be subject to tax in the Member State where such permanent establishment is located both under domestic and treaty law. The Directive does not envisage other types of permanent establishment provided for in Art. 5 OECD MC, such as the agency permanent establishment or the construction permanent establishment dealt with in Art. 5(5) and Art. 5(3), respectively, of the OECD MC. **448**

3. Objective and Territorial Scope

The analysis of the **objective scope** of the Directive will be divided in three main parts. The first part deals with the interpretation of the terms "distribution of profits" and "distributed profits". The second and the third part contribute to defining the objective and **territorial scope** of the Directive. In particular, the second part deals with a plain-vanilla bilateral situation, involving a qualifying parent company and its subsidiary. This situation will be analysed by taking into separate account the perspective of the two states involved, i.e. the parent company state and the subsidiary state. The third part deals with situations involving the presence of a permanent establishment – located in a state other than that of the subsidiary – to which the distributed profits are attributable. **449**

a) The Terms "Distribution of Profits" and "Distributed Profits"

The Directive uses the terms **"distribution of profits"** and **"profits distributed"** in Art. 1(1) and Art. 4(1), respectively, instead of making reference to the term "dividends". The terms "distribution of profits" and "profits distributed", however, are not defined in those provisions or elsewhere in the Directive. One must therefore wonder whether the terms have to be interpreted according to the domestic law of the Member States, or vice versa, and whether they should be given an autonomous interpretation regardless of any domestic law meaning. The latter interpretation must prevail, although it would not be possible to depart entirely from the characterization of the income under domestic law, which determines whether certain items of income are taxable or not.[455] **450**

The terms "distribution of profits" and "profits distributed" have a **broader scope** than the term "dividends". It has been argued that the term includes any kind of transfers of benefits – without consideration – from a qualifying subsidiary, resident in a Member State, to its qualifying parent company, resident in another Member State.[456] It has been argued that the Directive applies also to deemed distributions of profits such as those resulting from the application of thin capitalization rules, as well as those resulting from the application of trans- **451**

---

[455] Helminen, *The Dividend Concept in International Tax Law* (1999) p. 74.
[456] Helminen, *The Dividend Concept in International Tax Law* (1999) p. 74.

fer pricing rules. Such an extensive interpretation of the Directive seems therefore in line with its main goal, i.e. the elimination of economic double taxation.[457] On the other hand, one may argue that this interpretation contrasts with the *Les Vergers du Vieux Tauves SA* decision where the ECJ emphasized the existence of the shareholder status in the hands of the parent company.

452 The Directive is silent in the case of **disagreements** between the Member States concerning the characterization of certain types of income as profits distributed within the meaning of either Art. 4 or Art. 5 of the Directive.[458] In these cases, it is not possible, however, to exclude in advance the relevance of the EU Arbitration Convention.

453 In all such cases concerning **deemed distributions of profits**, it is necessary to distinguish the situations in which the parent company has a qualifying holding in the capital of the subsidiary from situations in which no such holding exists.[459] Such a distinction appears relevant for the purpose of applying Art. 4 and Art. 5 of the Directive, which deal with the elimination of economic double taxation in the state of the parent company and with the exemption from withholding tax in the state of the subsidiary, respectively.

454 Unlike Art. 5, Art. 4 of the Directive makes reference to the terms "**by virtue of association**", making it explicit that benefits provided by reason thereof are granted to the extent the qualifying parent company has holding stake in the capital of the qualifying subsidiary. It has been argued that the absence of such holding stake would render the Directive binding exclusively for the state of the subsidiary.[460]

455 However since the above *Les Vergers du Vieux Tauves SA* case, this position no longer has merit: the ECJ has indeed held that the application of the Directive requires a holding relationship between the companies involved. As a result, the benefits of the Directive should no longer be available with respect to deemed distributions of dividends or similar cases, at least insofar as this condition is not met (e.g. secondary transfer pricing adjustments between sister companies).[461]

b) Application of the Directive in the State of the Parent Company

456 In defining the objective scope of the Directive, Art. 1, first dash includes "distribution of profits **received by companies** which come from their subsidiaries of other Member States". Art. 1, first dash must be read together with Art. 4 and Art. 6, which impose two distinct obligations on the Member State of the parent company. Art. 4 affirms the obligation for the state of the parent company to

---

[457] Helminen, *The Dividend Concept in International Tax Law* (1999) p. 74.

[458] Thömmes/Nakhai, in Thömmes/Fuks (eds.) *EC Corporate Tax Law* (loose leaf) p. 26.

[459] Thömmes/Nakhai, in Thömmes/Fuks (eds.) *EC Corporate Tax Law* (loose leaf) p. 25.

[460] It has been argued that such an interpretation would allow the application of Art. 5 of the Directive to deemed distributions of profits, resulting from the transfer pricing adjustments operated between sister companies. See Maisto, *EC Tax Review,* 2004, p. 177.

[461] See Tenore, Taxation of dividends: a comparison of selected issues under Article 10 OECD MC and the Parent-Subsidiary Directive, *Intertax* 2009, in print.

eliminate economic double taxation arising in respect of such an inbound distribution profits, except for the case in which such profits result from the liquidation of the subsidiary.

In particular, the state of the parent company must **exempt** the profits received by the parent or, vice versa, must tax such profits while granting a **tax credit for the corporate tax** paid by the subsidiary and any lower-tier subsidiary, insofar as, in each tier, the requirements set out in Art. 2 and Art. 3 are fulfilled.[462] Art. 6 of the Directive prevents the Member State of the parent company from charging a withholding tax on the profits received by such a company. **457**

The Directive leaves the Member States free to decide between the exemption method and the credit method, depending on the **fiscal policy** pursued by the Member State concerned.[463] It is possible for a Member State to **adopt both methods** depending on the specific circumstances. For example, notwithstanding the application of the exemption method to inbound distributions of profits, the state of residence might be obliged to grant an indirect credit method, upon option of the parent company, whenever the double tax convention signed with state of the subsidiary explicitly provides for such a method. The same holds true whenever the application of the indirect credit method is envisaged in the domestic law of the Member State of the parent company. Such an obligation for the Member State of the parent company stems directly from Art. 7(2) of the Directive, which provides that "The Directive shall not affect the application of domestic or agreement-based provisions designed to eliminate or lessen economic double taxation of dividends ...". It is doubtful whether the same provision would allow the parent company to opt for the application of the exemption method, provided in domestic law or in a double tax convention, whenever the Member State has implemented the Directive by opting for the application of an indirect tax credit. **458**

Member States must **exercise the choice** between the exemption method and the credit method in a way that complies with **primary law**. In this respect, they may not disregard the method aimed at relieving economic double taxation in purely internal situations. The issue was touched upon in the *FII Group Litigation* **459**

---

[462] On 22 September 2011 the Economic and Monetary Affairs (ECON) Committee in the European Parliament issued a report on the recast of the Parent-Subsidiary-Directive proposing a minimum taxation requirement. According to this proposed amendment, the State of the parent company (or where the PE that receives the "distributed profits" is located) should refrain from taxing such profits only if they have been taxed in the country of the subsidiary at a corporate tax rate not lower than 70% of the average corporate tax rate in the EU, or should tax these profits at a corporate tax rate of not lower than 70% of the EU average corporate tax rate (i.e. 16% that amounts to 70% of the profits being taxed at the average EU corporate tax rate of 23.2%), while allowing a deduction of the tax paid in the State of the distributing subsidiary. This measure was meant to avoid the shifting of income to low-tax jurisdictions but it was ultimately rejected by the Council.

[463] In particular, the exemption method will achieve capital import neutrality (CIN) whereas the credit method will achieve capital export neutrality (CEN). See Terra/Wattel, *European Tax Law* (2008) p. 169.

case,[464] where the ECJ was confronted with the question of the compatibility with the EU law of the indirect credit system, applicable in cross-border situations, when domestic distributions of dividends were exempt from tax. The ECJ affirmed that the UK indirect credit system did not breach EU law insofar as the following conditions were met: (i) the tax rate applicable to inbound dividends could not be higher than that applicable to domestic distributions and (ii) the credit given in the residence state of the parent company had to be limited to the lower of the corporate tax paid by the subsidiary in its state of residence and the tax that levied in the state of the parent company upon a domestic subsidiary.

i. The Indirect Credit Method

460   Should the state of residence of the parent company opt for the **indirect credit method**, it will be obliged to allow a deduction – from the taxes due by such company – of the lower amount between the corporate tax paid by the subsidiary in its state of residence and the corporate tax, which would be levied in the case of purely internal distributions of profits.

461   The Member State of the parent company has the obligation to extend such a credit to corporate tax paid by **any lower subsidiary**, provided that the company can be regarded as "company of a Member State" and as "subsidiary" under Art. 2 and Art. 3 of the Directive, respectively. In particular, the minimum holding threshold will have to be satisfied by each subsidiary having regard exclusively to its holding stake in the capital of the lower-tier subsidiary.

462   The **extension of the indirect tax credit** to corporate tax paid by the lower-tier subsidiaries prevents economic double taxation, which would otherwise arise due to the fact that both the exemption method and the credit method may apply. For example, where a Member State (MS A) exempted the inbound distribution of profits received by a company resident therein from its subsidiary resident in another Member State (MS B), economic double taxation would not be eliminated should the former company pay the dividends on to its parent company resident in a third Member State (MS C), which relieves economic double taxation by means of the indirect credit method. Due to the exemption applicable in the former Member State (MS A), there would be no foreign corporate tax to offset the tax liability of the parent company resident in MS C.[465]

463   With respect to the indirect foreign tax credit, the Directive is silent on the **procedural and administrative issues** that could arise, such as the tracing of the profits distributed along the chain of companies. Neither does the Directive contain any guidance concerning the use of the excess foreign tax credit, which might arise for example when the foreign corporate tax rate is higher than the domestic one. All these issues are to be dealt with in domestic law of the Member States.

---

[464] ECJ 12 December 2006, C-446/04, *Test Claimants in the FII Group Litigation* [2006] ECR I-11753.

[465] Terra/Wattel, *European Tax Law* (2008) pp. 490-491.

ii. Tax Treatment of Charges Connected to the Holding in the Subsidiary

Art. 4(2), first dash provides the option for the Member States to deny the deduc- **464**
tion of any **charges or losses** connected to the distribution of profits. The second
part of the same provision, however, provides that whenever **management
charges** are determined by virtue of a flat rate, the amount so determined may
not exceed 5 % of the profits distributed by the subsidiary. Depending on whether
the state of the parent company exempts the inbound distribution of profits or
grants an underlying foreign tax credit, this state will accordingly reduce either
the amount of the profits exempted therein or the foreign dividends for the purpose of calculating the amount of the underlying foreign tax credit, by the same
percentage, i.e. 5 %.

With regard to the "dividend exemption" system under Art. 4.1 of the Direc- **465**
tive, the ECJ held in the *Cobelfret* case[466] that the rule is sufficiently clear and unconditional; therefore, it does not need to be implemented in domestic law and taxpayers may rely on this provision directly before national courts. In addition, the
Court upheld that the Belgian dividends deduction system was not compatible
with the aforesaid provision since it reduced the losses of the parent company,
thus leading to a *de facto* taxation of the foreign dividends.[467]

Art. 4(2) is **not worded in a clear way**.[468] Its first part makes reference to **466**
"any charges relating to the holding and any losses resulting from the distribution of the profits ...". Its second part refers to "management costs" only. It is
therefore clear that this second part, and the 5 % threshold it contains, is not relevant in the case of losses resulting from the distribution of profits. It is still
doubtful, however, whether this second part is strictly limited to "management
costs" or, vice versa, whether it also applies to other costs, such as interest expenses deriving from the loan taken out to finance the purchase of the holding.
A broad interpretation of Art. 4(2), second part can be derived from the *Bosal
Holding* case,[469] where the ECJ implicitly admitted the possibility for the Member
States to limit the deduction of interest expenses as a result of the exercise of the
option granted to such states in Art. 4(2).

In particular, the ECJ clarified in the **Bosal Holding** case that Member States **467**
are obliged to exercise the option provided for in Art. 4(2) in a way that complies

---

[466] ECJ 12 February 2009, C-138/07, *Cobelfret* [2009] ECR I-00731.

[467] In particular, according to the Belgian rules, dividends are first included in the company's
taxable income of the year. Afterwards, 95 % of their amount is deducted from the taxable
base (so-called Dividends-Received Deduction or DRD). This means that no DRD was
available to the extent that the company's taxable income, including the dividends received,
was lower than the DRD. This was the case e.g. if the parent company incurred operating
losses, which were reduced by the dividends received, thus leading to a de facto taxation of
the dividends. On the same issue, see also ECJ 4 June 2009, joined cases C-439/07 and
C-499/07, *KBC Bank NV* (not yet published).

[468] Brokelind, *ET* 2003, p. 455.

[469] ECJ 18 September 2003, C-168/01, *Bosal Holding* [2003] ECR I-9409.

with the fundamental freedoms.[470] It follows that a Member State would no longer be allowed to exercise the option, and accordingly to limit the deduction of expenses incurred with respect to holdings in companies resident in other Member States, insofar as such a limitation does not apply in purely domestic situations. Neither would the fact that inbound dividends are exempt – whereas domestic distributions are taxed – justify a different treatment of the costs connected to the holding.

468   In the *Banque Fédérative du Crédit Mutuel* case the ECJ held that Art. 4 of the Directive does not preclude the inclusion of tax credits – related to foreign withholding taxes applicable in some Member States during the transitional periods – in the fixed amount of the management costs relating to the holding of the parent company in the subsidiary.[471]

c) Application of the Directive in the State of the Subsidiary company

i. Exemption of Outbound Dividends

469   Art. 1, second dash includes in the objective scope of the Directive – amongst others – the **distributions of profits by subsidiary companies** in favour of their parent companies resident in other Member States. This provision must be read together with Art. 5 of the Directive, which contains the obligation for the Member State of the subsidiary to exempt such a distribution of profits from withholding tax.[472]

470   Such rules align the taxation of dividends in the state of the subsidiary to that of capital gains derived from the alienation of participations, normally also exempt from tax in under the provisions of Art. 13(5) OECD MC. By **exempting distributions of profits from withholding tax**, the Directive forbids the state of the subsidiary to collect a second layer of tax, in addition to corporate taxes levied in the hands of the subsidiary itself, thus preventing economic double taxation.[473]

471   Currently, **Estonia** is the only Member State that is allowed – till 31 December 2008 – to levy a withholding tax on outbound distributions of profits. The derogation is due to the fact that Estonian companies are not subject to corporate tax till the moment the income is distributed to shareholders.

---

[470] ECJ 18 September 2003, C-168/01, *Bosal Holding* [2003] ECR I-9409, para. 26.

[471] ECJ 3 April 2008, C-27/07, *Banque Fédérative du Crédit Mutuel* [2007] ECR I-02067.

[472] Art. 5 of the Directive was substantially revised by the 2003 Amending Directive, which eliminated the reference to a minimum holding threshold of 25 %, which had to be met by the parent in order to claim the exemption from withholding tax in the state of the subsidiary. It must be remarked that in the absence of the qualifying requirements for the withholding tax exemption the State of the subsidiary is nonetheless still obliged to apply its domestic law in a non-discriminatory manner. See ECJ 18 June 2009, C-303/07, *Aberdeen Property* (not yet published) para. 76.

[473] As we have seen in m.nos. 456 et seq., the state of the parent will be obliged either to exempt or to grant an in direct foreign tax credit.

The Directive is silent in respect of the **procedural issues** concerning the application of the exemption from withholding tax in the state of the subsidiary. In particular, Art. 5 of the Directive does not affirm explicitly whether such a state is obliged to the exempt the distribution of profits at the time of the payment, or vice versa, whether it is allowed to levy a withholding tax at the time of the actual distribution – according to domestic and tax treaty law – although it is under an obligation to refund the taxes so levied upon application of the parent company. Just like the procedural issues arising in respect of the holding period, such issues are also to be dealt with in the domestic law of the Member States concerned. However, Member States must still comply with the fundamental freedoms, not imposing more burdensome or stricter requirements for the parent company to obtain exemption from the withholding tax. **472**

ii. Definition of "Withholding Tax"

Neither in Art. 5 nor elsewhere in the Directive is it possible to find a **definition of withholding tax**.[474] The uncertainty resulting from the absence of such a definition has resulted in three cases brought before the ECJ, namely the *Epson* case,[475] the *Athinaiki Zithopiia* case[476] and the *Océ Van Der Grinten* case.[477] **473**

The *Epson* case dealt with the compatibility with Art. 5 of the Directive of Portuguese succession and donation tax, which was applicable in respect of transfers, without consideration, of shares in companies. This tax was levied upon the payment of dividends by companies having their seat in Portugal. It was collected in addition to the withholding tax, which Portugal was temporarily allowed to impose because of the transitional regime in Art. 5(4) that was included in the Directive before the 2003 amendments. The ECJ considered the Portuguese succession and donation tax as a withholding tax by regarding as immaterial the fact that it was called "succession and donation tax". The ECJ held that such a tax had in fact the same effect as a tax on income as it was being levied upon distributions of dividends, it was determined on the basis of income derived from the owning of shares and finally it was collected in hands of the holders of such shares.[478] **474**

The *Athinaiki Zithopiia* case concerned compensatory tax charges applicable in Greece upon the distribution of dividends in the hands of Greek subsidiaries, insofar as such dividends were distributed out of exempt income or income taxed under a more favourable regime. The ECJ took a very substantive approach by assimilating such compensatory tax charges to a withholding tax, despite the fact that they were levied on the subsidiary.[479] The Court considered decisive the fact that such tax was levied upon the payment of dividends and was **475**

---

[474] The term "withholding tax" is also found in Art. 6 of the Directive.
[475] ECJ 8 June 2000, C-375/98, *Epson* [2000] ECR I-4243.
[476] ECJ 4 October 2001, C-294/99, *Athinaiki Zithopiia* [2001] ECR I-6797.
[477] ECJ 25 September 2003, C-58/01, *Océ Van Der Grinten* [2003] ECR I-9809.
[478] Da Camara, *ET* 2001, p. 309.
[479] Stavropoulos, *ET* 2002, p. 97.

determined by reference to the size of the distribution. Finally, the Court dismissed the argument of the Greek Government, according to which these compensatory tax charges were authorized by Art. 7(2) of the Directive, as they were intended to eliminate or lessen economic double taxation. According to the ECJ, however, this was not the case because in fact economic double taxation resulted directly from the application of the charges themselves.

476   In the *Océ Van Der Grinten* case the ECJ endorsed the application of a withholding tax on the repayment of the underlying tax credit, to which Dutch shareholders of UK companies were entitled to under Art. 10(3) of the UK–Netherlands double tax convention. According to the ECJ, the application of a withholding tax on the repayment of the tax credit could not be assimilated to the application of withholding tax on distributed profits.[480]

477   In the light of the previous case law, the ECJ held that, in order to regard a tax on income levied in the State of the subsidiary as a "withholding tax" forbidden under Art. 5 of the Directive, three conditions must be cumulatively met.[481] In particular, the Court held that any tax on income received in the State in which dividends are distributed is a withholding tax on distributed profits where (i) the chargeable event for the tax is the payment of dividends or of any other income from shares, (ii) the taxable amount is the income from those shares and (iii) the taxable person is the holder of the shares.[482]

478   The case law above shows the tendency of the ECJ to prefer a **substance-over-form approach** in defining the term "withholding tax".[483] The term is in fact interpreted "autonomously", i.e. regardless of any definition contained in the domestic law of the Member States. In this respect, the ECJ has echoed the settled case law according to which "the nature of a tax, duty or charge must be determined by the Court, under Community law, according to the objective characteristics by which it is levied, irrespective of its classification under national law".

d) Application of the Directive to Permanent Establishments

479 Art. 1, third and fourth dash deals with:

- distributions of profits **received by permanent establishments** located in a state other than that of the subsidiary (third dash) and
- distribution of profits by subsidiary companies to permanent establishments located in another Member State and belonging to parent companies resident

---

[480] European Team of the IBFD, *ET* 2003, p. 396.

[481] ECJ 26 June 2008, C-284/06, *Burda* [2008] I-00170.

[482] ECJ 8 June 2000, C-375/98, *Epson* [2000] ECR I-4243, para. 23; ECJ 4 October 2001, C-294/99, *Athinaiki Zithopiia* [2001] ECR I-6797, paras. 28 and 29; ECJ 25 September 2003, 58/01, *Océ Van Der Grinten* [2003] ECR I-9809, para. 47; ECJ 24 June 2010, *joined cases C-338/08 – C-339/08, P. Ferrero e C. SpA v Agenzia delle Entrate – Ufficio di Alba (C-338/08) and General Beverage Europe BV v Agenzia delle Entrate – Ufficio di Torino 1 (C-339/08)* [2011] ECR I-05743, para. 26.

[483] Terra/Wattel, *European Tax Law* (2008) p. 503.

in a Member State, **whether or not resident** in the same Member State of the distributing subsidiary (fourth dash).

The **third dash** indeed requires the Member State of the permanent establishment – receiving the distribution of profits – to treat it like a parent company, thus either exempting or granting a tax credit according to Art. 4 of the Directive.[484] As argued by tax scholars, such a rule is a clarification of the principles deriving from the *Saint-Gobain* decision.[485] In particular, the third dash deals with a triangular situation, i.e. a situation involving three Member States, namely the Member State of the parent company, the Member State of the subsidiary and the Member State of the permanent establishment. In this case, (i) the Member State of the subsidiary is obliged to exempt from withholding tax the profits distributed by a company resident therein under Art. 1, second dash and Art. 5 of the Directive (ii) the Member State of the parent company is obliged to eliminate economic double taxation under Art. 1, first dash and Art. 5 of the Directive and finally (iii) also the Member State of the permanent establishment is obliged to eliminate economic double taxation according to the applicable method whenever the profits are received by resident parent companies. Such a result stems from the combined reading of Art. 1, first dash and Art. 4 of the Directive.

480

The **fourth dash** deals with a bilateral situation, in which the parent and the subsidiary are resident in the same Member State whereas the permanent establishment is resident in another Member State.[486] It was uncertain whether prior to the 2003 amendments this situation was covered by the Directive.[487] The main argument against the application of the Directive was the absence of a cross-border distribution of profits, as the parent company resides in the same state as the subsidiary.[488] However, one should take into account that the profits are also taxed in the permanent establishment state, as they are attributed to a permanent establishment therein. The application of the Directive in such a situation is therefore in line with its general aim, i.e. the elimination of economic double taxation. In particular, the permanent establishment state would be required to

481

---

[484] Should the permanent establishment belong to a non-EU parent, the Directive would no longer apply.

[485] For some Member States, which had meanwhile aligned their domestic law to the *Saint-Gobain* decision, the addition of such a third dash did not require any further amendment of the domestic law. See Maisto, *EC Tax Review* 2004, p. 166; Zanotti, *ET* 2004, p. 504; Thömmes, in Thömmes/Fuks (eds.) *EC Corporate Tax* Law (loose leaf) p. 32.

[486] Should the permanent establishment be located in a non-EU Member State, the Directive would no longer apply.

[487] Maisto, *EC Tax Review* 2004, p. 167; Zanotti, *ET* 2004, p. 505; Hausner, in Aigner/Loukota (eds.) *Source Versus Residence in International Tax Law* (2005) p. 496.

[488] Also in this case it could be argued that the denial of the application of the Directive in the state of source would hinder the freedom of establishment of the parent, which would be obliged to exercise such freedom by setting up a company instead of a permanent establishment. As for the state of the permanent establishment, once again the *Saint Gobain* decision would require such a state to treat it like a parent resident therein.

eliminate economic double taxation, as a result of Art. 1, fourth dash and Art. 4, whereas the state of the subsidiary will be required to exempt the distribution, according to Art. 1, fourth dash and Art. 5 of the Directive.

482   Two more **cases not covered by the 2003 amendments**, although still involving the presence of a permanent establishment, need to be analysed. First, one could wonder whether the Directive applies in case the permanent establishment is located in the same Member State as the subsidiary while the parent company is resident in another Member State. In such a scenario the distribution of profits would still be taxable in both the Member State of the subsidiary – which is also the state where the permanent establishment is located – and the Member State of the parent company.[489] As for the application of the Directive, different positions have been argued in the tax literature. According to some scholars, this scenario would fall outside the scope of the Directive, i.e. neither the state of the subsidiary would be obliged to exempt the profits nor would the state of the parent company be required to eliminate economic double taxation.[490] According to others, the Directive would only bind the state of the parent company to eliminate economic double taxation according to Art. 4.[491] Some others argue that the Directive would bind the state of the parent company and would prevent the state of the subsidiary from levying a withholding tax on the dividends. However, the latter state would not be prevented from taxing the dividends when received by the permanent establishment, according to domestic and tax treaty rules.[492] Finally, others argue that such a scenario should be dealt with under domestic law as suggested in Recital no. 8 of the amending Directive.[493]

483   Second, one could wonder whether the presence of a permanent establishment in a non-EU Member State is covered by the application of the Directive. Certainly, the definition of permanent establishment contained in Art. 2 makes reference exclusively to permanent establishments "situated in a Member State". Even though there are no specific provisions in this respect, the Directive should apply since the profits are still being distributed by a subsidiary resident in a Member State (Art. 4(1), second dash) and are still received by a company of a parent company resident in another Member State (Art. 4(1), first dash). The fact that the profits are attributable to a permanent establishment located in a non-EU Member State should therefore be immaterial.[494]

---

[489] According to the tax treaty between such two states, if any and if similar to the OECD MC, the dividends will be taxed in the subsidiary state (or the permanent establishment state) according to Art. 7(1) second dash. The state of the parent will have to grant double taxation relief according to Art. 23 OECD MC.

[490] Maisto, *EC Tax Review* 2004, p. 167.

[491] Garcia Prats, *ET* 1995, p. 181.

[492] Terra/Wattel, *European Tax Law* (2008) p. 481.

[493] Thömmes/Nakhai, in Thömmes/Fuks (eds.) *EC Corporate Tax Law* (loose leaf) p. 34.

[494] In such a case the Interest and Royalty Directive would not be applicable.

e) Overview of the Scope of the Directive (Art. 1)

484

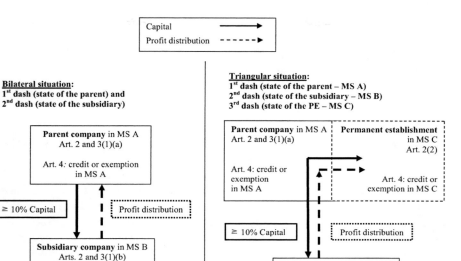

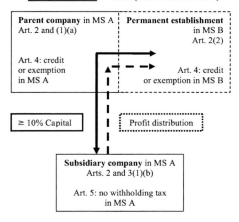

4. Abuse

485   Art. 1(2) of the Directive allows the application of domestic and agreement-based provisions aimed at preventing **"fraud or abuse"**. The wording of the provision very much echoes Art. 5(1) of the Interest and Royalty Directive. Art. 1(2) deals with both provisions existing before the date of the Directive's entry into force and provisions enacted after that date.

486   There is **no ECJ case law concerning the interpretation** of Art. 1(2), or on the interpretation of Art. 5(1). One must therefore wonder whether the case law on Art. 11 of the Merger Directive may apply, despite the difference in the wording.[495] In addition, one must furthermore wonder whether the case law of the ECJ concerning the prevention of abusive transactions would contribute to providing an interpretation of Art. 1(2) of the Directive.

487   There are no valid reasons to apply different standards for interpreting abuse under primary and secondary law. If this is true, one has to come to the conclusion that abuse should be given an **autonomous meaning**, i.e. regardless of whether the taxpayer intends to abuse a fundamental freedom, secondary legislation or a Member State's domestic law.[496] In this respect, any anti-abuse measure must allow the taxpayer to give evidence of the fact that a scheme or operation was not put in place for the purpose of benefiting from the more favourable regime of the Directive. In addition, the application of such anti-abuse measures must result from a case-by-case evaluation of the facts, whose findings must be subject to judicial review.[497] Finally, if the Member State does not make use of the option granted in Art. 1(2), the application of domestic law provisions or general principles – aimed at preventing the abuse of rights – or other provisions on tax evasion or tax avoidance should be taken into account.

488   Directive shopping is often based on the **interposition of a parent company** in an EU Member State in order to obtain the benefits of the Directive in situations that would otherwise fall outside its personal scope, i.e. distributions of profits to individual shareholders and distributions of profits to parent companies resident in a non-EU Member State.

---

[495] See Chapter V, m.nos. 520 et seq.
[496] See Chapter II, m.nos. 237 et seq.
[497] ECJ 17 July 1997, C-28/95, *Leur-Bloem* [1997] ECR I-4161, para. 44.

5. Overview of the Functioning of the Directive

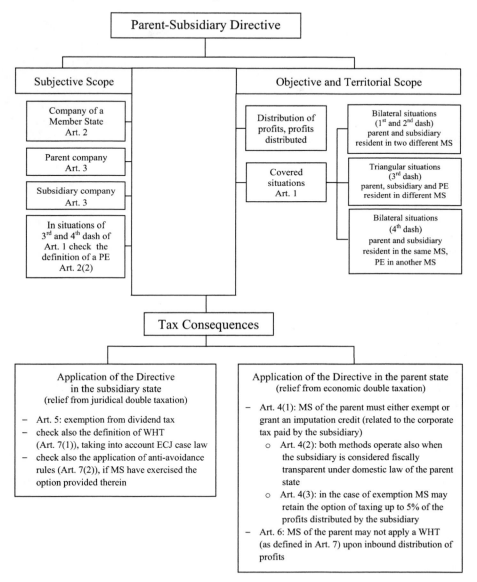

6. The Relationship with Double Tax Conventions

490   The application of the Directive prevails over domestic and tax treaty law. Art. 7(2), however, contains a derogation to this principle, where it is provided that the Directive may not affect the application of domestic or agreement-based **provisions aimed at eliminating or lessening economic double** taxation, such as the repayment of an indirect tax credit to foreign shareholders.[498]

491   Should the tax treatment of the distributed profits be **more favourable** under the regime provided for in a double tax convention, or eventually under that provided under domestic law, then parent companies may opt for the application of either regime instead of that provided for in the Directive.

---

[498] Usually, states adopting an imputation system only provide for an indirect tax credit in purely domestic dividend distributions. However, such states may exceptionally extend such tax credits to foreign shareholders, whether or not reciprocally, through a double tax convention.

V. The Merger Directive

Matthias Hofstätter/Daniela Hohenwarter-Mayr

Legal Basis: Council Directive 2009/133/EC of 19 October 2009 on the common system of taxation applicable to mergers, divisions, partial divisions, transfers of assets and exchanges of shares concerning companies of different Member States and to the transfer of the registered office of an SE or SCE between Member States (codified version), OJ L 310 of 25 November 2009.

Literature: Bezzina, The Treatment of Losses under the EC Merger Directive 1990, *ET* 2002, p. 57; Vinther/Werlauff, Community Law and the Independent Business as Interpreted by the ECJ in Andersen & Jensen *ApS*, *ET* 2002, p. 441; Schön, Tax Issues and Constraints on Reorganizations and Reincorporations in the European Union, *TNI* 2004, p. 197; Thömmes, EC Law Aspects of the Transfer of Seat of an SE, *ET* 2004, p. 22; Thömmes, Commentary on the Merger Directive, in Thömmes/Fuks (eds.) *EC Corporate Tax Law*, 28th suppl. (December 2004); Benecke, Vereinbarkeit der sogenannte doppelten Buchwertverknüpfung über die Grenze mit den Bestimmungen der Fusionsrichtlinie, *IStR* 2005, p. 283; Benecke/Schnitger, Final Amendments to the Merger Directive: Avoidance of Economic Double Taxation and Application to Hybrid Entities, Two Conflicting Goals, *Intertax* 2005, p. 170; Hofstätter, Änderungen der Fusionsrichtlinie, *ecolex* 2005, p. 824; Hofstätter, Internationale Einbringungen nach dem AbgÄG 2005 – Teil II: DBA- und Gemeinschaftsrechtliche Betrachtung, *RdW* 2006, p. 725; Kofler/Schindler, Grenzüberschreitende Umgründungen unter Beteiligung hybrider Gesellschaften, *SWI* 2006, p. 262; Russo/Offermanns, The 2005 Amendments to the EC Merger Directive, *ET* 2006, p. 250; Sørensen, Pending Cases Filed by Danish Courts: The Kofoed Case, in Lang/Schuch/Staringer (eds.) *ECJ – Recent Developments in Direct Taxation 2007* (2007) p. 23; Zalasinski, Case-Law-Based Anti-Avoidance Measures in Conflict with the Proportionality Test – Comment on the ECJ Decision in Kofoed, *ET* 2007, p. 571; Petkevica, The Concept of a "Branch of Activity" in the EC Merger Directive and Issues regarding its implementation in Portugal, *ET* 2008, p. 84; Furherr/Huber (eds.) *Internationale Umgründungen nach der Fusionsbesteuerungsrichtlinie* (2009); Hohenwarter, *Verlustverwertung im Konzern* (2009); Dourado/Pistone, Looking Beyond *Cartesio*: Reconciliatory Interpretation as a Tool to Remove Tax Obstacles on the Primary Right of Establishment by Companies and other Legal Entities, *Intertax* 2009, p. 342; Gusmeroli, The Conversion of a Branch into a Subsidiary under the EC Merger Directive: Still "Rarely Pure and Never Simple", *ET* 2009, p. 567; Helminen, *EU tax law* (2009); *Survey of the implementation of Council Directive 90/434/EEC (The Merger Directive, as amended)*, http://ec.europa.eu/taxation_customs/resources/documents/taxation/company_tax/mergers_directive/study_impl_direct.pdf; Lozev, Survey of Implementation of the EC Merger Directive – A Summary with Comments, *ET* 2010, p. 84; Petrosovitch, Abuse under the Merger Directive, *ET* 2010, p. 558; Helminen, Must EU Merger Directive Benefits Be Made Available where EEA States are involved?, *ET* 2011, p. 179; Helminen, Must the Losses of a Merging Company be Deductible in the State of Residence of the Receiving Company in EU?; *EC Tax Review* 2011, p. 172; De Broe, Belgium I: Preliminary Rulings Filed by Belgian Courts, in Lang/Pistone/Schuch/Staringer/Storck (eds.) *ECJ – Recent Developments in Direct Taxation 2011* (2012) p. 9; Helminen, The A Oy 1, A Oy 2 and K cases, in Lang/Pistone/Schuch/Staringer/Storck (eds.) *ECJ – Recent Developments in Direct Taxation 2011* (2012) p. 69; van den Broek/Meussen, *National Grid Indus* Case: Re-Thinking Exit Taxation, *ET* 2012, p. 190; Világi, Exit Taxes on Various Types of Corporate Reorganizations in the Light of EU Law, *ET* 2012, p. 346; Terra/Wattel, *European Tax Law*, 6th edition (2012); van den Broek, Cross-Border Mergers within the EU – Proposals to Remove the Remaining Tax Obstacles (2012).

1. The Necessity of Tax-Neutral Reorganizations in the European Union

492   **Reorganizations** in absence of any specific tax provisions will generally **trigger taxation of unrealized capital gains**. For **domestic reorganizations** Member States typically provide for tax deferrals of the capital gains tax levied on the hidden reserves of the transferred assets under their domestic tax law. Often, losses not yet utilized by the transferring company may also be carried over to the acquiring company in a domestic reorganization. Therefore, a domestic reorganization is tax neutral, i.e. it does not trigger immediate taxation at the time of reorganization since taxation of the capital gain is deferred until a later disposal of those assets.

Similar tax provisions for **reorganizations of companies of different Mem-** **493**
ber States are necessary for the completion of an internal market within the
European Union. Thus, cross-border reorganizations ought not to be hampered
by restrictions, disadvantages or distortions arising from the tax provisions of the
Member States. It is therefore necessary to introduce tax provisions that are neutral from the point of view of competition, in order to allow enterprises to adapt
to the requirements of the common market, to increase their productivity and to
improve their competitive strength at the international level. Consequently, tax
provisions that put cross-border reorganizations at a disadvantage in comparison
with reorganizations involving companies established in the same Member State
have to be abolished.

However, just extending the rules for domestic reorganizations to cross- **494**
border reorganizations was regarded as not feasible because of the differences
between the regimes in force in the Member States. (New) distortions were expected. According to the Council, only a **common tax system for cross-border**
reorganizations is able to provide a satisfactory solution. Therefore, the Council
adopted the Merger Directive.[499] In the absence of specific EU law provisions
Art. 115 TFEU (ex Art. 94 EC) seems to be an appropriate legal basis for the
Merger Directive.

The **aim** of the common tax system for cross-border reorganizations is to **495**
avoid the imposition of an income or capital gains tax in connection with
mergers, divisions, partial divisions, transfers of assets, exchanges of shares and
transfers of the registered office of an SE or SCE between Member States. At the
same time, the **financial interests of the Member State** of the transferring or
acquired company should be safeguarded. Thus, the taxing rights of the Member
States should be protected.[500]

Initial proposals for a Merger Directive date back to the year 1969. However, **496**
it took more than 20 years till the final text was **adopted by the Council in 1990**.
The Merger Directive adopted in 1990 covered mergers, divisions, transfers of
assets and exchanges of shares concerning companies of different Member States.

---

[499] Council Directive 2009/133/EC of 19 October 2009 on the common system of taxation
applicable to mergers, divisions, partial divisions, transfers of assets and exchanges of shares
concerning companies of different Member States and to the transfer of the registered office
of an SE or SCE between Member States (codified version), OJ L 310 of 25 November
2009, pp. 34–46; originally Council Directive 90/434/EEC of 23 July 1990 on the common
system of taxation applicable to mergers, divisions, transfers of assets and exchanges of
shares concerning companies of different Member States, OJ L 225 of 20 August 1990,
pp. 1–5.

[500] Council Directive 2009/133/EC of 19 October 2009 on the common system of taxation
applicable to mergers, divisions, partial divisions, transfers of assets and exchanges of
shares concerning companies of different Member States and the transfer of the registered
office of an SE or SCE between Member States (codified version), OJ L 310 of 25 November 2009, p. 34.

The Merger Directive required the Member States to **adjust their national legislation by 1 January 1992**.

497   A proposal for an amendment of the Merger Directive was drafted by the Commission in 1993.[501] This proposal was withdrawn in 2003 although the Commission issued a new proposal amending the Merger Directive.[502] A modified version of this proposal was adopted by the Council in 2005.[503] The changes in **2005** included a **broadening of the personal and the objective scope** of the Merger Directive. The personal scope was enlarged to include the SE, the SCE and several entities not covered by the former version of the Merger Directive as well as hybrid entities. With respect to the objective scope, partial divisions and the transfer of the registered office of an SE or SCE from one Member State to another were covered after the 2005 amendment of the Merger Directive. The changes of the 2005 amendment to the Merger Directive had to be **implemented in part by 1 January 2006 and in part by 1 January 2007**.

498   With the **accession of Bulgaria and Romania** to the European Union amendments were made so that Bulgarian and Romanian taxes and companies were covered.[504] Bulgaria and Romania had to adjust – like the ten Member States joining the European Union in 2004 – their national legislation immediately.

499   Because of the several amendments to the Merger Directive, the Merger Directive was codified in 2009 to enhance clarity and rationality. However, the codification did not lead to changes of the Merger Directive in terms of content.[505]

2. Scope

a) Personal Scope

500   The Merger Directive requires companies involved in the operations covered[506] to qualify as a "company from a Member State". To be characterized as a "company from a Member State", the respective company has to meet **three**

---

[501] COM(1993) 293.

[502] COM(2003) 613.

[503] Council Directive 2005/19/EC of 17 February 2005 amending Directive 90/434/EEC 1990 on the common system of taxation applicable to mergers, divisions, transfers of assets and exchanges of shares concerning companies of different Member States, OJ L 58 of 4 March 2005, pp. 19–26.

[504] Council Directive 2006/98/EC of 20 November 2006 adapting certain Directives in the field of taxation, by reason of the accession of Bulgaria and Romania, OJ L 363 of 20 December 2006, pp. 129–136.

[505] Council Directive 2009/133/EC of 19 October 2009 on the common system of taxation applicable to mergers, divisions, partial divisions, transfers of assets and exchanges of shares concerning companies of different Member States and the transfer of the registered office of an SE or SCE between Member States (codified version), OJ L 310 of 25 November 2009, p. 34.

[506] See m.nos. 505 et seq.

requirements: Firstly, the company has to take one of the legal forms listed in the annex to the Merger Directive. Secondly, the company has to be resident for tax purposes within the European Union. Thirdly, the company has to be subject to a certain kind of tax listed in the annex to the Merger Directive.

With respect to the first requirement (Art. 3(a)), the company has to be **incorporated in one of the legal forms listed in the annex** to the Merger Directive to be covered by the personal scope of the Directive. Under the 2005 amendment to the Merger Directive, the list of eligible legal forms was enlarged considerably to broaden the Directive's personal scope. Nevertheless, not all companies qualifying as companies for domestic corporate income tax purposes qualify as companies for the Merger Directive. **501**

The second requirement for qualifying as a company under the Merger Directive is that the company must be considered to be **resident for tax purposes in one Member State** on the basis of the **domestic tax law** of that state. Additionally, the company may not, according to a **tax treaty concluded with a third state** (non-Member State) be resident for tax purposes outside the EU. Therefore, the second requirement under Art. 3(b) deals with residence for tax purposes in two different respects. The company has to be resident under domestic tax law in one Member State and it must not be resident for tax treaty purposes in a third state based on the tax treaties concluded by the respective Member State. Companies resident for tax treaty purposes outside the European Union do not have access to the benefits of the Merger Directive. This is especially relevant for dual resident companies that are resident under the domestic tax law in one Member State but also resident under the domestic tax law in a third state. If there is a tax treaty similar to the OECD Model with the tie-breaker rule of the place of effective management, this company is not covered by the personal scope of the Merger Directive if the place of effective management is in that third state. However, dual resident companies having both of their place of effective management and their registered seat within the European Union are covered by the Directive's personal scope. Even if a dual resident company has its place of effective management in a third state this company may still benefit from the Merger Directive if there is no tax treaty in force between the respective Member State and the third state in which the place of effective management is located. **502**

According to Art. 3(c), the third requirement for being covered by the Merger Directive is that the company is **subject to a tax listed in the annex to the Merger Directive**, i.e. corporate income tax in the respective Member States without being exempt and without the possibility of an option. **503**

All three conditions have to be met to qualify as a company within the meaning of the Merger Directive. If one of the three requirements is not met, the company is not covered by the personal scope of the Merger Directive. However, it is **not required that all three conditions have to be met within one Member State**. **504**

b) Objective Scope

i. Operations Covered in General

505 Under Art. 1 of the Merger Directive, it is required that a "company from a Member State" is involved in operations covered and specified by Art. 2. The **list of operations** is **exhaustive**. Since the 2005 amendment to the Merger Directive mergers, divisions, partial divisions, transfers of assets, exchanges of shares and the transfer of the registered office of an SE or SCE from one Member State to another are covered. Other types of reorganizations are not covered.

ii. Mergers

506 For the purposes of the Merger Directive, Art. 2(a) defines a merger as an operation whereby one or more companies **transfer all of their assets and liabilities to another company**. The transferring companies are dissolved without going into liquidation. Therefore, the transferring companies cease to exist.

507 The **receiving company** is the legal successor of the assets and liabilities. In return for the assets and liabilities received, the receiving company **issues shares** to the shareholders of the transferring company or companies. An additional cash payment not exceeding 10 % of the nominal value, or in absence of a nominal value, of the accounting par value of those securities to match the values of the shares in the transferring and in the receiving company is allowed.

508 Under Art. 2(a), three different subtypes of mergers are defined. Firstly, one or more existing companies may **merge into another existing company**. Secondly, two or more existing companies may **merge into a newly formed company**. Thirdly, a wholly owned subsidiary may be **merged with its parent company (up-stream merger)**. Only for those mergers does the Merger Directive apply.

iii. Divisions and Partial Divisions

509 Divisions and partial divisions are covered under Art. 2(b) and (c). A division is an operation whereby **one company transfers all of its assets and liabilities**. The transferring company ceases to exist but is dissolved without liquidation.

510 The **transferring company transfers all the assets and liabilities to two or more new or existing companies in exchange for shares** representing the capital of the companies receiving the assets and liabilities. For matching the values of the shares of the transferring and the receiving company cash payments up to 10 % of the nominal value, or in absence of a nominal value, of the accounting par value of those securities, are eligible.

511 Although Art. 2(b) requires an "issue" of shares by the receiving company to qualify as division under the Merger Directive, thus implying that **new shares are required**, a division should also qualify if the receiving company transfers

existing shares to the shareholders of the transferring company.[507] The same rule applies for mergers covered by Art. 2(a).

Since the 2005 amendment, partial divisions are also covered by the Merger Directive. A partial division as defined under Art. 2(c) is an operation whereby a company **transfers, without being dissolved, one or more branches of activity to one or more existing or new companies,** leaving at least one branch of activity in the transferring company. Unlike the division, the transferring company does not cease to exist but is left with at least one branch of activity. The operation covered by Art. 2(c) is therefore also referred to as a split-off. However, for qualifying as a partial division under Art. 2(c) a transfer of at least one branch of activity has to take place while one branch of activity has to remain at the transferring company. **512**

The term **"branch of activity"** is defined under Art. 2(j) as all the assets and liabilities of a division of a company which from an organizational point of view constitute an independent business, i.e. an entity capable of functioning by its own means. Based on this definition, the transfer of a single asset is not covered by a partial division under Art. 2(c). **513**

iv. Transfer of Assets

Under Art. 2(d), a transfer of assets is covered by the objective scope of the Merger Directive. The transfer of assets is an operation whereby a **company transfers without being dissolved all or one or more branches of its activity to another existing or newly established company** in exchange for securities representing the capital of the company receiving the transfer. The transferring company continues to exist. **514**

The transferring company has to transfer at least one **branch of activity** defined under Art. 2(j). Otherwise it is not covered by the objective scope of the Merger Directive. Therefore, the transfer of unrelated assets does not result in access to the benefits of the Merger Directive. **515**

In return for the transfer of activities the transferring company receives shares in the capital of the receiving company. Unlike a merger, a division or a partial division it is the **transferring company itself that receives the shares as consideration** and not the shareholders of the transferring company. **516**

v. Exchange of Shares

In Art. 2(e), an exchange of shares is defined. An exchange of shares is an operation whereby the **acquiring company pays for the shares in the acquired company by issuing shares of its own capital** to the former shareholders of the acquired company. Thereby, the acquired company becomes a subsidiary of the acquiring company and the former shareholders of the acquired company become shareholders of the acquiring company. **517**

---

[507] Terra/Wattel, *European Tax Law* (2012) p. 660.

518 The application of the "exchange of shares" provision is made conditional upon the fact that the acquiring company obtains a **majority of the voting rights** in the acquired company, or, when already holding such a majority, acquires a further holding. Similar to mergers, divisions and partial divisions, cash payments not exceeding 10 % of the nominal value, and in the absence of a nominal value, of the accounting par value of the securities issued in exchange, do not exclude the application of the "exchange of shares" provision.

vi. Transfer of the Registered Office of an SE and SCE

519 With the 2005 amendment to the Merger Directive, the transfer of the registered office of an SE or SCE from one Member State to another became possible. Although Art. 1(b) includes such transfers in the objective scope of the Merger Directive, the transfer of a registered office has **nothing to do with merging or demerging**. Art. 1(b) deals with the emigration of an SE or SCE that is not a transaction but a movement of the management from one Member State to another. Under the other operations covered by the Merger Directive, e.g. a merger, there is only a transfer of the ownership, whereas there is usually no movement of the assets and liabilities.

3. Tax Consequences

a) Rationale of the Merger Directive

520 The essence of the Merger Directive is the **deferral of capital gains tax** on the occasion of a qualifying reorganization covered by the Directive. This is basically achieved **by a roll-over of basis**, i.e. by carrying over the value for tax purposes of the assets, liabilities and shares involved. In other words, the Directive requires the Member States to refrain from taxing any capital gains triggered by the cross-border merger, (partial) division, transfer of assets, exchange of shares or transfer of registered office of an SE or an SCE. However, the benefit of the Directive is not a tax exemption but a tax deferral. Thus, in a merger, (partial) division or transfer of assets the potential tax due on the hidden reserves accrued prior to the transaction (= latent tax claim) is shifted to the receiving company, which must enter the transferred assets and liabilities in its accounts at the same tax value as that assigned to them in the transferring company's accounts prior to the transfer. When the receiving company later on disposes of the assets transferred, tax may be due on the difference between the disposal value and the original value for tax purposes. As a matter of fact, this difference also encompasses those hidden reserves that have arisen prior to the reorganization, the tax on which was deferred by means of the Merger Directive. Similarly, shareholders who – in the course of a merger, (partial) division or exchange of shares – exchange shares they own in one company for shares in another company will not be taxed at the time of the swap, provided the same value for tax purposes of the substituted shares is attributed to the shares being substituted.

Also in this case, taxes only become due when the shares received are sold by the shareholder and thereby the hidden reserves are finally realized. Corresponding deferral rules also apply when an SE or SCE transfers its registered office from one Member State to another.

From the above, it becomes clear that with respect to the tax consequences the **521** Merger Directive distinguishes between **taxation at the level of the companies** involved and **taxation at the level of the shareholders** affected. This pattern will also be followed in the following discussion.

b) Taxation of the Companies Involved

i. Deferral of Capital Gains Tax and Carry-Over of Tax Values

Art. 4(1) provides the basic rule for taxation at the level of the transferring **522** company in the Member State of the transferring company.[508] Accordingly, a **merger, division or partial division may not give rise to any taxation of capital gains** calculated as the difference between the real values of the assets and liabilities transferred and their values for tax purposes. This "value for tax purposes" is defined as the value on the basis of which any gain or loss would have been computed by the transferring company if the assets or liabilities had been sold at the time of the reorganization but independently of it.[509]

However, Art. 4(4) makes the **tax deferral conditional upon** the receiving **523** company's computing any new depreciation and any gains or losses in respect of the assets and liabilities transferred according to the same rules that would have applied to the transferring company (or companies) if the merger, division or partial division had not taken place. This mechanism is therefore also known as **roll-over of basis**, since the tax values of the assets and liabilities of the transferring company have to be taken over by the receiving company in the Member State of the transferring company. Thereby the tax basis in the form of the hidden reserves accrued at the level of the transferring company until the merger or (partial) division is shifted to the receiving company.

Deviations in the value for tax purposes of the assets and liabilities trans- **524** ferred, such as a step-up in basis, partially frustrate the relief provided by the Directive. Consequently, as clarified by Art. 4(5), **where** – under the laws of the Member State of the transferring company – the **receiving company is entitled to have such a step-up in the tax value of the transferred assets**, the **tax neutrality** at the level of the transferring company as set out in Art. 4(1) **does not apply** to the assets and liabilities in respect of which the option was exercised.[510]

---

[508] Although Art. 4 does not explicitly state which Member State must apply the rules contained therein. From the scope, system and history of the Directive it becomes clear, however, that Art. 4 addresses only the State of the transferring company. See also Van den Broek, *Cross-Border Mergers within the EU* (2012) p. 203.

[509] Art. 4(2)(a) of the Merger Directive.

[510] Since Arts. 4(4) and 4(5) do not address the Member State of the receiving company, the valuation of the transferred assets and liabilities in that State is irrelevant for their valuation

525   Another important feature of Art. 4 of the Merger Directive is the "**remaining permanent establishment requirement**" as provided for by Art. 4(2)(b). Prima facie, it makes the tax deferral and the carry-over of values conditional upon the **transferred assets and liabilities remaining effectively connected with a permanent establishment** of the receiving company in the Member State of the transferring company. Furthermore, it is required that these assets and liabilities play a part in generating the profits and losses taken into account for tax purposes. The rationale of this remaining permanent establishment requirement is obviously the safeguarding of taxing rights and thereby the financial interest of the Member State of the transferring company, since under international tax (treaty) law, a state may only tax profits derived by non-residents if that profit is sourced within its territory. In the case of profits stemming from a business operation, this requirement is as a rule fulfilled if the business is carried on through a permanent establishment in that state. If the assets and liabilities transferred in a cross-border reorganization do not form part of a permanent establishment in the state of the transferring company, then that state as a rule loses its tax claim on the capital gains and fiscal reserves represented by those assets because at a later stage they belong to a non-resident taxpayer and their disposal cannot be taxed in the original source state. Art. 4(2)(b) is therefore regarded as "**claim saver**", ensuring that the future realization of the deferred capital gains will be part of the tax base allocated to the state of the transferring company;[511] thus, to the state under whose tax jurisdiction they were generated. However, in order to achieve this goal, it is not always necessary that the transferred assets remain effectively connected with a permanent establishment, such as in the case of immovable property. In this context the permanent establishment requirement is clearly excessive.

526   The **permanent establishment concept also fails when the state in which the permanent establishment is situated does not have the right to tax the permanent establishment** because of specific provisions in a tax treaty similar to the provision of Art. 8 of the OECD Model. To overcome this problem, the Commission and the Council agreed in the Council minutes that Art. 4 of the Directive should not prevent the Member State of a transferring company from taxing at the time of the merger or division gains that would otherwise, by virtue of tax treaty provisions, escape tax in that state altogether.[512]

527   The **crucial question in this respect is, however, whether an immediate taxation of hidden reserves** that would otherwise escape taxation in the state of the transferring company is **in line with the requirements of the fundamental**

---

in the Member State of the transferring company. Thus, even if the Member State of the receiving company grants a step-up in basis for the foreign assets and liabilities received, this does not frustrate the tax neutrality in the Member State of the transferring company according to Art. 4(1).

[511] Terra/Wattel, *European Tax Law* (2012) p. 676.

[512] Thömmes, in Thömmes/Fuks (eds.) *EC Corporate Tax Law* (December 2004) para. 163.

freedoms of primary EU law. Even though the Merger Directive seems to tolerate this, it has to be noted that the Merger Directive as a part of secondary EU law still has to comply with the higher-ranking fundamental freedoms.[513] As the cases on exit taxation of individuals[514] and legal entities[515] reveal, the compulsory immediate taxation of unrealized capital gains upon emigration to another Member State, whereas no such taxation is provided for in purely domestic situations, runs the risk of infringing the fundamental freedoms, primarily the freedom of establishment according to Art. 49 TFEU. If the arguments used by the ECJ in these cases are transposed to situations in which companies "emigrate" by means of a cross-border merger or (partial) division, **the remaining permanent establishment requirement** of Art. 4(2)(b) and Art. 10(1), if interpreted in such a way that it tolerated a compulsory immediate taxation, **would contravene the obligations imposed by the fundamental freedoms of primary EU law.**[516] The underlying object and purpose of such taxation – namely the safeguarding of tax claims – may be achieved by less restrictive measures than immediate taxation. These concerns, therefore, suggest an interpretation of Art. 4(2)(b) and Art. 10 (1) that is in conformity with primary EU law. The wording of the respective provisions is wide enough to do so.

For the time being it is, however, quite **unclear how such a system** of safeguarding the taxing rights of the Member State of origin (i.e. the Member State in which the hidden reserves accrued) in "exit scenarios" of corporate entities or business undertakings **has to be designed in order to meet the requirements of primary EU law.** At least the ECJ leaves no doubt that Member States are entitled to tax increases in value which were generated while the respective taxpayer or taxable object had a sufficient nexus to the taxing state. This is the result of a coherent understanding of the principle of fiscal territoriality linked to a tem-

528

---

[513] See e.g. ECJ 23 February 2006, C-472/04, *Keller Holding* [2006] ECR I-2107, para. 45.

[514] Such as ECJ 11 March 2004, C-9/02, *Lasteyrie du Saillant* [2004] ECR I-2409; ECJ 7 September 2006, C-470/04, *N.* [2006] ECR I-7409; ECJ 12 July 2012, C-269/09, *Commission vs. Spain* (not yet reported).

[515] Such as ECJ 29 November 2011, C-371/10, *National Grid Indus* (not yet reported); ECJ 6 September 2012, C-38/10, *Commission vs. Portugal* (not yet reported); see also the Opinion of Advocate General Mengozzi of 28 June 2012 in Case C-38/10, *Commission vs. Portugal* (not yet reported); the mandatory immediate taxation of increases in value when companies or other business undertakings transfer assets to fixed establishments in other Member States, even though no such taxation is provided for in corresponding domestic situations, is also challenged in the pending case C-261/11, *Commission vs. Denmark* (OJ C 238 of 13 August 2011, p. 5); corporate exit taxation is also the subject matter in the pending Cases C-65/11, *Commission vs. Spain*, (OJ C 113 of 9 April 2011, p. 8) and C-301/11, *Commission vs. Netherlands* (OJ C 252 of 27 August 2011, p. 10). As to the issue of capital taxes in the context of a transfer of seat see ECJ 6 September 2012, C-380/11, DI. VI. Finanziaria di Diego della Valle & C. (not yet reported).

[516] See Schön, *TNI* 2004, p. 202 et seq.

poral component.[517] Against the background of the principle of proportionality, the Court, however, rejects an immediate payment of the taxes due on the hidden reserves disclosed at the time of exit. At this point, the ECJ, interestingly, distinguishes between the establishment of the amount of tax due and its recovery. Whereas an immediate tax assessment is allowed, the immediate recovery of the tax is not. The **recovery of the tax debt has to be postponed until the time of actual realization** of the capital gain in the host Member State, instead. This, necessarily, requires that the assets (and liabilities) in respect of which the exit tax has been established at the time of transfer have to be traced in the host Member State or the Member State of the receiving company until an act of realization takes place. It goes without saying that such a system may be cumbersome, for both, the taxpayers and the tax authorities. Therefore, the **ECJ in** the *NGI* case **suggested an optional system**, offering taxpayers the choice between immediate payment of the tax or deferred payment, possibly together with interest in accordance with the applicable national legislation.[518] Furthermore, the Court indicated that the Member States might also take into account the risk of non-recovery of the tax in the case of deferral by measures such as the provision of a bank guarantee.[519] In contrast to the *N.* judgment, the ECJ further held that decreases in value which occur subsequently to the transfer need not be taken into account by the Member State that levies the exit tax. Thus, the amount of tax due on capital gains relating to the transferred assets may be fixed definitively at the time when the Member State of origin loses its tax jurisdiction.

529   Nevertheless, it is still open whether the *NGI* judgment can really be considered the ECJ's final word on the issue of corporate exit taxation. This is because the *NGI* case was unusual insofar as the company concerned held only a single financial asset. The cross-border tracing of such an individual asset was therefore easy. If, however, the assets and liabilities structure of a business undertaking is more complex, deferring the recovery of the tax debt until the time of actual realization is difficult. Moreover, the collection of the tax may be undermined if the assets are not destined for alienation but use in the ordinary run of the business. Difficulties also arise with respect to depreciable assets with different lengths of useful lives or self-developed intangibles. For these reasons it is not inconceivable that Member States are allowed to provide for other measures than the type of tax deferral suggested in the *NGI* case in order to safeguard the balanced allocation of taxing powers among them. One additional alternative could be an exit tax combined with staggered payments of the tax due to mitigate cash-flow disadvantages with the time period over which the payments are apportioned varying according to the type of assets transferred.[520] All in all, the

---

[517] ECJ 29 November 2011, C-371/10, *National Grid Indus* (not yet reported) para. 46 et seq.
[518] ECJ 29 November 2011, C-371/10, *National Grid Indus* (not yet reported) para. 73.
[519] ECJ 29 November 2011, C-371/10, *National Grid Indus* (not yet reported) para. 74.
[520] For alternative suggestions also Világi, *ET* 2012, p. 352.

currently pending cases on corporate exit taxation will definitely shed further light on these issues. Due to the structural relationship between exit taxation in situations of corporate emigration and the taxation of cross-border reorganizations, the findings of the Court will then also be relevant to the last-mentioned cases.[521]

Since Art. 9 explicitly refers to Art. 4, the **tax deferral rules of Art. 4** with **530** respect to mergers and (partial) divisions **also apply to transfers of assets.** Consequently, also in a qualifying transfer of assets, the transferring company may not tax any hidden reserves built into the assets and liabilities attributable to the branch of its activity that is transferred, provided the receiving company takes over the tax values attached to them prior to the transfer.[522]

For the **transfer of the registered office of an SE or an SCE or the cessation** **531** **of residence of such a corporation**, Art. 12(1) likewise provides that the emigration of the corporation **may not give rise to any taxation on capital gains** within the meaning of Art. 4(1). In analogy with the **remaining permanent establishment requirement** of Art. 4(2)(b), Art. 12(1)(b) also requires the assets and liabilities of the emigrating SE or SCE to remain effectively connected with a permanent establishment of that company in the Member State of departure for the tax deferral to apply. As a matter of fact, the same concerns as outlined in m.nos. 527 et seq. arise also with respect to Art. 12(1)(b). The second precondition for the tax neutrality of the transfer is – along the lines of Art. 4(4) – that the SE or SCE computes any new depreciation and any gains or losses in respect of the assets and liabilities that remain effectively connected with the permanent establishment in the Member State of departure in such a way as if the "corporate emigration" has not taken place.

ii. Carry-Over of Tax-Free Provisions and Reserves

According to Art. 5 of the Directive, the **Member State of the transferring** **532** **company** in a merger or (partial) division **must refrain from recapturing any** **tax-deductible provisions or tax-free reserves** formed by the transferring company in respect of assets and liabilities transferred to the receiving company. Such provisions and reserves must be carried over with the same tax exemption to the permanent establishments of the receiving company that are situated in the Member State of the transferring company. Thereby, the receiving company assumes the rights and obligations attached to the provisions and reserves and may continue to use them in the same way as the transferring company.

---

[521] See also Van den Broek/Meussen, *ET* 2012, p. 196.

[522] In this respect it is questionable whether a Member State may deviate from the Directive and make the tax neutrality of the transfer of assets conditional upon other requirements than that provided in Art. 9 in conjunction with Art. 4. Currently an Italian case is pending at the ECJ which could shed some light on that issue. Opinion of Advocate General Jääskinen of 10 July 2012 in Case C-207/11, 3D I Srl (not yet reported).

533   An **exception is made for provisions or reserves that were set up in connection with assets and liabilities of foreign permanent establishments of the transferring company**. As a result of the transfer, such permanent establishments become permanent establishments of the receiving company, which, however, is not a resident of the Member State of the transferring company. Consequently, the assets and liabilities concerned are not subject to tax in that state if they are disposed of or realized in the future. For this reason the Merger Directive allows the Member State of the transferring company to recapture and tax such provisions and reserves at the moment of the reorganization, i.e. when the Member State of the transferring company loses its taxing power over the foreign permanent establishments concerned. This, again, triggers the question whether such an immediate taxation is in line with the fundamental freedoms of EU law provided that a comparable domestic reorganization would not cause an immediate recapture.[523]

534   According to Art. 9, **Art. 5 also applies to the transfer of assets. Similar rules** as contained in Art. 5 **are also enshrined in Art. 13(1) concerning the transfer of the registered office of an SE or an SCE.**

iii. Takeover of Losses

535 The treatment of losses is in many cases decisive for the restructuring of business by means of mergers, divisions or other forms of reorganizations. This is also true for cross-border reorganizations. **Art. 6 of the Merger Directive addresses the issue of losses**, but only in a meagre way. If, for purely domestic mergers, (partial) divisions and asset-transfers,[524] the respective national laws allow losses connected with the transferred branches or branches of activity and not yet exhausted to be taken over by the receiving company to be set off there, such a takeover must also be available for the equivalent cross-border operation covered by the Merger Directive. Only then does the Merger Directive require the Member State of the transferring company to allow the takeover of such losses by the receiving company's permanent establishments situated within its territory. Thus, the Directive **only contains a non-discrimination rule** which, in the light of the case law of the ECJ on the fundamental freedoms, has to a large extent become obsolete.[525]

536   Like Art. 6 of the Merger Directive, Art. 13(2) requires the state of departure of an SE or SCE that transfers its registered office to another Member State to allow the remaining permanent establishment in its jurisdiction to set off the

---

[523] See m.nos. 527 et seq. Critical also Helminen, *EU tax law* (2009) p. 176; van den Broek, Cross-Border Mergers within the EU (2012) p. 359 et seq. and p. 394 et seq.

[524] This is the result of the references contained in Art. 9 on the transfer of assets for applying Art. 6 *mutatis mutandis.*

[525] See Bezzina, *ET* 2002, p. 59; Thömmes, in Thömmes/Fuks (eds.) *EC Corporate Tax Law* (December 2004) para. 189.

losses of the SE or SCE not yet utilized if it would allow such compensation in a comparable domestic situation in which the corporation continued to have its registered office or continued to be tax resident in that Member State.

From the above, it becomes clear that **Art. 6 and Art. 13(2)** of the Merger Directive **only address the treatment of losses in the Member State in which the permanent establishments** of the receiving company or emigrating SE/SCE **are located** but not by the state of residence of the receiving or emigrating company.[526] Discriminatory treatment resulting from cross-border reorganizations in these circumstances has to be resolved by primary EU law. The **crucial question** in this respect **is, whether losses that** as a result of the reorganization or emigration **can no longer be used** in the Member State of origin **have to be regarded as final losses under the *Marks & Spencer* doctrine**[527] and therefore have to be compensated in the Member State of the receiving company or in the new Member State of residence of the emigrating company. A first answer to this question is expected to be given by the ECJ in the pending *A Oy* case.[528] In her Opinion on this case, Advocate General *Kokott,* however, argues that such losses do not qualify as final losses within the meaning of *Marks & Spencer.* Consequently, the denial of cross-border loss compensation in merger scenarios does not constitute an infringement of the freedom of establishment.[529]

537

iv. Cancellation of Shares

The objective of Art. 7 is the relief of the tax burden of the receiving company in a special situation, namely that in which it has a holding in the capital of the transferring company (**up-stream merger**). Upon merging, the **participation the receiving company holds in the transferring company is cancelled**, since the transferring company ceases to exist. However, this cancellation of shares may trigger a taxable profit if the holding was assessed at a lower value than the value of the assets and liabilities which take the place of that holding in the balance sheet of the receiving company. **Art. 7(1)** of the Merger Directive now **prohibits any taxation** of gains that accrue **in connection with** such a **cancellation of shares**. The Directive only covers the cancellation of shares in cases of up-stream mergers. The reverse situation, where the transferring company holds a participation in the capital of the receiving company, as is the case in a **down-stream merger**, is **not covered** by the Directive, even though (book) gains may also arise in these circumstances.

538

---

[526] For an analysis of Art. 6 see also the Opinion of Advocate General Kokott of 19 July 2012, C-123/11, *A Oy*, points 25 et seq.

[527] ECJ 13 December 2005, C-446/03, *Marks & Spencer* [2005] ECR I-10837; see Hohenwarter, *Verlustverwertung im Konzern*, pp. 515 et seq. and pp. 255 et seq; Van den Broek, *Cross-Border Mergers within the EU* (2012) p. 391 et seq.

[528] Pending case C-123/11, *A Oy*, OJ C 145 of 14 May 2011, p. 17; Helminen, *EC Tax Review* 2011, p. 173 et seq.

[529] Opinion of Advocate General Kokott of 19 July 2012, C-123/11, *A Oy*, point 47 et seq.

539   Moreover, **Art. 7(2)** grants the Member States the **right to derogate from the tax exemption in Art. 7(1)** provided the amount of the shares held by the receiving company in the transferring company is below a certain threshold. This threshold corresponds to the **minimum shareholding** of Art. 3(1)(a) of the Parent-Subsidiary Directive.[530] Consequently, this minimum amount was reduced from the original 25 % to 10 % as of 1 January 2009.

v. Valuation of Shares Received in a Transfer of Assets

540   The Directive contains **no rules on how the transferring company** in a transfer of assets according to Art. 2(d) in conjunction with Art. 9 **should assess the value of the shares issued to it by the receiving company**. If, therefore, the transferring company has to enter those shares in its tax accounts at the book value of the transferred assets and liabilities, the **hidden reserves** contained in the transferred assets and liabilities **are doubled**. This means that both the receiving company (because of the roll-over of basis according to Art. 4) and the transferring company may later be taxed on the same capital gain; the receiving company when disposing of the assets and liabilities received and the transferring company when selling the shares in the receiving company that it obtained in exchange for the assets transferred.[531]

541   In order to avoid the doubling of hidden reserves and the economic double taxation that is thereby triggered, the proposal for the 2005 amendment of the Merger Directive included a change in Art. 9, adding a paragraph 2. These new rules should have provided that the transferring company had to attribute to the shares received in exchange the real value of the assets and liabilities transferred. However, no political agreement could be reached on this part of the proposal. Consequently, the proposed paragraph 2 was not included in Directive 2005/19/EC.

vi. Valuation of Shares by the Acquiring Company in an Exchange of Shares

542   Similarly, the **Directive does not include rules on the valuation of the shares acquired by the acquiring company in an exchange of shares** according to Art. 2(e). Art. 8(3) only provides for a roll-over of tax values at the shareholder level. In other words, this rule requires the shareholders of the acquired company to attribute to the shares received in exchange from the acquiring company the same value as attributed to the shares held in the acquired company before the exchange. Again, if the acquiring company is obliged to value the shares obtained from the former shareholders of the acquired company at their book value, economic double taxation due to a doubling of hidden reserves is the result. The same capital gain may be taxed twice, once in the hands of the former shareholders of the acquired company upon disposal of the shares received in ex-

---

[530] See Chapter IV, m.nos. 440 et seq.
[531] See also Opinion of Advocate General Jääskinen of 10 July 2012 in Case C-207/11, 3D I Srl (not yet reported) point 43 et seq.

change and once at the level of the acquiring company upon disposal of its shares in the acquired company. In this case as well, the proposal for the 2005 amendment of the Directive included its own valuation rule, according to which the acquiring company should be able to enter the shares acquired in its tax account at their real (market) value. Since no political agreement could be reached on this point either, this part of the amendment was dropped altogether.

More light on the issue of the valuation of shares in an exchange of shares was **543** shed by the ECJ in its decision in the case *A.T.*[532] The core of this case was the question whether Art. 8(1) and (2) of the Merger Directive preclude domestic tax rules under which, upon the transfer of shares in an EU company to another, the shareholders of the acquired company may maintain the book value of the shares transferred only if the acquiring company has itself valued the shares acquired at their book value. In other words, it was queried whether a **"double book value carry-over"** was in conformity with the Merger Directive. This was **denied by the ECJ**. In the light of the object and purpose of Art. 8(1) and (2) – providing for fiscal neutrality by ensuring that increases in the value of shares are not taxed until their actual realization – these provisions preclude national tax laws according to which, in consequence of an exchange of shares, the shareholders of the acquired company are taxed on the capital gains arising from the transfer,[533] unless the acquiring company carries over the historical book value of the shares transferred in its own tax balance sheet.[534] Besides the inadmissibility of making the taxation of the shareholders of the acquired company dependent on the valuation of their shares by the acquiring company in its Member State of residence, the issue of valuation at the level of the acquiring company is, however, still open.

vii. Transfer of a Foreign Permanent Establishment

Art. 10(1) sentence 1 in conjunction with sentence 3 of the Merger Directive **544** addresses the **transfer of a permanent establishment in a triangular situation**, in other words the transfer of a branch of activity in the form of a permanent establishment situated in one Member State by a company resident in another Member State to a company resident in a third Member State.

Tax neutrality in the Member State that hosts the permanent establish- 545 ment is achieved by Art. 10(1) sentence 3, which requires that the state of the permanent establishment and the Member State of the receiving company apply the provisions of the Merger Directive as if the transferring company was situated in the state of the permanent establishment. Consequently, the state of the permanent establishment may not tax any capital gains in the assets and liabilities of the permanent establishment and must allow the carry-over of tax-free

---

[532] ECJ 11 December 2008, C-285/07, *A.T* [2008] ECR I-9329.
[533] With these gains being deemed to correspond to the difference between the initial cost of acquiring the shares transferred and their market value.
[534] ECJ 11 December 2008, C-285/07, *A.T.* [2008] ECR I-9329, para. 39.

provisions and reserves, provided that within the permanent establishment the original book values and depreciation methods are maintained.

546   Art. 10(1) sentence 4 clarifies that the rules of Art. 10(1) providing for tax neutrality also apply to transactions commonly known as **incorporation of a branch into a subsidiary,** i.e. where the permanent establishment that is to be transferred is situated in the same Member State as that in which the receiving company is resident **(transfer of a permanent establishment in a bilateral situation).**

547   Even though the Member State of the transferring company may not tax any unrealized capital gains upon the transfer of the foreign permanent establishment, Art. 10(1) sentence 2 entitles that Member State to **recapture** any **loss deductions** granted in the past to the transferring company in respect of losses incurred by its foreign permanent establishment, provided these losses have not been recovered by the time of the transfer. Since after the transfer, the permanent establishment no longer belongs to the transferring company but is part of the receiving company's enterprise that is resident in another Member State this recapture rule is regarded as necessary to safeguard the financial interests of the Member State of the transferring company. The question in this respect is, however, whether an immediate claw-back of the losses concerned is also proportionate within the meaning of primary EU law.[535]

548   Art. 10(2) particularly addresses those Member States that apply the credit method for the avoidance of double taxation. By way of **derogation from paragraph 1,** the **Member State of the transferring company is allowed to include the capital gains** of the foreign permanent establishment's assets and liabilities **in the taxable income of the transferring company.** However, it is then **obliged to credit a notional amount of tax,** i.e. the amount of tax that the Member State in which the permanent establishment is situated would have levied on those gains, had it not been required to grant tax neutrality on the transaction under the rules of the Merger Directive. In this way double taxation should be avoided.

c) Taxation of the Shareholders Involved

549   **Art. 8(1)** of the Merger Directive **defers taxation** with respect to capital gains in the exchange of shares **at the shareholder level resulting from a merger, division or an exchange of shares** within the meaning of Art. 2(e) of the Directive. In the case of a merger or division the exchange of shares concerns the shareholders of the (dissolved) transferring companies, who in exchange for their shares get shares in the receiving companies, whereas in an exchange of shares transaction according to Art. 2(e), Art. 8(1) covers the shares in the acquired

---

[535] In the light of the ECJ case *Krankenheim Wannsee* this seems questionable. ECJ of 23 October 2008, C-157/07, *Krankenheim Ruhesitz am Wannsee – Seniorenheimstatt* [2008] ECR I-8061; see also Hohenwarter, *Verlustverwertung im Konzern* (2009) pp. 423 et seq; Van den Broek, *Cross-Border Mergers within the EU* (2012) p. 395 et seq.

company that are transferred to the acquiring company in return for new shares which are issued to the former shareholders of the acquired company. Similarly, **Art. 8(2) defers taxation of the allotment of shares issued in the course of a partial division**, where the receiving companies issue shares to the shareholders of the transferring company.

Consequently, no tax will be levied on the capital gain realized on the shares   **550** that were substituted or on the allotment of shares. This **deferral** is, however, **conditional upon the shareholders' carry-over of tax values**. According to Art. 8(4) and (5), the shareholders therefore have to attribute to the shares received in exchange the same value for tax purposes as that attached to the "old" shares. In most of the cases this mechanism ensures that the Member State in whose tax jurisdiction the hidden reserves built in the exchanged shares have accumulated is still able to tax them when the shareholder sells the shares in the acquiring or receiving company. Taxation at the time of subsequent disposal is also confirmed by **Art. 8(6)**, which **permits the Member States to tax the gain arising out of a subsequent transfer of the securities** received in exchange in the same way as gains arising out of the transfer of securities that existed before the acquisition. Not covered by the tax deferral is any additional cash payment that exceeds the 10 % limitation as provided for by Arts. 2(a) to (c) as well as Art. 2(e).[536]

If, however, the respective **national laws in which the shareholders are**   **551** **resident allow them to opt for a step-up in tax basis** concerning the shares received and the shareholders by exercising this option voluntarily choose to be taxed on the capital gain arising from the exchange of shares, then the **tax deferral rules**, of course, **do not apply**. This is provided for by Art. 8(8) of the Merger Directive.

The Directive lacks a comprehensive definition of the term "shareholder".   **552** From this lack of any further requirement as to the shareholder, it has been deduced that the benefits of the Merger Directive must also apply to shareholders resident in a third (non-EU) country. In the 2005 amendment, these issues should have been addressed by the insertion of a new Art. 8(12) which was supposed to extend tax neutrality to shareholders resident in third countries. In the final version of the amending Directive, this provision was, however, dropped, obviously because of the fear of negative revenue repercussions. Consequently, it is still not entirely clear whether the benefits of the Merger Directive have to be granted to shareholders resident in non-EU countries in the same way as to EU-resident shareholders.

Although a **transfer of the registered office of an SE or SCE** does not trig-   **553** ger an exchange of shares at the shareholder level, **Art. 14 also stipulates corresponding deferral rules** for the emigration of SEs or SCEs. The reason behind this is obviously the danger that the Member States could otherwise regard the

---

[536] Art. 8(9) of the Merger Directive; for the 10 % limitation see also m.nos. 507, 510 and 518.

act of emigration of an SE or SCE as a taxable event for the shareholders. Consequently, Art. 14(1) provides that the transfer of the registered office in itself may not give rise to any taxation of the shareholders of the emigrating company. There again the Directive does not preclude the Member States from taxing gains arising out of a subsequent alienation of the shares in the SE or the SCE that transferred its registered office previously (Art. 14(2)).

d) Special Case: Hybrid Entities

554 **Hybrid entities** are entities that are regarded as fiscally transparent by one Member State but non-transparent by another Member State. As of the 2005 amendment, the Merger Directive also includes special rules for cross-border reorganizations involving hybrid entities. These rules are contained in Arts. 4(3), 8(3) and 11.

4. Transactions Not Covered

555 The common tax system for cross-border reorganizations under the Merger Directive was introduced to create within the European Union conditions analogous to those of an internal market. However, the scope of the Merger Directive is **limited in several respects**.

556 The **personal scope** of the Merger Directive is restricted to companies specified under Art. 3. Therefore, entities not included in the list of the annex to the Merger Directive, entities not meeting the condition of residence for tax purposes under Art. 3(b) and entities not subject to one of the taxes listed in the annex to the Merger Directive do not qualify for the benefits of the Merger Directive.

557 The scope of the Merger Directive is also limited with respect to the **territorial scope**. Only the specified reorganizations under Art. 2 in which companies of two or more Member States are involved are covered by the Merger Directive. Therefore, in particular reorganizations with the involvement of third states' companies are not covered.

558 Under the **objective scope** of the Merger Directive, only the specified activities – mergers, divisions, partial divisions, transfers of assets, exchanges of shares and transfers of the registered office of an SE or a SCE – are covered.[537] Other reorganizations are not covered. Therefore, mergers of two companies resident for tax purposes in one Member State generally do not fall under the Merger Directive.

---

[537] Based on the *Cartesio* case (ECJ 16 December 2008, C-210/06 [2008] ECR I-9641) and the *Vale* case (ECJ 12 July 2012, C-378/10, *Vale* (not yet published)) the limitation of tax-neutral transfers of registered offices to an SE and a SCE seems to be too narrow. There is a discussion whether other legal forms should also have the possibility of tax-neutral transfers of registered offices. For a detailed discussion refer to Dourado/Pistone, *Intertax* 2009, p. 342 et seq. and Van den Broek, *Cross-Border Mergers within the EU* (2012) p. 100 et seq.

A merger, a division, a partial division and an exchange of shares are also not **559** covered if the consideration for the reorganization includes cash payments, if any, **exceeding 10 % of the nominal value** or, in absence of a nominal value, of the accounting par value of those securities.

In the ***Kofoed*** case the ECJ held that dividend distributions immediately after **560** an exchange of shares under Art. 2(e) of the Merger Directive do not necessarily have to be considered for determining the 10 % threshold for eligible cash payments. As there was no agreement between the participating parties in the exchange of shares that would characterize the dividend distribution as consideration for shares exchanged, the dividend distribution was not regarded as a "cash payment" under Art. 2(e) of the Merger Directive.[538] Consequently, the Merger Directive remained applicable since the threshold of 10 % was not exceeded. However, if the dividend distribution were regarded as a cash payment under Art. 2(e), the Merger Directive would not be applicable.

Although the scope of the Merger Directive is limited in several respects, for **561** cross-border reorganizations the **fundamental freedoms may offer a safety net**. As most Member States have provisions for domestic reorganizations not triggering immediate taxation at the time of the reorganization, under non-discrimination principles the Member States may in general not discriminate against comparable cross-border situations. Differences in treatment would only be permissible if they can be justified under the rule of reason doctrine. Furthermore, the measures taken have to be proportionate. A consistent application of the non-discrimination principles enshrined in the fundamental freedoms of the TFEU or the EEA-Treaty may, therefore, under certain circumstances, lead to an extension of the benefits of the Merger Directive to cases not covered.[539]

However, Member States are also **free to go beyond what is required by the** **562** **Merger Directive** by broadening its scope. Nevertheless, even by going beyond the scope of the Merger Directive, Member States have to apply those provisions in a non-discriminatory way. Furthermore, the provisions on the prohibition of State aid have to be obeyed.[540]

5. Withdrawal of the Benefits of the Directive[541]

a) Tax Evasion and Tax Avoidance

The Merger Directive includes in Art. 15 an anti-abuse clause providing that a **563** Member State may refuse to apply or withdraw the benefit of all or any part of

---

[538] ECJ 5 July 2007, C-321/05, *Kofoed* [2007] ECR I-5795, para. 33.
[539] To this end ECJ 19 July 2012, C-48/11, *A Oy* (not yet reported); see also Helminen, *ET* 2011, p. 179 et seq.
[540] See Chapter III, m.nos. 328 et seq.
[541] Whether the application of the Merger Directive can be made conditional upon filing a request on time was the issue in the *Pelati* case (C-603/10, *Pelati*, not yet reported). In its decision of 18 October 2012 the ECJ held that Art. 15(1)(a) of the Merger Directive (ex Art. 11(1)(a)), as

the Directive where it appears that the merger, the division, the partial division, the transfer of assets, the exchanges of shares or the transfer of the registered office of an SE or SCE has as its principal or as one of its principal objectives tax evasion or tax avoidance. Although the benefits of the Merger Directive may be withdrawn by the Member States, the Directive does not include a definition of tax evasion or tax avoidance. Even though the Member States are obliged to transpose the Merger Directive into domestic law, they are free with respect to the means to transpose the Merger Directive. Consequently, when transposing the Merger Directive into domestic tax law the Member States have implemented **different anti-abuse clauses reflecting the different views on what constitutes abuse**. The ECJ has already decided upon Art. 15(1)(a) and this shed some light on the interpretation of the anti-abuse clause of the Merger Directive.[542]

564   However, the implementation of the anti-abuse clause of the Merger Directive in domestic tax law does **not necessarily lead to legislative action**. The transposition of a directive may also be achieved through a general legal context so that a formal and express re-enactment of the provisions of the directive in specific national provisions is not necessary.[543]

565   If the Member States do not implement a specific anti-abuse provision based on the provision under Art. 15(1)(a) of the Merger Directive and also do not have any domestic anti-abuse clause that may be applicable for cross-border reorganizations covered by the Merger Directive, they may not neglect the application by the argument of abuse. Consequently, the **anti-abuse clause under the Merger Directive itself has no direct effect**. This is based on the case law of the ECJ that directives cannot of themselves impose obligations on an individual.[544] Rather it is necessary for the Member States that aim at neglecting the benefits of the Merger Directive by grounds of abuse, to provide for an anti-abuse provision in their domestic tax law.

566   Therefore, it is necessary for the Member States to **formulate their own anti-abuse clauses for purposes of the Merger Directive**. In formulating them the Member States are free to decide on the conditions that should apply and whether to withdraw the benefits of the Merger Directive entirely or only some of the benefits.

567   Art. 15(1)(a) provides that if an reorganization generally covered by the Merger Directive is not undertaken for valid commercial reasons, it may be **presumed that the whole reorganization has tax evasion or avoidance** as its prin-

---

a rule, does not preclude national legislation under which the grant of the tax advantages applicable to reorganizations in accordance with the directive is subject to the condition that an application relating to the respective operation is submitted within a specified period of time.

[542] ECJ 17 July 1997, C-28/95, *Leur-Bloem* [1997] ECR I-4161; ECJ 5 July 2007, C-321/05, *Kofoed* [2007] ECR I-5795. For a more detailed discussion on the anti-abuse clause of the Merger Directive refer to Petrosovitch, *ET* 2010, p. 558 et seq.

[543] ECJ 5 July 2007, C-321/05, *Kofoed* [2007] ECR I-5795, para. 44.

[544] ECJ 5 July 2007, C-321/05, *Kofoed* [2007] ECR I-5795, para. 42.

cipal objective or as one of its principal objectives. Therefore, these transactions may not be covered by the Merger Directive. Tax evasion or avoidance need not necessarily be the only goal behind the reorganization, as long as it is one of the main objectives. For merger operations between two companies of the same group, it was decided in the *Foggia* case that the operation is not carried out for valid commercial reasons if the acquired company does not carry out any activity, does not have any financial holdings and transfers to the acquiring company only substantial tax losses of undetermined origin, even though that operation has a positive effect in terms of cost structure.[545]

If a reorganization is not carried out for valid commercial reasons, this gener- **568** ally justifies the presumption of tax evasion or tax avoidance. However, in order to determine whether the planned operation has such an objective, the **application of general, predetermined criteria is not admissible**. In fact, an examination on a case-by-case basis has to take place that must be open to judicial review.[546]

Even if there are some **commercial reasons**, the attainment of a pure **tax** **569** **advantage** (like the utilization of losses) was and still is not accepted as a valid commercial reason by the ECJ.[547] In the *Zwijnenburg* case the question at stake was which tax advantages preclude the application of the Merger Directive. May the benefits of the Merger Directive be neglected if any taxes (e.g. transaction taxes on immovable property) are avoided or only if taxes are avoided to which the benefits of the Merger Directive relate. According to the ECJ, only the avoidance of taxes to which the benefits of the Merger Directive relate precludes the application of the Merger Directive.[548]

The laying down of a general rule automatically excluding certain operations **570** from the benefits of the Merger Directive would go further than is necessary for preventing tax evasion or tax avoidance. Therefore, such a **general exclusion would infringe the principle of proportionality**.[549]

b) Representation of Employees on Company Organs

Under Art. 15(1)(b), a provision was included that a Member State may withdraw **571** the benefit of all or any part of the Merger Directive if the transaction generally covered by the Merger Directive results in a **reduction or cancellation of employees' representation** on the companies' board of directors.

This provision, resulting in a denial of the application of the Merger Direc- **572** tive, was included at the request of Germany. The employees' representation on the company boards has **nothing to do with tax** deferrals granted for a qualifying reorganization under the Merger Directive. In fact, Art. 15(1)(b) is a provision dealing with labour law.

---

[545] ECJ 10 November 2011, C-126/10, *Foggia* (not yet published) para. 52.
[546] ECJ 10 November 2011, C-126/10, *Foggia* (not yet published) para. 37.
[547] ECJ 17 July 1997, C-28/95, *Leur-Bloem* [1997] ECR I-4161, para. 50 et seq.
[548] ECJ 20 May 2010, C-352/08, *Zwijnenburg* [2010] ECR-4303 para. 47 et seq.
[549] ECJ 17 July 1997, C-28/95, *Leur-Bloem* [1997] ECR I-4161, para. 52 et seq.

573 6. Overview of the Functioning of the Directive

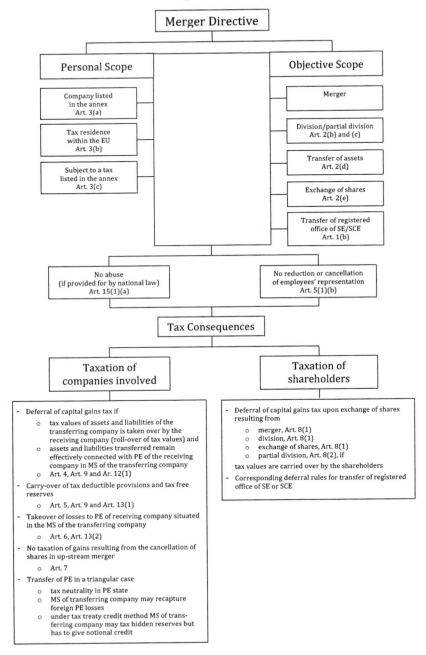

VI. The Interest and Royalty Directive

Dimitar Hristov

Legal Basis: Council Directive 2003/49/EC of 3 June 2003 on a common system of taxation applicable to interest and royalty payments made between associated companies of different Member States, OJ L 157 of 26 June 2003, pp. 49–54; Proposal for a Council Directive on a common system of taxation applicable to interest and royalty payments made between associated companies of different Member States of 11 November 2011, COM (2011), 714.

Literature: Weber, The proposed EC Interest and Royalty Directive, *EC Tax Review* 2000, p. 15; Brokelind, Royalty Payments: Unresolved issues in the Interest and Royalties Directive, *ET* 2004, p. 252; Cerioni, Intra-EC interest and royalties tax treatment, *ET* 2004, p. 47; Distaso/ Russo, The EC Interest and Royalties Directive – A comment, *ET* 2004, p. 143; Eicker/Aramini, Overview on the recent developments of the EC Directive on withholding taxes on royalty and interest payments, *EC Tax Review* 2004, p. 134; Rodriguez, Commentary on the EC Interest and Royalties Directive, in Thömmes/Fuks (eds.) *EC Corporate Tax Law*, 27th suppl. (October 2004); Gusmeroli, Triangular cases and the Interest and Royalties Directive: Untying the Gordian knot? – Part 1, 2 and 3, *ET* 2005, pp. 2, 39 and 86; Eberhartinger/Six, National Tax Policy, the Directives and Hybrid Finance, in K. Andersson et al. (eds.), *National Tax Policy in Europe* (2007), p. 225; Terra/Wattel, *European Tax Law* (2008); Report from the Commission to the Council in accordance with Article 8 of Council Directive 2003/49/EC on a common system of taxation applicable to interest and royalty payments made between associated companies of different Member States, COM (2009) 179; Bundgaard, Classification and treatment of hybrid financial instruments and income derived therefrom under EU Corporate Tax Directives – Part 1 and 2, *ET* 2010, pp. 442 and 490; Fernandes/Bernales/Goeydeniz/Michel/Popa/ Santoro, A comprehensive analysis of proposals to amend the Interest and Royalties Directive – Part 1 and 2, *ET* 2011, pp. 396 and 445; Riis, Danish tax authorities prevail in recent beneficial ownership decision, *ET* 2011, p. 184; van Dongen, Thin capitalization legislation and the EU Corporate Tax Directives, *ET* 2012, p. 20.

Case Law: ECJ 17 October 1996, joined cases C-283/94, C-291/94 and C-292/94, *Denkavit, VITIC and Voormeer* [1996] ECR I-5063; ECJ 17 July 1997, C-28/95, *Leur-Bloem* [1997] ECR I-4161; ECJ 18 September 2003, C-168/01, *Bosal Holding* [2003] ECR I-9409; ECJ 21 July 2011, C-397/09, *Scheuten Solar Technology GmbH* [2011] ECR I-0000.

1. Principles

574 On 1 January 2004 the Interest and Royalty Directive entered into force after long years of preparatory works and many disputes. The Interest and Royalty Directive is based on the notion that in the single market interest and royalty payments between associated companies of different Member States should not be subject to less favourable tax conditions than those applicable to the same payments carried out between associated companies of the same Member State. Less favourable tax conditions could consist in a double taxation of such EU cross-border payments since bilateral and multilateral tax treaties do not always ensure the elimination of double taxation. E.g. not all tax treaties provide for a reduction at source in the source state and credit in the residence state of the recipient; furthermore, bilateral tax treaties in particular do not contain solutions for triangular situations[550] and are not concluded between all EU Member States. Although in many cases double taxation is avoided through the application of tax treaties, the application of the particular tax treaty and especially source taxation often causes additional administrative burdens, cash-flow problems, interest and other opportunity costs.[551] Thus, according to Recital (1) of the Interest and Royalty Directive, an **equal treatment** of EU cross-border and domestic interest and royalty payments should be achieved by the Directive whereby less favourable tax conditions, as well as double taxation and double non-taxation could also be avoided. However, from a practical point of view it should be mentioned that due to the burdensome application requirements of the Interest and Royalty Directive companies often prefer to rely on a "zero" source tax rate (e.g. as provided for in Art. 12 OECD Model), if it is applicable under the respective double tax treaty.

575 The **main principle of the Interest and Royalty Directive** is found in Art. 1(1), which provides for an **exemption from source state tax** (which is in most cases a domestic withholding tax) **for interest and royalty payments** made by

(a) a **company** of a Member State or by
(b) a **permanent establishment** situated in another Member State of a company of a Member State,

---

[550] Terra/Wattel, *European Tax Law* (2008) p. 609; see on the issue of triangular cases, Gusmeroli, *ET* 2005, p. 2 et seq., p. 39 et seq. and p. 86 et seq.
[551] See e.g. Eicker/Aramini, *EC Tax Review* 2004, p. 134 et seq.

provided that the **beneficial owner** of the interest or royalty payments is
  (i) an **associated company** of another Member State or
  (ii) a **permanent establishment** situated in another Member State of an associated company of a Member State.

For the applicability of the benefits of the Interest and Royalty Directive it is **576** generally irrelevant whether a source tax was levied by deduction at "source" or by "assessment"; a source tax is generally abolished according to Art. 1(1) if the application requirements of the Interest and Royalty Directive are met (see m.nos. 583 et seq.).[552] In this context it has to be pointed out that according to the *Scheuten Solar Technology GmbH* case[553] Art. 1(1) does not preclude a provision of the national (in the concrete case: German) tax law according to which a loan interest paid by a (German) company to another associated (in the concrete case: Dutch) company is included into the assessment/tax base of the trade tax payable by the German company. Further, it is important to note that according to Art. 1(7) the company which is the **payer**, or the company whose permanent establishment is treated as the payer of the interest or royalty payment, has to be an **associated company** of the company that is the **beneficial owner**, or whose permanent establishment is treated as the beneficial owner, of that interest or royalty payment.

Art. 9 furthermore contains a **delimitation clause** whereby the applicability **577** of more favourable national or tax treaty provisions may not be excluded by the application of the Directive. This is also a tax harmonization clause[554] so that in such a way the harmonization obligations of the Member States are kept to a minimum. Moreover, when implementing the Interest and Royalty Directive into national law the Member States have to keep in mind the decision of the ECJ in the *Bosal Holding* case in which it was ruled that Member States must take into consideration the non-discrimination principle and the fundamental freedoms of the EU in the implementation of directives.[555]

Further, it has to be mentioned that the legal terms used by the Interest and **578** Royalty Directive are obviously similar to some definitions of the **OECD Model**, the **Parent-Subsidiary Directive** and the **Merger Directive**. The relation of the Interest and Royalty Directive to the OECD Model and the above-mentioned Directives will be discussed in more detail where the similarities have relevance for the interpretation and the application of the Interest and Royalty Directive. However, in any case it has to be pointed out that the terms used by the Interest

---

[552] Rodriguez, in Thömmes/Fuks (eds.) *EC Corporate Tax Law* (October 2004) para. 197 et seq.

[553] ECJ 21 July 2011, C-397/09, *Scheuten Solar Technology GmbH* [2011] ECR I-0000.

[554] Rodriguez, in Thömmes/Fuks (eds.) *EC Corporate Tax Law* (October 2004) para. 291.

[555] ECJ 18 September 2003, C-168/01, *Bosal Holding* [2003] ECR I-9409, para. 26 et seq.; Rodriguez, in Thömmes/Fuks (eds.) *EC Corporate Tax Law* (October 2004) para. 292.

and Royalty Directive have a meaning which is **autonomous** from the terms of the OECD Model.[556]

2. Historical Development

579 In 1990/91 the Commission prepared the **first proposal** on a common tax treatment of EU cross-border interest and royalty payments between parent companies and subsidiaries in different Member States.[557] As regards the personal scope, the scope of the first proposal was similar to the scope of the Parent-Subsidiary Directive and covered only payments made by parent companies holding directly a participation in a subsidiary company. The Ruding Committee mentioned in 1992[558] the necessity to achieve the quickest possible adoption of this first proposal for a Directive. Due to the fact that the Council was unable to agree on certain specific issues, the first proposal was withdrawn by the Commission in 1994.[559]

580 In 1997 the Commission was asked to submit a new proposal after the ECOFIN Council expressed the need for coordinated action at a European level to combat harmful tax competition and to reduce distortions in the single market.[560] Hence, in 1998 the Commission elaborated a **second proposal**[561] on a common tax treatment of interest and royalty payments made between associated companies. In comparison to the first proposal the personal scope of the second proposal was extended from payments between parent companies and subsidiaries to payments between associated companies. Henceforth, the term "associated companies" also covered indirect holdings of parent companies in subsidiary companies.

581 The final **adoption** of the Interest and Royalty Directive by the Council took place on 3 June 2003. Ultimately, the Directive was restricted to direct holdings, whereas the second proposal from 1998 also covered indirect holdings. The justification for this restriction was probably the apprehension of some Member States that the Directive as amended in the second proposal could have a major financial impact on the tax revenue of the Member States.[562] According to Art. 7(1), the final date for implementation was 1 January 2004. However, Art. 6

---

[556] van Dongen, *ET* 2012, p. 22.
[557] See Proposal for a Council Directive on a common system of taxation applicable to interest and royalty payments made between parent companies and subsidiaries in different Member States, COM(1990) 571 final of 6 December 1990, OJ C 53 of 28 February 1991, p. 26 et seq.
[558] Commission of the European Communities, *Conclusions and Recommendations of the Committee of Independent Experts on Company Taxation* (1992) p. 30.
[559] Commission press release IP/94/1023 of 8 November 1994.
[560] Rodriguez, in Thömmes/Fuks (eds.) *EC Corporate Tax Law* (October 2004) para. 5.
[561] See on this second proposal, Weber, *EC Tax Review* 2000, p. 15 et seq.
[562] Distaso/Russo, *ET* 2004, p. 144; Rodriguez, in Thömmes/Fuks (eds.) *EC Corporate Tax Law* (October 2004) para. 23.

provides for transitional rules for the Czech Republic, Greece, Spain, Latvia, Lithuania, Poland, Portugal and Slovakia. As regards Bulgaria and Romania the accession treaties contain transitional rules on the implementation of the Interest and Royalty Directive in these two Member States.

In **2011** the Commission adopted a **proposal containing amendments** for the **582** Interest and Royalty Directive.[563] The proposal has as its background in the 2009 Report from the Commission to the Council (which has its origins in Art. 8) on the functioning of the Interest and Royalty Directive.[564] The Commission intends by the proposal, on the one hand, to extend the list of companies (legal forms) covered by the Directive. On the other hand, the Commission wants to reduce the shareholding (threshold) requirements for associated companies from a 25% minimum direct holding to a 10% direct or indirect holding. Further, the Commission wants to make it clear that Member States would have to grant the benefits only to companies which are not exempt from corporate taxation; this addresses in particular companies which, while subject to corporate tax, also benefit from a special national tax (incentive) scheme exempting foreign interest or royalty payments received (e.g. "tax holidays" for a specific period of time, etc.).

3. Application Requirements

a) Personal Scope

i. Company of a Member State

As mentioned in m.no. 575, the exemption from source state tax is applicable **583** only if the payer of the interest or royalty is a company of a Member State or a permanent establishment of a company of a Member State and if the beneficial owner of the interest or royalty payment is an associated company of a Member State or a permanent establishment of an associated company of a Member State. Thus, in either case a **company of a Member State** is required for the applicability of the Directive. Art. 3(a) contains the definition of the term "company of a Member State" and makes the definition dependent on the fulfilment of three cumulative requirements.[565]

As a first requirement, according to Art. 3(a)(i), the company has to take one **584** of the legal forms listed in the annex to the Interest and Royalty Directive. The

---

[563] See the Proposal for a Council Directive on a common system of taxation applicable to interest and royalty payments made between associated companies of different Member States of 11 November 2011, COM (2011), 714.

[564] Report from the Commission to the Council in accordance with Article 8 of Council Directive 2003/49/EC on a common system of taxation applicable to interest and royalty payments made between associated companies of different Member States, COM (2009) 179; see further Fernandes/Bernales/Goeydeniz/Michel/Popa/Santoro, ET 2011, pp. 396 and 445.

[565] Distaso/Russo, *ET* 2004, p. 143.

annex provides an **exhaustive list of companies**[566] – similar to the (broader) list of the Parent-Subsidiary Directive – to which the Interest and Royalty Directive applies so that a legal entity not expressly mentioned may not benefit from the Directive, either as payer or as payee.[567] As regards the SE and the SCE, the Commission proposes to broaden the scope of the Interest and Royalty Directive to these two legal forms[568], which are not yet expressly contained in the Annex of the Directive.[569] Nevertheless, e.g. *Herzig/Griemla*[570] support the notion that the Interest and Royalty Directive is already applicable to the SE. For the potential future development regarding the list of companies see m.no. 582. Another important issue to which the tax literature pays attention is the question whether unincorporated **tax-transparent companies** (e.g. partnerships) may benefit from and fall within the scope of the Interest and Royalty Directive especially on the basis of Art. 54 TFEU (ex Art. 48 EC).[571] This question and the related problems do not yet seem to be resolved. In this context it further has to be mentioned that the Directive covers in any case some legal forms from the Eastern-European countries such as e.g. the Bulgarian "Командитно дружество" and "Събирателно дружество" or the Slovak "komanditná spoločnos" and "verejná obchodná spoločnos" which as commandit or open partnerships/companies are treated, in general, as tax-intransparent entities in their residence state but are characterized as tax-transparent entities in another foreign Member States (as e.g. this would be the case in Austria).

585 According to Art. 3(a)(ii), the second requirement is the necessity for the company – mentioned in the Annex of the Interest and Royalty Directive – to be **resident for tax purposes in a Member State** and not to be – within the meaning of a double taxation convention – a resident for tax purposes in a third state. This provision is especially of importance for dual resident companies. To solve the problem of dual residence the Interest and Royalty Directive refers to the relevant double taxation convention concluded with a third state. Normally double taxation conventions contain a tie-breaker-provision and provide – as Art. 4(3) of the OECD Model does – that with respect to dual resident companies the place of effective management is the preferred criterion. If according to the double taxation convention, the company is resident in a Member State, the Interest and Royalty Directive is applicable; otherwise, the benefits of the Directive are de-

---

[566] The list was amended at last by Council Directive 2006/98/EC of 20 November 2006 adapting certain Directives in the field of taxation, by reason of the accession of Bulgaria and Romania, OJ L 363 of 20 December 2006, p. 129 et seq.

[567] Rodriguez, in Thömmes/Fuks (eds.) *EC Corporate Tax Law* (October 2004) para. 25.

[568] See Proposal for a Council Directive on a common system of taxation applicable to interest and royalty payments made between associated companies of different Member States of 11 November 2011, COM(2011) 714, p. 7 et seq.

[569] Van Dongen, *ET* 2012, p. 22.

[570] Eicker/Aramini, *EC Tax Review* 2004, p. 144 footnote 53.

[571] Weber, *EC Tax Review* 2000, p. 17 et seq.

nied. As regards (especially Eastern-European) partnerships mentioned in the annex list of the Directive, the problem could arise that e.g. an interest-receiving partnership is characterized as tax resident by one Member State (e.g. where the interest or royalty payment is received) but not by the other Member State (where e.g. an interest or royalty payment is arising) as e.g. the other Member State does not recognize foreign partnerships as taxable entities (and therefore denies a residence status at all) or as e.g. the interest is received via a foreign permanent establishment of the partnership and the permanent establishment is situated in a Member State which does not recognize foreign partnerships as taxable entities either (and therefore denies their residence status at all). Nevertheless, in the author's opinion in all these situations the Directive will apply as the respective partnership (mentioned in the Annex of the Directive) is in any case tax resident of one Member State. Otherwise the aim of Art. 3(a)(i) to cover specific legal forms of companies may be circumvented by a Member State only on the background of its own national tax law by denying the residence status of a partnership mentioned in the Annex of the Directive.

The **subject-to-tax condition** of Art. 3(a)(iii) is the third and final require- **586** ment that has to be met in order for the Interest and Royalty Directive to be applicable. In this context the company has to be – as the Parent-Subsidiary Directive and the Merger Directive similarly provide – subject to one of the taxes listed in Art. 3(a)(iii) without being exempt, or to a tax which is identical or substantially similar and which is imposed after the date of entry into force of the Interest and Royalty Directive in addition to, or in place of the taxes listed in Art. 3(a)(iii). As regards the interpretation of the subject-to-tax requirement it was disputed in the tax literature whether the company itself may not be personally exempt from tax (subjective requirement)[572] or whether the income of the company may not be exempt from tax (objective requirement).[573] In my opinion, it is clear that the subject-to-tax requirement is a subjective one. This interpretation can be inferred from the wording of the introductory sentence of Art. 3(a) in conjunction with Art. 3(a)(iii), which defines the term "company of a Member State" as "any company: which is subject to tax to one of the following taxes without being exempt". "Without being exempt" obviously refers to the company itself and not to its income or to parts of its income. For the potential developments regarding the subject-to-tax-condition see m.no. 582.

ii. Permanent Establishments

According to Art. 1(1), the payer (see m.nos. 600 et seq.) or the beneficial owner **587** (see m.nos. 602 et seq.) of interest and royalty payments may also be a **permanent establishment belonging to** a company of a Member State that is situated in a

---

[572] Distaso/Russo, *ET* 2004, p. 143; Rodriguez, in Thömmes/Fuks (eds.) *EC Corporate Tax Law* (October 2004) para. 36.
[573] Weber, *EC Tax Review* 2000, p. 20 et seq.

different Member State. Thus, it is important to point out that according to Art. 1(8) the exemption from source state tax in Art. 1(1) is not applicable if the payer or payee is a permanent establishment situated in a third state of a company of a Member State and the business of that company is wholly or partly carried on through that permanent establishment. Correspondingly, Art. 3(c) defines a "permanent establishment" as a fixed place of business situated in a Member State through which the business of a company of another Member State is wholly or partly carried on. The similarity of this definition to Art. 5(1) of the OECD Model and Art. 2(2) of the Parent-Subsidiary Directive is obvious and the interpretation problems arising as a result of this definition (e.g. concerning building sites or construction or installation projects) have been discussed frequently in the tax literature.[574] Ultimately, the ECJ will have to find an autonomous interpretation of the term "permanent establishment".

588   By the extension of the personal scope, the Interest and Royalty Directive seems to resolve within the EU dual source problems in connection with **triangular and quadrangular cases** involving permanent establishments.[575] In such cases, a separate bilateral double tax convention generally does not contain real solutions due to its bilateral character. Nevertheless, it should be mentioned that the Interest and Royalty Directive resolves triangular and quadrangular situations only if the companies to which the payer or the payee-permanent establishment belongs are associated companies according to Art. 3(b) (see m.nos. 589 et seq.). Outside the scope of association, reference has to be made to the certain double taxation conventions concluded between the various Member States. Furthermore, in the tax literature it has been also noted that even within the scope of the Interest and Royalty Directive not all problems connected with triangular and quadrangular situations seem to be resolved.[576]

iii. Associated Companies

589   The source tax exemption applies only if the company that is the payer or the company whose permanent establishment is treated as the payer of interest or royalty payments is an **associated company** of the company which is the beneficial owner or whose permanent establishment is treated as the beneficial owner of that interest or royalty payment. This requirement is laid down in Art. 1(7) and made concrete in Art. 3(b). As mentioned in m.nos. 500 et seq., the association may only exist between companies of EU Member States within the meaning of Art. 3(a). To benefit from the Interest and Royalty Directive, companies of third states are excluded from the personal scope of the Directive.

---

[574] Distaso/Russo, *ET* 2004, p. 146 et seq.; Rodriguez, in Thömmes/Fuks (eds.) *EC Corporate Tax Law* (October 2004) para. 82 et seq.; Weber, *EC Tax Review* 2000, p. 23 et seq.; Terra/Wattel, *European Tax Law* (2008) p. 619.

[575] Eicker/Aramini, *EC Tax Review* 2004, p. 141.

[576] Gusmeroli, *ET* 2005, p. 2 et seq., p. 39 et seq. and p. 86 et seq.

Art. 3(b) provides for purposes of the Interest and Royalty Directive **two dif-** **590** **ferent forms of association**. The first form is a direct vertical association (Art. 3(b)(i) and (ii)), which requires that the company which is the payer or whose permanent establishment is treated as the payer of the interest or royalty payments has a direct minimum holding of 25 % in the capital of the company which is the beneficial owner or whose permanent establishment is treated as the beneficial owner of that interest or royalty payment (**downstream payments**). Vice versa, the vertical association covers the reverse situation, which requires that the company that is the beneficial owner or whose permanent establishment is treated as the beneficial owner of the interest or royalty payments has a direct minimum holding of 25 % in the capital of the company which is the payer or whose permanent establishment is treated as the payer of that interest or royalty payment (**upstream payments**). The second form of association is a direct horizontal association (Art. 3(b)(iii)), which requires that a parent company, which is neither the payer nor the beneficial owner of interest or royalty payments, has a direct minimum holding of 25 % both in the capital of the subsidiary company which is the payer or whose permanent establishment is treated as the payer of the interest or royalty payments and in the capital of the other subsidiary company which is the beneficial owner or whose permanent establishment is treated as the beneficial owner of that interest or royalty payment (**sidestream payments**). For the potential developments regarding the covered forms of associations see m.no. 582.

As regards the required **quality of the association**, attention should be paid **591** to the following three issues. First of all, the Interest and Royalty Directive requires a direct holding, in other words an indirect holding[577] is insufficient and the applicability of the Directive could be denied if the participation is not a direct one.[578] Secondly, Art. 3(b) allows the Member States to replace the requirement of a minimum holding in the capital with that of a minimum holding of voting rights. Thirdly, Art. 1(10) provides that a Member State has the option of not applying the Interest and Royalty Directive to a company in circumstances where the required forms of association "have not been maintained" for an interrupted period of at least two years (temporal criterion). In the tax literature the applicability of the ECJ's decision in the *Denkavit-VITIC-Voormeer* case[579] has been discussed due to similarity of Art. 1(10) to the provision of Art. 3(2) of the

---

[577] E.g. if a parent company is holding a participation in a subsidiary company through an intermediary (non-transparent) partnership or if a grandparent company is holding a participation in a sub-subsidiary through an intermediary company.

[578] See on this issue Distaso/Russo, *ET* 2004, p. 145 et seq.; Rodriguez, in Thömmes/Fuks (eds.) *EC Corporate Tax Law* (October 2004) para. 67 et seq.; Terra/Wattel, *European Tax Law* (2008) p. 617; see on the situation at the time of the second Interest and Royalty Directive proposal in 1998: Weber, *EC Tax Review* 2000, p. 22.

[579] ECJ 17 October 1996, joined cases C-283/94, C-291/94 and C-292/94, *Denkavit, VITIC and Voormeer* [1996] ECR I-5063, m.no. 445.

Parent-Subsidiary Directive and due to the fact that the Interest and Royalty Directive uses the past tense and the Parent-Subsidiary Directive uses the present tense. One of the opinions in the literature – and in the author's opinion the correct one – is that the *Denkavit-VITIC-Voormeer* decision is fully applicable to Art. 1(10), with the consequence that it is, in principle, not necessary for the required two-year holding period to have ended at the time the interest or royalty payment is made, provided the companies complete the required period of two years after the payment.[580]

b) Substantive Scope

i. Cross-Border Interest or Royalty Payments

592 On the one hand, the source tax exemption of the Interest and Royalty Directive applies to **interest** payments. According to the definition in Art. 2(a), interest payments mean "income from debt-claims of every kind, whether or not secured by mortgage and whether or not carrying a right to participate in the debtor's profits, and in particular, income from securities and income from bonds or debentures, including premiums and prizes attaching to such securities, bonds or debentures; penalty charges for late payment shall not be regarded as interest". The definition of "interest" in the Interest and Royalty Directive mirrors Art. 11(3) of the OECD Model and obviously refers to the definition in the OECD Model except for the exclusion of government securities.[581] Unlike the OECD Model, the Interest and Royalty Directive contains in Art. 4(1) an explicit catalogue of specific payments that are excluded from the definition of "interest" (see m.nos. 594 et seq.). Despite the similar definitions of Art. 2(a) of the Interest and Royalty Directive and Art. 11(3) of the OECD Model, EU law should be interpreted autonomously[582] although a reference of the ECJ to the interpretation concepts concerning Art. 11(3) of the OECD Model would seem to be an appropriate solution.[583]

593 On the other hand, the source tax exemption of the Interest and Royalty Directive applies also to **royalty** payments. According to the definition in Art. 2(b), royalty payments mean "payments of any kind received as a consideration for the use of, or the right to use, any copyright of literary, artistic or scientific work, including cinematograph films and software, any patent, trade mark, design or model, plan, secret formula or process, or for information concerning industrial, commercial or scientific experience; payments for the use of, or the right to use,

---

[580] Distaso/Russo, *ET* 2004, p. 151; Rodriguez, in Thömmes/Fuks (eds.) *EC Corporate Tax Law* (October 2004) para. 74 et seq; see, on the other hand, the opposite opinion of Terra/Wattel, *European Tax Law* (2008) p. 618.

[581] See e.g. Distaso/Russo, *ET* 2004, p. 149 et seq; Van Dongen, *ET* 2012, p. 23.

[582] Van Dongen, *ET* 2012, p. 22.

[583] See e.g. Rodriguez, in Thömmes/Fuks (eds.) *EC Corporate Tax Law* (October 2004) para. 105 et seq.

industrial, commercial or scientific equipment shall be regarded as royalties". Although the definition of royalty payments also seems to mirror the definition of Art. 12(2) of the OECD Model, the definition in the OECD Model is narrower since it does not mention software royalty payments and includes only payments for the information concerning industrial, commercial or scientific experience, but not for the use of, or the right to use, industrial, commercial or scientific equipment. In contrast, the Interest and Royalty Directive covers royalty payments for the use of, or the right to use, software[584] and also royalty payments for the use of, or the right to use industrial, commercial or scientific equipment.[585]

ii. Exclusion of Specific Payments

Art. 4(1) allows the source Member States to exclude specific – in the majority of cases, interest – payments from the benefits of the Interest and Royalty Directive. The **exclusion catalogue**[586] contains, in principle, hybrid financial instruments which fall between equity and debt.[587] In this context attention should be paid to the fact that if income received from these hybrid instruments does not fall under the scope of the Interest and Royalty Directive it could fall under the scope of the Parent-Subsidiary Directive.[588] In this case the requirements for application of the Parent-Subsidiary Directive should be scrutinized.[589] One of the aims of the exclusion catalogue could be the avoidance of "double-dip situations" (i.e. a situation where interest is paid without withholding tax and remains a tax-deductible expense in the payer's state; however, the interest is treated in the payee's state as a tax-exempt dividend).[590] However, in any case the exceptions mentioned in the catalogue of Art. 4(1) have to be **interpreted restrictively** as they are meant as exceptions to the general rule of application of the Directive stipulated in Art. 1(1) and 2.[591] It should further be mentioned that there could also be cases where hybrid financial instruments fall neither under the Parent-Subsidiary Directive nor under the Interest and Royalty Directive.

594

Art. 4(1)(a) refers to payments that are treated as a **distribution of profits or as a repayment of capital** under the domestic[592] law of the source Member

595

---

[584] See e.g. Brokelind, *ET* 2004, p. 255 et seq.; Rodriguez, in Thömmes/Fuks (eds.) *EC Corporate Tax Law* (October 2004) para. 125 et seq.

[585] See e.g. Brokelind, *ET* 2004, p. 252 et seq.; Rodriguez, in Thömmes/Fuks (eds.) *EC Corporate Tax Law* (October 2004) para. 136 et seq.

[586] See Distaso/Russo, *ET* 2004, p. 149 et seq.; Rodriguez, in Thömmes/Fuks (eds.) *EC Corporate Tax Law* (October 2004) para. 140 et seq.

[587] See for details Bundgaard, *ET* 2010, p. 442 et seq.

[588] Rodriguez, in Thömmes/Fuks (eds.) *EC Corporate Tax Law* (October 2004) para. 170 et seq; see also van Dongen, *ET* 2012, p. 20.

[589] Bundgaard, *ET* 2010, p. 445.

[590] Bundgaard, *ET* 2010, p. 445.

[591] Bundgaard, *ET* 2010, p. 445.

[592] Explicitly Distaso/Russo, *ET* 2004, p. 150.

State.[593] This exclusion has a wide scope by including several forms of hybrid financial instruments and especially **interest subject to thin capitalization rules** in the source state if the source state reclassifies the interest as dividend.[594] As regards the relationship between the Interest and Royalty Directive and domestic thin capitalization rules it has to be mentioned that according to *Van Dongen* the Interest and Royalty Directive is not applicable with respect to interest payments on which the respective domestic thin capitalization rule is applicable.[595] Art. 4(1)(a) mentions further the "repayment of capital". Despite the fact that in most Member States the repayment of capital should not be a taxable event (and should also not be a tax-deductible expense) subject to withholding tax, the Directive would, nevertheless, allow a withholding tax.[596]

596 Art. 4(1)(b) mentions payments from debt-claims that carry a right to participate in the profits of the debtor (i.e. **profit-sharing loans**).[597] This provision would potentially exclude some profit-participating loans, participating bonds, jouissance rights and silent partnerships from the scope of the Directive.[598] According to *Eberhartinger/Six*, this provision, in combination with the Parent-Subsidiary Directive, provides a Member State with the possibility of totally excluding jouissance rights and silent partnerships from the Directives by treating them as debt under domestic law.[599]

597 Furthermore, Art. 4(1)(c) contains the possibility for the source Member State to exclude payments from debt-claims that entitle the creditor to exchange his right to interest for a right to participate in the profits of the debtor (i.e. **convertible debt instruments**).[600] A literal interpretation of this provision would exclude convertible bonds/loans and warrant bonds/loans from the Directive.[601]

598 Finally, Art. 4(1)(d) enables the source Member State to exclude payments from debt-claims that contain no provision for repayment of the principal amount or where the repayment is due more than 50 years after the date of issue (i.e. **quasi-equity**).[602] Super-maturity debt and perpetual debt fall under the scope of this provision.[603]

---

[593] Rodriguez, in Thömmes/Fuks (eds.) *EC Corporate Tax Law* (October 2004) para. 153 et seq.

[594] Bundgaard, *ET* 2010, p. 444; see for details van Dongen, *ET* 2012, p. 20 et seq.

[595] See for details Van Dongen, *ET* 2012, p. 22 et seq.

[596] Bundgaard, *ET* 2010, pp. 445 and 446 for other questions with respect to the Directive.

[597] Rodriguez, in Thömmes/Fuks (eds.) *EC Corporate Tax Law* (October 2004) para. 156 et seq.

[598] Bundgaard, *ET* 2010, p. 445.

[599] Eberhartinger/Six, in K. Andersson et al. (eds.), p. 225 et seq.; see further Bundgaard, *ET* 2010, p. 445.

[600] Rodriguez, in Thömmes/Fuks (eds.) *EC Corporate Tax Law* (October 2004) para. 159 et seq.

[601] Distaso/Russo, *ET* 2004, note 16, p. 150; Eberhartinger/Six, in K. Andersson et al. (eds.), note 25, p. 228; see further Bundgaard, *ET* 2010, p. 445.

[602] Rodriguez, in Thömmes/Fuks (eds.) *EC Corporate Tax Law* (October 2004) para. 162 et seq.

[603] Bundgaard, *ET* 2010, p. 445.

Attention should also be paid to the provision of Art. 4(2), which follows the **599** arm's length approach of Art. 11(6) of the OECD Model and Art. 12(4) of the OECD Model and is very similar to these provisions. Thus, Art. 4(2) precludes the application of the Interest and Royalty Directive for payments that are not at arm's length. The Interest and Royalty Directive assumes payments not at arm's length where by "reason of a special relationship between the payer and the beneficial owner of interest or royalties, or between one of them and some other person, the amount of the interest or royalties exceeds the amount which would have been agreed by the payer and the beneficial owner in the absence of such a relationship".[604] In this case the Interest and Royalty Directive applies only to the amount that would have been agreed by the payer and the beneficial owner in the absence of such a relationship.

iii. Sourcing Rules

The sourcing rules are connected with the question where interest or royalty **600** payments arise. If the interest or royalty payment has been made by a **company** of a Member State (see Art. 3(b) and m.nos. 500 et seq.), Art. 1(2) provides that this payment is deemed to arise in that Member State. That Member State is also treated as the source Member State for purposes of the Interest and Royalty Directive. This sourcing rule seems to be self-evident.

As regards interest or royalty payments made by a **permanent establishment** **601** belonging to a company of a Member State that is situated in a different Member State Art. 1(2) provides for the same sourcing rule as for companies of a Member State. Thus, payments made by a permanent establishment belonging to a company of a Member State that is situated in a different Member State are deemed to arise in the first-mentioned (other) Member State where the permanent establishment is situated. That Member State is also treated as the source Member State for purposes of the Directive. The Interest and Royalty Directive re-emphasizes that aim in Art. 1(6) when pointing out that if a permanent establishment is treated as the payer of interest or royalty payments self-evidently no other part of the company, to which the permanent establishment in principle belongs, may be treated as the payer of that interest or royalty payments. However, in Art. 1(3) the Interest and Royalty Directive contains another more problematical requirement for permanent establishments. This provision provides that a permanent establishment is considered to be the payer of an interest or royalty payment only if that payment is a tax-deductible expense for the permanent establishment in the Member State where the permanent establishment is situated.[605] Otherwise, the source Member State may exclude the permanent establishment from the bene-

---

[604] See e.g. 2005 OECD Commentary, Art. 11 para. 32 et seq. and Art. 12 para. 22 et seq.

[605] As regards the relationship of this provision with the *Scheuten Solar Technology GmbH case* and thin capitalization rules see Van Dongen, *ET* 2012, p. 23.

fits of the Interest and Royalty Directive.[606] *Distaso/Russo* suggest that this rule could infringe EU primary law due to the different treatment of permanent establishments and companies resulting from this provision.[607]

iv. Beneficial Ownership

602   The beneficial ownership provisions in the Interest and Royalty Directive are related to the concept of "beneficial ownership" in the area of international tax law (see Art. 11(1) and Art. 12(2) of the OECD Model)[608] and concern the question which company or which permanent establishment should be treated as the effective payee of the interest or royalty payments and also (Art. 1(9)) which Member State has the right to ultimately tax the interest or royalty payments. For companies, Art. 1(4) provides that a company of a Member State is treated as the beneficial owner of these payments if the payments are received for the **company's own benefit** and not as an intermediary for another person (e.g. agent, trustee, authorized signatory). The aim of the provision is to prevent a circumvention of the goal of the Interest and Royalty Directive not to grant indirectly the benefits of the Directive to companies from third states.[609]

603   The determination of the beneficial ownership of permanent establishments is important due to Art. 1(6), which provides that if a permanent establishment of a Member State is treated as the beneficial owner of interest or royalty payments no other part of the company, to which the permanent establishment in principle belongs, may be treated as the beneficial owner of that interest or royalty payments. Concerning permanent establishments, the provisions on the determination of the beneficial ownership differ from the above-mentioned provisions for companies. In this context Art. 1(5) sets up **two exhaustive requirements** the fulfilment of which is necessary for the characterization of a permanent establishment as beneficial owner of interest or royalty payments.

604   The first requirement is the **effective connection** of the permanent establishment with the debt-claim or the right to use information (or equipment)[610] in respect of which the interest or royalty payments have been made (Art. 1(5)(a)). The

---

[606] The provision could have relevance especially where the tax base of the permanent establishment is a notional one or where it is based on the cost-plus method; furthermore if the payments have been made from a branch to the foreign head office or if the source Member State applies thin capitalization legislation. See on this issue e.g. Rodriguez, in Thömmes/Fuks (eds.) *EC Corporate Tax Law*, (October 2004) para. 187 et seq.; Terra/Wattel, *European Tax Law* (2008) p. 612 et seq.

[607] Distaso/Russo, *ET* 2004, p. 151; Van Dongen, *ET* 2012, p. 23.

[608] Distaso/Russo, *ET* 2004, p. 148 et seq.; Eicker/Aramini, *EC Tax Review* 2004, p. 142 et seq.; Rodriguez, in Thömmes/Fuks (eds.) *EC Corporate Tax Law* (October 2004) para. 191 et seq.; Terra/Wattel, *European Tax Law* (2008) p. 629 et seq.; Weber, *EC Tax Review* 2000, p. 22 et seq.

[609] See Terra/Wattel, *European Tax Law* (2008) p. 629 et seq.; see further Riis, *ET* 2011, p. 184 et seq. regarding a Danish case on beneficial ownership and international financing structures.

[610] Art. 1(5)(a) of the Interest and Royalty Directive does not explicitly mention the right to use equipment. However, Art. 2(b) of the Interest and Royalty Directive covers payments

tax literature interprets the term "effective connection" as a necessary genuine economic link[611] between the debt-claim or the right to use from which the interest or royalty payment arises and the permanent establishment. In other words, it is important e.g. whether the payments have been received for benefit of the permanent establishment, whether the interest or royalty income is attributable to the permanent establishment[612] or whether the debt-claim or the right to use is part of the business assets of the permanent establishment.[613]

Furthermore, Art. 1(5)(b) lays down a **subject-to-tax condition**. Thus, the interest or royalty payment has to represent income in respect of which the receiving permanent establishment is subject in the Member State in which it is situated to one of the taxes mentioned in Art. 3(a)(iii)[614] or to a tax that is identical or substantially similar and which is imposed after the date of the entry into force of the Interest and Royalty Directive in addition to or in place of the taxes in Art. 3(a)(iii). **605**

4. Fraud and Abuse

The Interest and Royalty Directive contains numerous specific anti-avoidance provisions (e.g. Art. 1(4), 1(5)(b), 1(8), 1(10), Art. 3(a)(iii) and Art. 4). Art. 5 contains two **general anti-avoidance provisions** whereas according to Art. 5(1) the application of the Interest and Royalty Directive does not preclude the application of domestic or agreement-based provisions for the prevention of fraud and abuse. According to Art. 5(2), the Member States have the option to withdraw the benefits of the Interest and Royalty Directive or to refuse to apply the Interest and Royalty Directive if the principal motive or one of the principal motives for transactions is tax evasion, tax avoidance or abuse. The obvious similarity of Art. 5(1) to Art. 1(2) of the Parent-Subsidiary Directive[615] and of Art. 5(2) to Art. 11(1)(a) of the Merger Directive[616] has often been discussed in the tax literature.[617] Thus, particularly the holdings of the ECJ in the *Leur-Bloem* and the *Kofoed* decision[618] and especially the proportionality principle[619] should be rele- **606**

---

for the right to use specific equipment. Thus, a systematic view results in the interpretation that Art. 1(5)(a) of the Interest and Royalty Directive also covers the right to use equipment.

[611] See e.g. Distaso/Russo, *ET* 2004, p. 149.

[612] Rodriguez, in Thömmes/Fuks (eds.) *EC Corporate Tax Law* (October 2004) para. 196.

[613] Terra/Wattel, *European Tax Law* (2008) p. 613.

[614] In the case of Belgium and of Spain permanent establishments are subject to a non-resident income tax to which Art. 1(5)(a) of the Interest and Royalty Directive refers.

[615] See Chapter IV, m.nos. 485 et seq.

[616] See Chapter V, m.nos. 563 et seq.

[617] See e.g. Rodriguez, in Thömmes/Fuks (eds.) *EC Corporate Tax Law* (October 2004) para. 225 et seq.

[618] ECJ 17 July 1997, C-28/95, *Leur-Bloem* [1997] ECR I-4161; ECJ 5 July 2007, C-321/05, *Kofoed* [2007] ECR I-5795.

[619] See m.no. 570.

vant to an interpretation of Art. 5 of the Interest and Royalty Directive.[620] Therefore, in general reference can be made to the explanations in Chapter V, m nos. 563 et seq. However, differentiations could arise due to the different wording of the anti-avoidance provisions in the Interest and Royalty Directive.

5. Procedural Provisions

a) Attestation of Fulfilment of Application Requirements

607 Art. 1(11) to (16) contains procedural provisions for the functioning of the Interest and Royalty Directive whereas Art. 1(11) to (14) regulates the **attestation procedure**.[621] In the attestation procedure the Interest and Royalty Directive differentiates between a simplified attestation procedure and an attestation procedure based on a decision. According to Art. 1(11), the simplified attestation procedure provides that the source Member State may require an attestation by which the fulfilment of the requirements laid down in Art. 1 and Art. 3 is established. The attestation must include the information listed in Art. 1(13) (proof of residence for tax purposes, proof of beneficial ownership of the receiving company, fulfilment of subject-to-tax requirement according to Art. 3(a)(iii), proof of minimum holding, proof of holding period).[622] In the attestation procedure based on a decision according to Art. 1(12), the source Member State has the right to make it a condition for the granting of the benefits of the Interest and Royalty Directive that its tax authority has issued a decision on source tax exemption based on the above-mentioned attestation. Thus, such a decision on source tax exemption is an optional additional requirement for the Member States for the attestation. It also should be mentioned that according to Art. 1(14) if the requirements for exemption cease to be fulfilled, the receiving company or permanent establishment has an obligation to immediately inform the paying company or permanent establishment and, if the source Member State so requires, the competent authority of that source Member State.

b) Repayment of Withheld Tax at Source

608 If the source tax exemption requirements have not been attested at the time of the interest or royalty payment, the source Member State may oblige the payer of the interest or royalty to withhold the tax at the time of the payment. As a con-

---

[620] See Distaso/Russo, *ET* 2004, p. 152; Eicker/Aramini, *EC Tax Review* 2004, p. 144 footnote 56; Rodriguez, in Thömmes/Fuks (eds.) *EC Corporate Tax Law* (October 2004) para. 241 et seq.; Terra/Wattel, *European Tax Law* (2008) p. 604 et seq.; Weber, *EC Tax Review* 2000, p. 28 et seq.

[621] Distaso/Russo, *ET* 2004, p. 152 et seq.; Rodriguez, in Thömmes/Fuks (eds.) *EC Corporate Tax Law* (October 2004) para. 252 et seq.

[622] In the literature it is not exactly clear by whom the attestation should be made; see on this issue Rodriguez, in Thömmes/Fuks (eds.) *EC Corporate Tax Law* (October 2004) para. 263 et seq.; Terra/Wattel, *European Tax Law* (2008) p. 614 et seq.

sequence of a later attestation, the source Member State has to provide for a **reimbursement procedure** the principles of which are laid down in Art.1(15) and (16).[623]

6. Overview of the Functioning of the Directive

609

Application Requirements of the Interest and Royalty Directive

---

A. Substantive Scope

A.1. Interest Payment:
- Income from debt-claims of every kind
- Income from securities bonds or debentures

A.2. Royalty Payment:
- Payment for the use or the right to use copyrights, trademarks, designs, models, plans, secret formulas,etc.
- Payments for the right to use industrial, commercial or scientific equipment

A.3. No exceptions by
- recharacterization of payments or by
- anti-avoidance provisions

B. Personal Scope

B.1. Payee (beneficial owner):
- Company of a Member State or
- Permanent establishment of a company of a Member State

B.2. Payer (source):
- Company of a Member State or
- Permanent establishment of a company of a Member State

B.3. Association of companies (at least 25 % and two years):
- Direct up-stream
- Direct down-stream
- Indirect side-stream

Full exemption from domestic source tax (withholding tax), if:
- **A.1. or A.2. and A.3. fulfilled** and
- **B.1., B.2. and B.3. fulfilled**

I. Exemption at source after Attestation Procedure
(if not procedure according to II.)

II. Repayment of withheld tax at source
(if not procedure according to I.)

---

[623] Distaso/Russo, *ET* 2004, p. 153; Rodriguez, in Thömmes/Fuks (eds.) *EC Corporate Tax Law* (October 2004) para. 265 et seq.

VII. The Savings Directive

Sabine Heidenbauer

Legal Basis: Council Directive 2003/48/EC of 3 June 2003 on taxation of savings income in the form of interest payments, OJ L 157 of 26 June 2003, p. 38; Council Decision 2004/587/EC of 19 July 2004 on the date of application of Directive 2003/48/EC on taxation of savings income in the form of interest payments, OJ L 257 of 4 August 2004, p. 7; Proposal for a Council Directive amending Directive 2003/48/EC on taxation of savings income in the form of interest payments, 13 November 2008, COM(2008) 727 final.

Literature: Dassesse, Will the Proposed "Taxation of Savings Income Directive" be the Victim of its Contradictions, *JIFM* 1999, p. 78; Lodin, What Ought to be Taxed and What Can be Taxed: A New International Dilemma, *Bulletin* 2000, p. 210; Bell, EU Directive on the Taxation of Savings Income, *British Tax Review* 2001, p. 261; Lodin, International Tax Issues in a Rapidly Changing World, *Bulletin* 2001, p. 2; Bell, Updated Proposal for a Council Directive on the Taxation of Savings Income, *British Tax Review* 2002, p. 32; Bell, EU Directive on the Taxation of Savings Income, *British Tax Review* 2003, p. 475 and *Bulletin* 2003, p. 201; Gilligan, Whither or Wither the European Union Savings Directive? A Case Study in the Political Economy of Taxation, *JFC* 2003, p. 56; Keen/Ligthart, Cross-Border Savings Taxation in the European Union: An Economic Perspective, *TNI* 2004, p. 539; McLure, Will the OECD Initiative on Harmful Tax Competition Help Developing and Transition Countries?, *Bulletin* 2005, p. 90; Oberson, Agreement between Switzerland and the European Union on the Taxation of Savings – A Balanced "*Compromis Helvétique*", *Bulletin* 2005, p. 108; Vanistendael, The interest-savings directive: European hide and seek, in van Arendonk/Engelen/Jansen (eds.) *A Tax Globalist: Essays in Honour of Maarten J. Ellis* (2005) p. 326; Gläser, *Handbuch der EU-Quellensteuer* (2006); Heidenbauer, Internationale Aspekte der EU-Quellensteuer, *SWI* 2006, p. 459; Jiménez, Loopholes in the EU Savings Directive, *Bulletin* 2006, p. 480; Aigner/Gläser/Tumpel (eds.) *The Taxation of Interest Savings Income in the European Capital Market – An Analysis of Council Directive 2003/48/EC and its Implications on the Member States of the EU and Third Countries* (2006); Gläser, Taxation of Cross-Border Savings: Options for Reviewing the European Approach, *Intertax* 2007, p. 726; Aigner, Europäische Kommission schlägt Änderungen der Sparzinsenrichtlinie zur Verhinderung der Steuerflucht, *SWI* 2008, p. 571; Lozev, Implementation of the Savings Directive in Bulgaria – Selected Issues, *ET* 2008, p. 534; Offermanns, The Functioning of the EU Savings Directive: Strategies for Improvement, *DFI* 2008, p. 189; Terra/Wattel, *European Tax Law* (2008) p. 625; Aigner, *Die Sparzinsenrichtlinie – Die Koordinierung der Besteuerung von Zinsen in Europa* (2009); Aigner, Problembereiche bei der Behandlung von Trusts und Stiftungen im Anwendungsbereich der Sparzinsenrichtlinie, *ZfS* 2009, p. 59; Czakert, Der Vorschlag der Kommission zur Revision der Zinsenrichtlinie, *IStR* 2009, p. 164; Helminen, *EU Tax Law – Direct Taxation* (2009) p. 303; Hemmelgarn/Nicodème, *Tax Co-ordination in Europe: Assessing the First Years of the EU-Savings Taxation Directive*, European Commission Taxation Papers, Working Paper No 18 (2009); Kubik/Titz, Das Zahlstellenkonzept der Zinsenrichtlinie, *ÖBA* 2009, p. 517; Panayi, The Proposed Amendments to the Savings Directive, *ET* 2009, p. 179; Vanistendael, The European Interest Savings Directive – An Appraisal and Proposals for Reform, *Bulletin* 2009, p. 152; Aujean, Savings Taxation: Is Automatic Exchange of Information Becoming a Panacea?, *EC Tax Review* 2010, p. 2; Pakarinen, EU Update, *European Taxation* 2012, p. EU-13; Stewart, Transnational Tax Information Exchange Networks: Steps towards a Globalized, Legitimate Tax Administration, *World Tax Journal* 2012, p. 152.

1. Introduction: Why Have a Savings Directive?

610 It all started with Directive 88/361/EEC,[624] which provided for the **liberalization of capital movements** within the European Community (now European Union). From 1993 capital liberalization even went beyond European borders when Art. 73b of the Treaty of Maastricht (eventually renumbered as Art. 56 EC and now Art. 63 TFEU) established an *erga omnes* liberalization of capital flows, i.e. liberalization also in relation to third countries. Under this legal framework, it became important to ensure a minimum level of taxation on interest income. This is best illustrated with an example:

611 A beneficial owner, resident in Member State R, receives an interest payment from a paying agent established in Member State P. In State P, the beneficial owner is only subject to limited tax liability; quite often, no source tax is levied. The beneficial owner's state of residence would tax the worldwide income, i.e. also the cross-border interest income, but where this income remains unreported, no tax will be levied in any of the states involved. The resulting **double non-taxation** distorts the capital movements between Member States and, as a consequence, threatens the balance of the internal market. On the same lines, capital flight to non-Member States may occur and needs to be prevented.[625]

612 In order to eliminate these distortions, the Council in 2003 adopted the **Savings Directive**[626] aimed at effective taxation of cross-border interest payments in the state of residence of the beneficial owner (Art. 1). The proposals leading to this directive, as well as the directive itself, were part of the larger tax package to

---

[624] Council Directive 88/361/EEC of 24 June 1988 for the implementation of Article 67 of the Treaty, OJ L 178 of 8 July 1988, p. 5.

[625] The countermeasures with respect to capital flight to non-Member States will be discussed below in section VII.5, m.nos. 644 et seq.

[626] Council Directive 2003/48/EC of 3 June 2003 on taxation of savings income in the form of interest payments, OJ L 157 of 26 June 2003, p. 38. The legal basis for this Directive was Art. 94 EC (now Art. 115 TFEU).

tackle harmful tax competition as presented by the Commission in 1997.[627] This, in turn, constituted a crucial part of the Commission's Single Market Action Plan targeted at a full and effective functioning of the single market. The Savings Directive's ultimate aim of bringing about effective taxation of interest payments in the beneficial owner's Member State of residence is to be achieved by obligatory and automatic **exchange of information** between the competent authorities of the Member States involved. The Savings Directive differs from all other direct tax directives insofar as it does not seek to remove obstacles; rather, it seeks to ensure effective taxation of savings income and to protect national revenue from attempted tax evasion and fraud by EU national individuals.

A previous proposal for a Savings Directive,[628] however, provided for a **co-existence model** (Art. 2), leaving each Member State the choice of either exchanging the relevant information with the other Member State concerned (Art. 7) or of applying a system of withholding taxation on cross-border interest payments and sharing the respective revenue with the Member State of residence (withholding tax system, Art. 8). The less ambitious aim at that time was the mere assurance of a minimum of effective taxation in the source state (Art. 1). While this coexistence model already seemed a political compromise, Member States nevertheless continued to support their own preferences with respect to the "right" system of dealing with cross-border interest payments: The Savings Directive, as it ultimately entered into force on 1 July 2005, now establishes a compulsory exchange of information system throughout the European Union and originally left the possibility of maintaining a withholding tax system to only three explicitly mentioned Member States that insisted on protecting their banking secrecy (Austria, Belgium, Luxembourg). On 12 March 2009, however, the Belgian Minister of Finance announced that Belgium will apply the exchange-of-information regime as from 2010. Hence, amongst the EU Member States, only Austria and Luxembourg apply the withholding tax regime.[629] **613**

Initially, it was envisaged that all Member States were obliged to apply the provisions of the (final draft of the) Savings Directive from 1 January 2005. This obligation, however, was subject to the concurrent application of measures *equivalent* to those contained in the Savings Directive by Switzerland, Liechtenstein, San Marino, Monaco, and Andorra. Each of these countries was to enter into agreements with the European Community (now European Union). Similarly, the Directive would not enter into force before all agreements were in place to ensure that all the relevant dependent or associated territories (which are not members of **614**

---

[627] The package further dealt with a code of conduct for business taxation, guidelines on the application of state aid rules on measures relating to business taxation, and the treatment of interest and royalty payments between companies.

[628] Proposal for a Council Directive to ensure a minimum of effective taxation of savings income in the form of interest payments within the Community, OJ C 212 of 8 July 1998, p. 13.

[629] Details on this in section VII.3.

the European Union but which have a close relationship to a Member State)[630] apply from that same date the *same* measures as are provided for in the Savings Directive. As these conditions were not met in due time, the date for the Directive's entry into force had to be reconsidered[631] and the Directive eventually entered into force on **1 July 2005**. Newly acceding Members States have to automatically exchange information from the outset as they are required to comply with the entire *acquis unionaire* upon accession. At the European Council summit in 2000, the Member States agreed that no derogation from the exchange of information requirement will be granted in enlargement negotiations with accession countries.[632]

2. Exchange of Information

a) The Basic Mechanism of Exchanging Information

615 The main feature of the exchange-of-information system is the **reporting obligation** imposed on the paying agent. This reporting obligation is triggered as soon as an interest payment is made (or received)[633] by a paying agent established in one Member State to an individual investor resident for tax purposes in another Member State. The paying agent is obliged to report to the competent authority of its own Member State of establishment the following **information** (Art. 8):

- the identity (name, address and, if there is one, tax identification number allocated by the Member State of residence) and residence of the beneficial owner,
- the name and address of the paying agent,
- the account number of the beneficial owner, and
- the amount of interest paid or credited.

616 The beneficial owner's **identity** is to be established on the basis of the passport or of the official identity card presented (Art. 3(2)). The beneficial owner's **residence** is considered to be located in the country where he has his permanent address. This is to be established with reference to the address mentioned on the

---

[630] The treatment of these dependent or associated territories is dealt with in more detail in section VII.5, m.nos. 644 et seq.

[631] The "Green light note" which triggered the application of the Savings Directive as well as that of the Savings Agreements between the European Community (now European Union) and five key European third countries and between the then 25 Member States and the ten relevant associated and dependent territories (see below in section VII.5, m.nos. 644 et seq.) was adopted by the Council of Ministers of the European Union on 24 June 2005.

[632] See Conclusions of the Presidency, Santa Maria da Feira European Council, 19 and 20 June 2000; Annex IV (Report from the ECOFIN Council to the European Council on the Tax Package).

[633] See the definition of "paying agent" below in section VII.2.b), m.nos. 624 et seq.

passport, on the official identity card, or, if necessary, on the basis of any documentary proof of identity presented by the beneficial owner. If the beneficial owner presents a passport or official identity card issued by a Member State but declares himself to be a resident of a third country, he is required to present a tax residence certificate issued by the competent authority of the said third country. Failure to do so results in the beneficial owner being considered a resident of the Member State that issued his passport or official identity card (Art. 3(3)).[634]

617 The competent authority of the Member State of the paying agent, in turn, is obliged to forward the information gathered to the competent authority of the beneficial owner's Member State of residence. This exchange of information is to take place automatically and at least once a year, within six months following the end of the tax year of the paying agent's Member State of establishment (**automatic exchange of information**, Art. 9). Having received this information, the competent authority of the Member State of residence of the beneficial owner is then in a position to tax the investor accordingly on his cross-border interest receipts.

618 The following chart illustrates the system of information exchange:

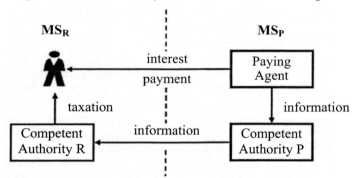

b) Essential Concepts of the Exchange of Information Mechanism

619 The whole concept of information exchange is based on a number of **technical terms** that are given a specific meaning within the scope of the Savings Directive. For the Directive's applicability, it is decisive that an *interest payment* is made by a *paying agent* to the *beneficial owner* of that interest payment. The system furthermore features the *competent authorities* as supporting actors.

620 First and foremost, it must be emphasized that a **beneficial owner** (Art. 2) of an interest payment can only be an individual in order for the Savings Directive

---

[634] Less stringent obligations with respect to establishing the beneficial owner's identity and residence are imposed on the paying agent as regards contractual relations entered into before 1 January 2004; refer to Art. 3(2)(a) and Art. 3(3)(a).

to apply. Interest payments to legal persons are not covered by the Savings Directive. Hence, a beneficial owner is any individual who either receives an interest payment or for whom an interest payment is secured.

621 **Exception**: The individual potentially considered the beneficial owner of a payment may, however, provide evidence that the interest payment was not received or secured for his own benefit. In order to succeed, he has to provide evidence that

- he acts as a paying agent,
- he acts on behalf of
  i. a legal person,
  ii. an entity that is taxed on its profits under the general arrangements for business taxation,
  iii. an undertaking for collective investment in transferable securities (UCITS),[635] or
  iv. a paying agent upon receipt, or
- he acts on behalf of another individual who is the beneficial owner. In this case, the identity of that beneficial owner has to be disclosed to the paying agent.

622 If one of these exceptions is applicable, the individual in question is not considered the beneficial owner. The interest payments received by him or secured for him are outside the scope of the Savings Directive.

623 It is the paying agent's responsibility to establish the identity of the real beneficial owner where it has information suggesting that the individual who receives an interest payment or for whom an interest payment is secured may not be the real beneficial owner. Where the paying agent does not succeed in determining the beneficial owner's identity, the individual in question is to be treated as the beneficial owner.

624 A **paying agent (upon payment**, Art. 4(1)) is any economic operator who pays interest to or secures the payment of interest for the immediate benefit of the beneficial owner. It is of no relevance whether this operator is the debtor of the debt claim from which interest is derived or not. It further makes no difference whether the operator is charged by the debtor or by the beneficial owner with paying interest or securing the payment of interest, respectively.

625 For anti-avoidance reasons, the Savings Directive extends the definition of paying agent to any Union-based entity (i.e. not an individual) to which interest is paid or for which interest is secured for the benefit of the beneficial owner (**paying agent upon receipt**, Art. 4(2)). Such an entity is regarded as a paying

---

[635] This exception presupposes that the UCITS is authorized in accordance with Council Directive 85/611/EEC of 20 December 1985 on the coordination of laws, regulations and administrative provisions relating to undertakings for collective investment in transferable securities (UCITS).

agent at the time the payment is made to this entity or secured by this entity for the beneficial owner's benefit (i.e. upon receipt of the interest payment), rather than at the time it makes an interest payment to the beneficial owner. This prevents the circumvention of the Savings Directive by interposition between the beneficial owner and the economic operator of fiscally transparent entities such as trusts or partnerships. Without the extension of the definition of the paying agent, the economic operator would not be considered a paying agent and, therefore, would not be required to comply with the Savings Directive. Art. 4(2) ensures that in such a situation the obligations of the paying agent are shifted from the economic operator to the entity concerned.

The economic operator paying interest to, or securing interest for, a paying **626** agent upon receipt is obliged to communicate the name and address of the entity and the total amount of interest paid or secured to the competent authority of its Member State of establishment. This competent authority, in turn, has to pass on the information received to the competent authority of the Member State where the entity is established. This actually leads to a **double reporting obligation** by the economic operator, on the one hand, and the paying agent upon receipt, on the other hand. The following chart illustrates this concept:

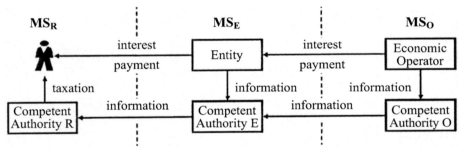

Exception: The entity, however, may produce official evidence that **627**
- it is a legal person,
- its profits are taxed under the general arrangements for business taxation, or
- it is a recognized UCITS.

Where one of these exceptions applies, the entity is not considered a paying **628** agent upon receipt. As a consequence, it does not have to comply with the obligations imposed by the Savings Directive.

An **interest payment** is, in the most elementary case, interest paid or credited **629** to an account, relating to debt claims of every kind. The term "interest payment" furthermore covers, for example, payments such as interest accrued or capitalized at the sale, refund or redemption of debt claims. In substance, these interest payments are similar to the definition of interest provided for in Art. 11 of the OECD Model. The Savings Directive, however, does not offer a general definition of "interest"; rather, it provides a list of what is considered to be interest under the Directive (Art. 6). In any case, penalty charges for late payments are explicitly excluded from the notion of interest payments and other types of income such as dividends, income from insurance and pension products as well as interest payments from certain grandfathered bonds are outside the scope of the Savings Directive.

630   The definition of the **competent authority** is, in contrast, rather straightforward: For Member States, the competent authority is simply the authority notified by the respective Member State to the Commission. For third countries, the competent authority is that which is also designated the competent authority for the purposes of tax treaties or, failing that, the authority which is competent to issue certificates of residence (Art. 5).

3. Withholding Tax System

a) The Basic Mechanism of the Withholding Tax System

631   Originally, Austria, Belgium,[636] and Luxembourg, all desiring to maintain their banking secrecy (or, as the preamble to the Savings Directive puts it: structural differences), were granted the concession of a transitional **withholding tax regime**. Instead of requiring paying agents, and competent authorities, established on their territory to exchange information, under the same circumstances and conditions, a source tax is to be withheld. During the transitional period, the **aim** of the Savings Directive is reduced to merely ensuring minimum effective taxation of savings in the form of interest payments made in one Member State to beneficial owners who are individuals resident in another Member State.

632   The rate of this withholding tax is progressively increasing in order to make it less and less attractive for a beneficial owner not to declare his cross-border interest income in his Member State of residence. From the Savings Directive's entry into force, and for a period of three years (i.e. until 30 June 2008) the **withholding tax rate** was fixed at 15 % of the amount of interest paid or credited; until 30 June 2011, 20 % had to be withheld; and since 1 July 2011, a tax rate of 35 % has been applicable. Note that, although withholding tax states do not provide information themselves during the transitional period, they are entitled to receive information from all other Member States (except, of course, from Austria and Luxembourg) in order to tax their residents receiving interest from abroad (Art. 10(1)).

633   75 % of the withholding tax has to be (anonymously) passed on to the beneficial owner's Member State of residence within six months from the end of the fiscal year concerned (**revenue sharing**, Art. 12). The residual 25 % may be retained by the Member State levying the withholding tax. This is intended to cover the cost of levying and transferring to the Member State of residence the

---

[636] Belgium has been applying the exchange of information regime as from 2010 (see m.no. 613).

withholding tax. It follows that during the first three years of the Savings Directive's applicability, the Member States applying the withholding tax regime generate tax revenue of 3.75 % of the interest income, then 5.00 % and 8.75 % from mid-2011.

As the Savings Directive's intention is not to levy an additional[637] tax on cross-border interest income, it also provides for appropriate **elimination of double taxation** (Art. 14). The Member State of residence is obliged to credit the entire amount of tax withheld against the income tax levied in this state or to refund the withholding tax (i.e. no maximum tax credit applies). Note that this obligation exists even though the Member State of residence only receives 75 % of the tax revenue. Obviously, the higher the withholding tax rate applying, the more attractive it is to report one's cross-border interest income in order to benefit from the tax credit or refund. **634**

The following chart illustrates the withholding tax procedure: **635**

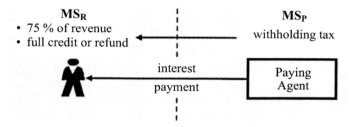

Beneficial owners explicitly desiring to be taxed by their Member State of residence only, rather than being subject to a withholding tax and a corresponding tax credit, must be given the opportunity to request that no tax be withheld. Austria and Luxembourg[638] are obliged to make available one or both of the following **exceptions to the withholding tax procedure** (Art. 13): The first alternative for a taxpayer simply is to expressly authorize the paying agent to disclose the relevant information to the tax authority of his state of residence. In this case, the normal exchange of information procedure applies. Another possibility is to authorize a beneficial owner to present to his paying agent a certificate of residence that confirms the competent authority's awareness of the interest payment. In both cases, there is no need for a withholding tax as the tax authorities of the beneficial owner's Member State of residence possess all the information required in order to accurately tax the beneficial owner. It is sufficient for a Member State to use one of these alternatives. **636**

---

[637] It has to be borne in mind that the withholding tax levied by the Member State of the paying agent's establishment does not exonerate the beneficial owner from his liability to tax in his Member State of residence.

[638] Before 1 January 2010, this was also true for Belgium.

637   The remaining two Member States admitted to the transitional withholding tax regime are certainly free to generally adopt the **exchange-of-information system** at any time before the end of the transitional period (see the example of Belgium). Remember that the Savings Directive's ultimate aim is to bring about effective taxation of cross-border interest payments in the beneficial owner's Member State of residence. In any case, as soon as

- bilateral agreements between the European Union and Switzerland, Liechtenstein, San Marino, Monaco, and Andorra that provide for the exchange of information upon request (i.e. not automatically) with respect to cross-border interest payments are in force in addition to the simultaneous application of a withholding tax on such payments, as well as
- the commitment of the United States to exchange information upon request with respect to the relevant interest payments has been confirmed by the Council,

the transitional period ends[639] and Austria and Luxembourg are required to switch to the automatic exchange of information system.

b) Relationship to Other Withholding Taxes

638   The Savings Directive allows the Member States to levy **other types of withholding tax** than the one imposed on the basis of the Savings Directive. These "other" withholding taxes may be levied in accordance with the Member State's **national law** or, if applicable, **double taxation conventions** (Art. 16).

639   If a beneficial owner's cross-border interest income has been subject to both the withholding tax to be imposed under the Savings Directive (because the paying agent is established in Austria or Luxembourg) and any other type of withholding tax (because, for example, the debtor of the interest payment is a resident of a third country), and the Member State of residence grants a tax credit for this other withholding tax under domestic or tax treaty law, this **other withholding tax is to be credited first**. Where not enough domestic income tax is levied on the interest payment so as to fully credit both types of withholding tax, this procedure leads to a maximum of refundable withholding tax: First, the other withholding tax is credited up to the maximum amount available; thereafter, a full refund with respect to the withholding tax imposed on the basis of the Savings Directive is granted.

640   Double taxation conventions concluded between the Member States of the European Union generally provide for a lower withholding tax rate than that provided for by the Savings Directive, which will eventually be as high as 35 %. The **precedence of EU law**, however, resolves this conflict in favour of the Savings

---

[639] The transitional period ends at the end of the first full fiscal year following the later of the two events mentioned.

Directive: The paying agent's Member State of establishment is obliged to impose the withholding tax as provided for by the Savings Directive and the beneficial owner's Member State of residence is obliged to credit, or refund, the full amount of tax withheld.

4. Proposed Amendments to the Savings Directive

Art. 18 obliges the Commission to report to the Council every three years on the operation of the Savings Directive. Accordingly, the Commission published its first **report** on 15 September 2008.[640] In this report, the Commission concluded that the Savings Directive has proven effective within the limits set by its scope. However, the extent of the Directive's current coverage appeared insufficient in order to meet the Directive's ultimate aim. The Commission identified a number of loopholes and shortcomings and presented to the Council – by means of a proposal for an **amending directive**[641] – the changes that prove necessary in order better to ensure effective taxation of savings income and to remove undesirable distortions of competition, as mandated by Art. 18. **641**

The most significant proposed amendments concerned the **definition of interest income**. In addition to savings income in the form of interest payments, other – substantially equivalent – income from a number of innovative financial products should also be covered by the Savings Directive. This is to avoid the possibility of "converting" savings income into income from financial instruments currently not covered by the Directive. Also, the concepts of "**beneficial owner**" and "**paying agent upon receipt**" are due to be significantly refined. In total, the Commission proposes changes to ten of the Directive's articles[642] as well as the addition of two new articles and four new annexes. **642**

In the aftermath of the second review of the Directive, the Commission adopted another **report** on 2 March 2012,[643] the main findings of which highlight **643**

---

[640] Report from the Commission to the Council in accordance with Article 18 of Council Directive 2003/48/EC on taxation of savings income in the form of interest payments, 15 September 2008, COM(2008) 552 final; and the accompanying document Commission staff working document presenting an economic evaluation of the effects of Council Directive 2003/48/EC on the basis of the available data, 15 September 2008, SEC(2008) 2420.

[641] Proposal for a Council Directive amending Directive 2003/48/EC on taxation of savings income in the form of interest payments, 13 November 2008, COM(2008) 727 final. See also the respective conclusions of the Council of the European Union of 2 December 2008 (Press 342, 16231/1/08 REV 1) and 9 June 2009 (Press 168, 10737/09), the European Parliament legislative resolution of 24 April 2009 (P6_TA-PROV(2009)0325) and the opinion of the European Economic and Social Committee of 13 May 2009 (ECO/242).

[642] Changes are proposed to Arts. 1, 2, 3, 4, 6, 8, 11, 13, 15, and 18.

[643] Report from the Commission to the Council in accordance with Article 18 of Council Directive 2003/48/EC on taxation of savings income in the form of interest payments; 2 March 2012, COM(2012) 65 final; and the accompanying document Commission staff working document presenting an evaluation for the second review of the effects of the Council Directive 2003/48/EC, 2 March 2012, SWD(2012) 16 final. As part of an on-going

"the widespread use of offshore jurisdictions for intermediary entities and the growth in key markets that provide products comparable to debt claims". These findings actually reinforce the arguments for extending the scope of the Directive and also of the relevant agreements concluded in accordance with Art. 17.[644] As the EU agreements in place with five key European third countries[645] are meant to largely reflect the measures applied within the European Union, the Commission intends to open respective negotiations with these countries.[646] The ECOFIN agreement on the proposed mandate to start negotiations is pending.[647] Regular updates on the progress of the Savings Directive Review are published on the Commission's website.[648]

5. Extending the Idea of the Savings Directive: Agreements with Dependent and Associated Territories and Third Countries

644 As mentioned previously, the free movement of capital also extends to third countries (Art. 63 TFEU; ex Art. 56 EC). It may well be the case that interest payments are received from an "agent" established in one of the dependent or associated territories of the Member States (which are not Member States of the European Union) considered to be tax havens or in another low-tax third country. As the **territorial scope of the Savings Directive is limited** to paying agents established within the territory as defined in Art. 52 TEU and Arts. 349 and 355 TFEU (Art. 7 still refers to former Art. 299 EC), it is not applicable to these interest payments. This certainly triggers the threat of capital flight to the financial markets mentioned. Therefore, the Savings Directive's entry into force was made subject to the concurrent application of measures equal to those contained in the Savings Directive by all relevant dependent or associated territories and equivalent measures by Switzerland, Liechtenstein, San Marino, Monaco, and Andorra.[649] Both types of the parallel agreements came into force on 1 July 2005.[650]

645 As regards the agreements with the Member States' **dependent or associated territories**, the following technique was chosen: Each Member State and each of

---

monitoring process, the report was preceded by a Commission staff working paper (Ad hoc report on the correct and effective application of Council Directive 2003/48/EC of 3 June 2003 on taxation of savings income, 14 June 2011, SEC(2011) 775 final) in which the Commission presented the results of its due diligence examination of Member States' implementing measures and the Member States' experience with the agreements with non-EU territories and countries.

[644] These agreements are discussed in section VII.5 below.

[645] See m.no. 644.

[646] See MEMO/11/493 of 8 July 2011.

[647] See MEMO/12/353 of 15 May 2012.

[648] See http://ec.europa.eu/taxation_customs/taxation/personal_tax/savings_tax/index_en.htm (last visited 15 September 2012).

[649] See also m.no. 614.

[650] 1 January 2007 for Bulgaria and Romania.

the dependent or associated territories[651] are to conclude bilateral agreements that provide for the same measures as those enshrined in the Savings Directive. This means that all relevant dependent or associated territories will either maintain an **exchange of information** regime[652] or, during the transitional period provided for by the Savings Directive, levy a **withholding tax**[653] on the same terms as Austria, previously Belgium, and Luxembourg – the actual mechanism applicable is to be negotiated individually in each bilateral agreement. After the transitional period, all dependent or associated territories providing for the withholding tax regime in their bilateral agreements will be expected to automatically exchange information. The majority[654] of the bilateral agreements concluded by the dependent or associated territories are applied on a reciprocal basis. This means that the Member States are not only entitled to receive information or their share in the withholding tax levied where an interest payment is made from a paying agent established in one of these territories to a beneficial owner resident in a Member State; they are also obliged to provide information or transfer a share of the tax withheld to a territory where a resident of which has received an interest payment from a paying agent established in the Member State concerned.

The agreements concluded by the European Community (i.e. not by the Member States, either collectively or individually) and each of the five key **European third countries**[655] mentioned provide for measures equivalent to those contained in the Savings Directive. Each of these agreements provides for a withholding tax to be levied by the third country where an interest payment is made from a paying agent established in the third country to a beneficial owner resident in a Member State of the European Union. The withholding tax rate corresponds to that levied by Austria, previously Belgium, and Luxembourg during the transitional period. The third countries are also obliged to share the revenue gen-

646

---

[651] As proposed by the Feira report, i.e. Anguilla, Aruba, British Virgin Islands, Cayman Islands, Guernsey, Isle of Man, Jersey, Montserrat, Netherlands Antilles (which were dissolved in October 2010), and the Turks and Caicos Islands.

[652] This option has originally been chosen by Anguilla, Aruba, the Cayman Islands, and Montserrat. Since then, Guernsey (as from 1 July 2011), Isle of Man (as from 1 July 2011), the British Virgin Islands (as from 1 January 2012), and Turks and Caicos Islands (as from 1 July 2012) have moved to automatic exchange of information. The three special municipalities emanating from the former Netherlands Antilles are now part of the Netherlands and hence also provide automatic exchange of information.

[653] A withholding tax will be levied by Jersey and the two constituent countries emanating from the former Netherlands Antilles (that is, Curaçao and Sint Maarten). As mentioned in the previous footnote, the British Virgin Islands, Guernsey, the Isle of Man, and the Turks and Caicos Islands have all recently moved to automatic exchange of information.

[654] Only the agreements with Anguilla, the Cayman Islands, and the Turks and Caicos Islands do not, for the time being, establish reciprocal rights and obligations.

[655] Andorra: OJ L 359 of 4 December 2004, p. 33; Liechtenstein: OJ L 379 of 24 December 2004, p. 84; Monaco: OJ L 19 of 21 January 2005, p. 55; San Marino: OJ L 381 of 28 December 2004, p. 33; Switzerland: OJ L 385 of 29 December 2004, p. 30.

erated by this withholding tax with the beneficial owner's Member State of residence in a ratio of 25:75. All agreements furthermore contain an option for voluntary disclosure by the beneficial owner; in such cases, no tax is withheld by the third country. Note that interest payments from a paying agent established within the European Union to taxpayers resident in the third country are not covered by the third country agreements – the agreements do not have reciprocal effect.

VIII. The Directives on Mutual Assistance in the Assessment and in the Recovery of Tax Claims in the Field of Direct Taxation

Michael Schilcher/Karoline Spies

Legal Basis: Council Directive 77/799/EEC of 19 December 1977 concerning mutual assistance by the competent authorities of the Member States in the field of direct taxation and taxation of insurance premiums, OJ L 336 of 27 December 1977; Council Directive 76/308/EEC of 15 March 1976 on mutual assistance for the recovery of claims resulting from operations forming part of the system of financing the European Agricultural Guidance and Guarantee Fund, and of agricultural levies and customs duties, and in respect of value-added tax, OJ L 73 of 19 March 1976; Council Directive 2008/55/EC of 26 May 2008 on mutual assistance for the recovery of claims relating to certain levies, duties, taxes and other measures, OJ L 150 of 26 May 2008; Council Directive 2010/24/EU of 16 March 2010 concerning mutual assistance for the recovery of claims relating to taxes, duties and other measures, OJ L 84 of 31 March 2010; Council Directive 2011/16/EU of 15 February 2011 on administrative co-operation in the field of taxation and repealing Directive 77/799/EEC, OJ L 64 of 11 March 2011; Commission Implementing Regulation (EU) No 1189/2011 of 18 November 2011 laying down detailed rules in relation to certain provisions of Council Directive 2010/24/EU concerning mutual assistance for the recovery of claims relating to taxes, duties and other measures, OJ L 302/16 of 19 November 2011.

Literature: Urtz, Exchange of Information according to the EC Mutual Assistance Directive and Tax Treaties in Austria, in Gassner/Lang/Lechner (eds.) *Tax treaties and EC law* (1997) p. 211; Grau Ruiz, *Mutual Assistance for the Recovery of Tax Claims* (2003); Hendricks, *Internationale Informationshilfe im Steuerverfahren* (2004); Seer, Die gemeinschaftsrechtliche Beurteilung der erweiterten Mitwirkungspflicht bei Auslandssachverhalten, *IWB* 2005, Fach 11 Gruppe 2, p. 673; Furuseth, Can Procedural Rules Create Obstacles to Fundamental Freedoms in European Law, *Intertax* 2007, p. 256; Herdin-Winter, Exchange of Information and Legal Protection: DTCs and EC Law, in Lang/Schuch/Staringer (eds.) *Tax Treaty Law and EC Law* (2007) p. 247; Terra/Wattel, *European Tax Law* (2012) p. 815; Caram, Enhancing International Cooperation among Tax Authorities in the Assessment and the Recovery of Taxes: The Proposals for New European Directives, *Intertax* 2009, p. 630; Hemels, References to the Mutual Assistance Directive in the Case Law of the ECJ: A Systematic Approach, *ET* 2009, p. 583; Troyer, A European Perspective on Tax Recovery in Cross-Border Situations, *EC Tax Review* 2009, p. 211; Baker/Czakert/van Eijseden/Grau Ruiz/Kana, International Assistance in the Collection of Taxes, *Bulletin* 2011, 281; Bal, Extraterritorial Enforcement of Tax Claims, *Bulletin* 2011, p. 598; Daurer, Die Amtshilfe in Steuersachen auf unionsrechtlicher Grundlage, in Lang/Schuch/Staringer (eds.) *Internationale Amtshilfe in Steuersachen* (2011) p. 13; Gabert, Council Directive 2011/16/EU on Administrative Cooperation in the Field of Taxation, *ET* 2011, p. 342; Nijkeuter, Exchange of Information and the Free Movement of Capital between Member States and Third Countries, *EC Tax Review* 2011, p. 232; Seer/Gabert, European and International Tax Cooperation: Legal Basis, Practice, Burden of Proof, Legal Protection and Requirements, *Bulletin* 2011, p. 88; Vascega/van Thiel, Council Adopts New Directive on Mutual Assistance in Recovery of Tax and Similar Claims, *ET* 2010, p. 231; Vascega/van Thiel, Assessment of Taxes in Cross-Border Situations: The New EU Directive on Administrative Cooperation in the Field of Taxation, *EC Tax Review* 2011, p. 148.

1. The Directive on Mutual Assistance in the Assessment of Taxes in the Field of Direct Taxation

a) Background and History

The first Directive on Mutual Assistance in the Assessment of Taxes in the field **647** of direct taxation (hereinafter: "**Exchange of Information Directive**") entered into force in December 1977.[656] The Directive was drafted with a view to providing for an efficient exchange of information between the Member States in order to counter new forms of tax evasion and avoidance, which are increasingly

---

[656] Council Directive 77/799/EEC of 19 December 1977 concerning mutual assistance by the competent authorities of the Member States in the field of direct taxation and taxation of insurance premiums, OJ L 336 of 27 December 1977.

assuming a multinational character.[657] Therefore, the Directive aims at **strengthening the collaboration between tax administrations** within the European Union in accordance with common principles and rules. The first Exchange of Information Directive has been **revised several times.** Its substantive scope was broadened to value added taxes in 1979,[658] excise duties in 1992[659] and insurance premiums in 2003.[660] As provisions covering administrative cooperation in the fields of VAT[661] and excise duties[662] had been regulated in separate legal instruments in the meantime, since 2003 the Exchange of Information Directive focused only on mutual assistance in the field of direct taxation and taxation of insurance premiums.[663] In 2004[664] changes were made that were intended to speed up the flow of information between Member States' tax authorities.

648   In 2009 the Commission put forward a proposal for a **completely new Directive** on administrative cooperation in the field of taxation.[665] This initiative was part of the "good governance" offensive by the European Union provoked by the successive financial crises.[666] In the Commission's view, the old Exchange of Information Directive was not efficient enough to ensure an appropriate administrative cooperation between the Member States. Also, the Directive no longer met the international cooperation standard of the OECD, a standard which had been developed further by the 2005 amendments to the OECD MC. Consequently, the new Directive creates a new legal base which should give Member States the powers to efficiently cooperate among themselves. The Council formally adopted the Directive on 15 February 2011.[667] The provisions of the new Directive will have to be implemented by the Member States **by 1 January 2013** (Art. 29), except for the provisions on automatic exchange of information (Art. 8) which will be implemented in phases starting on 1 January 2015.

649   The Exchange of Information Directive obliges Member States to exchange information on request, or even without a request, which appears relevant for the

---

[657] Preamble of the Council Directive 77/799/EEC of 19 December 1977.

[658] Council Directive 79/1070/EEC of 7 December 1979, OJ L 331 of 2 December 1979.

[659] Council Directive 92/12/EEC of 6 March 1992, OJ L 76 of 23 March 1992.

[660] Council Directive 2003/93/EC of 15 October 2003, OJ L 264 of 15 October 2003.

[661] Council Regulation 1789/2003 of 7 October 2003 on administrative cooperation in the field of value added tax and repealing Regulation (EEC) 218/92, OJ L 264 of 15 October 2003.

[662] Council Regulation (EC) 2073/2004 of 16 November 2004 on administrative cooperation in the field of excise duties, OJ L 359 of 4 December 2004.

[663] Council Directive 2003/93/EC of 15 October 2003, OJ L 264 of 15 October 2003.

[664] Council Directive 2004/56/EC of 21 April 2004, OJ L 127 of 29 April 2004.

[665] Proposal of 2 February 2009 for a Council Directive on administrative cooperation in the field of taxation, COM(2009) 29 final. See for a detailed analysis of the proposed Directive, Caram, *Intertax* 2009, p. 633 et seq.

[666] Communication from the Commission to the Council, the EP and the ESC of 28 April 2009, Promoting Good Governance in Tax Matters, COM(2009) 201 final.

[667] Council Directive 2011/16/EU of 15 February 2011 on administrative cooperation in the field of taxation and repealing Directive 77/799/EEC, OJ L 64 of 11 March 2011.

correct administration and enforcement of taxes covered by the Directive. Similar rules on the exchange of information can also be found in Art. 26 OECD MC (as well as Art. 26 UN MC), in the TIEA Model[668] and in the Multilateral Convention on Mutual Administrative Assistance in Tax Matters (MAATM Convention).[669] Since not all relations between the 27 Member States are covered by (up-to-date) bilateral or multilateral tax treaties, the Directive provides for a minimum standard of multilateral cooperation among the Member States.[670]

b) Scope of the Directive

i. Objective Scope

The Exchange of Information Directive has a **wide scope**: According to Art. 1(1),   **650** as a matter of principle any **information** that is **"foreseeably relevant"** to the **administration and enforcement** of the domestic laws of the Member States concerning taxes covered by the Directive must be exchanged. This wording permits exchange of information to the broadest possible extent. The cooperation is not limited to information relevant for the determination of the tax liability, but also includes e.g. information relevant for the recovery, the service of documents and the penalties with respect to taxes covered.[671] However, the wording is also intended to clarify that Member States are not at liberty to engage in "fishing expeditions" or to request information that is unlikely to be relevant to the tax affairs of a given taxpayer.[672] The wording "foreseeably relevant" has been copied from Art. 26 OECD MC. One could therefore argue that the Commentary to Art. 26 OECD MC may be taken into account as relevant material in interpreting this provision.

ii. Substantive Scope

According to Art. 2(1), the Exchange of Information Directive applies to **all**   **651** **taxes of any kind** levied by, or on behalf of, a Member State or its territorial or administrative subdivisions and local authorities. Art. 2(2) and (3), however, enumerate taxes that may not be covered by the Directive in an exhaustive list.

---

[668] Model agreement on exchange of information on tax matters (2002), developed by the OECD Global Forum Working Group on Effective Exchange of Information.

[669] Convention on Mutual Administrative Assistance in Tax Matters, developed by the Council of Europe (CoE) and the OECD. This Convention was opened to non-OECD and non-CoE member countries by an amending protocol in 2010, which increased its relevance.

[670] See in detail on the background Terra/Wattel, *European Tax Law* (2012) p. 815 et seq.

[671] The old Exchange of Information Directive was limited to information relevant for the "assessment" (determination of the tax liability) only. See Terra/Wattel, *European Tax Law* (2012) p. 825. As the Tax Collection Directive also obliges to exchange information foreseeably relevant for the recovery of a tax claim on request (see m.no. 702), there is an overlap in the scope of the two Directives concerning information relevant for the enforcement of taxes.

[672] See Recital 9 Directive 2011/16/EU.

According to these provisions, the Directive explicitly does not apply to value added tax, customs and excise duties covered by other Union legislation,[673] compulsory social security contributions (Art. 2(2)), fees for certificates and other public documents and dues of a contractual nature (Art. 2(3)). All taxes not listed in Art. 2(2) and (3) are covered by the Directive. This negative list approach adds to legal clarity.[674] The Directive, thus, covers in particular taxes on income and capital, including inheritance taxes,[675] real estate transfer taxes, car taxes and environmental taxes.[676]

iii. Personal Scope

652 In general, the nationality or residence of the taxpayers involved is not relevant. Therefore, even an exchange of information involving persons who are **neither nationals nor residents of any of the Member States** is possible.[677] Only the automatic exchange of information laid down in Art. 8 is limited to information concerning residents of a Member State. Moreover, the legal status of the persons affected – individuals, corporations or hybrid entities – is not relevant either. This may be derived from Art. 3(11), which defines the term "person" in a **very wide sense** including associations of persons and any other legal arrangements owning or managing assets which are subject to taxes covered.[678]

iv. Temporal Scope

653 The Directive only regulates the temporal scope for the application of **the automatic exchange of information and the admissibility of bank secrecy** as a ground for refusal of assistance. Art. 8(1) provides that the mandatory automatic exchange of information may include information regarding taxable periods as from 1 January 2014 only. With regard to bank secrecy, Art. 18(3) permits Member States to refuse the transmission of requested information held by a bank or financial institution where such information concerns taxable periods prior to 1 January 2011 and where the transmission of such information could have been

---

[673] Council Regulation (EU) No 904/2010 of 7 October 2010 on administrative cooperation and combating fraud in the field of value added tax, OJ L 268 of 12 October 2010; Council Directive 2004/106/EC of 16 November 2004 amending Directives 77/799/EEC concerning mutual assistance by the competent authorities of the Member States in the field of direct taxation, certain excise duties and taxation of insurance premiums and 92/12/EEC on the general arrangements for products subject to excise duty and on the holding, movement and monitoring of such products, OJ L 359 of 04 December 2004 and OJ L 333 of 11 December 2008; Council Regulation (EC) No 2073/2004 of 16 November 2004 on administrative cooperation in the field of excise duties, OJ L 359 of 4 December 2004.

[674] See Vascega/van Thiel, *EC Tax Review* 2011, p. 151 et seq.

[675] This was not clear under the old Directive. See Gabert, *ET* 2011, p. 342.

[676] Terra/Wattel, *European Tax Law* (2012) p. 826.

[677] See Terra/Wattel, *European Tax Law* (2012) p. 827.

[678] Such as e.g. partnerships, trusts, foundations and funds. See Terra/Wattel, *European Tax Law* (2012) p. 827.

refused on the basis of the old Directive. This means that for requests received after 1 January 2013, Member States applying domestic banking secrecy provisions (in fact, Austria and Luxembourg) will as a rule be forced to provide information resting with banks relating to taxable periods after 1 January 2011.

Besides these two provisions, no general rules on the taxable periods to which   **654** the requested information has to be related are included in the Directive. Thus, in all cases not regulated it seems to be **immaterial to which taxable period** a request relates, even if that tax year predates the entry into force of the Directive.[679] This conclusion can also be drawn from the *Tsalapos and Diamantakis* case, in which the ECJ held that the old Tax Collection Directive is to be interpreted as applying to customs claims which arose in one Member State before the Directive entered into force in the other Member State.[680]

c) Organization (Art. 4)

The Directive distinguishes between **four types** of entities engaged in the co-   **655** operation proceedings: the **competent authority, the single central liaison office ("CLO"), liaison departments and competent officials**. Each Member State has to designate a single competent authority for the purposes of the Directive which will be made public by the Commission.[681] The Member State's competent authority must then designate a single central liaison office which has the principal responsibility for contact with other Member States.[682] In addition, the competent authority is permitted, but not obliged, to appoint liaison departments and competent officials in any number. The central liaison office should keep the list of appointed liaison departments and competent officials up-to-date and make the list available to the other Member States and the Commission.

The Directive, thus, provides, as opposed to the old Directive,[683] a legal basis   **656** for a **direct communication between two internal revenue services** of different Member States, on the basis that these authorities are appointed as liaison departments or competent officials by the Member States' competent authorities.[684] *Terra/Wattel* point out that direct communication between the national delegated departments and officials should be the rule.[685] If liaison departments or com-

---

[679] See Terra/Wattel, *European Tax Law* (2012) p. 829.
[680] ECJ 1 July 2004, joined cases C-361/02 and C-362/02, *Tsapalos and Diamantakis* [2004] ECR I-6405, para. 23.
[681] See List of competent authorities referred to in Article 4(1) of Council Directive 2011/16/EU, OJ C 177 of 17 June 2011, p. 4.
[682] See Gabert, *ET* 2011, p. 342 et seq. The same approach can be found for cooperation in the field of VAT (Art. 3(2) Council Regulation No. 1798/2003) and excise duties (Art. 3(2) Council Regulation No. 2073/2004).
[683] See Terra/Wattel, *European Tax Law* (2008) p. 667.
[684] See Gabert, *ET* 2011, p. 343.
[685] See Terra/Wattel, *European Tax Law* (2012) p. 828.

petent officials are in direct contact with authorities of other Member States, they have to inform the central liaison office (Art. 4(6)).

d) Exchange of Information

657 The Directive distinguishes between three types of exchange of information: exchange on request (Arts. 5 et seq.), mandatory automatic exchange (Art. 8), and spontaneous exchange (Art. 9).

i. Exchange on Request (Arts. 5 et seq.)

658 Any designated authority laid down in Art. 4 of a Member State **may** request from a designated authority of another Member State **any information** according to Art. 1(1) (see m.no. 650). Although the opportunities for making a request are very extensive, it is necessary that a request must relate to a specific case (Art. 3(8)).[686] So-called "fishing expeditions" should, thus, not be permitted under the Directive.[687] In order to demonstrate the foreseeable relevance of the information requested, the request has to include at least the **identity of the person** under investigation and the **tax purpose** for which the information is sought (Art. 20(2)). Additional information such as the name and address of persons that might be in possession of the requested information and other helpful elements must be provided by the requesting authority only to the extent known and in line with international developments.[688] If these conditions are met, the requested State is, in principle, **obliged** to answer such a request, unless it can rely on a ground for refusal provided for in the Directive (discussed in m.nos. 672–677).

659 Art. 6 obliges the requested State to carry on **any** enquiries necessary to obtain such information and the same procedures as it would when acting for its own purposes, which also includes audits.[689] It is immaterial to this obligation that the requested information is irrelevant for the requested State's own tax purposes (Art. 18(1)). The requesting authority is also permitted to ask the requested authority to carry out a specific administrative enquiry upon a reasoned request (Art. 6(2)).

660 According to established ECJ case law, Member States are **not obliged** to make use of the Directive and request information from another Member State if

---

[686] See also on the old Directive ECJ 11 June 2009, C-155/08 und C-157/08, *X and Passenheim* [2009] ECR I-5093, para. 64.

[687] See Recital 9 Directive 2011/16/EU.

[688] One, however, has to wonder how these wording, in particular "in line with international developments", should be interpreted and what the meaning and the consequence of this provision should be. The developments on the OECD level, in particular in Art. 26 OECD MC, the TIEA Model and the corresponding commentaries could be of relevance here. This approach, however, would lead to a dynamic interpretation depending on the future decisions in a non-EU body which could be criticized from a democratic and policy point of view.

[689] See Terra/Wattel, *European Tax Law* (2008) p. 669.

the taxpayer has not provided or is even not in position to provide the necessary evidence for applying a certain tax benefit.[690] The burden of proof as a rule lies in the hands of the taxpayer.[691]

ii. Mandatory Automatic Exchange of Information (Art. 8)

As opposed to the old Directive which only permitted the Member States to introduce a system of automatic exchange of information for categories of cases,[692] under the scope of the new Directive automatic exchange of information becomes mandatory for specific categories of income and capital. Only with regard to interest payments to individuals has a mandatory automatic exchange of information already been established under the Savings Directive (see m.nos. 615 et seq.). The new Exchange of Information Directive introduces a **systematic communication** of predefined information to another Member State, without prior request, **at pre-established regular intervals** (see on the time limits m.no. 667), for specific categories of income, phased in over a longer period of time. According to Art. 8(1), the competent authority of each Member State must[693] communicate to the competent authority of another Member State information that is **"available"** concerning residents in that other Member State on the following **five specific categories of income and capital:** income from employment, director's fees, life insurance products not covered by other Union legislation, pensions, and the ownership of and income from immovable property.[694]

661

This obligation is, however, based on several **preconditions:** Regarding the temporal scope, automatic exchange of information will only be mandatory as **from 1 January 2015** including **information** regarding taxable periods **as from 1 January 2014** (see also m.no. 653). In addition, the relevant information has to be **"available"**, which means retrievable in the tax files in accordance with national procedures for gathering and processing of information of the Member State communicating the information (Art. 3(9)). This precondition may lead to significant imbalances of exchange content among the Member States.[695] The Member States have to inform the Commission of the categories of which they have information available by 1 January 2014. Member States may also indicate

662

---

[690] ECJ 27 September 2007, C-184/05, *Twoh International* [2007] ECR I-7897, para. 32; ECJ 27 January 2009, C-318/07, *Persche* [2009] ECR I-359, para. 64; ECJ 10 February 2011, C-436/08 and C-437/08, *Haribo and Österreichische Salinen* [2011] ECR I-305, para. 102; Critical see e.g. Furuseth, *Intertax* 2007, p. 256 et seq.

[691] See Nijkeuter, *EC Tax Review* 2011, p. 233 et seq. See also m.nos. 289 et seq.

[692] Art. 3 Directive 77/799/EEC.

[693] In connection with the heading to Section II "Mandatory automatic exchange of information" in the Directive, the word "shall" amounts to an obligation. See also ECJ 13 April 2000, C-420/98, *W.N.* [2000] ECR I-2847, para. 13.

[694] For the specific definitions of the categories listed the understandings under the national legislation of the Member State which communicates the information may be relied on.

[695] Terra/Wattel, *European Tax Law* (2012) p. 831 et seq.

that they do not wish to receive information on certain categories of income and capital listed or that they do not wish to receive information not exceeding a certain threshold.[696] In such a case, other Member States are not under any obligation to provide this information automatically to this specific Member State. In addition, if a Member State has no information on any single category of income or capital listed available in its tax files, this Member State will be considered to not wish to receive any information automatically. This rule serves as an '**anti-free-riding**' provision motivating the Member States to make at least one category available. If they do so, they are entitled to receive information on all categories from all other Member States.[697] Of course, the Member States are free to agree on an extended automatic exchange by bi- or multilateral agreements (Art. 8(8)). Further practical arrangements for the automatic exchange of information are to be adopted by "comitology" procedure (see m.no. 678) before entering into force on 1 January 2015.

663   The Directive also includes specific provisions on **future improvements**: In a second phase of the automatic exchange system, the Commission will submit a report providing an overview and assessment on the automatic proceeding and, if appropriate, also a proposal for revision before 1 July 2017. The mid-term goal is that **by 2017** all Member States will exchange information automatically for at least three categories of income and capital listed, and, in addition, that the list should be extended to **include dividends, capital gains and royalties** (Art. 8(5)).

iii. Spontaneous Exchange of Information (Arts. 9 et seq.)

664   In Art. 9(1) the Directive also mentions other cases in which a Member State "**shall**" inform the other State without prior request. These provisions largely correspond to the provisions on spontaneous exchange in the old Directive for which the ECJ has already clarified that this amounts to an **obligation** for the Member States.[698] A Member State **must** therefore of its own motion forward information in the five cases listed below:[699]

- a possible loss of tax in another Member State (not necessarily certain or proven, reasonable expectation is enough; a "loss of tax" refers to an **unjustified saving of tax** in another Member State);[700]
- a taxpayer obtains a tax reduction or exemption which should be followed by a corresponding tax liability or increase in another Member State (e.g. a tax in the source state is subsequently reduced, which should lead to a higher

---

[696] This seems to serve the goal of exchanging only relevant information that actually will and could be analysed and not just to "produce paper". See Gabert, *ET* 2011, p. 343.

[697] See Vascega/van Thiel, *EC Tax Review* 2011, p. 153 et seq.

[698] ECJ 13 April 2000, C-420/98, *W.N.* [2000] ECR I-2847, para. 13.

[699] See Terra/Wattel, *European Tax Law* (2012) p. 832 et seq; Urtz, in Gassner/Lang/Lechner (eds.) *Tax treaties and EC law* (1997) p. 225.

[700] ECJ 13 April 2000, C-420/98, *W.N.* [2000] ECR I-2847, paras. 22–24.

tax liability in the residence state, as the amount of the tax credit would be reduced);[701]

- business dealings between taxpayers in two different Member States in a way liable to reduce tax (tax planning, not necessarily "tax avoidance");
- a possible loss of tax as a result of artificial transfers of profits within groups of enterprises (transfer pricing not in line with the arm's length principle);
- *do ut des*: when information obtained from Member State B enabled Member State A to get new, interesting information, which is also relevant for Member State B, Member State A has to forward that new information to State B.

In addition, Art. 9(2) **allows** a Member State in all other cases to forward any **665** information of which it is aware to another Member State by spontaneous exchange, if this information might be useful to the other Member State. Finally, it has to be kept in mind that the Tax Collection Directive also permits the Member States to spontaneously exchange information in specific situations (see m.no. 703).

e) Time Limits for Forwarding Information (Arts. 7, 8 and 10)

The Directive sets up time limits for all three types of exchange of information **666** in order to make exchanges quicker. With regard to the exchange upon request, the requested authority has to provide the information as quickly as possible, **at any rate within six months** from the date of receipt of the request. If the requested authority is already in possession of the relevant information, the information even has to be transmitted within two months (Art. 7(1)). In addition, the requested authority is obliged to confirm the receipt of the request (within seven working days at the latest, Art. 7(3)), to inform the requesting authority about any deficiencies or the need for additional information (within one month at the latest, Art. 7(4)), to provide information about the inability to respond within time (within three months at the latest) or about the refusal of assistance and the reason thereof (within one month at the latest, Art. 7(6)).

In case the preconditions for mandatory automatic exchange are met (see **667** m.no. 662), the Member State is obliged to communicate the relevant information **at least once a year, within six months** following the end of the tax year during which the information became available (Art. 8(6)). The first exchange, therefore, will take place before 1 July 2015.

If one of the circumstances for spontaneous exchange under Art. 9(1) is at **668** hand, the competent authority must forward the information to the competent authority of the other Member State concerned as quickly as possible, and **no later than one month** after the information has become available (Art. 10(1)).

---

[701] See Urtz, in Gassner/Lang/Lechner (eds.) *Tax treaties and EC law* (1997) p. 225. Concerning this obligation, there is an overlap with the spontaneous exchange of information under the Tax Collection Directive see m.no. 703.

The receipt of the information has to be confirmed by the competent authority receiving the information within seven working days at the latest.

f) Other Forms of Cooperation

i. Collaboration by Officials in the State Concerned (Art. 11)

669 Under international public law, tax officials of one Member State may not conduct investigations in another Member State on their own.[702] The Exchange of Information Directive does not revoke that principle, as it merely provides for an exchange of information. Thus, a Member State is still dependent on the information it gets from the other State, which might not be sufficient in any case. However, Art. 11 offers the opportunity to **authorize the presence of tax officials of the requesting State** in the offices of administrative authorities or during administrative enquiries carried out in the territory of the requested Member State. This could be helpful when the premises of the taxpayer must be inspected, where individuals must be interviewed or where books must be examined (audit).[703] Note that the opportunity conceded in Art. 11 is subject to prior bilateral agreement by the Member States concerned. In addition, the officials involved need to be authorized by the requesting Member State and be able to produce written confirmation of their identity and authorization at any time (Art. 11(1) and (3)). The admission to be a part of the domestic proceedings could, however, be in conflict with taxpayers' rights under national law, since if foreign officials already know about relevant facts because of their presence at the investigations, it is of little use for the taxpayers concerned to file for an injunction or get involved in a litigation proceeding.[704]

ii. Simultaneous Controls (Art. 12)

670 Art. 12 provides for the procedures and rules for simultaneous controls of one or more persons of interest in different Member States. Simultaneous controls are tax audits, where the audited persons, the audited cases and the time schedules are coordinated between two or more states. However, the Member States still remain sovereign, as they still conduct these coordinated audits **only in their own territory**. Only the information thus obtained will be exchanged between the Member States involved. Simultaneous audits can be more effective than controls conducted by one Member State alone in particular in the case of multinational enterprises (e.g. transfer pricing issues between a German parent company and its Belgian subsidiary).

iii. Request for Notification (Art. 13)

671 Beside presence in the territory of another Member State and simultaneous controls, Member States may also ask for assistance in notification to addressees.

---

[702] See Hendricks, *Internationale Informationshilfe im Steuerverfahren* (2004) p. 54.
[703] See Terra/Wattel, *European Tax Law* (2012) p. 834.
[704] See Terra/Wattel, *European Tax Law* (2012) p. 834 et seq.

The object of notification may be **any instrument and decision** which emanates from the administrative authorities of the requesting Member State. The requested Member State has to carry out the notification as if it were its own similar decision or instrument. A valid request is, however, subject to certain prerequisites: First, an authority may only make a request when it is unable to notify in accordance with the national rules governing the notification, or where such notification would lead to **disproportional difficulties** (Art. 13(4)). In this respect, the Directive explicitly allows competent authorities to also notify documents directly to addressees in another Member State by registered mail or electronically. In addition, the requesting Member State must indicate at least the subject of the instrument or decision to be notified and the name and address of the addressee in the request for notification (Art. 13(2)).

g) Grounds for Refusal of Assistance

i. Invalid Grounds

The Directive leads to a far-reaching obligation of Member States to exchange information among one another. Such an obligation to cooperate is not only derived from the Directive itself, but also from EU law, namely the principle **of Union loyalty** (Art. 4(3) TEU, ex Art. 10 EC).[705] The Directive explicitly refers to two important invalid grounds for refusal of assistance: Art. 18(1) provides that Member States cannot refuse to cooperate on the ground that they have **no domestic interest** in the information asked for. In addition, according to Art. 18(2) **national bank secrecy** is no longer recognized as a valid ground for refusal.[706] Information resting with banks or financial institutions, therefore, has to be exchanged if the other prerequisites of the Directive are fulfilled. However, the Directive itself also lists five specific grounds that give the requested State the right to refuse cooperation (Art. 17).

672

ii. Requesting State Has Not Exhausted Its Domestic Means of Information Prior to the Request (Art. 17(1))

Art. 17(1) allows the requested State to refuse its cooperation if it appears as if the requesting State has not exhausted its own usual sources of obtaining the information sought prior to the request, in as far as these means could be utilized without jeopardizing the result desired. The provision leads to a number of **uncertainties**: It seems unclear how the requested State can verify whether this requirement is met.[707] Furthermore, there are doubts whether "usual sources" also cover more burdensome increased procedural obligations for taxpayers in cross-

673

---

[705] See also Hendricks, *Internationale Informationshilfe im Steuerverfahren* (2004) p. 96 et seq.
[706] This had been a valid ground for refusal under the old Exchange of Information Directive. See Schilcher in Lang et al. (eds.), *Introduction to European Tax Law on Direct Taxation* (2010) m.no. 617.
[707] See Terra/Wattel, *European Tax Law* (2012) p. 838.

border situations than in purely domestic situations (e.g. Art. 90(2) German Tax Code).[708] If this were the case, it is doubtful whether this understanding is fully in line with EU law, as procedural obligations can also lead to a breach of the fundamental freedoms.[709] However, the ECJ seems to accept increased procedural obligations in cross-border situations.[710]

iii. National Treatment (Art. 17(2))

674 The Directive does not oblige the requested State to carry out enquiries or to provide information if this would be **contrary to its domestic law**. However, if information is already readily available at the requested State and there is consequently no need to conduct enquiries to collect it, the wording of Art. 17(2) does not seem to provide grounds for refusal of forwarding that specific information, although the collection would be contrary to the national law of the requested State.[711] In addition, it has to be kept in mind that Member States can no longer rely on national bank secrecy provisions in order to refuse assistance (Art. 18(2)). Bank secrecy merely works as valid ground for refusal if the request concerns tax periods prior to 2011.

iv. Reciprocity (Art. 17(3))

675 The principle of reciprocity allows a Member State to refuse to provide information when the requesting State itself is **legally unable** to provide similar information on request. This provision only covers reasons of law, but not reasons of fact. This means if a competent authority does not have the necessary administrative possibilities to collect the information requested, that is no valid excuse.[712] In fact, this provision permits Member States in particular to decline the forwarding of banking information to Austria and Luxembourg related to tax years prior to 2011.[713]

---

[708] See, however, Seer, *IWB* 2005, Fach 11 Europäische Gemeinschaften, Gruppe 2, p. 677 et seq., who argues that this provision makes clear that a Member State is even not allowed to make a request before exhausting all domestic means of obtaining the information.

[709] See e.g. ECJ 15 May 1997, C-250/95, *Futura Participations* [1997] ECR I-2471; ECJ 28 April 1998, C-118/96, *Safir* [1998] ECR I-1897.

[710] ECJ 27 January 2009, C-318/07, *Persche* [2009] ECR I-359; ECJ 10 February 2011, C-436/08 and C-437/08, *Haribo and Österreichische Salinen* [2011] ECR I-305, paras. 95 et seq.

[711] See Terra/Wattel, *European Tax Law* (2012) p. 839.

[712] Under the old Directive declination for reasons of law and for reasons of fact had been possible. See Terra/Wattel, *European Tax Law* (2012) p. 839.

[713] Note that the obligation to exchange information on interest payments under the Savings Directive prevails over the provision of Art. 17(3) Exchange of Information Directive (Art. 9(3) Savings Directive). Consequently, Austria and Luxembourg, which currently do not provide information on interest payments to other Member States themselves under the Savings Directive, are nevertheless entitled to receive information from other Member States on interest payments under the scope of the Savings Directive.

v. Commercial Secrets (Art. 17(4))

Member States may refuse to provide information if this would lead to the dis- **676** closure of a commercial, industrial or professional secret or a commercial process. The aim of this provision is to protect the legitimate competitive edges of the undertakings concerned.[714] Art. 18(2) clarifies that banking secrets and ownership secrets are not covered by this exception.

vi. Ordre Public (Art. 17(4))

Member States may refuse to exchange information whose disclosure would be **677** contrary to **public policy**. The public policy reservation allows a Member State to refuse an exchange of information if one of its fundamental interests would be affected.[715]

h) Standard Forms and Language (Arts. 20 and 21)

To guarantee efficient information exchange, Art. 20 sets up **standard forms** **678** **and computerized formats**, which must be used for all types of exchange. The use of these standard forms is accompanied by provisions concerning the use of the Common Communication Network (**CCN**), an electronic data exchange system.[716] Information communicated must "as far as possible" be provided by electronic means using this network. This reflects the Commission's intention to get all tax systems using the same channel.[717] The standard forms and other practical arrangements should be developed in the implementation stage under the "**comitology**" procedure, which allows for a "light" delegated qualified majority decision-making by a Committee composed of representatives of the Member States.[718]

The Directive does not give priority to a particular language. Requests and **679** documents may be made in **any language** agreed between the cooperating authorities. Asking for translations into the official language of the requested State is only permitted in "special cases" where the requesting authority gives reasons for the necessity of the translation (Art. 21(4)).[719]

---

[714] See Terra/Wattel, *European Tax Law* (2012) p. 840.

[715] The public policy reservation is also included in the fundamental freedoms. The ECJ holds the opinion that it must be interpreted strictly in EU law; see ECJ 27 October 1977, C-30/77, *Bouchereau* [1977] ECR I-1999, paras. 33–35.

[716] This system is already in use for value added tax and excise purposes.

[717] See Terra/Wattel, *European Tax Law* (2012) p. 825.

[718] See Art. 21(1) and 26(2) in conjunction with Regulation (EU) No. 182/2011 (which repealed Decision 1999/468/EC). See on this procedure Terra/Wattel, *European Tax Law* (2012) p. 24.

[719] See on the potential effects Gabert, *ET* 2011, 346.

i) Use of Information Received and Secrecy Provisions

680 Art. 16(1) provides that all information made known to a Member State under this Directive must be kept secret in that State in the same manner as information received under its domestic legislation ("**national treatment**" of the information). In addition, Art. 25 clarifies that all exchange of information pursuant to the Directive is subject to the provisions of the Data Protection Directive 95/46/EC.[720] Besides these provisions, the Directive does not contain any provision on the judicial protection for taxpayers. Persons potentially affected by an exchange of tax information can thus rely only on domestic legislation for injunction or claim of damages in the case of unlawful exchange.[721]

681 Information received may be used for the **administration and enforcement** concerning taxes covered by the Directive and compulsory social security contributions. In addition, the requesting State may also use the information received for the assessment and enforcement of taxes covered by the Tax Collection Directive, which extends the use notably to value added tax, excise duties and customs; and for judicial and administrative proceedings involving penalties, meaning criminal proceedings against tax offenders, provided their defence rights are respected.[722] Any other use legally permitted in the requesting State is only allowed under consent of the requested State. Permission, however, has to be granted if the envisaged use is legal in the requested State as well (Art. 16(2)).

682 **Forwarding of information to other Member States** is as a rule permissible if the information seems to be useful for the administration and enforcement of taxes in this third Member State. The Member State of origin must be informed beforehand about the intention of forwarding, in order to be in the position to oppose such a sharing of information (within ten working days of receipt at the latest, Art. 16(3)). **For forwarding of information to third states** see m.no. 684.

j) Exchange of Information and Third Countries

683 The Directive also gives guidance on the exchange of information with regard to third countries. According to Art. 24(1), Member States may also **forward information received from a third country to other Member States**, upon request or spontaneously, if this information is "foreseeably relevant" for the administration or enforcement of the other Member State and in so far as the agreement with that third country so permits. The scope of this provision seems rather narrow, since under the current OECD standard a contracting State to a DTC or TIEA is only permitted to request information which is needed for **its own tax**

---

[720] Directive 95/46/EC of the European Parliament and of the Council of 24 October 1995 on the protection of individuals with regard to the processing of personal data and on the free movement of such data, OJ L 281 of 23 November 1995, p. 31.

[721] Terra/Wattel, *European Tax Law* (2012) p. 840.

[722] Terra/Wattel, *European Tax Law* (2012) p. 837.

purposes (not for the purposes of another State). In addition, under the prevailing opinion, the current OECD standard does not permit the passing on of information received from a contracting State to another State not party to the treaty, unless explicitly stipulated otherwise. Art. 24 will, thus, probably not have much relevance.[723]

Vice versa, Art. 24(2) regulates the **forwarding of information received** 684 **from a Member State to third countries**. Information received from another Member State can be provided to a third country, provided that the Member State of origin agrees, and the third country is prepared to reciprocate by exchanging information for the purposes of tax avoidance.

Art. 19 sets up a **most-favoured nation clause** with respect to third countries. 685 If a Member State thus agrees on a wider cooperation with a third country than that provided for under the Directive, this Member State is obliged to extend this cooperation to any other Member State asking for it. This most-favoured nation clause does not apply within the European Union: Therefore, if two Member States decide to cooperate more extensively, they are not obliged to grant the same preferential treatment to other Member States.[724]

k) Relevance of the Directive in the ECJ's Case Law on the Fundamental Freedoms

The Exchange of Information Directive also influenced the ECJ's judgments 686 concerning the relationship between Member States' direct tax systems and the **fundamental freedoms**. Repeatedly, the ECJ referred to the Directive and held that Member States may rely on it in order to obtain from another Member State all the information enabling it to ascertain the correct amount of income or all the information it considers necessary to ascertain the correct amount of income tax payable by a taxpayer according to the legislation that it applies.[725] Thus, Member States cannot justify discriminatory tax measures for cross-border situations within the European Union by the need to ensure the **effectiveness of fiscal controls**. However, the ECJ also mentioned the possibility to ask taxpayers to provide sufficient information to ensure the effectiveness of fiscal controls. Although, one might challenge whether it is in line with the **fundamental freedoms** to apply more burdensome procedural rules for cross-border situations compared to domestic situations, as long as the facts of the case can also be

---

[723] See on a different view Nijkeuter, *EC Tax Review* 2011, p. 241.

[724] Terra/Wattel, *European Tax Law* (2012) p. 824.

[725] ECJ 28 January 1992, C-204/90, *Bachmann* [1992] ECR I-249; ECJ 11 August 1995, C-80/94, *Wielockx* [1995] ECR I-2493; ECJ 15 May 1997, C-250/95, *Futura Participations* [1997] ECR I-2651; ECJ 28 October 1999, C-55/98, *Vestergaard* [1999] ECR I-7461; ECJ 3 October 2002, C-136/00, *Danner* [2002] ECR I-8147; ECJ 26 June 2003, C-422/01, *Skandia* [2003] ECR I-6817; ECJ 14 September 2006, *Stauffer* [2006] ECR I-8203; ECJ 29 March 2007, C-347/04, *Rewe Zentralfinanz* [2007] ECR I-2647; ECJ 11 October 2007, C-451/05, *Elisa* [2007] ECR I-8251.

established by means of the Exchange of Information Directive,[726] the ECJ seems to accept increased procedural obligations for taxpayers in cross-border situations,[727] as long as the evidendentiary requirements are not too formalistic.[728] The Member States are, thus, not obliged to make use of the Directive,[729] but may ask the taxpayer to provide evidence in advance. In case a taxpayer is not willing or even not in a position to provide the necessary information, Member States are permitted to refuse a tax benefit.[730] The Directive seems to serve the goal of verifying information already provided by the taxpayer only.

687   However, the ECJ accepts the justification of effectiveness of fiscal control for discriminatory tax measures in third-country situations, as the Directive is not applicable vis-à-vis third countries, including EEA Member States.[731] Third countries may, thus, only escape discriminatory treatment of capital movements in the tax law systems of the Member States if they agree on an exchange of information system equivalent to the Directive with the respective Member State (see m.nos. 280 et seq.).[732]

l) Comparison and Relationship to Bi- and Multilateral Provisions on the Exchange of Information

688   Alongside the national provisions based on the Exchange of Information Directive, bilateral provisions based on Art. 26 OECD MC as well as on the TIEA Model, and the MAATM Convention also allow for an exchange of information. Art. 26 OECD MC and the MAATM Convention are **to a large extent comparable** to the Exchange of Information Directive, as they provide for an exchange of information upon request, automatically or spontaneously. The TIEA Model, however, only permits exchange upon request. The OECD, the TIEA Model and the MAATM Convention also contain secrecy provisions (Art. 26(2) OECD MC, Art. 8 TIEA Model, Art. 22 MAATM), which are to a large extent similar to Art. 16 of the Directive. Furthermore, the OECD MC provisions allow the requested State to refuse its cooperation (Art. 26(3) OECD MC) in situations

---

[726] See e.g. Furuseth, *Intertax* 2007, p. 256 et seq.

[727] ECJ 27 January 2009, C-318/07, *Persche* [2009] ECR I-359; ECJ 10 February 2011, C-436/08 and C-437/08, *Haribo and Österreichische Salinen* [2011] ECR I-305, paras. 95 et seq.

[728] ECJ 30 June 2011, C-262/09, *Meilicke II* (not yet published) para. 46; ECJ 15 September 2011, C-310/09, *Accor* (not yet published) para. 99.

[729] ECJ 27 September 2007, C-184/05, *Twoh International* [2007] ECR I-7897, para. 32; ECJ 27 January 2009, C-318/07, *Persche* [2009] ECR I-359, para. 64.

[730] ECJ 10 February 2011, C-436/08 and C-437/08, *Haribo and Österreichische Salinen* [2011] ECR I-305, para. 102.

[731] ECJ 18 December 2007, C-101/05, *A* [2007] ECR I-11531; ECJ 27 January 2009, C-318/07, *Persche* [2009] ECR I-359; ECJ 19 November 2009, C-540/07, *Commission vs. Italy* [2009] ECR I-10983; concerning EEA states see ECJ 28 October 2010, C-72/09, *Etablissements Rimbaud* [2010] ECR I-10659.

[732] See e.g. ECJ 27 October 2011, C-493/09, *Commission vs. Portugal* (not yet published) para. 50.

that are equal to Art. 17 Exchange of Information Directive. The TIEA Model and the MAATM Convention, however, include more grounds for refusal of cooperation than the Directive.[733] In addition, it seems to be easier to produce a valid request under the Directive than under the TIEA Model, since the requirements to exclude fishing expeditions are less strict in the Directive.[734] The Directive also sets up a mandatory automatic exchange for specific categories of income and capital, whereas the OECD MC and the MAATM Convention leave automatic exchange to bilateral arrangements by the contracting states. In addition, Art. 26 OECD MC, the TIEA Model and the MAATM Convention do not contain any time limits for responding to a request and are less specific when it comes to organizational and procedural aspects.

Bilateral provisions based on Art. 26 OECD MC may either provide for a restricted "**small**" exchange of information or an unrestricted "**broad**" exchange of information. The difference between these two types of exchange of information can be explained as follows: Under a "small" information clause only information that is relevant for the proper application of the respective convention can be exchanged. However, under a "broad" information clause information that is only relevant for the correct application of domestic law can be exchanged as well. Thus, a "broad" information clause equals the standard set in Art. 5 Exchange of Information Directive. If a DTC between Member States only provides for a "small" information clause, the possibilities for exchanging information are broadened by the Exchange of Information Directive. **689**

As a rule, the **most effective rule applies** between EU Member States, since the EU rules are the minimum level of cooperation to be extended.[735] Art. 1(3) Exchange of Information Directive refers to the relation between the Directive and wider-ranging bilateral (e.g. in a DTC or TIEA) or multilateral provisions (e.g. in a multilateral convention on the exchange of information) on the exchange of information. Art. 1(3) clarifies that **provisions with a broader scope** than the Exchange of Information Directive are not in any way affected by the provisions of the Directive.[736] Member States are, thus, free to agree on an exchange of information with other Member States on a wider scale, without being forced to extend the same provisions to all other Member States (see on the most-favoured nation clause m.no. 685). **690**

---

[733] E.g. declining a request is also permitted in the case of discrimination against a national of the requested state as compared with a national of the applicant state in the same circumstances. See Terra/Wattel, *European Tax Law* (2012) p. 842.

[734] The Directive as opposed to the TIEA Model e.g. does not ask about the nature and form of the information sought and the ground for believing that the requested information is held by the requested state. Compare Art. 20(2) Directive 2011/16/EU and Art. 5(5) TIEA Model. See Vascega/van Thiel, *EC Tax Review* 2011, p. 152 et seq.

[735] See Terra/Wattel, *European Tax Law* (2012) p. 843.

[736] See on the old Directive ECJ 11 October 2007, C-451/05, *Elisa* [2007] ECR I-8251, paras. 42–48.

m) Relationship to the Savings Directive

691 The Savings Directive provides for a **compulsory automatic exchange of information** system between the Member States on certain interest payments to individuals and currently leaves the possibility of maintaining a withholding tax system only to Austria and Luxembourg. Consequently, the Savings Directive should be understood as *lex specialis* in relation to the Exchange of Information Directive.[737] This could be derived from Art. 9(3) Savings Directive, which precludes Member States from relying on the limitations on the exchange of information provided for by Art. 8 old Exchange of Information Directive, especially the reciprocity clause (see m.no. 675).

692 ## n) Overview of the Exchange of Information Directive

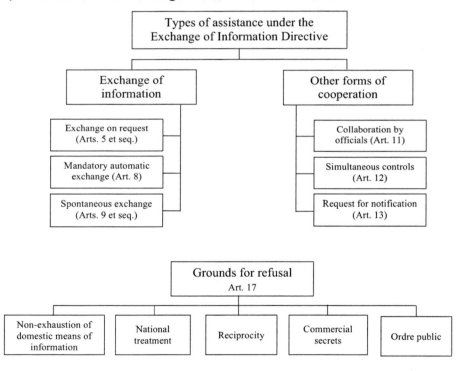

---

[737] See Terra/Wattel, *European Tax Law* (2012) p. 828 et seq.

2. The Directive on Mutual Assistance in the Recovery of Tax Claims

a) Background and History

On 16 March 2010 the Council adopted Directive 2010/24/EU on Mutual Assist- **693** ance in the Recovery of Tax Claims (hereinafter: the "**Tax Collection Directive**"), which came into force as from 1 January 2012. National provisions relating to recovery are applicable only within national territories, which could be in itself an obstacle to the establishment and functioning of the common market.[738] Thus, the Tax Collection Directive provides for common rules on mutual assistance for the cross-border recovery of tax claims. Similar rules on the assistance in the recovery of tax claims can also be found in Art. 27 OECD MC and in the Multilateral Convention on Mutual Administrative Assistance in Tax Matters (MAATM).

The new Tax Collection Directive 2010/24/EU replaces the old Tax Collection **694** Directive 2008/55.[739] Currently, the recovery ratio only amounts to 5% of the amounts for which recovery assistance is requested.[740] Consequently, the new Tax Collection Directive 2010/24/EU allows for an improved recovery assistance system within the internal market which should guarantee swift, efficient and uniform recovery assistance procedures among Member States compared to the old Directive. The old Directive came into force in 1976 and initially only applied to the recovery of agricultural subsidies and levies and customs duties.[741] In 1979 its scope was extended to value added taxes and excise duties,[742] and in 2001 to taxes on income and on capital as well as taxes on insurance premiums.[743]

b) Scope of the Directive

i. Objective Scope

The Tax Collection Directive has a **wide scope**, since, it covers assistance be- **695** tween the Member States for the recovery of any claims covered by the Directive (Art. 1).

---

[738] Recital of the Council Directive 76/308/EEC.
[739] Council Directive 2008/55/EC of 26 May 2008, OJ L 150 of 26 May 2008 on mutual assistance for the recovery of claims relating to certain levies, duties, taxes and other measures.
[740] COM(2009) 28 final.
[741] Council Directive 76/308/EEC of 15 March 1976 on mutual assistance for the recovery of claims resulting from operations forming part of the system of financing the European Agricultural Guidance and Guarantee Fund, and of agricultural levies and customs duties, and in respect of value-added tax, OJ L 73 of 19 March 1976.
[742] Council Directive 79/1071/EEC of 7 December 1979, OJ L 331 of 27 December 1979.
[743] Council Directive 2001/44/EC of 15 July 2001, OJ L 175 of 28 June 2001.

ii. Substantive Scope

696 In contrast to the old Directive, which listed the taxes and duties for which collection assistance could be requested, the new Directive covers **all taxes and duties of any kind** levied by or on behalf of a Member State or its territorial or administrative subdivisions, or on behalf of the Union (Art. 2(1)(a)). It also applies to refunds, interventions and other measures forming part of the system of total or partial financing of the European Agricultural Guarantee Fund (EAGF) and the European Agricultural Fund for Rural Development (EAFRD), including sums to be collected in connection with these actions (Art. 2(1)(b)) and to levies and other duties provided for under the common organization of the market for the sugar sector (Art. 2 (1)(c)). Moreover, the Tax Collection Directive also covers fees and surcharges relating to these claims, fees for certificates and similar documents issued in connection with administrative procedures related to taxes and duties as well as interest and costs relating to these claims (Art. 2(2)). The Tax Collection Directive does not apply to compulsory social security contributions, dues of a contractual nature and criminal penalties (Art. 2(3)).

iii. Personal Scope

697 The **definition** of "*person*" in the Directive (Art. 3(c)) is aligned with the Exchange of Information Directive (Art. 3(11)).[744] This wide definition should allow Member States to carry out cross-border assistance for all possible debtors, as the Directive does not include any limitations on its personal scope.[745] Only the spontaneous exchange of information laid down in Art. 6 between Member States is limited to information concerning residents of a Member State.

iv. Temporal Scope

698 As the new Tax Collection Directive applies since 1 January 2012, any request on recovery assistance by a Member State as from 1 January 2012 is based on the provisions of the new Tax Collection Directive, whereas requests made prior to 1 January 2012 are still based on the provisions of the old Tax Collection Directive. As there are no general rules in the Directive on the taxable periods requested, recovery assistance has to be related to, it should be **immaterial to which tax year** a request relates, even if that tax year predates the entry into force of the Directive provision on which the requesting State is relying.[746]

c) Organization (Art. 4)

699 Art. 4 provides for detailed rules on the designation of the competent authorities for applying the Tax Collection Directive which are similar to the rules on or-

---

[744] See m.no. 652.

[745] See Vascega/van Thiel, *ET* 2010, p. 235.

[746] ECJ 1 July 2004, joined cases C-361/02 and C-362/02, *Tsapalos and Diamantakis* [2004] ECR I-6405, para. 23. See already m.no. 654.

ganization included in the Exchange of Information Directive. The key aspect of Art. 4 is the designation of a **single central liaison office ("CLO")** in each Member State which is to have principal responsibility for any administrative cooperation with other Member States covered by the Tax Collection Directive (Art. 4 (2)). Every communication between the Member States based on the Directive must in principle be sent by or on behalf of the central liaison office which is to ensure effectiveness of communication (Art. 4(7)). Apart from the CLO, Member States may designate liaison offices that have responsibility for particular types or categories of taxes and duties (Art. 4(3)) and liaison departments that have limited territorial or operational competences (Art. 4(3) and (4)).

d) Types of Assistance

The Tax Collection Directive provides for **four main types of assistance** in the recovery of tax claims, which include the exchange of the relevant information in relation to a tax claim (Arts. 5–7), the notification to the addressee of a tax claim (Art. 8), the recovery of a tax claim upon request (Arts. 10–15) as well as the enforcement of precautionary measures (Arts. 16–17). **700**

i. Exchange of Information (Arts. 5 et seq.)

The Directive distinguishes between three types of exchange of information: exchange on request (Art. 5), spontaneous exchange (Art. 6) and the presence of officials of the requesting Member State in the requested Member State (Art. 7). **701**

a. On Request (Art. 5)

At the **request** of the requesting authority, the requested authority **must** provide **any information** which is **foreseeably relevant** to the requesting authority in the recovery of its tax claims.[747] For the purpose of providing that information, the requested authority must arrange for the carrying out of any administrative enquiries necessary to obtain it. **702**

b. Spontaneous Exchange of Information (Art. 6)

Art. 6 of the Directive allows for a spontaneous exchange of information on refunds of tax other than VAT relating to a resident of another Member State which is similar to the spontaneous exchange under the Exchange of Information Directive. It is worth noting that the spontaneous exchange of information on refunds of taxes covered by the Exchange of Information Directive is mandatory under Art. 9(1) Exchange of Information Directive. In the authors' view the wider obligation to exchange information under the Exchange of Information Directive in such cases takes precedence over the permission under Art. 6 Tax Collection Directive according to Art. 24(1) Tax Collection Directive. **703**

---

[747] The wording „foreseeably relevant" is also used in the Exchange of Information Directive. See m.nos. 650 and 658 for its interpretation.

c. Collaboration by Officials in the State Concerned (Art. 7)

704   In order to promote the exchange of information under this Directive, Art. 7 offers the opportunity to authorize the presence of tax officials of the requesting Member State in the offices of administrative authorities or during administrative enquiries carried out in the territory of the requested Member State as well as the assistance of the competent officials during court proceedings in the requested Member State.[748]

ii. Notification to Addressee (Art. 8)

705   At the request of the requesting Member State, the requested Member State must notify to the addressee all documents issued by the requesting Member State which relate to a tax claim or its recovery. This includes, e.g. (additional) assessments, distress warrants, judgments, court orders, writs of attachment. The request for notification must be accompanied by a standard form including information on the name and address of the addressee, the purpose of the notification and a description of the attached document (Art. 8(1)). Similar to the Exchange of Information Directive, Member States may notify documents under the Tax Collection Directive directly to addressees in another Member State by registered mail or electronically (Art. 9(2)) and, therefore, may only request notification assistance subsidiary to its domestic notification rules (Art. 8(2)).[749]

iii. Recovery upon Request (Arts. 10–15)

706   Arts. 10–15 lay down the rules for the collection and cross-border enforcement measures of a tax claim. Art. 10 provides that, at the request of the requesting authority, the requested authority must recover claims that are the subject of an instrument permitting their enforcement. Moreover, the tax claim must be treated by the requested State as if it were a domestic claim (Art. 13(1)). Any request for recovery assistance must be accompanied by the EU uniform instrument permitting enforcement in the requested State (Art. 12(1)).[750]

707   According to Art. 11(2), the requesting State **must**, as a rule, first use its domestic recovery remedies before requesting recovery assistance. However, there are two cases listed where a Member State is permitted to ask for assistance under the Directive without actually using domestic remedies beforehand: First, when it is obvious that there are no recoverable assets in the requesting State and the requesting authority has specific information indicating recoverable assets in the requested State. Second where using its own remedies would be disproportionately difficult. A request may not be made if the tax claim and/or the in-

---

[748] Apart from the assistance of the competent officials during court proceedings in the requested Member State the provision is aligned with Art. 11 Exchange of Information Directive. For more details see m.no. 669.

[749] See Vascega/van Thiel, *ET* 2010, p. 235. See m.no. 671.

[750] See in detail m.no. 709.

strument permitting enforcement is legally challenged by the taxpayer in the requesting State (Art. 11(1)). However, despite such a challenge, the requesting State may insist that the requested State proceeds anyway if the law of both States nevertheless allow enforcement (Art. 14(4) 3rd subpara.). If the result of that challenge is successful for the taxpayer, the requesting State will be liable to pay the reimbursement and all damages required under the laws of the requested State (Art. 14(4) 3rd subpara.).[751]

iv. Precautionary Measures on a Reasoned Request (Arts. 16 and 17)

At the request of the requesting authority, the requested State must take **pre-cautionary measures** to ensure recovery where a claim is contested in the requesting State if the law of both States allows such measures (Art. 16(1)). The Directive also allows for **early action** to guarantee recovery of a future claim when an instrument permitting enforcement has not yet been issued (Art. 16(1) 1st subpara.).[752] The original document permitting precautionary measures in the requesting Member State forms the sole basis for the precautionary measures and may not be subject to any act of recognition, supplementing or replacement in the requested Member State (Art. 16(1) 2nd subpara.). **708**

e) Uniform Instrument Permitting Enforcement (Art. 12)

One of the **main advantages** of the new Tax Collection Directive is the **uniform instrument permitting enforcement** in the requested State.[753] Any request for recovery assistance must be accompanied by the EU uniform instrument permitting enforcement in the requested State (Art. 12(1)). The uniform instrument must reflect the content of the original domestic enforcement instrument (e.g. warrant, writ or judgment) and constitutes the **sole basis for recovery and precautionary measures** in the requested State. Thus, its validity may not be dependent on any act of recognition, supplementing or replacement by judicial or other authorities of the requested State.[754] **709**

f) Standard Forms and Language (Arts. 21 and 22)

Like the Exchange of Information Directive, the Tax Collection Directive sets up **standard forms** and **computerized formats**, which must be used for all types of assistance. These documents are to be sent by electronic means as far as possible. Notification requests are based on the **uniform notification form,** which is transmitted to the addressee of the notification. Recovery requests are based on the **uniform instrument permitting enforcement** in the requested State. Both documents are available in all official languages and are annexed to the Com- **710**

---

[751] See Terra/Wattel, *European Tax Law* (2012) p. 849.
[752] See Vascega/van Thiel, *ET* 2010, p. 236.
[753] See also Baker et al, *Bulletin* 2011, p. 285.
[754] See Terra/Wattel, *European Tax Law* (2012) p. 848.

mission Implementation Regulation No. 1189/2011, which lays down detailed rules in relation to certain provisions of the Tax Collection Directive.[755] All requests for assistance, standard forms for notification and uniform instruments permitting enforcement in the requested State must be sent in, or must be accompanied by a translation into the **official language of the requested State** (Art. 22). Documents for which **notification assistance** is requested do not need to be translated in the official language of the requested State (Art. 22(2)). The same is true for any other accompanying documents of a request (e.g. the original domestic instruments permitting enforcement of a claim).[756] However, the requested State may, where necessary, require a translation of such accompanying documents (Art. 22(3)) from the requesting State.

g) Grounds for Refusal of Assistance

i. Invalid Grounds

711 Like the Exchange of Information Directive, the Tax Collection Directive leads to a far-reaching obligation of the Member States to provide the four main forms of assistance covered by the Directive. Contrary to the old Directive according to the new Tax Collection Directive national bank secrecy is no longer recognized as valid ground for refusal.[757]

ii. National Treatment

712 The Directive does not oblige the requested State to provide information requested if it would not be able to obtain the information for its own recovery purposes (Art. 5(2)(a)).

iii. Commercial Secrets

713 A Member State may refuse to provide information if this would lead to the disclosure of any commercial, industrial or professional secrets (Art. 5(2)(b)).

iv. Ordre Public

714 Member States may also refuse to provide information if such disclosure would jeopardize security or public policy.

v. Serious Economic or Social Difficulties

715 The requested State is not obliged to grant recovery assistance or to take precautionary measures if the recovery of the claim, because of the situation of the debtor, creates serious economic or social difficulties in the requested State,

---

[755] Commission Implementing Regulation (EU) No. 1189/2011 of 18 November 2011, OJ L 302 of 19 November 2011.

[756] See Vascega/van Thiel, *ET* 2010, p. 236.

[757] This provision is aligned with Art. 18(2) Exchange of Information Directive, see m.no. 672.

provided national law also allows for such exceptions for national claims (Art. 18(1)).[758]

vi. Claims older than 5 Years

The requested State is not obliged to grant any assistance under the Directive if the claim is more than five years old (Art. 18(2)).   **716**

vii. Amount of Claim less than EUR 1,500

There is also no obligation for the requested State to grant any assistance under the Directive if the total amount of the claim is less than EUR 1,500 (Art. 18(3)).   **717**

h) Statute of Limitation (Art. 19)

The periods of limitation of a claim are solely governed by the **law of the requesting State** (Art. 19(1)). However, suspension, interruption or prolongation of that period is in principle determined by the law of the requested State, unless that law does not provide for suspension, interruption or prolongation, in which case the steps taken in the requested State are deemed to have been taken in the requesting State in so far as they would produce suspension, interruption or prolongation under the law of the requesting State (Art. 19(2)).   **718**

i) Costs (Art. 20)

The requested State must seek to **recover from the debtor** and retain for itself the costs linked to the recovery that incurred according to its national rules applicable to similar domestic claims (Art. 20(1)). No reimbursement of costs from the requesting State arising from any assistance is allowed under the Directive, unless for exceptional cases creating a specific problem, concerning a very large amount in costs or relating to organized crime in which the Member States involved may agree reimbursement on a case-by-case basis (Art. 20(2)). However, the requesting State remains liable for costs and losses resulting from actions held to be unfounded in case the tax claim or the enforcement proves to be legally invalid (Art. 20(3)).   **719**

j) Use of Information Received and Secrecy Provisions (Art. 23)

Art. 23 Tax Collection provides for rules on the allowable use of information received under the Directive in a similar way to Art. 16 Exchange of Information Directive.[759] Any information received under the Directive by a Member State must be kept secret in that state in the same manner as information received under its domestic law (**"national treatment"** of the information). Information   **720**

---

[758] According to Engelschalk, in Vogel/Lehner (eds.) *DBA*, 5th edition, Art 27. para. 6 this provision may apply e.g. in case the debtor would become insolvent due to the enforcement of the tax claim and a significant number of employees would, thus, lose their jobs.

[759] See already m.nos. 680–682.

received under the Directive may be used for the purpose of **enforcement or precautionary measures** for claims covered by the Directive and, additionally, for the assessment and enforcement of **compulsory social security contributions**.

721   Like under the Exchange of Information Directive, the requesting Member State is also permitted to use the information received for any other purposes, provided that such information could be used for similar purposes in the requested State (Art. 23(3)). Information can also be transmitted to other Member States if that information seems to be useful for the purposes of taking enforcement or precautionary measures in recovery claims or assessing and enforcing compulsory social security contributions subject to prior information of the requested Member State which may oppose such sharing of information (within ten working days after receipt at the latest; Art. 23(4)).

k) Relevance of the Directive in the ECJ's Case Law on the Fundamental Freedoms

722   Member States cannot justify discriminatory tax rules (e.g. exit taxes) in cross-border situations within the European Union[760] with the **need to ensure the recovery of tax claims**, as according to the ECJ's case law the Tax Collection Directive – in a less restrictive way for the taxpayer – enables them to get assistance in the cross-border recovery of tax claims.[761]

l) Comparison and Relation to Bi- and Multilateral Provisions on the Recovery of Tax Claims

723   Beside the national provisions based on the Tax Collection Directive, bi- and multilateral provisions based on **Art. 27 OECD MC as well as the MAATM Convention** allow for assistance in the recovery of tax claims. Art. 27 OECD MC and the provisions on recovery assistance in the MAATM Convention are to a large extent comparable to the Tax Collection Directive. However, Art. 27 OECD MC and the MAATM Convention are less specific when it comes to organizational and procedural aspects than the Directive.

---

[760] However this justification may be relevant in third country-situations as the Tax Collection Directive is not applicable vis-à-vis third countries. ECJ 6 October 2011, C-493/09, *Commission vs. Portugal* (not yet published) para. 49.

[761] ECJ 6 October 2011, C-493/09, *Commission vs. Portugal* (not yet published) para. 49; ECJ 29 November 2011, C-371/10, *National Grid Indus BV* (not yet published) para. 78; Similarly, the ECJ also held that a prohibition of a Member State on a managing director of a company from leaving that State on the ground that a tax liability of the company has not been settled may infringe the freedom of movement of a Union citizen provided that said tax claim could also be enforced by the means of mutual assistance provided under the Tax Collection Directive (ECJ 17 November 2011, C-434/10, *Aladzov* (not yet published) para. 48). See also m.nos. 294 and 297.

Furthermore, Art. 27 OECD MC and the MAATM Convention primarily differ from the Directive in respect of the **grounds for refusal of assistance**:[762]   **724**

- Art. 27(8)(c) OECD MC allows for refusing assistance if the requesting State has not pursued all reasonable measures of collection or conservancy, whereas under the Tax Collection Directive the requesting State may already ask for recovery assistance prior to using its domestic recovery remedies if it is obvious that there are no recoverable assets in the requesting State and it has specific information indicating recoverable assets in the requested State, or where using its own remedies would be disproportionately difficult (Art. 11(2) Tax Collection Directive).[763]
- Art 27(2) OECD MC and Art. 21(2)(e) MAATM[764] permit restricting assistance in cases where the underlying taxation is contrary to the respective DTC, whereas a similar provision is not included in the Tax Collection Directive.
- In contrast to Art. 27 OECD MA and the MAATM, the Tax Collection Directive allows for refusing assistance in case the tax claim is older than five years, or the amount of the claim is less than 1,500 EUR or the recovery of the claim, because of the situation of the debtor, creates serious economic or social difficulties in the requested State.
- Art. 27(8)(d) OECD MC allows for refusing assistance in those cases where the administrative burden for that state is clearly disproportionate to the benefit to be derived by the other contracting State, whereas such a grounds for refusal is not explicitly mentioned in the Tax Collection Directive. However, the de minimis threshold of 1,500 EUR in the Tax Collection Directive seems to serve a similar goal.

Bi- or multilateral provisions on the recovery of tax claims and national provisions based on the Tax Collection Directive can be applied **in parallel** by Member States. Like the Exchange of Information Directive, the Tax Collection Directive does not limit in any way wider bi- or multilateral forms of cooperation (Art. 24(1)).   **725**

---

[762] See Herdin-Winter, in Lang/Schuch/Staringer (eds.) *Tax Treaty Law and EC Law* (2007) p. 256.

[763] See Daurer, Die Amtshilfe in Steuersachen auf unionsrechtlicher Grundlage, in Lang/Schuch/Staringer (eds.) *Internationale Amtshilfe in Steuersachen* (2011) p. 40 et seq.

[764] The MAATM Convention also permits restricting assistance if taxation would be contrary to generally accepted taxation principles or against any other convention which the requested state has concluded with the requesting state.

726 m) Overview of the Tax Collection Directive

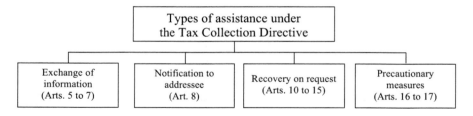

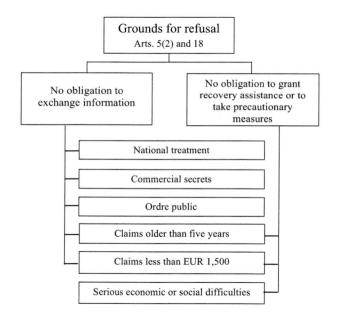

IX. The EU Arbitration Convention

Patrick Plansky

Legal Basis: Convention on the elimination of double taxation in connection with the adjustment of profits of associated enterprises (90/436/EEC), OJ L 225 of 20 August 1990, pp. 10–25.

Literature: Kilius, The EC Arbitration Convention, *Intertax* 1990, p. 447; Hinnekens, The Tax Arbitration Convention. Its significance for the EC-based Enterprise, the EC itself, and for Belgian and International Tax Law, *EC Tax Review* 1992, p. 94; Thömmes/Hagenbucher/Hasenoehrl, Commentary on the EC Arbitration Convention, in Thömmes/Fuks (eds.) *EC Corporate Tax Law*, 4th suppl. (October 1992); Züger, The ECJ as Arbitration Court for the New Austria-Germany Tax Treaty, *ET* 2000, p. 101; Züger, ICC Purposes Arbitraton in International Tax Matters, *ET* 2001, p. 221; Züger, *Schiedsverfahren für Doppelbesteuerungsabkommen* (2001); Tillinghast, Issues in the Implementation of The Arbitration of Disputes Arising under Income Tax Treaties, *Bulletin* 2002, p. 90; Ribes Ribes, Compulsory Arbitration as a Last Resort in Resolving Tax Treaty Interpretation Problems, *ET* 2002, p. 400; Lang/Züger, *Settlement of Disputes in Tax Treaty Law* (2002); Wilkie, Prior Consultation in the Application of the EC Arbitration Convention, *ITPJ* 2003, p. 151; Carreño/Canta, Proposal to Construct Obligation of Prior Consultation in the Application of the EC Arbitration Convention, *ITPJ* 2003, p. 154; Adonnino, Some Thoughts on the EC Arbitration Convention, *ET* 2003, p. 403; Huibregtse/Offermanns, What Is the Future of the EU Arbitration Convention?, *ITPJ* 2004, p. 76; Rousselle, The EC Arbitration Convention – An Overview of the Current Position, *ET* 2005, p. 14; de Hert, A New Impetus for the Arbitration Convention?, *ITPJ* 2005, p. 50; Thömmes/Hagenbucher/Hasenoehrl, Commentary on the EC Arbitration Convention, in Thömmes/Fuks (eds.) *EC Corporate Tax Law*, 32nd suppl. (December 2006); Terra/Wattel, *European Tax Law* (2008) p. 563; Thömmes/Rasch/Hammerschmitt/Nakhai, *Commentary on the Arbitration Convention* (2009); Damsma, Proposed Changes to the Code of Conduct for the Arbitration Convention, *ITPJ* 2009, 34; Helminen, EU Tax Law – Direct Taxation, *IBFD Publications* 2009, 259 et seq. Hinnekens, The Uneasy Case and Fate of Article 293 Second Intent EC, *Intertax* 2009, 602; Nieminen, Abolition of Double Taxation in the Treaty of Lisbon, *Bulletin* 2010, 330; Smit, *Freedom of Investment between EU and Non-EU Member States and its Impact on Corporate Income Tax Systems within the European Union, Volume one* (2011), 177 et seq.

1. Aim and History

727 The aim of the Arbitration Convention[765] is to establish a procedure to **eliminate double taxation** resulting from a profit adjustment by the competent authorities in one contracting state without a corresponding adjustment in the other contracting state.

728 The following simplified **example** illustrates the issue:

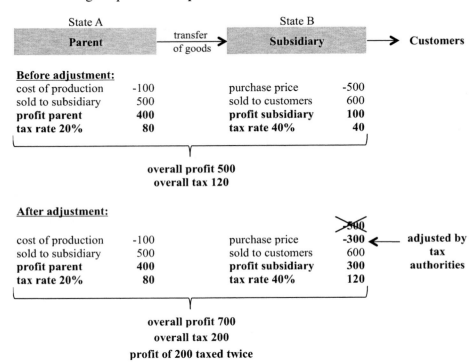

A group of companies is operating in State A and State B. State A's tax rate is 20 % whereas the tax rate of State B is 40 %. A parent company in State A is engaged in the production of certain products in State A whereas the wholly owned subsidiary, resident in State B, is responsible for the sales function and the customer relationship management. Products are purchased by the subsidiary and further on sold to final customers. The costs of the products in State A amount to 100. They are sold to the sales company in State B for a price of 500. The sales price for third-party customers for subsequent sales is 600. Thus, 400 of the overall profit of 500 (600 sales price − 100 costs of goods sold) are taxed in

---

[765] Convention on the elimination of double taxation in connection with the adjustment of profits of associated enterprises (90/436/EEC), OJ L 225 of 20 August 1990, pp. 10–25.

State A, only 100 of the profits are considered to arise from sales and customer relationship management in the subsidiary in State B. The reason for choosing the price of 500 at the time of the transfer could be due to the fact that the overall profit of the sale of the product should be shifted to the state with the lower tax rate. State B's authorities are suspicious and question the arm's length price of 500 for the transfer of the product from the parent in State A to the subsidiary in State B. For them, the appropriate arm's length price would have been 300 and they adjust the price downward from 500 to 300. This leads to the result that the subsidiary now earns a profit of 300 (600 sales price − 300 cost of acquisition). If this adjustment in State B is not followed in State A, meaning that State A also accepts the transfer price of 300 and therefore reduces its tax base from 400 to 200, double taxation may arise. State A would still tax 400 (500 transfer price − 100 costs goods sold) and State B would tax 300 (600 sales price − 300 cost of acquisition (= transfer price after adjustment)). Whereas the overall profit is 500 (600 sales price − 100 costs of goods sold), after the adjustment carried out in State B, the tax base of the group of companies would amount to 700 in total (400 in State A and 300 in State B). Therefore, a portion of 200 would be taxable in both states.

Besides the Arbitration Convention, the **Mutual Agreement Procedure** **729** **(MAP)** in Art. 25 of the OECD Model is also available to resolve transfer pricing disputes. Nevertheless, at present these **mechanisms in tax treaties** do not necessarily lead to satisfactory results. There are many reasons for this.[766] The most important reason is that the authorities of the contracting states are not obliged to actually come to a solution that eliminates double taxation under Art. 25 of the OECD Model.[767] Furthermore, there are no time constraints for a dispute settlement. Although there are already some tax treaties that contain a provision on arbitration procedures they do not necessarily solve the problem of eliminating double taxation. While the OECD Commentary states that it is a duty of the authorities to set in motion the mutual agreement procedure,[768] some authors are of the opposite opinion.[769] Moreover, not in all possible situations within the European Union are there tax treaties concluded. Additionally, not all tax treaties that have been concluded between Member States contain the cor-

---

[766] See Thömmes/Hagenbucher/Hasenoehrl, in Thömmes/Fuks (eds.) *EC Corporate Tax Law* (October 1992) para. 34 et seq.; Ribes Ribes, *ET* 2002, p. 400 with further references.

[767] See Terra/Wattel, *European Tax Law* (2008) p. 564 et seq. Under Art. 25(3) of the OECD Model the authorities of the contracting states must only "endeavour" to resolve by mutual agreement any difficulties or doubts arising as to the interpretation or application of the convention. For a detailed comparison between the EU Arbitration Convention and the Mutual Agreement Procedure under Art. 25 of the OECD Model, see Thömmes/Hagenbucher/Hasenoehrl, in Thömmes/Fuks (eds.) *EC Corporate Tax Law* (October 1992) para. 55.

[768] See OECD Commentary 2008, Art. 25 para. 33.

[769] Thömmes/Hagenbucher/Hasenoehrl, in Thömmes/Fuks (eds.) *EC Corporate Tax Law* (October 1992) para. 58.

responding adjustment requirement of Art. 9(2) of the OECD Model. But even if there is a provision equivalent to Art. 9(2) of the OECD Model in the respective tax treaty, double taxation may arise due to the different views on the correct interpretation of the arm's length principle. As a result of all of the above, and other deficiencies in tax treaties (and also in domestic law), the Arbitration Convention offers an alternative solution to eliminate double taxation as a result of an adjustment of transfer prices between related parties by the tax authorities in one contracting state, without a corresponding adjustment being carried out in the other contracting state.

730　In 2007, the OECD issued a report[770] proposing a new provision (Art. 25(5)) on an arbitration process for the OECD Model. For new tax treaties modelled along the lines of this new paragraph 5 of Art. 25 of the OECD Model, the level of protection of the taxpayer increases. The **arbitration process of Art. 25(5) of the OECD Model** will cover all disputes arising from "taxation not in accordance with the Convention" and will therefore have a wider scope than the EU Arbitration Convention, which deals with transfer pricing issues only. The main differences between Art. 25(5) of the OECD Model and the Arbitration Convention are set out in the following chart:[771]

	Art. 25(5) OECD Model Convention	Arbitration Convention
Dispute subjects	Competent authority disputes	Only transfer pricing disputes
Arbitration trigger	Disputes that remain unsolved after two years	Disputes that remain unsolved after two years
Potential parties	The two competent authorities	Taxpayer and the two competent authorities
Tribunal	Each competent authority appoints an arbitrator; the two arbitrators appoint a third arbitrator who chairs the panel	Advisory commission composed of independent president, two authority representatives and two independent members
Decision	Panel may issue its own opinion or chose between the two settlements proposed by the competent authorities (dependent on respective tax treaty)	Advisory commission delivers opinion
Binding decision	Decision binding on the competent authorities	Competent authorities may find alternative solution; if they fail, they are bound by opinion

---

[770] OECD, Improving the Resolution of Tax Treaty Disputes (Report adopted by the Committee on Fiscal Affairs on 30 January 2007), February 2007.

[771] For a more detailed comparison see Thömmes/Rasch/Hammerschmitt/Nakhai, *Commentary on the Arbitration Convention* (2009).

In 1976 the Commission already proposed a directive for the elimination of double **731** taxation as regards profit adjustments in transfer pricing scenarios.[772] This directive was never implemented but in 1990 the Arbitration Convention was concluded. The **legal base** for the Arbitration Convention is not Art. 115 TFEU (ex Art. 94 EC) (as it would have been for the proposed directive), but Art. 293 EC (deleted in the TFEU). The Arbitration Convention is therefore not an EU law instrument, but a multilateral international law convention. In the literature, Art. 293 EC has been seen as an obligation to abolish double taxation within the EU by some authors and as a mere declaration of intent by others. Art. 293 EC simply encouraged Member States to conclude, *inter alia,* the Arbitration Convention as an international agreement. In case an agreement is put in place, Art. 293 EC did not have any further consequences. Therefore, the deletion of Art. 293 EC in the course of the TFEU is of no relevance for the ongoing application of the Arbitration Convention. Even after the abolition of Art. 293 EC the Arbitration Convention forms ordinary treaty law and is still part of the *acquis communitaire*.[773]

The most important **consequences** for the Arbitration Convention resulting **732** from its legal nature as convention are the following:[774]

- No jurisdiction is conferred on the ECJ. The ECJ cannot therefore interpret provisions of the Convention. Questions may only be brought before the national courts.
- The effectiveness of the Convention is dependent on national (constitutional) law. It does not have of itself direct and self-executing effect and in principle does not take priority over national law.
- For the Convention implementation is not required but rather a ratification process.

In total, a convention in general, and the Arbitration Convention in particular, represents a more **limited level of integration** in relation to a directive. As a consequence, a greater degree of tax sovereignty remains in the hands of the contracting states.

The initial validity of the convention was limited to five years from the rati- **733** fication of the last EU Member State, but was then first extended and then made subject to an implicit periodical renewal. Parallel to the three enlargements of the European Union the personal scope of the Arbitration Convention has also been extended three times. In the course of the accession of Austria, Finland and Sweden

---

[772] Proposal for a Council directive on the elimination of double taxation in connection with the adjustment of transfers of profits between associated enterprise (Arbitration Procedure), COM(1976) 611 final.

[773] See Hinnekens, *Intertax* 2009, 604.

[774] See Thömmes/Hagenbucher/Hasenoehrl, in Thömmes/Fuks (eds.) *EC Corporate Tax Law* (October 1992) paras. 54 et seq. including an illustrative table of the weaknesses of a convention in relation to a directive; see also Terra/Wattel, *European Tax Law* (2008) p. 568.

to the European Union it has been decided that the Arbitration Convention will enter into force between the contracting states that have already ratified it.[775] Therefore, the Convention has already partially entered into force.

734   The Commission has identified difficulties in the practical implementation and established the **EU Joint Transfer Pricing Forum** (JTPF) in 2001 to examine possibilities to enhance, *inter alia,* the implementation of the Arbitration Convention. The JTPF prepared a **Code of Conduct** for the effective implementation of the Convention on the elimination of double taxation in connection with the adjustment of profits of associated enterprises, which was adopted by the Council in 2004.[776] The Code of Conduct is a mere political commitment and does not affect rights and obligations of the contracting states. Although the Code of Conduct is a soft law tool, it can be a useful instrument for the interpretation of the Arbitration Convention. In 2009 a Revised Code of Conduct which aims at resolving more cases within a three-year time frame was adopted by the Council.[777] The improvements of the Revised Code of Conduct cover penalty issues, interest charged or credited by tax administrations for cases being dealt with under the Arbitration Convention, the scope and the functioning of the Arbitration Convention as well as the interaction of the Arbitration Convention and domestic litigation. As a last step in the evolution of the EU strategy to resolve transfer pricing disputes, in addition to the *ex post* resolution of transfer pricing disputes by way of the Arbitration Convention, the Commission (JTPF) has issued Guidelines for Advance Pricing Agreements (APA) and thereby also promotes the *ex ante* possibility of preventing transfer pricing disputes. Thus, the possibilities to resolve transfer pricing disputes under the Arbitration Convention are now complemented by Guidelines for APAs within the European Union.

2. Scope and Principles

735   The Arbitration Convention has a **wide scope**. As regards the substantive scope, the Arbitration Convention covers taxes on income, in particular income tax and corporate tax.[778] As regards the personal scope, it applies to any situation in which profits of an enterprise of one contracting state are also included in the profits of an enterprise in another contracting state. The term "enterprise" is not

---

[775] Convention on the accession of the Republic of Austria, the Republic of Finland and the Kingdom of Sweden to the Convention on the elimination of double taxation in connection with the adjustment of profits of associated enterprises – Minutes of the signing, OJ C 026 of 31 January 1996.

[776] Code of conduct for the effective implementation of the Convention on the elimination of double taxation in connection with the adjustment of profits of associated enterprises (2006/C 176/02), OJ C 176 of 28 July 2006, p. 8.

[777] Revised Code of Conduct for the effective implementation of the Convention on the elimination of double taxation in connection with the adjustment of profits of associated enterprises (2009/C 322/01), OJ C 322 of 30 December 2009.

[778] Art. 2 of the Arbitration Convention.

defined in the Convention but it contains a broad concept and also covers permanent establishments of an enterprise of another contracting state.[779] Two constellations are covered by the Convention:

- violations of the arm's length principle between associated enterprises (Art. 4(1) of the Arbitration Convention) and
- violations of the arm's length principle between independent parts of an enterprise, i.e. head office and permanent establishment or between permanent establishments (Art. 4(2) of the Arbitration Convention).

The Arbitration Convention allows for an **adjustment of profits** that are not **736** determined in accordance with the arm's length principle. Adjustments other than arm's length profit adjustments are not covered by the Convention.[780]

Art. 4(1) of the Arbitration Convention is a literal rendition of Art. 9(1) of the **737** OECD Model. These arm's length profit adjustments for **associated enterprises** are applicable in two constellations: first, where an enterprise of a contracting state participates directly or indirectly in the management, control or capital of an enterprise of another contracting state (horizontal affiliation) and, second, where the same persons participate directly or indirectly in the management, control or capital of an enterprise of one contracting state and an enterprise of another contracting state (vertical affiliation).

As regards **independent parts of an enterprise**, Art. 4(2) of the Arbitration **738** Convention, which is a literal rendition of Art. 7(2) of the OECD Model (old version before 2010), provides that those profits must be attributed to the permanent establishment that it might be expected to make if it were a distinct and separate enterprise, engaged in the same or similar activities under the same or similar conditions and dealing wholly independently with the enterprise of which it is a permanent establishment. Violations of these principles may lead to profit adjustments and to the following procedures.

3. Procedural Issues

a) The Notification (Art. 5)

Where one contracting state intends to adjust the profits of an enterprise in **739** accordance with the arm's length principle, the tax authorities are **obliged to inform** the respective enterprise of the intended step and give the enterprise the possibility to inform the other enterprise in the other contracting state of the in-

---

[779] Art. 1(2) of the Arbitration Convention; see also joint declaration on Art. 4(1) in the annex of the Convention which states that Art. 4(1) of the Arbitration Convention applies also to permanent establishments of the other enterprise situated in a third country.

[780] Therefore, if one contracting state adjusts the profit of an enterprise as a result of the recharacterization of income or costs, this adjustment may lead to double taxation as the other contracting state possibly will not follow this recharacterization by that state.

tended step. This enterprise must, on its side, be able to inform its contracting state of the intended step of the other contracting state. The contracting state wishing to adjust the profits does not need to wait for a reaction of the other contracting state to adjust the profits; nevertheless, the Revised Code of Conduct, which is just a soft law tool, proposes to suspend the collection of taxes deriving from the profit adjustment.[781] If both states agree to the adjustment, there is no need for a further mutual agreement or arbitration procedure. In this case, of course, the second contracting state would have to adjust its profits correspondingly.

b) The Mutual Agreement Procedure (Art. 6)

740 If no agreement can be reached after the notification and the enterprise is of the opinion that the arm's length principle has not been observed, it may present its case (a **complaint**) to the competent authority of the contracting state in which the enterprise is situated. This complaint must be made within three years after the first notification. In this context the Revised Code of Conduct refers to the "date of the first tax assessment notice or equivalent" that results or may result in double taxation as the starting point for the calculation of the three-year period.[782] At the same time the enterprise must notify which other contracting states may be involved so that the competent authority in the other contracting state can be informed.

741 It is possible that the competent authority is not willing or not able to give a unilateral solution.[783] In this case, Art. 6(2) of the Arbitration Convention obliges the contracting state to open a **mutual agreement procedure**. While the notification phase did not leave the domestic level, the opening of the mutual agreement procedure is at cross-national level. If the competent authorities fail to reach a solution that eliminates double taxation within two years after submitting the case to the competent authority,[784] the **arbitration procedure** must be initiated.

---

[781] See Point 8 of the Revised Code of Conduct for the effective implementation of the Convention on the elimination of double taxation in connection with the adjustment of profits of associated enterprises (2009/C 322/01), OJ C 322 of 30 December 2009, p. 10.

[782] See Point 4 of the Revised Code of Conduct for the effective implementation of the Convention on the elimination of double taxation in connection with the adjustment of profits of associated enterprises (2009/C 322/01), OJ C 322 of 30 December 2009, p. 3.

[783] Art. 6(2) of the Arbitration Convention uses the wording "if the complaint appears to be well-founded" which seem to confer the discretionary power to the competent authorities. Nevertheless this phrase has to be interpreted as just enabling the competent authorities to "dismiss manifestly ill-founded applications"; see Terra/Wattel, *European Tax Law* (2008) p. 576.

[784] Point 5 of the Revised Code of Conduct contains more details on the starting point of this two-year-period; see Revised Code of Conduct for the effective implementation of the Convention on the elimination of double taxation in connection with the adjustment of profits of associated enterprises (2009/C 322/01), OJ C 322 of 30 December 2009, p. 3 et seq.

c) The Arbitration Procedure (Arts. 7 et seq.)

If no satisfactory result as regards the elimination of double taxation in the **742** mutual agreement procedure is reached, the first step in the arbitration procedure is to set up an **advisory commission** that has to deliver an opinion on the dispute submitted for arbitration.[785] According to the Revised Code of Conduct, the contracting state that issued the first tax assessment on the additional income takes the initiative for the establishment of the advisory commission and arranges for its meetings.[786] Additionally, the enterprises involved may appeal before national courts in parallel. In this case, the two-year period for reaching a solution starts only after the judgment of the final court of appeal.

The **composition** of the advisory commission is laid down in Art. 9(1) of the **743** Arbitration Convention. The advisory commission consists of (i) a chairman, (ii) (one)[787] or two representatives of each competent authority and (iii) an even number of independent persons. Independent persons within the meaning of Art. 9 of the Arbitration Convention are appointed by mutual agreement or by the drawing of lots. In the case of drawing of lots each competent authority may under certain circumstances object to the appointment of any independent person.[788] For each independent person one alternate has to be appointed. These independent persons must be nationals of a contracting state and resident in one of the signatory countries of the Arbitration Convention. Moreover, they must be competent and independent.[789] The chairman is then elected by the representatives and independent persons. The chairman of the advisory commission must have the highest qualifications, i.e. possess the qualifications for the highest judicial office or be a jurisconsult of recognized competence.[790] There is always an uneven number of members. Usually the advisory commission consists of five persons (one chairman, one representative of each competent authority and two independent persons). As a consequence of this composition, the votes of the independent persons will normally be decisive.[791]

Art. 10 of the Arbitration Convention lays down the **procedure before the** **744** **advisory commission.** All the members of the advisory commission have to keep secret what has come up during the procedure. On the one hand, the enterprises concerned may provide the advisory commission with any information,

---

[785] Art. 7(1) of the Arbitration Convention.

[786] See Point 7.2. of the Revised Code of Conduct for the effective implementation of the Convention on the elimination of double taxation in connection with the adjustment of profits of associated enterprises (2009/C 322/01), OJ C 322 of 30 December 2009, p. 8.

[787] Art. 9(1) of the Arbitration Convention proposes two representatives of each competent authority but also allows this number to be reduced to one representative per competent authority by agreement.

[788] Art. 9(3) of the Arbitration Convention.

[789] Art. 9(4) of the Arbitration Convention.

[790] Art. 9(5) second sentence of the Arbitration Convention.

[791] See Terra/Wattel, *European Tax Law* (2008) p. 578.

evidence or documents that seem to be of use for an opinion of the advisory commission. On the other hand, the enterprises are obliged to present all the information, evidence or documents requested by the advisory commission. Oral hearings may also be held.

745   After the investigation, the advisory commission is obliged to **deliver an opinion** within a period of six months from the date on which the case was referred to it. The term "referred to it" is not defined in the Convention. Under the Revised Code of Conduct, the matter "is referred to" the advisory commission as soon as the chairman confirms that its members have received all relevant documentation and information.[792] The opinion must be adopted by a simple majority of its members. The costs of the enterprises are borne by the enterprises. The costs of the procedure are shared equally by the competent authorities.

746   The advisory commission must base its opinion on Art. 4 of the Arbitration Convention, which lays down the arm's length principle in the exact wording of Art. 9(1) of the OECD Model. Although the Arbitration Convention does not provide special rules for the modality, the procedures and the criteria other than those laid down in Art. 4 of the Arbitration Convention, the **OECD transfer pricing guidelines** must be taken into consideration.[793]

747   As a last step in the arbitration procedure, the competent authorities have to take a **decision** within six months after having received the opinion of the advisory commission. The competent authorities may reach an agreement that deviates from the opinion of the advisory commission. In case they cannot reach an agreement, they are bound by the opinion of the advisory commission.[794] The decision may be published if the competent authorities as well as the enterprises involved agree.

---

[792] See Point 7.3.(b) of the Revised Code of Conduct for the effective implementation of the Convention on the elimination of double taxation in connection with the adjustment of profits of associated enterprises (2009/C 322/01), OJ C 322 of 30 December 2009, p. 8.

[793] Adonnino, *ET* 2003, p. 403.

[794] Art. 12 of the Arbitration Convention.

d) **Chart illustrating the Procedure**

The chart illustrates and summarizes the procedure laid down in the Arbitration **748**
Convention.[795]

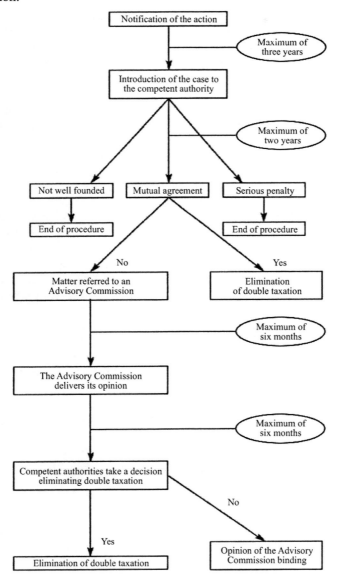

---

[795] Diagram taken from Rousselle, *ET* 2005, p. 16.

4. Critical Issues

749   Although the Arbitration Convention does not have the legal form of a directive, it is a positive **step forward in integration** in the tax area, especially in transfer pricing. The Arbitration Convention is based on the mutual agreement procedure in the OECD Model. Although there generally are mechanisms for mutual agreement procedures in bilateral tax treaties, the Arbitration Convention is the only tool that can be used if no agreement is reached in the mutual agreement procedure. The arbitration phase has therefore been novelty in relation to tax treaties (as Art. 25(5) is a rather new provision in the OECD Model) and is an effective tool to actually eliminate double taxation in the area of transfer pricing.

750   There are some important **strengths** of an arbitration procedure that are of major importance. First, states that have ratified the Arbitration Convention oblige themselves to eliminate double taxation. This is not just an endeavour, but a commitment. The second important advantage of the Arbitration Convention is that the advisory commission is an independent body of experts. Due to its composition, it is independent persons that are decisive. Thirdly, an important strength of the Arbitration Convention is the time-frame. The procedures must be completed within a three-year period. All this leads to a higher degree of legal certainty. Additionally, the costs for the enterprises are considerable. Finally, a multilateral convention is a far better means to eliminate double taxation as a result of profit adjustments than bilateral tax treaties.

751   In addition to all these strengths of the Arbitration Convention there are also weaknesses. Some **weaknesses** of the Arbitration Convention due to its legal nature as convention have already been mentioned. One is that its interpretation is in the hands of national courts, which may not uniformly interpret the provisions. The ECJ does not have any competence in the interpretation of the provisions of the Arbitration Convention. Therefore, no uniform interpretation and application of the Arbitration Convention can be secured. Another weakness deriving from the legal nature of the convention is the ratification process, which, as experience shows, may slow down integration. Additionally, although double taxation must be eliminated, the Arbitration Convention does not eliminate any interest payments or penalties resulting from the transfer pricing dispute.[796] Finally, the effectiveness of the Revised Code of Conduct, as a soft law tool, for the interpretation of the Arbitration Convention may be questioned.

---

[796] In contrast to the previous Code of Conduct, the Revised Code of Conduct includes a stronger recommendation not to levy interest.

List of Authors

Łukasz Adamczyk

Former Mondi Packaging researcher at the Institute for Austrian and International Tax Law, WU; Ph.D. candidate in Tax Law at the University of Warsaw and tax advisor.

Vanessa E. Englmair, LL.M.

Lecturer and former research assistant at the Institute for Austrian and International Tax Law, WU; former staff member of the International Tax Unit at the Austrian Federal Ministry of Finance and currently tax expert at LeitnerLeitner, Linz.

Dr Marie-Ann Kronthaler

Former lecturer and research assistant at the Institute for Austrian and International Tax Law, WU; currently staff member at the Austrian Financial Market Authority (FMA).

Yinon Tzubery, LL.M.

Research assistant at the Institute for Austrian and International Tax Law, WU.

Dr Mario Tenore, LL. M.

Former lecturer at the Institute for Austrian and International Tax Law, WU and research assistant at the University of Salerno, Italy; currently tax advisor at Maisto e Associati, Milan (Italy).

Matthias Hofstätter

Lecturer and former research assistant at the Institute for Austrian and International Tax Law, WU; currently tax expert at LeitnerLeitner, Vienna.

Dr Daniela Hohenwarter-Mayr, LL.M.

Hertha Firnberg-research associate at the Institute for Austrian and International Tax Law, WU.

Dr Dimitar Hristov

Lecturer and former research assistant at the Institute for Austrian and International Tax Law, WU; currently associate at Toifl Kerschbaum Rechtsanwälte GmbH, Linz.

Dr Sabine Heidenbauer, LL.M.

Lecturer and former research assistant at the Institute for Austrian and International Tax Law, WU; currently senior consultant at BDO Graz.

Dr Michael Schilcher

Lecturer and former research assistant at the Institute for Austrian and International Tax Law, WU; tax consultant; currently tax expert at a company of chartered accountants and tax consultants.

Karoline Spies

Deloitte research project assistent at the Institute for Austrian and International Tax Law, WU.

Dr Patrick Plansky

Lecturer and former research assistant at the Institute for Austrian and International Tax Law, WU; certified tax advisor, Tax Manager at Ernst & Young, Vienna.

Tables of Equivalences
of Relevant Treaty Provisions for Direct Taxation

Treaty on European Union (TEU)		
	Old numbering	New numbering
EU Institutions	Art. 7 EC	Art. 13 TEU
EU loyalty	Art. 10 EC	Art. 4(3) TEU

Treaty on the Functioning of the European Union (TFEU)		
	Old numbering of the Treaty establishing the European Community (EC)	New numbering of the Treaty on the Functioning of the European Union (TFEU)
General non-discrimination provision	Art. 12	Art. 18
Free movement and residence of EU citizens	Art. 18	Art. 21
Free movement of goods	Arts. 23 et seq.	Arts. 28 et seq.
Free movement of workers	Arts. 39 et seq.	Arts. 45 et seq.
Freedom of establishment	Arts. 43 et seq.	Arts. 49 et seq.
Freedom to provide services	Arts. 49 et seq.	Arts. 56 et seq.
Free movement of capital and payments	Arts. 56 et seq.	Arts. 63 et seq.
State aid	Arts. 87 et seq.	Arts. 107 et seq.
Legal basis for harmonization	Arts. 93-95	Arts. 113-115
Legal basis for international agreements	Arts. 300 et seq.	Arts. 216 et seq.
Infringement procedure	Arts. 226 et seq.	Arts. 258 et seq.
Right to sue	Art. 230	Art. 263
Preliminary ruling	Art. 234	Art. 267
Double taxation convention	Art. 293	repealed

Table of ECJ Case Law

This table contains all ECJ judgments mentioned in the book, listed alphabetically in the first column, with relevant information on the marginal number of the book and the chapter in which they are quoted.

ECJ cases listed alphabetic	Date	Case	General	Funda-mental Freedoms	State Aid	Parent-Subsidi-ary Directive	Merger Directive	Interest and Royalty Directive	Mutual Assistance Directives
			Chapter I	Chapter II	Chapter III	Chapter IV	Chapter V	Chapter VI	Chapter VIII
A	18 December 2007	C-101/05		118, 211, 280, 298					687
A and B	10 May 2007	C-102/05		135					
Accor	15 September 2011	C-310/09		137, 291					
A.G.M.-COS.MET	17 April 2007	C-470/03	36						
Air Liquide Industrica Belgium	15 Juni 2006	C-393/04 C-41/05			367				
A.T.	11 December 2008	C-285/07					543		
Aberdeen Property	18 June 2009	C-303/07		152, 159		469			
Adria-Wien Pipeline	8 November 2001	C-143/99			316, 330, 336, 356, 361, 367, 370, 372				
Aladzov	17 November 2011	C-434/10							722
Altmark	24 July 2003	C-280/00			333				
Amurta	8 November 2007	C-379/05		251					
Athinaiki Zithopiia	4 October 2001	C-294/99				473, 477			
Atzeni and others	23 February 2006	C-346/03 C-529/03			387				

ECJ cases listed alphabetic	Date	Case	General	Fundamental Freedoms	State Aid	Parent-Subsidiary Directive	Merger Directive	Interest and Royalty Directive	Mutual Assistance Directives
			Chapter I	Chapter II	Chapter III	Chapter IV	Chapter V	Chapter VI	Chapter VIII
Baars	13 April 2000	C-251/98		113					
Bachmann	28 January 1992	C-204/90		223					686
Banco Bilbao	8 Dezember 2011	C-157/10		269					
Banco Exterior de España	15 March 1994	C-387/92			329, 330, 397, 399				
Banque Fédérative du Crédit Mutuel	3 April 2008	C-27/07				468			
Becker	19 January 1982	8/81	6						
Biehl	8 May 1990	C-175/88		155					
Block	12 February 2009	C-67/08		269					
Bosal Holding	18 September 2003	C-168/01				466, 467		577	
Bouanich	19 January 2006	C-265/04		156, 194					
Bouchereau	27 October 1977	C-30/77							677
British Aggregates v Commission	22 Dezember 2012	C-487/06			356				
Burda	26 June 2008	C-284/06				477			
Cadbury Schweppes	12 September 2006	C-196/04		113, 177, 241, 242					
Cartesio	16 Dezember 2008	C-210/06					558		
Cassa di Risparmio di Firenze SpA	10 Jänner 2006	C-222/04			342, 344, 348, 349				
CELF	12 February 2008	C-199/06			425				

ECJ cases listed alphabetic	Date	Case	General	Funda-mental Freedoms	State Aid	Parent-Subsidi-ary Directive	Merger Directive	Interest and Royalty Directive	Mutual Assistance Directives
			Chapter I	Chapter II	Chapter III	Chapter IV	Chapter V	Chapter VI	Chapter VIII
Centro Equestre	15 February 2007	C-345/04		139, 161					
CILFIT	6 October 1982	283/81	20						
Ciola	29 April 1999	C-224/97	1						
CLT-UFA	23 February 2006	C-253/03		184					
Cobelfret	12 February 2009	C-138/07				465			
Cofaz	28 January 1986	169/84			414				
Columbus Container	6 December 2007	C-298/05		179, 195, 269					
Comité d'entreprise de la Société française de production and others	23 May 2000	C-106/98			414				
Commission v Austria	16 Juni 2011	C-10/10		217					
Commission v Austria	29 September 2011	C-387/10		272					
Commission v Belgium ("flat-rate transference duty")	5 May 1970	77/69	36						
Commission v Belgium ("deductibility of insurance contributions")	28 January 1992	C-300/90		223					
Commission v Belgium ("Maribel")	17 June 1999	C-75/97			370				
Commission v France ("Avoir Fiscal")	28 January 1986	270/83		97, 163, 266					

ECJ cases listed alphabetic	Date	Case	General	Funda-mental Freedoms	State Aid	Parent-Subsidi-ary Directive	Merger Directive	Interest and Royalty Directive	Mutual Assistance Directives
			Chapter I	Chapter II	Chapter III	Chapter IV	Chapter V	Chapter VI	Chapter VIII
Commission v France	26 September 1996	C-241/94			368				
Commission v France ("FIM")	13 July 1988	C-102/87			334				
Commission v France ("Boussac")	14 February 1990	C-301/87			418, 419				
Commission v France ("vineyards in Charentes")	12 December 2002	C-456/00			387				
Commission v Germany ("The New German Länder")	19 September 2000	C-156/98			321, 367				
Commission v Germany	20 Oktober 2011	C-284/09		157, 251, 255					
Commission v Gibraltar	15 November 2011	C-106/09 C-107/09			316, 329, 330, 353, 354, 356, 361, 365, 366, 367, 371, 372, 378				
Commission v Greece	20 Jänner 2011	C-155/09		120					
Commission v Italy ("family allowances in the textile industry")	2 July 1974	173/73			330				
Commission v Italy ("Italgrani")	30 June 1992	C-47/91			397, 418				

ECJ cases listed alphabetic	Date	Case	General	Fundamental Freedoms	State Aid	Parent-Subsidiary Directive	Merger Directive	Interest and Royalty Directive	Mutual Assistance Directives
			Chapter I	Chapter II	Chapter III	Chapter IV	Chapter V	Chapter VI	Chapter VIII
	5 October 1994								
Commission v Italy	28 April 1993	C-364/90			378				
Commission v Italy ("EFIM group")	23 February 1995	C-349/93			427				
Commission v Italy ("Alfa Romeo II")	4 April 1995	C-348/93			427				
Commission v Italy ("conditions of recovery")	9 December 2003	C-129/00	36						
Commission v Italy ("Friuli-Venezia Giulia Region")	29 April 2004	C-372/97			378, 397				
Commission v Italy ("outbound dividends")	19 November 2009	C-540/07		251, 283, 285, 298					687
Commission v Netherlands ("The MINAS System")	29 April 2004	C-159/01			365				
Commission v Netherlands ("outbound dividends to EEA")	11 June 2009	C-521/07		120, 182, 284					
Commission v Philip Morris	17 September 1980	730/79			343, 387				
Commission v Portugal ("Azores and Madeira")	6 September 2006	C-88/03			352, 535, 356, 358, 359, 360				
Commission v Portugal	5 Mai 2011	C-267/09		120, 121, 285					

ECJ cases listed alphabetic	Date	Case	General	Funda-mental Freedoms	State Aid	Parent-Subsidi-ary Directive	Merger Directive	Interest and Royalty Directive	Mutual Assistance Directives
			Chapter I	Chapter II	Chapter III	Chapter IV	Chapter V	Chapter VI	Chapter VIII
Commission v Portugal	6 Oktober 2011	C-493/09		246, 290, 297					687, 722
Commission v Portugal	6 September 2012	C-38/10					527		
Commission v Spain ("Cook II")	14 January 1997	C-169/95			387				
Commission v Spain ("VAT – services by a settlement office of a mortgage district")	12 November 2009	C-154/08	36						
Commission v Spain	3 Juni 2010	C-487/08		214					
Commission v Spain	12 Juli 2012	C-269/09					527		
Conijn	6 July 2006	C-346/04		175					
Costa v. E.N.E.L.	15 July 1964	6/64	1		404				
D.	5 July 2005	C-376/03		175, 199					
Damseaux	16 July 2009	C-128/08		195, 270					
Danner	3 October 2002	C-136/00		228					686
De Gezamenlijke Steenkolenmijnen	23 February 1961	30/59			330, 334				
De Groot	12 December 2002	C-385/00		175					
Demesa and Territorio Historico de Alava	11 November 2004	C-183/02 C-187/02			427				
Denkavit International & Denkavit France	14 December 2006	C-170/05		157, 249					

ECJ cases listed alphabetic	Date	Case	General	Funda-mental Freedoms	State Aid	Parent-Subsidiary Directive	Merger Directive	Interest and Royalty Directive	Mutual Assistance Directives
			Chapter I	Chapter II	Chapter III	Chapter IV	Chapter V	Chapter VI	Chapter VIII
France Télécom SA	8 Dezember 2011	C-81/10			335, 371, 426, 427				
Francovich	19 November 1991	C-6/90 C-9/90	22, 34						
Futura Participations	15 May 1997	C-250/95		232					673, 686
Gaz de France	1 October 2009	C-247/08				436			
Gerritse	12 June 2003	C-234/01		139, 157, 157, 175					
Gielen	18 März 2010	C-440/08		158					
Gilly	12 May 1998	C-336/96	39						
Glaxo Wellcome	17 September 2009	C-182/08		136					
Grundig Italiana	24 September 2002	C-255/00	22						
Gschwind	14 September 1999	C-391/97		175					
Halley	15 September 2011	C-132/10		137, 292					
Haribo Lakritzen and Österreichische Salinen	10 Februar 2011	C-436/08 C-437/08		137, 204, 217, 273, 283, 285, 289, 291, 297					673, 686
Holböck	24 May 2007	C-157/05		215					
Ianelli & Volpi	22 März 1977	74/76			321				
Intermills	14 November 1984	323/83			414				

ECJ cases listed alphabetic	Date	Case	General	Funda-mental Freedoms	State Aid	Parent-Subsidi-ary Directive	Merger Directive	Interest and Royalty Directive	Mutual Assistance Directives
			Chapter I	Chapter II	Chapter III	Chapter IV	Chapter V	Chapter VI	Chapter VIII
Internationale Handels-gesellschaft	17 December 1970	11/70	1						
Kapferer	16 March 2006	C-234/04	28						
KBC Bank NV	4 June 2009	C-439/07 C-499/07				465			
Keller Holding	23 February 2006	C-471/04		111, 122					
Kerckhaert-Morres	14 November 2006	C-513/04		142, 269					
Köbler	30 September 2003	C-224/01	36						
Kofoed	5 July 2007	C-321/05					560, 563, 564, 565	606	
Konle	1 June 1999	C-302/97		216					
Krankenheim Ruhesitz am Wannsee-Senioren-heimstatt	23 October 2008	C-157/07		223, 230			547		
Kühne & Heitz	13 January 2004	C-453/00	25						
Kwekerij Gebroeders van der Kooy and others	2 February 1988	68/85 69/85 70/85							
Laboratoires Fournier	10 März 2005	C-39/04		271					
Lakebrink	18 July 2007	C-182/06		175					
Lankhorst-Hohorst	12 December 2002	C-324/00		239					
Lasertec	10 May 2007	C-492/04		132					
Lasteyrie du Saillant	11 March 2004	C-9/02		140			527		

ECJ cases listed alphabetic	Date	Case	General	Funda-mental Freedoms	State Aid	Parent-Subsidi-ary Directive	Merger Directive	Interest and Royalty Directive	Mutual Assistance Directives
			Chapter I	Chapter II	Chapter III	Chapter IV	Chapter V	Chapter VI	Chapter VIII
Lawrie-Blum	3 July 1986	66/85		109					
Les Vergers du Vieux Tauves SA	22 December 2008	C-48/07				439			
Leur-Bloem	17 July 1997	C-28/95				487	569, 570	606	
Lidl Belgium	15 May 2008	C-414/06		276					
Lindman	13 November 2003	C-42/02		221					
Littlewoods Retail	19 Juli 2012	C-591/10	32						
Lorenz	11 December 1973	120/73			404, 408, 421				
Lucchini	18 July 2007	C-119/05	29						
Manninen	7 September 2004	C-319/02	18	235, 265					
Marks & Spencer	13 December 2005	C-446/03		152, 189, 275			537		
Meilicke	6 March 2007	C-292/04		102					
Meilicke II	30 Juni 2011	C-262/09		289, 291					
MOTOE	1 Juli 2008	C-49/07			347				
N.	7 September 2006	C-470/04		120, 140, 293			525		
National Grid Indus	29 November 2011	C-371/10		277, 293, 294			527, 528		722
Océ van der Grinten	25 September 2003	C-58/01				473			
Ospelt	23 September 2003	C-452/01	56						

ECJ cases listed alphabetic	Date	Case	General Chapter I	Fundamental Freedoms Chapter II	State Aid Chapter III	Parent-Subsidiary Directive Chapter IV	Merger Directive Chapter V	Interest and Royalty Directive Chapter VI	Mutual Assistance Directives Chapter VIII
Oy AA	18 July 2007	C-231/05		275, 276					
Papillon	27 November 2008	C-418/07		261					
Pavlov and others	12 September 2000	C-180/98 C-184/98			347				
Persche	27 January 2009	C-318/07		154, 291					660, 673, 686, 687
Philip Morris v Commission	17 September 1980	730/79			343, 387				
Point Graphos	8 September 2011	C-78/08 C-80/08			329, 330, 344, 356, 363				
Polydor and others	9 February 1982	270/80	8						
Prunus	5 Mai 2011	C-384/09		117					
Ratti	5 April 1979	148/78	6						
Regione Sardegna	17 November 2009	C-169/08			321				
Renneberg	16 October 2008	C-527/06		175					
Rewe	16 December 1976	33/76	22						
Rewe Zentralfinanz	29 March 2007	C-347/04		275					686
Rewe-Zentral "Cassis de Dijon""	20 February 1979	120/78		222, 244					
Safir	28 April 1998	C-118/96		166					
Saint-Gobain	21 September 1999	C-307/97							673
San Giorgio	9 November 1983	199/82	31						

ECJ cases listed alphabetic	Date	Case	General	Funda-mental Freedoms	State Aid	Parent-Subsidi-ary Directive	Merger Directive	Interest and Royalty Directive	Mutual Assistance Directives
			Chapter I	Chapter II	Chapter III	Chapter IV	Chapter V	Chapter VI	Chapter VIII
Savaş	11 May 2000	C-37/98	8						
Schempp	12 July 2005	C-403/03		105					
Scheuten Solar Technology	21 July 2011	C-397/09						576	
Schröder	31 März 2011	C-450/09		175					
Schumacker	14 February 1995	C-279/93		151, 168					
Scorpio	3 October 2006	C-290/04		139, 160, 161					
SFEI and others	11 July 1996	C-39/94			419				
Simmenthal	9 March 1978	106/77	1						
Skandia	26 June 2003	C-422/01							686
Sloman Neptun	7 March 1993	C-72/91 C-73/91			333				
Société de Gestion Industrielle	21 Jänner 2010	C-311/08		137, 277					
Stahlwerk Ergste Westig	6 November 2007	C-415/06		135					
Stauffer	14 September 2006	C-386/04		261					
Test Claimants in Class IV of the ACT Group Litigation	12 December 2006	C-374/04		152					
Test Claimants in the FII Group Litigation	12 December 2006	C-446/04		204, 215, 216		459			
Test Claimants in the Thin Cap Group Litigation	13 March 2007	C-524/04	31	113					

ECJ cases listed alphabetic	Date	Case	General	Fundamental Freedoms	State Aid	Parent-Subsidiary Directive	Merger Directive	Interest and Royalty Directive	Mutual Assistance Directives
			Chapter I	Chapter II	Chapter III	Chapter IV	Chapter V	Chapter VI	Chapter VIII
Traghetti del Mediterraneo	13 June 2006	C-173/03	35						
Transalpine Ölleitung	5 October 2006	C-368/04			424				
Truck Center SA	22 December 2008	C-282/07		149, 152, 160					
Tsapalos and Diamantakis	1 July 2004	C-361/02 C-362/02							
Turpeinen	9 November 2006	C-520/04		107					
Twoh International	27 September 2007	C-184/05							660, 686
Unión General de Trabajadore de La Rioja (UGT-Rioja) v Juntas Generales del Territorio Histórico de Vizcaya	11 September 2008	C-428/06 C-434/06			358, 359				
Vale	12 July 2012	C-378/10					558		
van Calster	21 October 2003	C-261/01			424				
Van Duyn	4 December 1974	41/74	6						
Van Gend & Loos	5 February 1963	26/62	6						
Verkooijen	6 June 2000	C-35/98		122					
Vestergaard	28 October 1999	C-55/98							686
W.N.	13 April 2000	C-420/98							661, 664
Wallentin	1 July 2004	C-169/03		175					
Weber's Wine World	2 October 2003	C-147/01	24						
Westzucker	14 March 1973	57/72			387				

ECJ cases listed alphabetic	Date	Case	General	Funda-mental Freedoms	State Aid	Parent-Subsidi-ary Directive	Merger Directive	Interest and Royalty Directive	Mutual Assistance Directives
			Chapter I	Chapter II	Chapter III	Chapter IV	Chapter V	Chapter VI	Chapter VIII
Wielockx	11 August 1995	C-80/94		229					721
X Holding	25 February 2010	C-337/08		153, 190, 252					
X and Passenheim	11 June 2009	C-155/08 C-157/08		292					
X AB and Y AB	18 November 1999	C-200/98		122					
X and Y	21 November 2002	C-436/00		239, 241					
Zanotti	20 Mai 2010	C-56/09		114					
Zurstrassen	16 May 2000	C-87/99		175					
Zwijnenburg	20 May 2010	C-352/08					569		

Index

(The numbers refer to the marginal numbers in the text)